This important contribution to comparative economic history examines different countries' experiences with different monetary regimes, laying particular emphasis on how the regimes fared when placed under stress such as wars and/or other changes in the economic environment. Covering the experience of 10 countries over the period 1700–1990, the contributors employ the latest techniques of economic analysis in their studies. Several papers are concerned with the transformation from bimetallism to gold monometallism in the nineteenth century and the determinants of monetary regimes' transformation in the core countries of Britain, France, and the United States. Others focus on the successful and unsuccessful gold standard experiences of Canada, Australia, and Spain, while yet others examine the experience of wartime and postwar stabilizations surrounding the two World Wars and the Napoleonic Wars.

T0312097

Monetary regimes in transition

Studies in Monetary and Financial History

Editors: Michael Bordo and Forrest Capie

Monetary regimes in transition

Edited by

MICHAEL D. BORDO

Rutgers University

FORREST CAPIE

City University Business School

CAMBRIDGE UNIVERSITY PRESS
Cambridge, New York, Melbourne, Madrid, Cape Town, Singapore, São Paulo

Cambridge University Press
The Edinburgh Building, Cambridge CB2 2RU, UK

Published in the United States of America by Cambridge University Press, New York

www.cambridge.org
Information on this title: www.cambridge.org/9780521419062

First published 1993
This digitally printed first paperback version 2006

A catalogue record for this publication is available from the British Library

Library of Congress Cataloguing in Publication data

Monetary regimes in transition / edited by Michael D. Bordo, Forrest
  Capie.
        p.   cm. – (Studies in monetary and financial history)
     ISBN 0 521 41906 9 (hc)
     1. Money – History. 2. Gold standard – History. I. Bordo, Michael
  D. II. Capie, Forrest. III. Series.
  HG231.M58 1993
  332.4′9 – dc20   92–43109   CIP

ISBN-13 978-0-521-41906-2 hardback
ISBN-10 0-521-41906-9 hardback

ISBN-13 978-0-521-03042-7 paperback
ISBN-10 0-521-03042-0 paperback

Contents

Figures

Tables

Contributors

PROFESSOR MICHAEL D. BORDO
Rutgers University

PROFESSOR CHARLES CALOMIRIS
University of Illinois, Urbana-Champaign

PROFESSOR FORREST CAPIE
City University Business School

PROFESSOR ALESSANDRA CASELLA
University of California, Berkeley

PROFESSOR TREVOR DICK
University of Lethbridge

PROFESSOR BARRY EICHENGREEN
University of California, Berkeley

PROFESSOR JOHN FLOYD
University of Toronto

PROFESSOR GIULIO GALLAROTTI
Wesleyan University

PROFESSOR LARS JONUNG
Stockholm School of Economics

PROFESSOR PABLO MARTÍN-ACEÑA
Programa de Investagiones Publica, Madrid

PROFESSOR DAVID POPE
The Australian National University

PROFESSOR ANGELA REDISH
University of British Columbia

DR ANNA J. SCHWARTZ
National Bureau of Economic Research

PROFESSOR PIERRE SIKLOS
Wilfred Laurier University

PROFESSOR EUGENE WHITE
Rutgers University

1 Introduction

MICHAEL D. BORDO AND FORREST CAPIE

We planned this volume of essays as an exercise in comparative economic history. Our objective was to examine different countries' experiences with different monetary regimes. What, if anything, might be said about how different regimes fared when placed under stress? For example, when war broke out, or when there was some other change in the economic environment, how did that lead to a change, or perhaps a breakdown in a regime? If neither occurred, what was it that preserved the existing system? What was it, in short, that made some monetary regimes stable and durable, and others not?

Any comparison of the broad range of monetary regimes and experiences requires an analytic framework. In this Introduction we outline briefly some basic themes in the evolution of a monetary economy, discuss some of the basic kinds of stress that have commonly occurred, define "regime," and consider the kinds of conditions that bring about transition to a new regime. We then turn to some associated themes for modern macroeconomics – the themes include credibility in policy stance, time inconsistency in policy, and the desirability of independence of monetary authorities. We conclude with a brief synopsis of the papers in the volume.

Some basic themes in the evolution of the monetary economy

Monetary economics have evolved slowly over a long period. The path is well known and is closely connected to the functions of money: as a medium of exchange, a unit of account, and a store of value (Morgan, 1965; Clower, 1967; Hicks, 1970). In the very earliest forms of exchange, transactions were carried out by barter. The inefficiencies of such a system are obvious and were well understood at an early date. Primitive money arose to combat the basic deficiency of matching needs. All manner of forms of primitive money emerged – cattle, shells, bales of tobacco, and kegs of rice. Some forms of commodity money were clearly superior to others and the next stage in the evolutionary process was the emergence of something we would recognize as money: metals that fulfilled many or most of the basic requirements of a useful medium of exchange and a store of value – durability, storeability, portability and divisibility. It was a short step from this type of commodity money to the issue of paper money or bank notes that represented a claim on metal and then to paper money that could simply be printed by decree – fiat money. A variety of means of transmission has accompanied the development of these monies, the most obvious and widely used being the bank check.

A key theme in the literature is the social saving, by the issue of fiduciary money, of the resources tied up in commodity money. However, the benefits of low-cost fiduciary money depended on its convertibility on demand into specie to provide a nominal anchor. In times of stress such as wars, convertibility had to be suspended, to allow governments access to additional resources by use of the inflation tax. Indeed, the issue of fiat money in wartime is one of the most common monetary regime transformations in history. While nations typically returned to a specie standard after a war, for the first time in history the world after 1971 adopted a peacetime fiat money regime.

When a shift in regime occurs, a major question is whether it is a permanent or a temporary change. The papers in this volume by Bordo and White and by Jonung (chapters 8 and 11) are concerned in part with this issue. Even enduring peacetime regimes are subject to stress, notably a financial crisis that may force a change. In many countries the basic regimes survived stresses unchanged. Monetary regimes in Britain, Australia (Pope, chapter 7 in this volume) and Canada (Dick and Floyd, chapter 6 in this volume) withstood shocks in the nineteenth century but in other countries, for example Argentina (Cortés-Conde, 1991), Chile (Llona, 1991) and Italy (Fratianni and Spinnelli, 1984), they did not.

Definition of a regime

The definition of a regime is a necessary prerequisite to any discussion of the transition from one regime to another, and whether a regime has "survived." The word "regime" originally meant a system of government, and was gradually extended to apply to any institution that was widely recognized. The term may be neutral but it is nevertheless not easy to define, as some recent attempts illustrate. For political scientists a suggested definition of a regime has been given as "the norms, rules and procedures that guide the behavior of states and other important actors" (Keohane, 1980, p. 152). When taken together as a package this could be empirically useful, but there are difficulties since some small change in procedures might be seen as constituting a change in regime and yet such changes are taking place all the time. For example, during the Great Depression of 1929–33 a number of countries made many small policy changes. How were these read at the time? Some of them could have been taken to be a change of regime, and may have brought about a widespread change in expectations. But there was seldom any dramatic change that was obvious at the time. How big, then, would such a change have to be before it qualified, and how should it be measured? For economists, Eichengreen has suggested a more robust version of this approach. In his words a regime is: "an equilibrium in which a set of rules or procedures governing the formulation of public policy generates stable expectations among market participants" (Eichengreen, 1991, p. 1). This may be still some way from being precise enough for empirical testing, but it helps focus attention on the essential elements.

The difficulties of definition increase when we turn to a consideration of a *monetary* regime. There remains considerable divergence of view over what constitutes a "monetary regime." Eichengreen suggests that one possible reason for this is that since money has three functions (store of value, means of payment, and unit of account) there could be occasions when factors affecting the store of value function leave unaffected the means of payment and the unit of account functions. Against that there can be occasions when all three functions are affected. There remain differences, therefore, on what should constitute the essential distinguishing feature.

It thus remains problematical to settle on a definition that will be both accurate and useful. For example, should the regime be defined at the national or at the international level? In a fundamental sense, the gold standard was a domestic monetary regime based on the rule of a fixed price of gold. However, because many nations in the period 1880–1914 fixed the prices of their currencies (defined the weights of their coins) in terms of gold the gold standard became an international monetary regime – a fixed exchange rate regime.

As is often the case, it is easier to point to what is being discussed than it is to define it. A whole range of commodity money standards (for example silver/gold bimetallism, silver monometallism) functioned similarly to the gold standard and seemed to attract wide acceptance as descriptive of regimes. The abandonment of any tie with commodity money leads to a fiat money regime. It then becomes possible to move to discussion of fixed exchange rate and floating exchange rate regimes. In this sense, can a period of hyperinflation be viewed as a monetary regime? It may even fit Eichengreen's definition – an equilibrium in which participants adapt and expectations are validated. But how long would this last – how long should stable expectations hold in order to qualify as a regime? Can there be regimes within regimes (Capie, 1986)?

Our own preference for a definition of a monetary regime is: a set of arrangements governing the monetary system. This definition covers rules such as the gold standard rule or Palmer's Rule, a specific form of the gold standard rule, embracing both enabling institutional arrangements and policies. To complete the definition we need to add the public's perception of the arrangements in terms of their operation and possible impact, as well as the likely durability of the arrangements. These issues are tackled by Gallarotti (chapter 2) and Siklos (chapter 9) in this volume (also see Sargent, 1986).

For the reasons enumerated above, strict definition is not insisted upon in this volume. Some authors have chosen to write on the experience of a particular country during what would be accepted as a specific regime – such as the gold standard (Dick and Floyd, chapter 6, Pope, chapter 7). Others, such as Calomiris (chapter 4) have elected to attempt definition and work within that, and others again have taken what might be considered more controversial positions. This diversity of approach reflects some of the complexity of the subject.

Finally, the definition of a monetary regime is important because of the behavior under different regimes of basic macro variables such as the price level, interest rates, and exchange rates. Thus under a commodity money regime the price level tends to be mean-reverting and the inflation rate tends to be free of persistence. This is compared to a fiat regime where inflation often exhibits persistence (Barsky, 1987).

Transition

What constitutes a transition? The extent of change and whether change means discontinuity are at the heart of historical enquiry. This question then turns out to be as difficult as that of defining "regime" itself. While not all the authors in this volume explicitly treat this question, Calomiris (1990, p. 2) tackles it, stating that a "Monetary regime change refers to a change in the forcing process that governs policy – including changes in the reaction function of monetary authorities, perceived changes in credibility of a fixed exchange rate or changes in the random component of the money supply disturbance." The difficulty with implementing this type of definition is obvious: while the abandonment of the gold standard is easily observed, not all changes are quite so straightforward to identify.

Once some agreement on what is meant by "transition" is settled, interesting questions can be pursued. Why does a country, either suddenly or slowly, decide to change its monetary regime – for example, to fix or float its exchange rate? Does it matter whether the transition is effected quickly or slowly? These are the kinds of questions that are of vital interest in the 1990s, both in the West and in Eastern Europe.

No regime has ever been permanent. How a regime appears to contemporaries is, however, another matter. A variety of factors and changing circumstances will necessitate or provoke change. Some changes will be the result of long years of persuasion; others perhaps simply of fashion; and others will be the result of simply accepting what appears to be a demonstrably better arrangement.

In the great sweep of world history there are some obvious breaks in the type of monetary regime in place. Across most of history, commodity money has been used, and the more refined versions of this were bimetallic systems using gold and silver in combination. In the modern industrial world economy that dates from the eighteenth century the monometallic gold standard has probably predominated. Britain is often said to have adopted gold in 1717, and while that may be the *de facto* case, 1821 is the correct *de jure* date (see Redish, 1990). By the late nineteenth century most industrial and many primary producing countries had adopted gold. That regime lasted until the 1930s, and in a watered down version until the 1970s. Thereafter, there has been a mixture of floating and pegged exchange rates.

There can be no doubt that the gold standard was one of the most striking regimes in all history. Commodity money had been around in various forms from earliest times, and as we noted, gold in some form was present, but the classical gold standard emerged in the course of the nineteenth century and reached its high point in the 30 or 40 years prior to the First World War (Bordo and Schwartz, 1984; Eichengreen, 1985; Bordo and Kydland, 1992). What accounts for the adoption of that particular monetary regime by so many countries in the world?

One strand in the literature seems simply to assert that gold was more stable. But the main account given by economists depends on relative prices and therefore is that gold displaced silver after a change in Mint parities caused silver to be relatively overvalued. However, these parities had often changed in the past, depending as they did on demand and supply, and there had been large discoveries in the past. The interesting question is why governments in the 1870s acted to demonetize silver. Gallarotti (chapter 2) gives a fascinating explanation that rests heavily on politics, and is closer to Schumpeter's "mark of a civilized society."

The gold standard was an obvious well-defined regime, and its disappearance should therefore at least be easy to see. Why did it last so long and why did it disappear? To some extent the answer might be thought to be the reverse of the answer as to why it emerged. Had conditions so changed that it was time for a break? The proximate cause of its demise was the First World War. But it should also be remembered that even in its heyday the gold standard did not go unchallenged. There was quite widespread disillusionment with the standard in the United States and a move to a bimetallic standard was not entirely ruled out in the 1890s (see Friedman, 1990). Gold was blamed for the long deflation of 1873–96, and that in turn was blamed for the depression in the real economy. Other assessments of gold have concluded that while it worked well for some countries – especially those such as Britain and other industrial countries at the hub of the world economy – it did not work so well for primary producers (price takers) at the periphery of the world economy (Ford, 1962). Some countries adopted it, abandoned it and then rejoined. Certainly after the massive disruption to the world economy in the years 1914–18 the re-establishment of the old gold standard proved impossible, and the modified version was either unable to meet the requirements of the changed world, or was badly handled.

In summary, the question we put is: what is it that makes a regime (the set of monetary arrangements, together with the public's reaction to them) stable (see Eichengreen, 1991)? A prerequisite is that they must be internally consistent: that is, monetary policy, fiscal policy and the exchange rate must be in agreement with each other. Furthermore, the public must find the combination of these policies credible. That being the case, what would lead to their requiring alteration? Various possibilities may arise that result in a change in the underlying economic/monetary environment, and that bring about a necessary change in the basic relationship. In other words, something could happen that alters the money/income relationship or the budgetary position or the exchange rate. Pressures can then emerge for government to capture resources – either because of war as mentioned above or perhaps because of some distributional conflict. Take, for example, the exchange rate. Over a certain time differences in productivity differentials can develop, or differences in comparative advantage emerge. Or on the demand side tastes may undergo a major change. An extreme example would be where an important staple, such as rubber in Brazil, experiences a collapse in the market, placing pressure on the government to maintain producers' incomes (Fishlow, 1989).

Shocks such as war need not have permanent effects. Fiat money may be issued to cope with the emergency but if the public's perception is that this is temporary (see Bordo and White, chapter 8 in this volume) then a different outcome will emerge from that which will emerge where the public does not trust the government to restore the status quo. Similarly, the lender of last resort can act to save the market when it is under liquidity pressure. But post-crisis behavior is important, too, as is the public's view of what it will be.

We have suggested, then, that changes in the underlying environment provide reasonable cause for the need for a regime change. But it could be that the regime itself is fundamentally flawed and survives only because of a particularly favorable environment. A good illustration of this can be found in the Bretton Woods system. The design of the Bretton Woods system was based on particular perceptions of how the international economy operated in the 1930s. These perceptions were to some extent faulty, and therefore a flawed system was designed. For example, in the 1930s there was capital flight and therefore capital controls were seen as being a necessary part of the new system. But capital controls could not work in the post-1945 world. The conception of the system was fatally flawed in this important respect (Bordo, 1993).

Some related themes for macroeconomics

Many of the issues raised by the historical examples in this volume have a direct application to modern macroeconomics. Where a regime breaks down it may be as a result of a change in the environment or a flaw of the regime coming to light, or some combination of the two – a flaw being exposed by reason of a change in the environment. The related themes that we now wish to consider briefly are: the credibility of policies, the possible time inconsistency of policies, and the possible need for independence of monetary authorities.

Credibility

The important role that rational expectations have come to play in macro-economics has meant that policies must be assessed for their credibility. When economic agents are rational they make decisions based on what they believe will happen, given the best information available. For example, if it becomes clear that in certain circumstances there are gains to be derived from inflationary monetary growth, the rational private sector will see that, and base their actions on the anticipated inflation rather than on the announced inflation rate that the authorities may have set. The only way this could be avoided would be if governments had a reputation for reliability – if they always kept to their declarations unfailingly, or at least if they could be counted on to keep to a particular course once they had set it.

An extreme version of this view is that belief is, of itself, sufficient to bring about a change of action by the private sector. For example, Sargent (1986) claims that some of the worst inflations of all time, those of the 1920s in Europe, were brought to a halt not when monetary growth stopped, but in spite of continuing monetary growth, when the authorities announced that a new regime was being instituted to bring about stabilization. The fact that the public believed the announcement was sufficient to change their expectations, private sector behavior, and hence inflation. The reason the public believed the announcement was that a fiscal policy stance was announced that was capable of backing monetary policy, and the personnel imple-menting policy had good reputations. These views have not gone unchallenged and Siklos' chapter 9 in this volume is a specific rejection of this for the case of Hungary.

Time inconsistency

At the core of the problem is whether monetary authorities should be constrained by rules or be allowed discretionary action. This is a very old issue in monetary economics. Those favoring rules tend to assume foolish administrators; they assume the possibility of sensible rules. Discretion presumes all-wise administrators, good information, and the low likelihood of formulating good rules. A variety of rules can obtain, extending from something very general like the gold standard that provides a basic operational framework, to something much narrower such as the Palmer Rule proposed in England in the 1830s, whereby when a certain reserve/deposit ratio was reached all fluctuations in the Bank's notes and deposits should thereafter be equal to the changes in the Bank's holding of specie, to the Friedman-type monetary growth rule of x percent per annum. Such rules diminish the monetary authorities' freedom of movement. Their duty is to manage the currency/money supply in relation to the gold reserves in the first case, or in the second to issue money at a steady rate consistent with the growth of the real economy.

The objections to such rules are that some of the pain that may occasionally come from living under them could be avoided if some flexibility were introduced – if the authorities could exercise some discretion (Fischer, 1990). For example, if over the business cycle the authorities could relax policy in the downswing and tighten it in the upswing, the cycle could be smoothed out and some costs of recession and boom could be avoided. However, this freedom may allow the authorities to cheat. For example, if the authorities adopt a particular policy based on the correct state of the economy, and declare at that time that they will behave in a certain way, from that point onwards the danger is of their reneging on that declaration at a later date, when new information is revealed. There is the further difficulty that it can be hard to distinguish discretion from cheating. Such time inconsistent actions arise whenever there is the possibility of short-term benefits being placed alongside longer-term loss. Kydland and Prescott (1977), who were among the first to formalize these views, gave examples such as: revoking existing patent rights widening the available existing knowledge but deterring future devotion of resources to invention and research and development; and capital levies – a non-distortionary method of financing the government now which deters future saving.

In monetary matters, the story is often presented along the following lines (Barro and Gordon, 1983; Persson and Tabellini, 1990). Governments have incentives to inflate: they gain revenue from money creation, and they also want to win elections. It is widely accepted that monetary policy ultimately affects only the general price level, and quite widely accepted that unexpected monetary fluctuations have temporary effects on output. Low inflation is desired by the public but increased output is, too. Where voters' expectations are rational, politicians have an incentive to promise zero inflation. But they also have an incentive to produce an inflationary surprise. The reason for the latter is that if voters believe the promise on inflation, then prices – particularly wages – are set in the expectation of zero inflation. Once that is the case there is an incentive for government to deliver the inflationary surprise. The only thing stopping it will be if the expected loss of votes from high inflation outweighs the gains in votes from higher output. An equilibrium will be reached with positive inflation and no change in output.

Independent monetary authorities

Given the time inconsistency problem, an effective rule binding politicians' actions over time is required to make the policy action time consistent. The classical gold standard and to a lesser extent Bretton Woods provided such a commitment mechanism (Bordo and Kydland, 1992, Bordo, 1993). In 1971–73, following the breakdown of the Bretton Woods system, there was a major monetary regime change: the world as a whole severed its link with commodity money and adopted fiat money. Since then there have been limitless possibilities for expanding the money supply. In the light of the subsequent poor price level performance in many countries around the world the issue of political involvement in monetary arrangements has emerged as a topic of concern in macroeconomics. Modern game theoretic studies have shown that one way of avoiding the kind of inflationary surprises described above is to have an independent monetary authority whose only function is to deliver stable prices (Persson and Tabellini, 1990; Rogoff, 1985, 1987; Capie and Wood, 1991). Few of the chapters in this volume discuss the issue of central bank independence, although Siklos' study (chapter 9) is concerned with it. One part of the explanation for the omission is that the studies are primarily concerned with a world of fixed exchange rates where there is less room for maneuver on the part of the monetary authorities.

The studies in this volume

There is currently a great deal of concern amongst economists, policy makers and businessmen about the part that money and monetary policy play in the economy, and the possibilities that there might be for reducing uncertainty, stabilizing prices and smoothing the path of economic progress. We have to turn to historical experience for guidance on these questions. The studies in this volume deal with various aspects of monetary regimes and how these actually operated; why they succeeded or failed; and why they were consciously adopted or altered. The studies range over the experiences of several countries and over the time period 1700–1990. The investigations are carried out by a variety of means, but almost always employing the most recent techniques available from economic analysis.

Several chapters are concerned with the transformation from bimetallism to gold monometallism in the nineteenth century and the determinants of monetary regime transformation in the core countries of England, France, and the United States. Whether gold should be considered a different regime to silver is open to debate, but it is nevertheless interesting to discover the path that was taken from one to the other and indeed to explore why gold came to dominate the world's economies of the late nineteenth century. This particular issue may not have a straightforward economic explanation and it is the contention of Gallarotti in chapter 2 that political forces were potent. Calomiris in chapter 4 focuses on monetary regime transformations in the late nineteenth century US experience. His main point is that expected deflation during the "greenback" episode, in anticipation of resumption, and expected inflation during the silver episode in anticipation of the collapse of the gold standard, were unrelated to current changes in monetary aggregates or exchange rates. Redish in chapter 3 explores the rationale for the ill-fated Latin Monetary Union. She views it as a step on the path to gold monometallism – not as a dead end attachment to bimetallism.

Other chapters focus on the gold standard experience of three countries at the periphery of the world economy, where the experience has been said to be less than ideal: Canada (Dick and Floyd, chapter 6), Australia (Pope, chapter 7) and Spain (Martín-Aceña, chapter 5). The degree of commitment to the monetary regime may be an important determinant of the successful adherence to convertibility by Canada and Australia. The less successful adherence by Spain makes an interesting contrast. Some chapters center on the upheavals in monetary regimes during wartime. Topics covered include: the abandonment of gold convertibility in favor of paper money, postwar attempts at stabilizations and the imposition and ultimate restoration of credit controls.

Two jointly authored chapters (Bordo and White, chapter 8 and Casella and Eichengreen, chapter 10) draw comparisons between two countries' experience with a similar problem. Bordo and White show the contrasting experience in Britain and France in the Napoleonic Wars as these countries sought to finance an expensive war. One moved from gold to paper, the other clung to a commodity standard. Casella and Eichengreen compare the stabilization process in France and Italy after the Second World War. Siklos (chapter 9) takes the most dramatic of monetary episodes, the Hungarian inflation of the 1920s, and examines the issue of credibility when an abrupt change in regime is proposed. Finally, Jonung (chapter 11), examines the mid-twentieth century experience of Sweden with monetary controls – a country whose experience since 1939 is paralleled by many other industrial economies. In this chapter explanations are offered for the movement into regulated markets in the 1940s, 1950s, and 1960s and then to deregulation in the 1970s and 1980s.

Finally there is an overview study by Anna J. Schwartz (chapter 12). She addresses the main theories of successful and unsuccessful monetary regimes, the forces underlying regime transformations and the historical experiences covered in the book.

Note

For helpful comments and suggestions we thank Eugene White and Geoffrey Wood.

References

Barro, R.J. and D.B. Gordon, 1983. "Rules, discretion and reputation in a model of monetary policy," *Journal of Monetary Economics*, 12 (July): 101–121.

Barsky, R.B., 1987. "The Fisher hypothesis and the forecastability and persistence of inflation," *Journal of Monetary Economics*, 19 (January): 3–24.

Bordo, M.D., 1993. "The Bretton Woods international monetary system: a historical overview," in M.D. Bordo and B. Eichengreen (eds.), *A Retrospective on the Bretton Woods System*, Chicago: University of Chicago Press.

Bordo, M.D. and F.E. Kydland, 1992. "The gold standard as a rule," Federal Reserve Bank of Cleveland, *Working Paper*, 9205 (March).

Bordo, M.D. and A.J. Schwartz, 1984. *A Retrospective on the Classical Gold Standard: 1821–1931*, Chicago: University of Chicago Press.

Calomiris, C.W. 1990. "Policy regimes, the price process, and the Phillips Curve: the United States, 1862–1913," Northwestern University, Department of Economics, unpublished mimeo. (August).

Capie, F., 1986. "Conditions in which very rapid inflation has appeared," *Carnegie Rochester Conference Series on Public Policy*, 24 (Spring): 115–168.

Capie, F. and G.E. Wood, 1991. "Central bank dependence and performance: a historical perspective," City University of London Business School (mimeo).

Clower, R.L., 1967. "Editor's introduction," *Monetary Theory*, London: Penguin.

Cortés-Conde, R., 1991. "The gold standard in Argentina in the XIX century," Buenos Aires (mimeo).

Eichengreen, B., 1985. "Editor's introduction," in B. Eichengreen (ed.), *The Gold Standard in Theory and History*, New York: Methuen.

1991. "Editor's introduction," *Monetary Regime Transformations*, Cheltenham: Edward Elgar.

Fischer, S., 1990. "Rules versus discretion in monetary policy," in B.M. Friedman and F.H. Hahn, *Handbook of Monetary Economics*, vol. II, Amsterdam: North-Holland.

Fishlow, A., 1989. "Conditionality and willingness to pay: some parallels from the 1890's", in B. Eichengreen and P. Lindert (eds.), *The International Debt Crisis in Historical Perspective*, Cambridge MA: MIT Press.

Ford, A.G., 1962. *The Gold Standard 1880–1918: Britain and Argentina*, Oxford: Clarendon Press.

Fratianni, M. and F. Spinelli, 1984. "Italy in the gold standard period 1861–1914," in M.D. Bordo and A.J. Schwartz (eds.), *A Retrospective on the Classical Gold Standard 1821–1931*, Chicago: University of Chicago Press.

Friedman, M., 1990. "Bimentallism revisited," *Journal of Economics Perspectives*, 4 (Fall): 85–104.

Hicks, J.R., 1970. *A Theory of Economic History*, Oxford: Clarendon Press.

Keohane, P., 1980. "The thesis of hegemonic stability and changes in international economic regimes, 1967–1977," in O.R. Holsti, R.M. Siverson and A.L. George (eds.), *Change in the International System*, Boulder, CO: Westview.

Kydland, F.E. and E. Prescott, 1977. "Rules rather than discretion: the inconsistency of optimal plans," *Journal of Political Economy*, 85: 473–491.

Llona, A., 1991. "Chile during the gold standard: a successful paper money experience," Buenos Aires (mimeo).

Morgan, E.V., 1965. *A History of Money*, London: Penguin.

Persson, T. and G. Tabellini, 1990. *Macroeconomic Policy Credibility and Politics*, New York: Harwood Academic Publishers.

Redish, A., 1990. "The evolution of the gold standard in England," *Journal of Economic History*, 50(4) (December): 789–805.

Rogoff, K., 1985. "The optimal degree of commitment to an intermediate monetary target," *Quarterly Journal of Economics*, 100.

1987. "Reputational constraints on monetary policy," *Carnegie Rochester Conference Series on Public Policy*, 26 (Spring): 141–181.

Sargent, T.S., 1986. *Rational Expectations and Inflation*, New York: Harper & Row.

Part I

Commodity money standards in transition

2   The scramble for gold: monetary regime transformation in the 1870s

GIULIO M. GALLAROTTI

Introduction

Economists and political scientists have long interested themselves in the regimes that govern economic and political systems. Both have become interested in regimes as a set of policy tools, institutions, and norms which organize political and economic relations into orderly patterns. An encompassing definition is found in Krasner (1982, p. 185): "principles, norms, rules, and decision-making procedures around which actor expectations converge in a given issue-area." More recent scholarship has shown greater emphasis on how regimes are formed and transformed.[1] Disciplinary parochialism has, however, fragmented the study of regime formation and transformation. Economists have been wont to take an apolitical approach to regimes: of principal interest have been the relative efficiency of competing institutional structures, and the changes in economic relations as catalysts for institutional change.[2] Political scientists have been limited in the opposite direction: approaching regime change and formation as necessarily a political phenomenon. Regimes form and are transformed through the exercise of power or changes in political power structures.

   This study takes a more integrated approach in considering the formation of the classical gold standard as the resultant of a prevailing mode of transformation in domestic monetary standards during the 1870s.[3] Beginning with the Reichstag's mandate to make the gold mark the basic unit of account and restrict the minting of territorial silver coin in Germany in 1871, the transition from bimetallic and silver standards to a gold standard represented a compelling trend in the monetary systems of developed nations in the 1870s. Following Germany's lead, Norway, Denmark, and Sweden signed a convention in December 1872 instituting a gold standard in each nation, with silver and bronze coinage as subsidiary (i.e., token coin). By 1875 all three were members of the Scandinavian Monetary Union which was configured around central monetary status for gold (krone), with silver and bronze coin relegated to subsidiary roles. In that year Holland continued the provisional suspension (which had begun in 1873) of coining silver and introduced the 10-gulden gold coin as the central coin. This ad hoc gold standard was formally institutionalized in 1877 when the coinage of silver was definitively suspended.

The United States, having arguably perpetrated a transition from bimetallism to gold in 1853, in the 1870s mirrored the European trend of legislation against the central monetary status of silver.[4] The *de facto* gold standard already existing was consolidated. The Law of 1873 demonetized the 412.5-grain silver dollar, thus making the gold dollar the central legal unit of account. The Act of 1878 reinstituted the silver dollar but under a policy of limited government purchase and coinage. In the following year Austria–Hungary closed its mints to silver, although its formal adoption of a gold standard was still more than a decade away.

Belgium, reacting to an enormous influx of silver in 1873, limited the coinage of 5-franc silver pieces at the Brussels mint. A similar influx into France caused the coinage of 5-franc pieces at the Paris mint to be limited in the same year. In the following year, the Latin Monetary Union (whose principal members were France, Switzerland, Italy, and Belgium) instituted 5-franc coinage limits for all its members. The limits were renewed and adjusted in 1875 and 1876. In 1876 France and Belgium suspended the coinage of 5-franc pieces. In 1878 the coinage of the 5-franc piece was suspended over the entire Latin Union membership.[5] With this cessation of the coining of the Union's central coin, noted Helfferich, "the fate of silver as a money metal was sealed, insofar as [economically developed] European countries were concerned," (1927, p. 181).[6] What began as a decade which saw only two nations of note (Great Britain and Portugal) legally on a gold standard ended with the developed world firmly entrenched in the practice of gold monometallism. This "scramble for gold," as White called it (1893, p. 27), had in one short decade abrogated the practices of centuries.[7]

The formation of an international gold standard was a natural outcome of redundance in domestic monetary standards. As more nations adopted a gold standard domestically, a greater international gold bloc crystallized. In this case, the creation of an international regime was an additive process. As Ludwig Bamberger argued, "a world monetary union would be superfluous if all countries based their currencies on gold."[8] Things equal to the same thing are equal to each other. And gold monometallist orthodoxy was fairly uniform over those nations practicing such a standard. Each nation could be expected to maintain a stable value in the central monetary unit by defending convertibility. Each could be expected to maintain a high level of private discretion over the management and movement of gold stocks (i.e., individuals were free to hold gold in various forms as well as to import and export it freely). Thus a stable set of exchange rates and expectations regarding monetary relations emerged from a convergence of monetary practices at the domestic level.

It is difficult to impute any international consciousness in the national policies that marginalized silver in monetary standards of this period. The creation of an international gold standard showed neither intention nor the exercise of international power. Monetary cooperation in this period, primarily embodied in the International Monetary Conferences of 1867 and 1878, was unsuccessful at creating any kind of formal international monetary agreement. The latter conference, in fact, was initiated by the US to discuss the possibility of an international bimetallist union. As for the four core (i.e., dominant) monetary powers of the period – the United States, France, Great Britain, and Germany – none exercised any political or economic power (aside from initiating international discussion) in bringing about an international regime, either individually or collectively. Great Britain, the so-called monetary hegemon of the period, not only avoided any unilateral initiatives at creating international institutions, but was exceedingly uncooperative at supporting any initiatives in the Conferences of 1867 and 1878.[9] Thus, the creation of this regime cuts against the standard political-science vision. It can best be described as a decentralized or diffuse process, where the formative elements and rationalization of an international monetary system were dispersed among a number of individual national monetary standards, rather than deriving from international conference rooms where nations conceived of and collectively coordinated their monetary practices.[10]

For the political scientist, understanding the formation of the international gold standard represents a study in the formation of diffuse regimes. This pertains particularly to the interests of international-relations specialists and students of comparative monetary history. For the former, it illuminates a much neglected area in the study of regimes. For the latter, it illuminates processes in which the confluence of shared external and internal pressures filter through domestic political and economic structures to create uniformities in national policy styles. This bears directly upon how comparative monetary systems converge upon common institutions. For the economic historian, who has been more concerned with how the gold standard worked than with how it formed, it proposes and answers an alternative set of questions regarding how monetary systems crystallize.[11]

The scramble for gold in the 1870s can principally be understood as a resultant of two types of forces: structural and proximate. The former refer to long-term and developmental forces in the nineteenth century that compelled nations away from silver-based standards toward gold. Specifically, these were (1) a growing ideological attraction to gold and aversion to silver, (2) industrialization and economic development, and (3) changes in political power structures. Proximate forces represent critical developments in the 1860s and 1870s that served as the immediate catalysts for legal changes in monetary standards. Structural forces incrementally compelled the shift to gold, but it was these critical developments that accounted for the timing of the transformation.

The chapter is organized as follows. The first section discusses the structural foundations of the movement toward gold. The proximate foundations of the movement are then considered, and a final section concludes the article with a discussion of some central implications for monetary regime theory.

The structural foundations of the classical gold standard

As the nineteenth century progressed, three sets of structural forces increasingly compelled national monetary authorities toward gold and away from silver as central monetary metals. First, nations came to see monetary standards as economic and political status symbols: gold monometallism came to confer high status, while silver and bimetallism came to confer low status. Second, industrialization, economic development, and the growth of international trade encouraged the greater use of the more convenient metal (gold).[12] Finally, the spectrum of class politics changed significantly in the nineteenth century. The rise of liberalism was a manifestation of the political rise of an urban–industrial class and a challenge to the traditional dominance of an agricultural class. With the shift in the political balance of power came a concomitant shift in monetary preferences from a standard oriented around a bulky and inflationary metal to one oriented around a light and non-inflationary metal.

The ideology of gold

According to Joseph Schumpeter (1954, p. 770) it is difficult to explain prevalent cases in the transition from paper standards to gold standards in the last two decades of the nineteenth century independently of a "non-economic" factor: the quest for monetary "prestige." Italy, Austria–Hungary, and Russia shifted from a non-metallist regime where paper was depreciated in terms of silver to one in which monetary units were raised to an arbitrary gold parity, all of this occurring in decades exhibiting low or negative inflation. Moreover, some of the dominant economic interests in those nations were opposed to fixing exchange rates. This is explicable, Schumpeter argued, when we realize that gold monometallism as a standard had become a "symbol of sound practice and badge of honor and decency," and that national monetary authorities were compelled by the "admired example of England." In other words, gold monometallism had become an ideological focal point. As a standard, it was imputed a value which was independent of purely economic advantages (e.g., non-inflationary standard, low transaction costs in exchange). What Schumpeter attributed to monetary authorities of the 1880s and 1890s, can no less be attributed to authorities of earlier decades.

The Marquis de Moustier, presiding at the International Monetary Conference of 1867, stated that "sentiments" independent of economy held sway over monetary institutions, and that such sentiments were largely based on ideological attachments to certain practices (e.g., fondness for certain coins, fear of innovation). Gold monometallism, he suggested, generated such sentiments, and it was desirable for the Conference to assure that these sentiments were fulfilled.[13] The sentiments in this period generated an ideological attraction for gold and an ideological aversion to silver, so it is not surprising that the Conference ended with a unanimous call for a monetary union founded on gold.[14]

The ideological attachment to gold emanated primarily from a propensity on the part of monetary authorities to make associations between national monetary practices and greater achievements in the global economic and political order. Authorities became sensitized to a prevailing association: there was a strong relationship between the importance which gold played in national monetary systems, and the levels of economic development and political importance of those nations. By the later 1860s it became clear that gold was perceived as "the natural standard of the stronger and richer nations, and silver of the weaker and poorer nations."[15] Ernest Seyd of the United States, in his letter to the US Monetary Commission (US Congress, Senate, 1876, vol. II, p. 115), cited the prevalence of the belief that "civilized nations" should use gold and "uncivilized nations" silver.[16] The Swiss monetary diplomat Charles Feer-Herzog went so far as to call silver the "inferior metal."[17]

The unanimous support for gold monometallism at the International Conference of 1867 was taken by many as the most overt manifestation of a growing monetary division of the world. Feer Herzog's own assessment of this development was widely accepted. It was acknowledged that the Conference split the world into two monetary spheres: a gold sphere characterized by nations that were "civilized, rich, and active" and a silver sphere of "less advanced" nations.[18] The perceived relation between international political/economic status and monetary practices provided potent ammunition for the supporters of gold both in national and international monetary debates. Supporters of gold at meetings of the French Monetary Commission of 1868, for example, were not reserved in their use of this association in trying to discredit silver and bimetallism as future standards for France.[19] At the International Monetary Conference of 1878 the Dutch representative Mees expressed his pessimism about the possibility of a bimetallist alliance forming among the US and European states, but added that the US might look for monetary "allies" in the less-developed world (Central and South America, Asia, Dutch and English Indies). Russell (1898, p. 224) noted that Mees' comment may have contained some quiet ridicule of the United States' attempts to resuscitate silver by intimating that the US could be monetarily classified in a group of underdeveloped nations. One US delegate (Horton), in fact, requested a clarification of what Mees intended when he cited these prospective US monetary alliances.[20]

The status of gold derived disproportionately from the British example. That Great Britain was not only a monetary role model but also an economic-policy role model in the nineteenth century is generally acknowledged in the historical literature on the period.[21] Michel Chevalier (1859) underscored how readily French and other European authorities imitated British financial innovations.[22] On all dimensions of monetary policy, nations would "turn to England for financial wisdom."[23] The compelling nature of the British example is attributable to what Jervis (1976) called "overlearning from history": i.e., hastily attributing a cause and effect relationship to a simple existing association.

In explaining the attraction of gold after 1850, Edward Atkinson and William Sumner's testimonies to the US Monetary Commission (1876, vol. II, pp. 274, 275, 356) representatively conveyed the prevailing lesson.

The tendency of opinion in Europe had been for 20 years in favor of the mono-metallic system. From the example of England it was seen that the English by the mono-metallic system of a gold standard enjoyed great advantages, and the Continental nations, especially Prussia, seeing this, decided to go into the mono-metallic system . . .

the prosperity of England is due largely to its monetary standard . . . [T]hose [nations] who adopted gold as their standard of value have . . . been most permanently prosperous.

Certainly there were many who were skeptical about the nature of the causal link. Disraeli, in fact, saw causation in reverse. The gold standard, he averred, "was not the *cause* but the *consequence* of our commercial prosperity."[24] For the US monetary diplomat Dana Horton the purported causal link became a "doctrinaire propaganda" used by the advocates of gold to drive out silver.[25] Horton added that irrespective of its propagandistic nature, the lesson drove nations to transform their monetary standards.[26] This lesson was especially compelling for Germany.

For Germany, this was certainly one of the principal factors underlying its strong predilection toward gold after 1860. The period marked, in fact, a high point in what Stolper (1940, p. 33) called Germany's "Western orientation." It was most visible in liberal–elite circles championed by Ludwig Bamberger and Delbrück, and supported strongly by Bismarck who had venerated Western styles in policy from his early years. Bamberger himself, the single most important influence on German monetary unification in the early 1870s, saw the Western trend as being one characterized by the growing displacement of silver by gold.[27] Bamberger, Camphausen, Delbrück and other leading Liberals were "dazzled by the universal sway of gold" in developed countries.[28] These men saw gold (in that it was a fundamental part of the Liberal economic-policy agenda) as a means of what one publicist of the period referred to as putting Germans "in the same position as the citizens of the great industrial states."[29]

Within the Western bias, the British precedent was especially compelling, and it was as strong in trade as monetary policy, German trade liberalization in the 1840s being encouraged by the British example.[30] Bismarck's banker and financial advisor Bleichröder noted the prevalence of a desire in certain elite circles "to tailor our [monetary policies] to the British pattern."[31] The gold mark became a symbol of the German challenge to the politico–economic hegemony of the British, as "the [gold] mark could take its place besides the pound as the mainstay of stability in the West."[32] The importance of monetary status was made all the more evident by the questionable economic rationality of a sudden transformation of six Germanic monetary systems traditionally founded on silver and paper circulation (only Bremen was on a gold standard). US Secretary of the Treasury McCulloch (1879, p. 16), in fact, argued that a rapid transition to gold monometallism was a mistake. Germany, he added, paid a great price for "[placing] herself along side of Great Britain." She risked severe deflation and could not match Britain's capacity to keep gold and thus maintain convertibility.[33]

Monetary ideology also had a place in US monetary history in the eighteenth and nineteenth centuries. White (1893, p. 6) argued that Hamilton's advocacy of bimetallism in the late eighteenth century was founded on a veneration of the policies of prominent European nations. Some of the most powerful political forces behind the Gold Bill of 1834 (which changed the legal ratio from 15:1 to 16:1, thus overvaluing gold at the mint and causing the displacement of silver) advocated increasing gold circulation based on tradition ("[our] fathers once possessed it") and prevailing practices elsewhere ("the subjects of European kings now possess [it]").[34] The Act of 1853 was preceded by Congressional diatribes in the early 1850s against bimetallism, citing such practices as being antithetical to what the leading political economists of the day approved.[35] Representative Dunham, who on behalf of the Ways and Means Committee introduced the bill that would become the Act of 1853, associated various economic advantages with a gold standard based on the "experience of every nation which has attempted it."[36]

It is not clear, however, that gold held an ideological advantage over silver throughout the nineteenth century in the US. The US was consistently metallist, but the balance of ideology among silver and gold tended in general not to be skewed.[37] Friedman and Schwartz (1963, p. 109) identify regional attachments to metals, the East being sympathetic to gold, and the West and South being sympathetic to silver.[38] One can add to this division urban versus rural attachments. And although US monetary legislation in the 1870s appeared not to have the same ideological force behind it that legislation in Germany did, evidence suggests that both supporters of gold and silver came to the realization that gold was becoming the universal standard, and that this represented a compelling factor in Congressional decisions over appropriate policies.[39]

French metallist ideology seems to have been amenable to bimetallism throughout the nineteenth century. Much of the ideological attachment was founded on tradition, i.e., venerating the monetary practices of their revolutionary ancestors as manifest in the legislation of 1803 and 1811.[40] Napoleon III's Saint-Simonian policy leanings and personal veneration for British economic policy styles appeared to create the seeds of an ideological attachment to gold in the Second Empire.[41] But his dependence on the Bank of France for financing his foreign campaigns sensitized him to the Bank's (as well as the Finance Ministry's and haute finance's) advocacy of bimetallism, an advocacy sustained by a history of lucrative arbitrage in the two metals.[42]

Like France, the metallist ideologies of Latin Union members Italy, Switzerland, and Belgium seemed somewhat ambiguous, and the ideological factors underlying their policies in the 1870s are difficult to tease apart from other structural and proximate factors. Italy's adoption of the French monetary system in 1862 was stimulated by gratitude to Napoleon III for facilitating unification, as well as Victor Emmanuel's loyalty to the monetary practices of his native Sardinia. The Belgian Chambers in 1847 sought to introduce a gold circulation based on a "patriotic desire."[43] Holland, if anything, was ideologically silverite and bimetallist, with a strong royal and popular attachment to silver,[44] although, as with Latin Union countries, the strength and independence of ideology in the Dutch case are problematic. Evidence on the Scandinavian countries did not show any overwhelming ideological stimuli in their conversion to gold.

Of the nations that experienced policy transformations in the 1870s, the structural effects of ideology seem to have been strongest in Germany, and somewhat less compelling in other nations.

Industrialization and economic development

Laughlin (1886), White (1893), and Helfferich (1927) all accounted for the scramble of the 1870s as part of a general monetary evolution that continually causes inconvenient monies to be replaced by more convenient monies. The impetus for a more convenient metal was the result of the industrial revolution. The size and amount of economic transactions grew with economic development, and growing economic activity spilled out internationally as the level of foreign trade increased. This naturally increased the burden of using silver, the metal with much higher transaction costs in exchange.

At the time, O.D. Ashley noted that

[Gold] is less bulky and easier to transport, more convenient to carry upon the person, and more easily guarded against theft or destruction. Ten dollars in silver would be an uncomfortable weight in the pocket, while in gold it would make no perceptible difference ... If there were no other reasons than these, they seem strong enough to give gold the preference as the principal measure of value.[45]

Chevalier (1859, pp. 39, 40, 94, 95) argued that just as Rome stopped using bronze when silver became sufficiently abundant, gold came to displace silver when it became available in sufficient amounts in the 1850s. For Parieu the events of the latter nineteenth century fit perfectly into a pattern that saw "mineralogical, industrial, and commercial circumstances" lead to metals of superior "portability and density" replacing those of inferior portability and density. It is perfectly natural, he argued, that "silver first took the place of iron and copper, and . . . silver is now displaced by gold."[46] According to Edward Atkinson of the US, the rise of gold in the 1870s was a process of "natural selection."[47] Helfferich (1927, p. 118) pointed out that the increased use of gold after 1650 was contemporaneous with the spurt in international trade in the seventeenth century [48] He further identified the British commitment to gold monometallism in the late eighteenth and early nineteenth centuries as deriving from a concern over the convenience of exchange.[49] "Great civilized communities," argued Chevalier (1859, p. 95), "modify the machinery of their exchanges, in proportion as commerce extends its operations and enlarges its spheres."

Laughlin (1886, pp. 168–170) identified a "one-way" trend in the evolution of monetary policy in the nineteenth century. Nations, he said, allowed gold to displace silver in circulation in the 1850s and 1860s, but would not tolerate the opposite trend in the 1870s.[50] Nations were more troubled by a lack of gold than by a lack of silver. Russell (1898, p. 202) referred to this nineteenth century policy bias as "the natural tendency with advancing civilization to give to gold a quality as a measure of values which it denies to silver."[51]

This suggests that there was a systematic instability in bimetallism after 1850 that would have made it difficult to sustain cyclical shortages of gold emanating from the workings of Gresham's Law. Such cyclical shortages affected both metals in bimetallist regimes throughout the nineteenth century, which essentially rendered the practice of bimetallism an alternating monometallist standard.[52] Under any hypothetical bimetallist regime, if the market bimetallic ratio is distributed randomly around the prevailing legal (i.e., mint) ratio over time, and divergences between the two ratios make arbitrage in metals profitable (i.e., are greater than the transaction costs of arbitrage), then Gresham's Law will produce alternating abundances in one metal (the bad money, or that money whose mint value exceeds its intrinsic value) and shortages in the other (the good money, or that money which is undervalued at the mint). It is clear that nations' one-way orientation toward media of exchange in this period would have tolerated periods of de facto gold standards more than periods of de facto silver standards.[53] In this respect, preferences seemed to "tip" toward gold as a central metallic medium of exchange.[54] Hence, it appears that bimetallism after the 1850s might not have been as stable as Friedman (1990a, 1990b) has contended. Nations would have instituted restraints against recurrent shortages of gold, and in the 1870s, this took the form of demonetizing silver.[55]

The transformation of monetary standards was not independent of the greater evolution of financial institutions in the nineteenth century. Rapid industrialization and economic development after 1850 shaped financial institutions in the developed world according to new imperatives. Nowhere was this more evident than in Germany and France where the development of banking systems capable of handling long-term industrial lending was a response to the needs of the new industrial economies on the Continent.[56] Bouvier's term for the transformation of French banking in the nineteenth century ("cosmopolitan") aptly fits the transformation of monetary standards. Gold was the more cosmopolitan standard and silver the more rustic since gold was better adapted to an urban–industrial economy and silver to an agricultural economy (where transactions are fewer and smaller). As an issue of the Economist (1866, p. 1252) of the period pointed out, "Gold money is becoming the money of commerce . . . The large obligations of modern times are best settled in a costly metal. Gold is . . . the wholesale money of mercantile nations." H.R. Linderman testified to the

US Monetary Commission (1876, vol. II, p. 199) that irrespective of what standard nations adopted in the 1870s, people would not transact in silver. If they could not use gold, he argued, they would use paper.[57] Transactions in coin after 1850 were still sufficiently abundant to make convenience in domestic exchange an important issue. As late as 1856, 80 percent of French payments were effected in metal (50 percent gold and 30 percent silver), while only 20 percent were effected in bank notes. By 1891 France still had 160 million pounds' worth of coin in circulation. In Italy in 1865 only one-tenth of the money in circulation represented bank notes.[58] Even in Great Britain the need for gold in transactions was pronounced up until the First World War.[59]

If we differentiate between the early and/or rapid industrializers of the nineteenth century and the late and/or slow industrializers, we see a division of monetary actions in the 1860s and 1870s that is roughly consistent with the expected structural preferences. The early and/or rapid industrializers, Great Britain, Germany, Sweden, Denmark, Switzerland, and Belgium, can be said, as a group, to have fought harder to attain and retain gold standards in the 1860s and 1870s. The late and/or slow developers, France, the US, Italy, and Holland, fought less hard.[60] Holland was the only nation at the International Monetary Conference of 1867 to oppose the overwhelming call for the international adoption of gold monometallism. The US and Italy fought the hardest at the International Conference of 1878 to bring nations back to bimetallism. France, of course, stayed *de jure* with a bimetallist standard through the first half of the 1870s, as other nations turned to gold.[61]

In Germany, the call for gold on grounds of convenience was seen as early as the 1830s from the economist J.G. Hoffman, in the South German States Union (1837), and in the Dresden Agreement (1838). This was part of an ongoing call for a rationalization of German monetary and economic systems to bring Germany more into line with economic modernization on the Continent. The call was most visible in resolutions issued by the Congress of German Economists which met regularly throughout the nineteenth century.[62] The supply of gold in Germany before 1850, however, was far too small to institute a gold standard. The father of German monetary unification Ludwig Bamberger himself believed in the inevitability of the movement toward more convenient mediums of exchange in Germany. Under any dual-standard system, he reasoned, the more convenient standard will displace the less convenient.[63] Both White (1893, pp. 14, 15) and Helfferich (1927, p. 149) saw convenience as a principal factor behind the course of German monetary unification in the 1870s.

In the US, monetary experts questioned the rationality of maintaining a standard with silver coins in large denominations. John Sherman (1895,

p. 696) argued that even if the American silver dollar were remonetized in the 1870s, Americans would shun it due to its inconvenience; they would opt for paper instead.[64] By the 1870s the US was indeed showing the normal developed-nation structure of exchange: larger transactions moving away from silver.[65]

In the Latin Union states of Switzerland, France, Belgium, and Italy, the infusion of gold coin during the 1850s and 1860s was received quite favorably, especially among commercial groups.[66] In France, the Finance Ministry in 1858 underscored how tolerant the French were of the situation of the 1850s when gold flowed in and silver departed.[67] White (1893, p. 19) noted how the French after 1850 were happy to rid themselves of the inconvenience of carrying around heavy sacks of 5-franc silver pieces in cabs and handcarts. Chevalier (1859) argued that the French acceptance of gold in the 1850s was functionally similar to the British situation earlier in the century, diverting to a more convenient medium of exchange once it became abundant.[68] The French economist Levasseur saw the 1850s and 1860s in France as a time of monetary evolution. He added that practices should conform to evolutionary realities, and that the more fit metal (gold) should be made the central money.[69]

In Belgium in the 1840s, one of the principal factors encouraging the Belgian Chambers to introduce a gold coin in 1847 was a concern for the preferences of business for a more convenient medium of exchange.[70] In Switzerland the proliferation of French gold coins in the early 1850s was greatly welcomed by Swiss business interests who found the new coins much less cumbersome. Swiss chambers of commerce, and banking and mercantile associations put constant pressure on the Bundesrath in the 1850s and 1860s to insure a convenient standard. The financial community actually based its transactions on French gold through the Bankvaluta system which dictated, among other things, that bills were payable in French gold.[71]

Among Scandinavian nations it became a major imperative to replace a burdensome silver standard with more convenient money.[72] Holland was less resolute in making the transition to gold, and evidence regarding the compelling convenience of gold appears less for Holland than for other Western European nations.

The growth of an international economy in the nineteenth century compounded the effects of domestic economic development on the choice of a monetary standard. For Unger (1964, p. 331), "the strong, world-wide current for an international gold standard [was a response to the] rational needs of a developing international economy." The enormous growth of trade in the middle decades of the century naturally conferred a greater attractiveness onto the superior trade-clearing metal.[73] Gold's importance in foreign trade had historically preceded its importance as a domestic medium of exchange. It was not uncommon for nations on standards other than gold to clear their trade payments in gold. In Sweden, for example, the silver rix thaler was the central monetary coin, but trade was cleared in gold ducats. A dual standard was also practiced in Argentina where gold became the medium for international payments, while paper became the domestic medium of exchange.[74]

One major concern behind the attempt at an international monetary union at the Conference of 1867 was with reducing the transaction costs of foreign trade through the institution of a common gold standard. Laughlin (1886, p. 152) underscored the pressure put on French monetary authorities to use gold as a result of the growth of trade after 1848. In Belgium, where the trade sector was large relative to the economy, the pressure for gold was especially acute.

The growth in trade also served to compel nations toward Great Britain's standard because most of the world's trade was cleared in London. Moreover, with the growth and internationalization of finance, the standard used by Great Britain became more compelling as financial institutions were drawn into an international market place for financial services and investments dominated by the London market.

Here again, gold was part of a greater movement at the time: that for international standardization. Russell (1898, pp. 82, 83) talked of the consensus at the International Monetary Conference of 1867 for gold as being reflective of a "spirit of the times." Part of this *Zeitgeist* was a movement toward reducing the transaction costs of international interdependence by standardizing the means of transportation, communication, and exchange.[75] It was visible as early as the 1850s in the agitation for the standardization of weights and measures.[76] The sentiment extended in the 1860s to calls and initiatives for international monetary unification, of which the International Monetary Conference of 1867 was the highpoint.[77] Ludwig Bamberger and John Sherman argued that with the growth of commerce, nations would be increasingly compelled toward conformity in their monetary systems.[78] The complex calculations required in determining the values of foreign currencies without standardization, and the foreign exchange charges incurred by merchants became more burdensome as trade grew.

For reasons both of growing domestic and international exchange, therefore, silver was increasingly perceived to be obsolete as a central monetary metal.

The politics of gold

The victory of gold over silver in the 1870s was as much a political as it was a practical and ideological victory. As with most economic institutions, monetary practices exhibited a consistency with ongoing political developments in the world. The growing attraction of gold over silver partly reflected changing political power structures across the nineteenth century. A rising urban–capitalist class (professionals, business, banking) was displacing an agricultural class (farmers and landowners) in the political hierarchy, and the monetary victory of gold over silver and bimetallism was in many ways coterminous with the political victory of the bourgeoisie.[79] It is not surprising that Great Britain was the first to go to gold, given that this political struggle was first resolved there.

Clough and Cole (1946, p. 358) argue that the liberalism of the nineteenth century was the "class philosophy" of a rising urban–industrial class. Monetary philosophies can also be differentiated according to particular class preferences in this period. The virtues of gold were best adapted to urban–industrial interests, while silver and bimetallism were better adapted to agricultural interests. Gold was naturally the preferred metal for business interests given that its convenience most efficiently expedited transactions.[80] Creditor (banking) classes would naturally favor the metal that was perceived to be historically most stable, and the nineteenth century witnessed a widespread perception that gold was that metal.[81] Starting in the 1860s the value of silver began a secular and precipitous decline, thus definitively casting pro-inflation (agricultural) interests on the side of silver, and stable-money (urban–industrial) interests on the side of gold. But even before the 1870s, many creditors had been collecting debts in gold.[82] Moreover, stable-money interests sided with monometallism, while pro-inflation interests sided with bimetallism. First, there was the conviction that a multiple metallic standard would encourage a larger money supply. Second, under bimetallism debtors had the benefit of accepting loans in an appreciating metal and liquidating in a depreciating metal.[83] To some extent, this narrowed the monetary menu to a choice between gold and silver monometallism in a period when the silver standard was the least acceptable (ideologically and economically) metallist option.[84] By the 1880s, the creation of an international bimetallist league to abate the decline of silver had become politically impossible.[85]

Germany's political transition in the nineteenth century was less complete than that of other Continental nations, but with respect to the structure of influence over monetary issues, it fitted well into the Continental trend. The rise of the urban industrial classes on the Continent manifested itself in the rise of liberal parties. In Germany the party of note was the National Liberal Party which, according to Stern (1977, p. 177), came to represent the interests and ideals of the German middle class (academics, industrialists, urban professionals, bankers, merchants). It crystallized from the fracture of liberal politics in the 1860s and emerged as the principal challenger to the German Conservatives, a party strongly grounded in agricultural interests (peasants and landowners). In the 1870s liberals became the dominant party in the Reichstag (they had as many as 40 percent of the seats in 1874).

The political struggle between classes, in Germany and on the Continent as a whole, was coterminous with the struggle between autocratic government and parliamentary government. In Germany it was specifically between the Crown (the conservative bases of power were the army, bureaucracy, and the Crown) and the Reichstag. Bismarck, whose own leanings dictated a conservative government in Germany, was intent on resolving this dispute in a way that would bring about unification founded on a clear conservative hierarchy which was supported by an urban–industrial class; he felt no government was sustainable without the backing of the two economic pillars of the German state (agriculture and industry).[86] He therefore orchestrated a quid pro quo which configured domestic economic policy according to the preferences of liberals in exchange for liberal support of a conservative government. Led by Bamberger, the liberals were able to impose their monetary agenda onto reluctant conservatives.[87]

In the Latin Union and Northern European nations, there was much more continuity between real political influence and economic policy. The Second Empire (1852–71) saw France make major strides toward a government consistent with liberal principals.[88] Politics became inextricably tied to the preferences of the rising economic classes. Napoleon III's own power elite (appointed ministers) came disproportionately from the grand bourgeoisie (merchants, financiers, and industrialists). The legislature (Deputies) came to be dominated by former civil servants and the grand bourgeoisie, each more numerous than landowners.[89] Napoleon's political agenda was not functionally dissimilar to Bismarck's. Both men courted a broad-based coalition of political movements under a fundamentally conservative banner, Napoleon seeking a union of the masses, aristocracy, and bourgeoisie under a Bonapartist masthead. Both courted the middle classes through economic reforms in the full realization that no French or German government could be viable in the absence of bourgeoisie support.

Switzerland and Belgium, after many years of liberal agitation, saw the entrenchment of liberal governments by the 1870s. Belgium's liberal constitution, founded after independence from Holland in 1830, set a European precedent. Liberals, representing the large-town bourgeoisie, dominated Belgian politics from 1847 to 1870, and the Liberal party under M. Frere-Orban took formal control of the government in 1878.[90] Switzerland, even before federation in 1848, was dominated by liberal politics through regional control in the cantons; the constitution of a united Switzerland

was, in fact, the creation of liberal forces.[91] This institutionalization of
liberal politics was crucial in moving the Bundesrath in a direction that was
consistent with the demands of business and banking in the mid- and late
1850s. One of these demands was the monetization of gold consistent with
the French system.

Post-unification Italy in the 1860s and early 1870s was dominated by a
liberal elite. The political system was an extension of Piedmonte's which
had had a liberal constitutional system from the late 1840s. This essentially
reflected Cavour's own political and economic leanings, which were
strongly configured around the English example. Up until 1876 when the
Left took power, leaders tended to be Cavour clones, reflecting both his
political and economic agendas.[92]

The Scandinavian nations and Holland followed the Continental trend.
Sweden saw the rise of liberal politics in the 1840s as a function of the
political rise of a business class. As in France and Germany, liberals used
this leverage to promote economic reforms. In Sweden the rise of liberal
politics was especially pervasive, manifesting itself in the management of
political, economic, judicial, and social systems.[93] For Denmark, like
Sweden, the 1840s was also a crucial period in the growth of liberalism.
Liberals became a national party in 1842 and by the late 1840s gained
significant influence in state assemblies. The 1840s also saw Christian VIII
undertake extensive economic reforms. By the 1850s the National Liberal
Party came to dominate the Royal Council and the Landsting.[94] In
Holland 1848 proved to be a crucial political turning point. Led by
Thorbecke, liberals imposed a constitution (on the government of William
II) which reflected a middle-class political agenda and the system, consolidated under William III (1848–90), carried on a typically Continental style
of economic policy.[95] Holland also showed the same political dynamics
over monetary issues that France had in the 1870s: a split between a Crown
or executive which sympathized with silver versus a coalition of capitalist
groups pushing strongly for gold. The reluctance to relinquish silver and
bimetallist regimes *de jure* in these nations in the 1870s can be largely
explained by a liberal lag in coopting the executive on monetary practices.[96]

Norway did not reflect the typical Continental timing in the transformation of politics, although the Norwegian political struggle was indeed
typically Continental (liberal coalition versus a conservative government
led by the Crown). Party politics remained relatively underdeveloped, and
it was not until the mid-1880s that liberals and conservatives formed viable
political parties. And although liberals gradually gained some power
throughout the century, it was not until 1884 that they took formal control
of the governmment.[97] Much of this is explained by the fact that Norway
did not experience the same socio–economic transformation that other

Continental nations did: it remained predominantly a small peasant farming economy throughout the nineteenth century.[98]

In the United States, the politics of money after the Civil War were coterminous with the politics of inflation. The monetary factions seemed to crystallize into three partly overlapping sets of opposing forces: by class, region, and party politics. With respect to class, the factions fundamentally mirrored the European style: stable money was the preference of an urban–capitalist class (commercial bankers, professionals, merchants, manufacturers, gentlemen reformers, respected literati) and was confronted by an inflationist–rural–agricultural class of farmers, landowners, and miners.[99] Regionally, the issue often split along a North and East (stable money) versus South and West (inflationist) cleavage. With respect to party politics, it was the "hard-money" Republicans versus "soft-money" Democrats.[100] Unlike Europe, where the shift in monetary politics in favor of stable money was incremental, the shift in the US power structure emerged abruptly from the ashes of the Civil War which, by enhancing industrialization and sectionally polarizing party politics, created rigidities favoring stable-money interests in the American political system for the rest of the century.[101]

In sum, the politics of money, as a reflection of the greater political struggle within the developed world, showed that monetary issues were increasingly resolved in favor of a convenient and stable money, which by the end of the 1860s and early 1870s was equated with gold.

The proximate foundations of the scramble for gold: chain gangs and regime transformation

The 1860s: A decade of growing nervousness

The compelling structural changes in the developed world in the nineteenth century created an environment ripe for monetary regime transition after 1850.[102] It was not until the late 1860s and early 1870s, however, that a structurally predisposed developed world encountered the proximate catalysts that consummated the transformation of monetary standards. These catalysts represented various critical events (which were principally coterminous with developments in the market for precious metals) that created and compounded nervousness over future trends in the value of silver.

The policy changes of the 1870s that demonetized silver were part of a common trend in the monetary history of the nineteenth century which saw nations protecting their monetary systems against disturbances in the market for metals. The gold strikes in the late 1840s and 1850s, for example, led to a depreciation of gold which caused Belgium, Spain, Naples, Switzerland, and Holland to protect their silver circulations by limiting gold convertibility. For similar reasons, Great Britain demonetized gold in India in the 1850s.[103] The Act of 1834 changed the legal bimetallic ratio in the United States from 15:1 to 16:1 in order to abate a shortage of circulating gold coin resulting from a market bimetallic ratio that undervalued gold and overvalued silver at the mint.[104] The Act of 1853 reduced the weight of small silver coins to abate the effects of the gold discoveries on silver circulation.[105] Like other metallist monetary regimes, the regimes of the 1870s were thus subject to vagaries in the market for precious metals, but the constellation of policy responses of the 1870s was far broader on a national level, and far more pervasive on an international level, than any similar phenomena before it.

The 1870s version of this trend showed policy responses to the displacement of gold by silver in circulation owing to a depreciation of the latter metal. This reversed the pattern which had prevailed in the 1850s and early 1860s when the depreciation of gold led to the displacement of silver. By the late 1860s, with the movement of the market bimetallic ratio to a level which overvalued silver and undervalued gold at mints, it became profitable to import and coin silver, and melt and export gold. A continuation of this trend had two severe consequences. First, national monetary systems would be dominated by silver circulation, and gold would be scarce. Second, with the inflow of silver, nations would be on *de facto* standards based upon what John Sherman pejoratively referred to as a "depreciated currency" (1895, p. 541). Nations had difficulty tolerating the first, given their greater dependence on gold for larger-coin transactions. As for the second, a depreciating currency carried the possibility of multiple undesirable consequences: a depreciating exchange rate *vis-à-vis* gold-standard nations, depletion of international reserves (silver-standard nations would deplete their reserves when adjusting with nations on gold), and inflation. The stable-money monetary officials of the period were quite hostile to any such possibilities, especially inflation.[106] Chevalier (1859, p. 201) noted that it was destabilizing for nations to shift (either *de jure* or *de facto*) to a standard "at the very moment when it is impaired in value and launched in a movement of depreciation."[107]

Like metallist regimes of the past, therefore, the regimes of this period were sensitized to developments in the market for precious metals. Given the strong structural predisposition toward gold, any developments in the supply and demand for metals that suggested a secular decline in the value of silver in the face of a stable or rising gold value, was the cause of grave concern. The worst-case scenarios portrayed the maintenance of silver and bimetallist standards when the decline in the value of silver was large, rapid, and secular. The nervousness over the market for metals became significant in the 1860s when the expressions of the preferability of gold over silver and bimetallist standards became pronounced, thus suggesting that a major shift in the demand for gold (whose value promised to rise) and silver (whose value promised to decline) was on the horizon. These expressions became more intense and international, and thus more visible, as the decade progressed, and with the visibility came a higher level of apprehension.[108]

At the national level, the calls for a legal gold standard were widespread. The Congress of German Economists and Chambers of Commerce (Handelsstag) had been advocating a gold standard in German states throughout the 1860s. Toward the end of the decade Prussian legislators, the German Customs Parliament, and various business groups (trade congresses) were calling for German membership in an international union based on gold.[109] In 1869 a strong movement in Belgium arose to demonetize silver.[110] Norway in 1869 began transforming its reserves from silver to gold. And in Sweden, a specially formed monetary commission in 1869 unanimously called for monetary union among Scandinavian nations based on a gold standard.[111] French Chambers of Commerce and public opinion advocated a gold standard in France.[112] Similarly, in Switzerland, commercial and banking groups, along with the various canton administrations and economists, strongly supported the move to gold. The Swiss National Council, in fact, interpreted the Act of 1860 which monetized gold as reflecting an intention to institute a gold standard in Switzerland.[113]

At the international level, there were two major gatherings of nations considering monetary union: the Latin Monetary meeting in 1865 and the International Monetary Conference of 1867. The Latin meeting, which was originally called in response to disturbances in subsidiary silver circulation among the franc-bloc nations, ended up consummating a broader monetary union among France, Belgium, Switzerland, and Italy. The delegates of all four nations originally advocated union based on gold monometallism, with the French delegates eventually changing their preference to bimetallism after strict instructions from the French government.[114] The Latin Union was founded on *de jure* bimetallism, but in actuality maintained a *de facto* gold standard by instituting a legal bimetallic ratio of $15\frac{1}{2}:1$.[115] While the Latin Union meeting was regional, that of 1867 was truly international (inviting 20 nations that represented the developed world at the time) and unanimously proclaimed gold monometallism as the only appropriate standard for economically developed nations.[116] The Conference proved to be one of the more crucial events in convincing nations that a major disturbance in the market for metals was imminent. Monetary experts of the period and historians have identified the Conference as a fundamental turning point in the scramble for gold. According to Feer-Herzog, the

Conference "sowed precious seed . . . which the future would cause to germinate."[117] For the US monetary diplomat Francis A. Walker "The Conference of 1867, in proclaiming the crusade against silver . . . did [initiate the demonetization of silver], the consequences of which are even yet only half unfolded."[118] As a direct consequence of the Conference, the Bank of Norway, for example, was authorized to change its reserves from silver to gold.[119] The Conference also proved to be a principal catalyst of Germany's movement to gold. Its proclamation of an impending monetary transformation in the developed world made a German transformation seem ever more necessary in the Reichstag because of the large amount of silver in German states which would have to be liquidated.[120]

In addition to the proliferation of appeals for a legal gold standard, developments in India also bode poorly for the future of silver. India had emerged as one of the principal silver markets in the world. Indian silver imports relative to world production exhibited an enormous increase after 1854. From 1855 to 1865, with the exception of the year 1860, yearly Indian net imports of silver were either greater or slightly below the entire yearly production of silver in the world. (The net imports in 1865 were almost twice the world production of silver.)[121] The period 1866–70 saw a decline in yearly net silver imports relative to world production to levels lower than the quinquennial imports of 1856–60 (see table 2.1).[122] Even though the price of silver showed little immediate sensitivity to shifts in Indian demand, these developments presaged difficult times for silver in the future because the conditions leading to a lower demand for silver were not perceived as reversible.[123] First, with the return of US cotton onto the world market, Indian exports would never again reach the levels achieved in the years 1861–65. Furthermore, less silver was flowing into India because of an increasing use of council bills to clear payments, a practice which was expected to continue in the future.[124] It became apparent that the decline of one of the world's largest markets for silver might be secular rather than cyclical, given that significant changes in net silver imports before 1860 were never the result of systematic uses of new financial instruments.

On the supply side, the production of silver had been secularly increasing from the second decade of the century, with especially large increases after 1850.[125] The average yearly increases from the period 1856–60 to that of 1861–65 and from 1861–65 to 1866–70 were both 22 percent. Even in the latter quinquennia, however, the average yearly increase from the previous quinquennia was still well below the average yearly net imports of silver into India.[126] But aside from contributing to a mild decline in the price of silver in the late 1860s, the increase added more concern about the market for metals, especially in light of the fact that the production of gold during the 1860s was declining. Gold production declined from the middle to the

Table 2.1 *Silver: net imports into India and world production, 1851–79*

Year	Net imports of silver into India (1) (000)	World production of silver (2) (000)	Net imports as a percentage of world production
1851	$14,327		36
1852	23,025		58
1853	11,529	$39,875	29
1854	148		< 1
1855	40,972		103
1856	55,366		136
1857	61,095		150
1858	38,641	40,725	95
1859	55,738		137
1860	26,640		65
1861	45,432		92
1862	62,751		127
1863	63,984	49,550	129
1864	50,394		102
1865	93,343		188
1866	34,815		58
1867	27,970		46
1868	43,005	60,250	71
1869	36,602		61
1870	4,710		8
1871	32,564		37
1872	3,523		4
1873	12,257	88,625	14
1874	23,211		26
1875	7,777		9
1876	35,994		32
1877	73,382	112,500	65
1878	19,853		18
1879	39,349		35

Notes:
1. Estimates in *Report to House of Commons*, 1876 and French Report of Conference of 1881, both reprinted in Laughlin (1886, pp. 252, 253).
2. Soetbeer's estimates, reprinted in Laughlin (1886, p. 218).

end of the decade, and total decadal production in the 1860s was 7 percent lower than production in the 1850s. These differential trends in supply promised to compound the effects of prevailing demand conditions in moving the values of gold and silver in directions that would threaten national gold supplies. And, in fact, the latter half of the decade saw the price of silver dip and remain below 61ppp, and the market bimetallic ratio move from a level that was below the legal ratio in Latin Union nations (thus encouraging a large gold circulation because gold was overvalued at the mints) to one that was above the legal ratio (thus threatening to drive gold out of circulation).[127]

In sum, the latter half of the 1860s witnessed the emergence of a nervousness over conditions prevailing in the market for metals. The principal concerns centered around supply and demand conditions that carried important consequences for monetary standards, and these conditions tended to be perceived as permanent rather than transitory. Gold would continue to dominate larger-coin transactions, the Indian market for silver was declining, and monetary authorities were compelled by the practice of gold monometallism. Critical events embodied in national and international proclamations of the superiority of gold monometallism as a standard for developed nations were perceived to carry important secular demand consequences. In the short run, the supply of precious metals showed an increase in the production of silver and a decline in the production of gold, the price of silver was declining, and the market bimetallic ratio was moving above the legal ratio prevailing in the bimetallist nations of Europe. It became commonly perceived that the world was moving toward conditions which would make it impossible concurrently to circulate silver and gold at par, and that any such attempts at concurrent circulation under the traditional practice of a fixed legal ratio would result in a scarcity of the most convenient metal: gold. Furthermore, any nation remaining on a silver standard would be faced with the possibility of a depreciated currency. In a fundamental sense, the 1860s initiated a contraction of the metallist menu in the eyes of monetary authorities. With prevailing conditions increasingly delegitimating the practices of orthodox bimetallism (i.e., with a fixed legal ratio) and silver monometallism, the choice was converging toward gold.

But as the decade ended no significant policy initiatives had been enacted that would legally eliminate silver as a central monetary unit, or significantly limit the convertibility of silver. Latin Union nations were still legally bimetallist, as was the United States, which was continuing a suspension of convertibility. Sweden, Denmark, Norway, Holland, and Germany were legally on silver standards. As long as the value of silver had only depreciated slightly and mints remained open, fears of gold depletion and floods of silver were not overwhelming. This created a holding pattern in the late 1860s. Critical developments in the 1870s would turn this disposition of "watchful waiting" into a scramble for gold.

The monetary chain gang

In terms of pervasive economic policy changes, the transition to gold in the 1870s was relatively rapid. The decision to move to gold monometallism had been consummated in Germany and the Scandinavian nations by the end of 1872. For members of the Latin Union the transition was initiated in 1873–74, first with the limitation on the coinage of 5-franc silver pieces in Belgium and France in 1873, and then with the institution of limits over the entire membership of the Latin Union in 1874.[128] Holland limited the purchase of silver ingots at the Netherlands Bank in 1872 and temporarily suspended the coinage of silver in 1873. The United States was still on a paper standard, but did legally demonetize its central silver coin in 1873 and further marginalized silver by instituting a regime of limited silver coinage with the Bland–Allison Act of 1878. It thus took three years from the time Germany moved to gold in 1871 for all these nations to eliminate silver as a central monetary metal.

This speed was a natural outcome of conditions that created a monetary "chain gang" among these nations: the movement of any one or a few nations to gold in this period of nervousness would assure that the others would follow suit. The chain gang structure of monetary policy emanated from two types of interdependence. The first I refer to as speculative interdependence; the second was of a monetary and trade nature.

As for speculative interdependence, conditions in the market for silver in the late 1860s and early 1870s were functionally similar to conditions in markets which find themselves at the height of a speculative boom (i.e., bubble), where investors are holding assets or commodities whose values are threatened with sharp and rapid declines. The liquidation of assets or commodities in such markets at what is considered a peak is typically one of contagious liquidation or "running with the herd," where one or two significant liquidations will create an urgency for other investors to follow.[129]

Monetary experts of the period described the late 1860s and early 1870s as a period of "alarm and apprehensions" and even "panic" over developments in the market for metals that could have grave consequences for national monetary systems.[130] Any compelling signs that market conditions were turning against silver, either by a sharp decline in its value or crucial events (like legal changes in monetary practices) that signalled an impending decline, created a sense of urgency to pre-empt others in demonetizing silver, or to follow closely behind the demonetization initiatives of other nations. Any lag was considered with the greatest concern. Feer-Herzog's description of a common perception shortly before 1871 is representative:

There are two milliards of silver in Germany and Austria demanding that they be converted into gold, because the states that possess them are resolved to adopt the gold standard. The state that demonetizes first will do so with but little loss, while the state which shall have hesitated and waited will undergo the losses resulting from the demonetizations which have preceded its own, and so will pay for all the rest. The German authors have perfectly understood . . . the advantages which will accrue to their country from acting speedily . . .[131]

From the late 1860s, both France and Germany acknowledged the advantages of pre-empting others onto gold and the disadvantages of lagging behind. France, as noted, was prevented by the deft political maneuvering of the Ministry of Finance, but defenders of gold in the French Monetary Commission of 1869 stressed that the North German states were committed to gold, and that France dare not delay its transition in a world which appeared on the verge of a scramble. Germany's own movement to gold was formulated in an environment in which monetary authorities accepted the inevitability of a global movement toward gold, and were therefore more disposed toward a strategy of early transition.[132] Sumner's assessment of the scramble of the 1870s noted that as soon as nations became convinced of the inevitability of a widespread transition to gold and away from silver (thus assuring a declining value of silver), "they seemed to be running over one another's heels as fast as they could to get rid of silver, because the one who sold first would get the best price."[133]

The chains linking the monetary standards of nations were strengthened by trade and monetary interdependencies which created greater urgency to monitor and respond to changes in the monetary practices of other nations. Nations were concerned with keeping uniformity in their standards so as not to disturb trading relations with their principal partners.[134] Holland would have found it extremely difficult to sustain a silver standard once Germany and Great Britain, its two major trading partners, were both practicing gold standards. The Dutch monetary diplomat Mees stated that as long as Holland stood between Germany and Great Britain financially and geographically, she must conform to their monetary practices.[135] In the United States, it was acknowledged in elite monetary circles that the movement to gold by the major trading nations of the world necessitated a gold standard.[136] From the 1870s onwards John Sherman (1895, pp. 470, 1190) continued to argue against central monetary status for silver on the grounds that such a practice would "detach the United States from the monetary standards of all the chief . . . nations of the world . . . with which [the United States had its] chief commercial and social relations." In France there was grave concern over carrying on exchanges with the "great commercial nations" in a depreciated currency.[137]

In the greater constellation of developed nations that made transitions to gold in the 1870s, trade and monetary dependence most visibly manifested itself in two economic "satellite" systems: (1) Germany and its Northern European satellites (Sweden, Denmark, Norway, and Holland) and (2) France and its principal Latin satellites (Switzerland, Belgium and Italy). Each of these satellite systems itself formed a small monetary chain gang centered around the monetary and trade hegemony of Germany and France. Within these systems the monetary policies of hegemonic economies were compelling: any changes in monetary practices in the core were quickly exported to the satellite economies. Germany's Northern satellites stayed historically close to German monetary practices principally due to trade dependence; they, like Germany, were on silver standards before the 1870s. At the International Monetary Conference of 1867, the Norwegian delegate Broch made it clear that given Norway and Sweden's dependence on their trade with Northern German states (especially Hamburg), any decision these nations reached on a monetary standard must be conditional upon Germany's selection of the same standard.[138] M.J. Cramer, a US diplomat reporting on the monetary situation among Scandinavian nations following Germany's move to gold in 1871, identified an overwhelming perception that because of Germany's new standard, "a corresponding change in the money system of the Scandinavian North had become an absolute necessity."[139] Holland, too, as noted, found the German move compelling.[140] Compounded by an already large British trade, the Northern nations found themselves in a bloc whose monetary practices were essentially contingent upon the preferences of Germany. The Scandinavian Monetary Union and monetary legislation in Holland were strong manifestations of Germany exporting her monetary standard onto economically dependent nations.[141]

The Latin Union nations showed the same historical conformity in monetary standards. The Union's formation in 1865 merely consolidated an already existing monetary bloc (the franc bloc).[142] In fact, Switzerland, Belgium, and Italy inaugurated the monetary systems of their newly unified or independent nations based exactly upon the French system as legislated in the Law of 1803. In Belgium's case, the Law of 1832 inaugurating a monetary policy was a "word for word" recreation of the French Law of 1803.[143] By the 1860s, monetary and trade dependence within the Latin constellation had grown so as to preclude any significant deviations from French monetary practices.[144] The Swiss monetary diplomat Kern's statement putting forward his nation's position on monetary unification at the International Monetary Conference of 1867 is representative of the fate of Latin satellites. He said that Switzerland itself preferred union based on a gold standard, but that its ultimate decision would be dictated by the preference of France.[145] The Latin Union found itself in a situation in which "as soon as France gave up its double standard and accepted the gold standard . . . [i]t was certain that Switzerland, Belgium, and Italy would express their absolute adherence to such a step."[146]

The late 1860s and early 1870s thus found the developed world in a nervous environment and configured in a structure of monetary and trade interdependence that dictated a conformity in monetary practices. Such a situation was ripe for a transition onto gold en bloc once the holding pattern of the 1860s had been broken by critical developments in the 1870s which increased the urgency of demonetizing silver.

The 1870s

Nations that adopted *de jure* gold standards in the 1870s did nothing but legally sanction that which they had been practicing throughout the 1850s and 1860s. Values in the market for metals in these decades had been such that gold had displaced silver in circulation (gold was overvalued and silver undervalued at mints). No laws protecting gold circulations were necessary until market conditions changed so as to encourage the displacement of gold. But the overvaluation of gold and undervaluation of silver at mints by the late 1860s was still moderate, and as yet there were no definitive national commitments on the part of major economic powers that threatened the convertibility of silver. The 1870s changed these conditions of watchful waiting into a more intense nervousness. The period of greatest apprehension was initiated by Germany's legal adoption of a gold standard in 1871: Germany's transition can be regarded as the unilateral policy initiative that pulled the monetary chain gang onto gold.[147]

Of the nations that eventually made the transition onto gold after 1870, Germany was perhaps the most structurally predisposed. Pro-gold ideology was most developed in Germany's elite monetary circles. The agitation of interest groups calling for monetary practices better adapted to industrializing economies was most visible in Germany, and politics were strongly conducive to a gold policy given Bismarck's sensitivity to the liberal economic policy agenda. At the proximate level, Germany was anxious not to lag behind a Continental monetary transformation that it perceived as inevitable,[148] and the large inflows of silver in 1871, according to Helfferich (1927, pp. 155, 156), wiped out whatever uncertainty still remained in Germany about the exact course of monetary unification. The swelling silver circulation directly led the government to institute a reduction in the purchase price of silver at the Berlin mint (the largest in Germany). When this failed to abate the influx of silver, the purchase of silver from private persons was suspended at the mint. As Helfferich (1927, p. 156) noted, the exact legislation of monetary unification was now "prejudiced by the pressure of events."[149]

The German move had both immediate psychological and real impacts on its Northern satellites. These nations immediately faced significant influxes of silver.[150] In 1872 a Joint Scandinavian Monetary Commission was formed to consider the monetary question following Germany's transition to gold. The report of the Commission established the foundations of the Scandinavian Monetary Union. It recommended that these nations follow the German policy and institute gold standards. In December 1872 a convention founded on the report was signed by Norway, Sweden, and Denmark. By 1873 all three nations had gold standards. Denmark and Sweden immediately became members of the Union, with Norway deferring membership (but remaining on gold) until 1875.[151] In Holland, the German action caused the King immediately to appoint a monetary commission to consider the question of an appropriate standard for Holland in the wake of the new monetary conditions. The commission concluded that the silver standard had become untenable given the direction of monetary developments in the world. It cited the double standard as theoretically best, but said that it was not possible unless Germany instituted such a standard. It recommended that silver coinage be suspended. In December 1872, the Netherlands Bank stopped purchasing silver; a law instituting a temporary (six-month) suspension of silver coinage was enacted in 1873.[152]

The fall of the German chain gang from silver was consummated by 1873. Fears of the scenario which had gained international attention with the International Monetary Conference of 1867 were beginning to be realized. The world was demonetizing silver: the convertibility of silver on a global scale was becoming restricted as Continental mints were closing. Moreover, the entire net silver imports into India from 1870 to the beginning of 1873 were barely more than they had been in the single year of 1869, and they were approximately half the net imports of the year 1865. Except for the years 1847–49 and 1854, net imports in the year 1872 were the lowest of the century up to that time (see table 2.1). The precipitous decline in Indian silver demand in the 1870s was the source of even more pessimistic expectations about the future demand for silver.

On the supply side, the early 1870s experienced a significant increase in silver production and an equally significant decline in gold production. The increase in silver production from 1870–71 was the single biggest one-year increase of the century (roughly 20 percent by most estimates).[153] Moreover, it was believed that the mines in the United States were still short of their highest yield potential.[154] The following year saw the most significant one-year decline in gold since the 1850s.[155] Especially compelling were fears of the supply consequences of Germany's move to gold.[156] Throughout the 1870s the German silver supply was perceived as a major proportion of an increasing global pool of silver chasing fewer and fewer buyers as nations closed their mints.[157] Fears of what France's Léon Say referred to as Germany's "enormous mass of silver . . . [being thrown] upon the metal market" permeated the decade.[158]

By 1873 the course of events had brought market conditions to a state that put intense pressure upon Latin Union nations, which until this time were still in a holding pattern. In 1872 the price of silver breached two important thresholds. On the London market it had dropped below 60ppp for the first time since 1849.[159] In September 1873 the market bimetallic ratio hit the 16:1 level for the first time since April 1845.[160] The resulting influx of silver and outflow of gold from Latin Union nations assumed "alarming" proportions.[161] The net imports of silver into France in the first three months of 1873 alone reached 52 million francs. Net gold exports more than doubled from 105 million in 1872 to 225 million francs in 1873, and assumed an amount which was greater than one-third of the gold holdings of the Bank of France in 1873. In the years 1872 and 1873, with the exception of Italy, no gold was coined in the Latin Union. The total silver coinage of France and Belgium went from 26,838,370 francs and 10,225,000 francs respectively in 1872 to 156,270,160 and 111,740,795 in 1873. Italy experienced only a 20 percent increase in silver coinage.[162] Switzerland continued its policy of coining little of its own money, but found the influx of silver and the outflow of its foreign gold coin destabilizing. Monetary conditions could not continue in this situation.

Agitation was strong in both Belgium and France to check this unfavorable flow of metals. Belgium was the first among Latin Union nations to begin unilateral action in response to the alarming developments of 1873 by reviving early in that year an old decree (of 1867) that limited the daily coinage of silver to 150,000 francs for the public and an equal amount for the National Bank. Calls for stronger measures followed and the Ministry of Finance addressed the question to a group of monetary authorities, which declared that the Latin Union should move to a gold standard. A law quickly followed empowering the government to limit or suspend the coinage of 5-franc silver pieces until January 1, 1875. France in September 1873 instituted a limit on silver coinage up to 250,000 francs per day (lowered to 150,000 in November). In that same month the Bank of France stopped making advances on deposits of silver bullion, and practically refused to accept Belgian and Italian 5-franc pieces for deposit. These measures, especially the limitations on coinage which were secret, did little to stem the speculation in France.[163]

A collective Latin Union response to the problem became inescapable, and in November 1873 the Swiss issued a request to the French government to convoke a Latin Union meeting to form a new regime based on gold. The request was founded on a shared belief that since Germany and her Northern European satellites were adopting gold, it would be "folly" for Latin Union nations to continue their present policy of bimetallism.[164] The meeting of the Latin Union in January 1874 led to the institution of yearly limits on the coinage of the Union's central silver coin, the 5-franc piece. The limits placed Latin Union nations in a somewhat safer holding pattern from which trends in the market for metals could be assessed before determining an optimal long-term standard for the Union.[165] The measures resulted in a greater flow of gold into Latin Union nations, thus granting some relief, although in France, net silver imports in 1874 were substantially larger than those in 1873.[166]

In Holland the temporary suspension of silver coin instituted in 1873 ran out in May 1874, and the Utrecht mint was again open to silver purchase. The resulting flood of silver into Holland forced the government to once more suspend silver coinage in December of that year.[167] The pressures to make a more complete transition to gold became especially intense in this period as a suspension of convertibility caused the gulden to depreciate significantly. It was also obvious that as long as market conditions remained the same or worsened, conventional silver and bimetallist standards were not feasible. In June 1875 Holland established a gold (10-gulden) coin and continued the provisional suspension of silver until December 1877, when suspension was made definitive, thus formally instituting a gold standard.[168]

The Latin Union met again in 1875 to adjust the limits agreed upon for the coinage of 5-franc pieces in 1874. The holding pattern was still viable as a favorable movement of gold which resulted from these measures continued,[169] but it was clear that market conditions were worsening as the value of silver continued to fall. The decline in the price of silver in London was now dramatic. It dropped from $58\frac{5}{16}$ppp in 1874 to $56\frac{7}{8}$ppp in 1875, and the market bimetallic ratio pushed to its highest level of the century, 16.62:1. Indian net silver imports were well below 1874 levels. The belief that the depreciation of silver was not a cyclical but a secular phenomenon became more compelling, and monetary authorities began to look for a more definitive standard for the Union.[170] The urgency to move to gold was enhanced by an even more drastic decline in the value of silver in 1876. In July the London price had actually been quoted as low as $46\frac{3}{4}$ppp, and the market ratio in that month had surpassed the 19:1 level. Following another adjustment of the Latin Union coinage quotas in early 1876, the silver question finally reached the French Chambers.[171] The result was a law in August of that year suspending both the coinage of 5-franc pieces at the French mint and the further reception of bullion for deposit.[172] The influx of gold into France from both Union and non-Union nations now accelerated. Belgium responded to France's policy and her loss of gold to France with a law in December providing for complete and indefinite suspension of the 5-franc piece. This policy was extended *de jure* to the Union as a whole in 1878.[173] The lag in the Union's formal adoption of gold reflects the asymmetrical interdependence in the Latin Union system. The main force behind the lag was France, whose own preference for watchful waiting through the turbulent market conditions of the 1870s reflected the economic policy agenda of the Ministry of Finance and haute finance. Satellites were calling for gold as early as 1865, and once France formally fell into the gold club in 1876, its Latin Union allies followed closely behind.

The United States was more removed from this specific monetary turbulence of the 1870s, as it continued on an inconvertible paper standard. Events on the Continent thus did not elicit immediate responses. The US policy evolution toward gold in the 1870s was not of the drastic-reactive type seen in Europe. It was a less frantic and more reflective response to compelling developments in the United States and the world. Above all, elite concerns gravitated around resuming convertibility with a viable long-run standard. Much of the input into decisions underlying monetary options were considerations of trends in Europe and the general movement of market conditions for precious metals. The management of the money supply and monetary institutions in the United States in the 1860s and 1870s were configured around stable-money preferences. Behind much of the hard-money assault on bimetallism were fears over events in Europe and prevailing global market conditions. The principal fear centered around secular trends in the world creating a "depreciated currency" in a bimetallist United States.[174] Behind the Allison revisions of the Bland Bill of 1877 were sensitivities to the perils of resuming specie payments on bimetallism in a world bent on gold. Allison warned about the growing demand for gold in Europe and the destabilizing flows of silver into France. He affirmed the folly of being the only nation to open its doors to silver in a world which was frantically redeeming its excess silver to increase gold circulations. Each of the concerns manifested itself in the final Bland–Allison Act of 1878, which assured resumption on a gold standard.[175] Although the pull was milder, the United States also followed the chain gang onto gold.

By the late 1870s with the transition to gold consummated, any unilateral initiatives toward silver or bimetallist standards were seen as impossible. Like a Prisoner's Dilemma game in a non-cooperative Nash equilibrium, any unilateral move toward cooperation (opening mints to unlimited silver coinage) exposed the cooperating nation to exploitation. The new open mints would be a tempting target for the mass of silver on the world market, as the Dutch experiment of 1874 had showed.[176] With the rapid decline in the value of silver and the now irresistible conviction that silver *qua* central monetary metal was at a point of no return (barring some grand international agreement), the potential flood of silver was expected to be devastating. Sherman's concern for the United States (1895, p. 541) was felt by all recent converts to gold. "The general monetizing of silver now . . . would be to invite to our country, in exchange for gold or bonds, all the silver of Europe."[177] Nothing better characterized this strategy than France's "expectant policy." It dictated that French policy would follow upon the initiatives of the community of developed nations in any attempt to stabilize the price of silver. In essence, it committed France to being a follower, not a leader.[178] All nations still sympathetic to bimetallism (the United States, Holland, France, and Italy) shared this view. Any movement back toward silver would have to be en bloc.

The International Monetary Conference of 1878, convened by the United States as a mandate of the Bland–Allison Act, gave the world a viable forum to discuss the resuscitation of silver. But it was doomed at the outset. Germany would not consider a change in monetary standards, it refused even to attend the Conference; this automatically froze its Northern European satellites' position. Since the threat of Germany's large silver pool persisted, France would not resume her old policy of silver convertibility. Great Britain reiterated its commitment to gold. And the United States would consider a bimetallist standard only if it were part of an international agreement, which was not forthcoming. The Conference failed. With its failure fell the final curtain on the silver question. The metal which had dominated exchanges for centuries was reduced to token status. In the words of Ludwig Bamberger, it was the "dethroning of a world-monarch."[179]

When the scramble for gold began in the first years of the 1870s, it was as much a psychological as a real phenomenon. When Germany turned to gold, market conditions were far from intolerable. The price of silver had declined little, Indian silver demand was only then beginning its precipitous drop, and mints on the Continent remained open to silver. Germany's own move appeared to be structurally driven, with the anticipation of a Continental scramble and some market disturbances enhancing the urge toward gold. Political unification conveniently appeared as a means of realizing its monetary predispositions. Germany's Northern satellites were driven by the anticipation of adverse consequences on their trade relations with Germany, as well as disturbances in the flow of precious metals. From 1873 on, however, market conditions became intolerable for any mints fully open to silver. Latin Union nations found themselves deluged with silver, and Holland's experiment with silver-convertibility resumption in 1874 failed. What was at first driven by cognitive dispositions (i.e., pessimistic projections about conditions in the market for metals) became exclusively sustainable by real conditions as the decade progressed.

There is no question that self-fulfilling prophecy manifested itself in the scramble, specifically in the nervousness of the late 1860s and early 1870s which contributed to the sharp decline in the value of silver in the 1870s.[180] It is clear, however, that the market itself was in the midst of secular trends that augured poorly for the value of silver. Gold production showed a declining trend after the 1850s, which was to continue until the 1890s. Silver production had been secularly increasing across the century, especially sharply after 1850. Also, with the passing of the Civil War and the increasing use of council bills, India would never again be the market for silver that it had once been. Compounding these market conditions were, of course, the structural factors driving nations away from silver. The changing nature of economic exchange made silver increasingly archaic as a medium of exchange for large transactions. Growing trade and the internationalization of finance enhanced the desirability of emulating the British standard, which continued to generate appeal on ideological grounds. Shifting political structures created a more hostile environment against an inconvenient and inflationary metal like silver.[181] It is therefore apparent that, self-fulfilling prophecy notwithstanding, the transformation of monetary regimes after 1850 was irresistible: self-fulfilling expectations merely hastened an inevitable outcome. Structural and market forces had brought the developed world to a state where any significant real and/or psychological disturbances which threatened national gold circulations would bring about the demonetization of silver.

Conclusions: the gold standard and monetary regime theory

As with most broad overviews of historical trends comprising the actions of many nations, this study aspires more to the illumination of important forces that played a role in the scramble for gold, than definitively to model the correlates of monetary practices in that period. The latter would require a detailed study of the nations that did not join in the scramble for gold (i.e., those that maintained silver-based and paper standards). Although such an enterprise lies beyond the scope of this study, some pertinent observations can be offered. It is apparent that the scramble for gold was essentially a phenomenon that characterized the developed world (Western Europe and the United States). With some exceptions, nations outside of the developed world tended to remain on non-gold standards. This is consistent with the logic in this study. First, the more numerous and larger transactions in developed nations made gold more attractive as a medium of exchange, while countries with lower incomes did not find silver as inconvenient.[182] Second, the change of political structures which redistributed power from high-inflation groups (agricultural interests) to low-inflation groups (urban–capitalists) was more pronounced in economically advanced nations. The underdeveloped world (where silver and paper retained their central positions) featured more traditional political power structures. Finally, it may be the case that monetary status was a necessity for the developed world, while it was only a luxury for less-developed nations. Developed nations may have felt more pressure to conform to the practices of leading nations. Ford, for example (1962, p. 134), notes how Argentina did not feel the same shame that Great Britain would have felt in breaking the gold link, while Keynes ([1913] 1971, p. 5) observed that when the Reichsbank found it necessary to limit convertibility, it did so "covertly and with shame."

These observations, however, are not free of anomalies. Portugal, a relatively underdeveloped nation with traditional political structures, pre-empted other Western European nations onto a *de jure* gold standard.[183] Austria–Hungary and Russia in the 1890s also made the gold link in the face of traditional political structures which resisted fixing the exchange rate.[184] Argentina resumed gold convertibility in the twentieth century under the leadership of landed oligarchs.[185] Italy, although following the Latin Union onto a *de facto* gold standard in 1865, found it necessary to break the gold link in 1866 and resume it again in 1884. And Spain, of course, did not conform to the behavior of its Western European neighbors in the 1870s.

These anomalies and the case studies in this chapter suggest first that additional factors need to be imputed into any comprehensive explanation of the selection of monetary standards in this period, and second that greater attention needs to be paid to the relative influence of each factor. Some nations found it easier to follow the structural–proximate compulsion and formally adopt gold standards. In this respect, there appear to have been permissive factors which influenced to what extent structural and proximate catalysts could dictate the choice of a monetary standard. Permissive factors such as the development of capital markets and central banking institutions, and the management of money supplies and fiscal policies played important roles in determining whether nations could successfully institute and maintain the gold link. Nations with more developed capital markets and central banking institutions, and which practiced fiscal and monetary restraint (i.e., low inflation and low budget deficits) found it easier to institute and maintain a gold standard. These permissive factors need to be more fully identified and understood.[186] Assessing the relative influence of each factor was difficult in these case studies because the structural and proximate forces usually tended in the same direction. More definitive conclusions about relative influence in causation could be generated by carefully considering crucial cases (e.g., cases in which two factors encouraged different responses).[187]

Notwithstanding these limitations, the findings of this study carry some important implications for the study of monetary regimes. As a process of regime transformation through multiple evolutions in national monetary standards, the scramble of the 1870s represented the culmination of a shrinking monetary menu. By the 1870s, structural and proximate forces had eliminated silver from the list of viable long-run standards in the developed world. Whatever superiority paper possessed over gold with respect to convenience was strongly counteracted by the stable-money and metallist orientations prevailing among monetary authorities of the period. Gold won by default. In the study of comparative political and economic systems, this convergence in monetary institutions is indeed unique. Nations rarely face such restricted options in confronting regime disturbances. As Gourevitch (1978, p. 911) notes, "some leeway in [policy] response is always possible." Although silver politics in the United States and the strategic political coups of the French Ministry of Finance were successful in providing some of this "leeway" in the short run, the course of monetary events was compelling. The growing redundance in monetary practices is attributable to the fact that nations were exposed to a common set of internal and external forces. Moreover, these forces were homogeneous (i.e., complemented each other) with respect to their influence on the choice of monetary standards.[188] To borrow an analogy from Wolfers (1962), the developed world found itself in a burning house with a single exit. In terms of theories explaining comparative monetary regimes, the gold standard demonstrated that when comparative regimes are exposed to international environments which generate common and homogeneously influential forces, the likelihood of uniformities in rules and institutions will be high.

The scramble for gold also demonstrated that the proliferation of common national responses to disturbances is especially rapid among groups of nations that are highly interdependent. The monetary chain gangs which prevailed in the nineteenth century made an en bloc response to the depreciation of silver inevitable. Trade and monetary interdependence were keenly felt among core nations, especially in the satellite systems that crystallized around the economic hegemony of France and Germany. These cases suggest that domestic monetary regimes can more easily transmit themselves internationally in constellations of interdependent nations. The sensitivity shown in the French and German satellites is not unlike that which we see today in pegging blocs where key currency nations essentially export their monetary policies to trade-dependent satellites.

In terms of the interconnections between domestic regimes, common developments in monetary practices in this period were influenced by transformations in both political and economic systems. The gold standard, therefore, attests to the endogeneity of monetary institutions. The fundamental structure of economic exchange and production shifted to one which required a more "cosmopolitan" standard. The political rise of urban–industrial society encouraged a monetary standard that facilitated exchange and encouraged stable money. Interestingly, the monetary orientation of politics has changed over the last century, from one of stable money to one of inflation. With the politicization of the budget (through the rise of the welfare state) and the electoral impact of unemployment, inflation has become a fundamental means through which elites gain and maintain office.[189] Those advocating a shift in monetary policies away from the inflationary fiat regimes of today should take special note of the interconnections between politics and money. Any such policy shift would have to overcome very strong political rigidities.

Finally, the scramble for gold showed that the convergence of monetary practices at the domestic level can generate a regime at the international level. The confluence of structural and proximate forces influencing monetary practices in this period did what none of the four major international monetary conferences after 1850 could do: create uniformity in the monetary standards of developed nations. Nations failed to bring a gold union about through multilateral managerial initiatives. And unilateral managerial (i.e., hegemonic) initiatives were not attempted. In this case, the formative process was diffuse rather than centralized.[190] The scramble for gold showed that monetary hegemony and broad multilateral cooperation are not necessary conditions for the creation of international regimes. Consequently, social scientists should consider more than hegemonic intentions and the use of power when explaining the processes through which international monetary institutions emerge. Furthermore, the diffuse nature of the international gold standard suggests that we can sometimes learn as much about international relations from studying prevailing domestic developments among nations as we can from observing the direct interactions between them.

Notes

I gratefully acknowledge the comments of Michael Bordo, Forrest Capie, Jeff Frieden, Richard Grossman, Philip Pomper, Jaime Reis, and Anna Schwartz.
 1 Keohane (1984) and Young (1982).
 2 See, for example, Campbell and Dougan (1986) and Dorn and Schwartz (1987).
 3 Economists are more likely to think of monetary regimes in terms of the rules governing the money supply, while this study looks at broad changes in monetary standards as constituting a regime transformation. Although the two are distinct, we should remain sensitized to the possible interdependencies between them. Being on one standard or another may carry consequences for the outcomes which monetary policy aims at, such as stability in exchange rates or inflation. In fact, in this period much of the political battle between silver and gold revolved around different expectations about inflationary consequences of selecting a standard.
 4 Martin (1973) and Laughlin (1886, pp. 79–85) see 1853 as the real end of bimetallism given that the monetary legislation of that year failed to make coinage adjustments that would bring the silver dollar (which had disappeared owing to a higher intrinsic than nominal value) back into circulation, and followed up this so-called (by silverites) "neglect" with a further marginalization of silver coin through changes in weights and legal tender regulations.
 5 Willis (1901) and Redish (chapter 3 in this volume). Italy was the only exception, being allowed to coin a limited amount of pieces the following year.
 6 This could also be said of the United States by the late 1870s.
 7 By 1885 there was not a mint open to the unlimited coinage of silver in Europe and the United States. See Laughlin (1886, p. 160).
 8 See Zucker (1975, p. 65).
 9 On the conferences, see Russell (1898). For further discussion of the managerial void in the emergence of the international gold standard, see Gallarotti (forthcoming).
10 Young (1982) calls such regimes "spontaneous."
11 For recent studies of the gold standard, see Bordo and Schwartz (1984) and Eichengreen (1985).
12 Since the value per bulk of gold was roughly 15 times greater than that of silver, gold would naturally become more important as a medium of exchange in environments where the size and frequency of transactions and incomes were growing. In this case, the metal with lower transaction costs would grow in importance *vis-à-vis* the metal with higher transaction costs. As Redish (1990b) notes, however, the success of a gold standard in the period depended upon an effective system of token coinage (i.e., one which minimized counterfeiting and shortages of token coin). Silver retained an important role in this function throughout the nineteenth century.
13 See US Congress, Senate (1867, p. 51) (hereafter *International Monetary Conference*).

14 National monetary authorities in this period were strongly metallist. Paper rated lower in the monetary hierarchy than either silver or gold. As John Sherman (1895, p. 387) noted, an irredeemable paper currency was a "national dishonor." The prevailing ideological preference ordering of the period with respect to monetary standards was: gold preferred to bimetallism preferred to silver preferred to paper.

15 Russell (1898, p. 148).

16 In this period, the term "civilized nations" was commonly used as a synonym for economically developed nations.

17 Russell (1898, p. 239). Other foundations for ideological prejudices such as gold's intrinsic superiority or rarity seem to have been much less compelling in this period. Although Alexander Hamilton did acknowledge some such sources of attraction in the latter eighteenth century. See Laughlin (1886, pp. 13, 14).

18 US Congress, Senate (1879, p. 80) (hereafter *International Monetary Conference*).

19 Willis (1901, p. 103).

20 *International Monetary Conference* (1879, pp. 53, 54, 91).

21 Kindleberger (1975, p. 51) notes that the British example was central to the proliferation of free trade policies in Europe from 1850 to 1875. In monetary matters, Clough and Cole (1946, p. 623) identify Great Britain as a monetary model which, through example, exported practices governing currency, note issue, and circulation.

It is interesting to note here that although both laissez-faire/free trade and gold standards compelled for similar reasons, monetary practices did not see the same reversals (i.e., away from laissez-faire) that other issue areas experienced. In this respect money can be considered the last bastion of nineteenth century liberalism. This may have had something to do with the fact that states had greater institutional obstacles (i.e., central banks) in the area of money, while in trade and social policy, for example, there were few pre-existing institutions to overcome.

22 Great Britain looked to the Dutch two centuries earlier when developing its own banking system. See Kindleberger (1984, p. 52).

23 Farmer ([1886] 1969, p. 45). See also Friedman (1990a, p. 1168, 1990b, p. 94).

24 Quoted in Slater (1886, p. 45).

25 *International Monetary Conference* (1879, pp. 241, 242).

26 *International Monetary Conference* (1879, pp. 241, 242).

27 This displacement strongly manifested itself in the developed world in the 1850s and 1860s. Massive gold discoveries (the average yearly world production of gold in fine ounces increased almost fourfold from the 1840s to the 1860s, while the production of silver on yearly average increased less than twofold) altered the market bimetallic ratio so as to overvalue gold and undervalue silver at mints, thus causing the circulation of gold to swell at the expense of the circulation of silver, as it became profitable to import and coin gold, and melt down and export silver.

The organization of German monetary unification in the Reichstag in the early 1870s was the most pronounced example of an individual personally orchestrating a policy agenda. Bismarck, in a political quid pro quo, allowed Liberal discretion over monetary policy (by relegating the question to the Reichstag where Liberals dominated), and the Liberals deferred to the monetary expertise of Bamberger, who emerged as the financial leader of the Reichstag. So pronounced was his influence over the course of German monetary unification that he lost on only one major issue (in 1874): linking the expansion of government note issue to the retirement of silver. Interestingly, the setback occurred because it violated the stable-money imperatives of the Reichstag. See Zucker (1975, pp. 65, 74–76).

28 Stern (1977, p. 180).
29 Quoted in Hamerow (1972, p. 60).
30 Rosenburg (1962, p. 14) and Kindleberger (1975). More generally, the policies liberalizing exchange were perceived as the reason for the prosperity enjoyed in Great Britain and the United States. See Hamerow (1972, p. 346).
31 Stern (1977, p. 180).
32 Hamerow (1958, p. 254).
33 Willis (1901, p. 111) argued that a component of Germany's gold ideology was that France was a *de jure* bimetallist, political competition leading to a preference for a different standard.
34 Senator Thomas Benton, quoted in White (1893, pp. 7, 8). On the politics behind the Bill, see Friedman (1990a, p. 1162).
35 Martin (1973, p. 839).
36 Quoted in Russell (1898, p. 16). Friedman (1990a, 1990b) sees the British example as compelling for the United States.
37 Sherman (1895, p. 491).
38 Unger (1964) identifies a strong ideological attachment to silver in the rural South. Friedman (1990a, p. 1162), however, observes that similar regions could manifest differing preferences for standards across time, as the Jacksonian coalition favoring gold in the 1830s and the Bryan coalition favoring silver in the 1890s drew their support from the same regional classes.
39 Sherman (1895, pp. 468, 492); O'Leary (1960, p. 389); and Laughlin (1886, pp. 100, 101).
40 White (1893, p. 21) and Chevalier (1859). But Kindleberger (1984, p. 115) argues that France in the nineteenth century greatly admired and strove to emulate British financial institutions.
41 Chapman (1962, p. 122) and Plessis (1985, p. 62).
42 Willis (1901, p. 57).
43 Willis (1901, pp. 16, 37).
44 Helfferich (1927, p. 131).
45 US Congress, Senate (1876, vol. II, p. 61) (hereafter *US Monetary Commission*).
46 Russell (1898, pp. 84, 85) and *US Monetary Commission* (1876, vol. II, p. 137).
47 *US Monetary Commission* (1876, vol. II, p. 273).

48 Kindleberger (1984, p. 23) links the origin of gold coins in Italy (the florin and genoin) in the thirteenth century to the commercial revolution which increased the need for high-value/low-bulk money.

49 The British closed the mints to silver in 1798, argued Helfferich, because they were reluctant to allow a mint-undervalued gold to be displaced in circulation by silver (1927, pp. 121, 122)

Redish (1990b, p. 805) asks why the monetary standard of Great Britain (gold as the central monetary metal with token silver), being the most convenient in the early nineteenth century, was not copied by more nations at the time. Much of the reason, I believe, is to be found in differential rates of economic development. To the extent that monetary institutions are endogenous (i.e., conditions of economic exchange influence monetary institutions), it is only natural to expect Great Britain to be the first to opt for this more convenient monetary standard because it was the first to experience the industrial revolution. Other nations were less compelled in this period, given the nature of their transactions; their industrial revolutions came in the mid-to-latter half of the century. In fact, the French Monetary Commission of 1790 resolved that gold was the natural standard of commercial nations because it was "easy of carriage," but that France at the time had neither the scale of domestic nor international trade to warrant a gold standard. See White (1891, p. 314). Helfferich (1927, p. 125) noted that the German compulsion toward gold in the early nineteenth century was mitigated by low incomes and the large number of small transactions. In addition, it was easier for Great Britain to attain and maintain gold stocks since London was the center of both the global gold and capital markets.

50 Laughlin argued that when the production of gold increased enormously, it was eagerly absorbed. But when the production of silver was increased to the same extent, it was not permitted to displace gold in developed nations.

51 Evidence suggests that this bias must be qualified. Both France and Belgium tolerated a displacement favoring silver from 1832 to 1847 when the market ratio caused silver to be overvalued at their mints. In the period of 1849–54 Belgium, Switzerland, Naples, Spain, and India instituted policies limiting the use of gold in response to large gold influxes into circulation. France instituted monetary commissions in 1851 and 1857 to discuss solutions to the problems of declining silver circulation. The United States in 1853 and the Latin Union nations in the 1860s reacted to a shrinking silver circulation by altering coinage laws. It should be noted, however, that the greatest concerns relating to the retention of silver in this period were over silver as a subsidiary coin. These practices and policies defending silver were principally stimulated by shortages in small coin. Laughlin's "bias," therefore, is truer of central money metals than of metals in general. Developed nations showed a propensity to protect gold as a central monetary metal and protect silver as a subsidiary-coin metal. See Willis (1901, pp. 18, 19); Helfferich (1927, p. 139); and Martin (1973).

52 See the most recent debate over whether the practice of bimetallism in the nineteenth century led to alternating monometallism (Greenfield and Rockoff,

1991 and Redish, 1990a) or in fact maintained both metals in circulation (Rolnick and Weber, 1986). I find Redish and Greenfield and Rockoff's evidence more compelling.

53 Of course, even under a gold standard, nations required a stable token-coin system. See Redish (1990b).

54 On the use of the concept of "tipping" in the selection of money, see Greenfield and Rockoff (1991). My use of tipping does not suggest, as Greenfield and Rockoff's use does, that Gresham's Law might not work (when tipping occurs), but only that people would have found its workings undesirable if these workings resulted in gold shortages.

55 Of course, if the market ratio were kept close to the mint ratio, then bimetallism could maintain itself. But this assumes that people would not systematically discriminate against silver as a medium of exchange, which events in this period suggest is not the case. Furthermore, and as Friedman (1990a, 1990b) acknowledges, maintaining bimetallism would require price support schemes for silver when it was losing its value and threatening to drive gold out of circulation. In the 1870s and 1880s, given the severity of events in the silver market, it is dubious that any small core of nations could have stabilized the price of silver. In any case, nations were afraid to begin a price support scheme unilaterally. In fact, in discussing such support schemes at international monetary conferences, the most powerful nations (especially Great Britain) preferred to free-ride by keeping their mints closed to silver while others opened theirs. The schemes failed to be instituted for typically collective-action reasons. See Russell (1898).

56 Milward and Saul (1973, p. 422) and Bouvier (1970, p. 342).

57 In Germany, the stable-money Liberals in the Reichstag perceived a greater urgency to go to gold just for this reason. They believed that a silver standard or bimetallism would be more inflationary because people would not transact in silver, thus putting pressure on the government to orchestrate greater issue of bank notes. See White (1893, pp. 14, 15).

58 Kindleberger (1984, pp. 108, 120) and Clare (1909, p. 113).

59 Keynes ([1913] 1971, p. 12) cited the customary traditions of collecting railway fares and paying wages in gold.

60 Neither the categorization of development nor the links to monetary diplomacy developed here is unproblematic. Norway appears as an exception. It did not experience an industrial revolution in the nineteenth century, but pursued monetary practices consistent with the Scandinavian trend. Holland may represent an anomaly in this logic as well. Finally, the United States developed roughly as fast as or faster than all of the other nations except for Great Britain.

61 Russell (1898) and Willis (1901). The recent literature on bimetallism has shown greater sensitivity to the effects of transaction costs on the working of Gresham's Law, but has underplayed the effects of social preferences based on convenience (i.e., whether society will accept the displacement of a convenient medium of exchange). See Friedman (1990a, 1990b) and Redish (1990a). An exception to this is Greenfield and Rockoff's (1991) use of the concept of tipping.

62 Flotow (1941).
63 Zucker (1975, p. 65).
64 This view is supported by Joseph Ropes in his testimony to the US Monetary Commission (1876, vol. II, p. 199).
65 *US Monetary Commission* (1876, vol. I, p. 33) and Sherman (1895).
66 Helfferich (1927, p. 137).
67 Willis (1901, p. 6). In a survey conducted by the French Monetary Commission of 1867, results showed a disproportionate support of gold on the part of French chambers of commerce and tax collectors. See Helfferich (1927, p. 146).
68 See also Laughlin (1886, p. 152).
69 White (1891, p. 334).
70 Willis (1901, p. 17).
71 Willis (1901, p. 28, 29).
72 Nielsen (1933, p. 598).
73 From 1844 to 1864 the aggregate trade of France, Great Britain, and the United States increased threefold from $11.5 to $32.7 billion. See *US Monetary Commission* (1876, vol. I, pp. 22, 23).
74 Ford (1962, p. 94).
75 Chevalier (1859, p. 207).
76 Such initiatives came out of the International Exhibition in London in 1851 and the International Statistical Congresses in Brussels in 1853 and 1855.
77 The German Trade Congress in 1867 called for international monetary unification based on a gold franc. The Reichstag in 1868 and the Customs Parliament in 1869 called for German entrance into international union. See Helfferich (1927, pp. 151, 152).
78 Zucker (1975) and US Congress, Senate (1868, p. 2) (hereafter *Report of the Committee on Finance*).
79 Cecco (1974, pp. 58, 59) and Clough and Cole (1946, p. 688).
80 Laughlin (1886, p. 114). More generally, the nature of urban versus rural transactions created a natural division of preferences. Urban interests, which transacted more often and in larger amounts, preferred gold, while rural dwellers, who transacted less frequently, were less burdened by the use of silver. Almost all rural areas in the developed world before 1850 transacted principally in silver. Russell (1898, p. 15), in fact, noted that it was the "plain people" in America that complained of the disappearance of silver after changes in the coinage ratio in 1837. Of course, neither exclusively transacted in their preferred metal, given the need for token coins in cities and larger-coin transactions in rural areas. See Redish (1990b).
81 Laughlin (1886, p. 114).
82 Even in the 1850s, when gold depreciated *vis-à-vis* silver, French creditors preferred to be paid in gold. See Willis (1901, p. 8). Although Russell (1898, p. 85) noted that creditors in this period were not uncomfortable accepting silver as well. However, by the 1870s there was little question regarding creditors' preferences. Whatever ambivalence was created by cheap gold in the 1850s and 1860s, was gone by the 1870s when silver depreciated precipitously *vis-à-vis* gold.

83 See the statement of the Belgian delegate Pirmez in *International Monetary Conference* (1879, p. 124). It is interesting that the Bank of France maintained its preference for bimetallism even in the 1870s. In this instance, its own historical success in bimetallic arbitrage overcame a natural disdain for a depreciating metal (silver). But it should also be noted that it traditionally adhered to silver when its gold reserves were abundant. Once the gold drain became serious in the 1870s, the Bank was quick to reverse its traditional defense of bimetallism. See Willis (1901, p. 60).

84 Monetary authorities in developed nations during this century were far too wedded to metallism ever to consider a paper standard as a long-run option.

85 Laughlin (1886, p. 6).

86 Essentially, he was attempting to sustain a pre-capitalist political structure in what had become a capitalist society. See Stern (1977, pp. 177–183) and Rosenburg (1962).

87 Kindleberger (1984, p. 120).

88 Zeldin (1958, p. 2).

89 In 1852, landowners made up 19 percent of the legislature, while former civil servants and the grand bourgeoisie made up 26 percent and 24 percent respectively. See Plessis (1985, pp. 31–37).

90 Cammaerts (1921, pp. 317, 318).

91 Dandliker (1899).

92 Albrecht-Carrie (1950, p. 192) and Lovett (1982, p. 47).

93 Stromberg (1931, pp. 647–667).

94 Birch (1938, pp. 322–351).

95 Barnouw (1944, pp. 187–192).

96 The royal attachment to silver in Holland appears to have been strongly based on ideology, i.e., maintaining monetary tradition. In France, executive advocacy of bimetallism was founded on strong ties to the Bank of France.

97 Derry (1968, p. 177).

98 Milward and Saul (1973, p. 520).

99 Inflationist groups were able to coopt urban labor by convincing them that the expanded metallic base assured by bimetallism was more conducive to high wages.

100 The taxonomy shows numerous anomalies. Western bankers and businessmen commonly advocated bimetallism, and Republicans and Democrats often reversed roles on issues of resumption and the management of greenbacks. Also, Southern urban interests showed a long history of stable-money preferences. These anomalies were often founded on some conflict of interests. Among the capitalist class, it was the bankers and businessmen that had disproportionate ties to agriculture, land speculation, or rural development (i.e., investments in railroads) that were the most likely supporters of inflation. Unger (1964, pp. 158, 159), in fact, argues that such reversals among businessmen over resumption were not rare. The structure of monetary preferences dictated by this taxonomy did, however, crystallize often enough to maintain the taxonomy's usefulness as a means of categorizing the foundations of

competition in monetary politics. See Sherman (1895, pp. 509–520, 540, 570, 1147); Laughlin (1886, pp. 187, 188); Friedman and Schwartz (1963, pp. 45–49); Stern (1964, pp. 4, 5, 53); Blaine (1884, vol. I, p. 421; vol. II, pp. 391, 392); Upton (1884, pp. 157–162); Beard and Beard (1927, p. 297); and Clark (1920, pp. 322, 484).

101 Friedman and Schwartz (1963, pp. 54, 55, 111) cite the trends in the money stock in the 1870s as reflective of a political balance skewed toward stable money. Later in the 1890s, they add, the political balance was still anti-inflation as evidenced by the policy rigidity of maintaining convertibility in the face of financial crisis.

102 In his testimony to the US Monetary Commission (1876, vol. II, p. 356), William Sumner argued that Europe was ready to move to gold at any time after 1850, but that it took Germany's transition to compel the rest of the Continent.

103 Willis (1901, pp. 18, 19) and McCulloch (1879, pp. 18, 19).

104 Friedman (1990a, p. 1162) underscores the politics of the Act: a "golden club" which Jacksonian sympathizers could use against Biddle's Bank of the United States. The intention was to reduce the demand for the Bank's notes by introducing more gold into circulation.

105 Laughlin (1886).

106 See Sherman (1895, p. 541). Whether or not these outcomes would have been pervasive is subject to speculation. It is clear, however, that forecasts of future outcomes tended in this direction. Hence, whether the threat was real or not, it was perceived as real.

107 His concerns, like Sherman's, derived primarily from a concern with stable money.

108 Those who argue that bimetallism has the capacity automatically to reverse gold or silver shortages through a stabilizing mechanism that works via the substitution of metal between monetary and non-monetary uses (see Bordo, 1987 – such substitution will automatically bring the market ratio back to the mint ratio), assume that metals are perfectly substitutable as mediums of exchange. If they are not, people will institute coinage laws which prevent their preferred medium from being displaced (as happened in the 1870s).

109 Russell (1898, pp. 89, 90); Flotow (1941, p. 114); and Helfferich (1927, pp. 151, 152).

110 Willis (1901, p. 105).

111 Russell (1898, p. 103).

112 Willis (1901, p. 38) and Helfferich (1927, p. 146).

113 *International Monetary Conference* (1879, p. 190). By the time this act was passed, at least a majority of the metallic transactions in Switzerland were in gold.

114 Redish (chapter 3 in this volume) suggests the possibility that Napoleon III may have been using the bimetallist position as a bargaining chip to be later traded away to the community of nations in return for considering international monetary union around the franc at the Conference of 1867. This is

problematic, given that Napoleon would have had correctly to predict that the community of nations would accept the idea of the franc but reject international bimetallism. See Russell (1898).

115 This assured that silver would not displace gold in circulation since it was undervalued and gold overvalued at Latin Union mints. In this respect, the Union did not intend (in the short run, anyway) to deviate from gold monometallism in practice. See Willis (1901, pp. 40–46) and Redish (chapter 3 in this volume).

116 Helfferich (1927, p. 143) noted that the Conference definitively conveyed that "gold was the standard of the future." Willis (1901, p. 135) regarded it as the beginning of a global consensus on the desirability of a gold standard.

117 *International Monetary Conference* (1879, p. 81). John Sherman (1895, p. 412) expressed the same view.

118 Quoted in Slater (1886, p. 39). See also Russell (1898, pp. 84, 236).

119 Russell (1898, p. 103).

120 Helfferich (1927, p. 149).

121 The extraordinary rise in silver imports from 1861 to 1865 is due to the fact that Indian cotton took up the slack of declining US cotton exports caused by the American Civil War.

122 Greater use of notes, a less favorable balance of trade, and the greater use of council bills to clear payments with Great Britain were responsible for a drop-off in silver imports after 1865.

The US Monetary Commission of 1876 cited the drop in India's net imports as one of the major factors (along with policy changes in Europe and silver production) accounting for the depreciation of silver in the 1860s and 1870s. The Commission's conclusion was representative of a widespread belief of this period.

123 The price of silver on the London market changed by only $\frac{9}{16}$ppp (pence per ounce) from 1865 to 1871 (from $61\frac{1}{16}$ppp to $60\frac{1}{2}$ppp) when India's net silver imports went from \$93 million (in 1865) to almost \$5 million (in 1870). Furthermore, the price of silver did not change by more than $\frac{1}{16}$ppp from 1869 to 1872, years which saw extremely sharp swings in the level of net imports (see Table 2.1). In these cases, changes in flows did not produce large enough changes in the stock of silver to alter the price significantly. See Laughlin (1886, p. 224).

124 Council bills were bills of exchange sold by the India Council (the government of India residing in London) for the purpose of making payments to Great Britain for public expenses such as interest on debt and pensions. Since these bills represented claims on silver in India, they increasingly substituted for shipments of silver, as they would be purchased by those in Great Britain who needed to send silver to India in payment for goods. On the effects of council bills on silver flows, see Laughlin (1886, pp. 126, 127).

125 John Sherman (1895, p. 412) attributed the decline in the value of silver in the 1860s solely to the increased production of silver.

126 The average yearly quinquennial increase in the production of world silver

from 1861–65 to 1866–70 was equal to 36 percent of the average yearly net silver imports into India in the period 1866–70.

127 The market ratio changed from 15.44:1 in 1865 to 15.57:1 in 1870. The legal ratio in Latin Union nations was 15½:1. After 1866, the market ratio never again dropped below 15½:1. See Laughlin (1886, pp. 223, 224).

128 Actually, the Latin Union nations might have pre-empted Germany onto gold if it had not been for the strategic political maneuvers of the French Ministry of Finance, and the Franco–Prussian War. From 1865, Belgium, Switzerland, and Italy had been advocating a Latin Union based on gold monometallism. Even the French delegates at the founding of the Union in 1865 had requested a gold union. French society and the legislature were strongly behind gold. The perpetuation and exportation of a bimetallist standard to the Union in the mid- and late 1860s resulted from the deft actions of the Ministry of Finance at keeping the matter out of the legislature and under the jurisdiction of the Ministry. In 1869, for example, Minister Magne responded to a call for assessing France's monetary standard by referring the matter to the Conseil Supérier of Agriculture, Commerce, and Industry rather than the Chambers, which was overwhelmingly predisposed to pass a gold bill. The Ministry further protected bimetallism by not making public the Conseil's decision supporting gold over silver and bimetallism (by 26 to 11) until 1872. With the advent of the Franco–Prussian War and the problem of the indemnity, any meaningful changes had to wait until after 1873. The Ministry was successful at keeping the matter out of the Chambers until 1876, when a law was passed suspending the coinage of 5-franc silver pieces. A Ministry more sympathetic to gold could have had France and the Latin Union (since Latin Union nations configured their monetary standards to that of France) officially on a gold standard well before Germany. See Willis (1901, pp. 105–107).

It is difficult to impute motives other than support for haute finance and the Bank of France to the French Ministry in its defense of bimetallism. Arguments that suggest France was holding out to get into a more advantageous position as leader of a gold bloc on the Continent fail to address the fact that France's intransigence threatened to drive her Latin Union satellites into a gold union with Germany, certainly an undesirable outcome for the French government and Ministry of Finance.

129 Such contagion was not an issue in the working of bimetallism before 1860 because perceptions attributed a cyclical rather than secular character to the market for metals.

130 See the testimonies of William Sumner and Joseph Ropes in *US Monetary Commission* (1876, vol. II, pp. 312, 355).

131 Quoted in Russell (1898, p. 105).

132 Willis (1901, p. 113); Russell (1898, p. 89); and Helfferich (1927, p. 149).

133 *US Monetary Commission* (1876, vol. II, p. 356). The urgency of early liquidation of silver was all the more enhanced by the desire to maximize gold stocks for the impending legal transition to a full gold standard. This necessitated exchanging silver at its maximum purchasing power, which was perceived to be

at the beginning of a secular decline.

134 Helfferich (1927, p. 444). Helfferich (p. 149) contended that one of the principal considerations driving Germany to gold was a fear of being "isolated" in a world destined to move toward gold monometallism.

135 US Congress, House (1878, p. 5) (hereafter *Report of the Commissioners*).

136 See O.D. Ashley's letter in *US Monetary Commission* (1876, vol. II, p. 61).

137 Willis (1901, p. 163).

138 The Swedish rix thaler, in fact, exactly corresponded with the Hamburg rix thaler. See *International Monetary Conference* (1867, p. 35); Russell (1898, p. 58); and Helfferich (1927, p. 144).

139 *US Monetary Commission* (1876, vol. I, pt. 2, p. 170).

140 White (1893, p. 23) and Upton (1884, p. 230).

141 See Nielsen (1933, p. 598) and Holmboe's statement in *US Monetary Commission* (1876, vol. I, pt. 2, p. 518).

142 Willis (1901, pp. 56, 57, 143) argued that the Union was engineered by France and Napoleon III as a means of extending France's monetary hegemony on the Continent. The proximate reason of the Union's formation, of course, was a response to disturbances in subsidiary silver coin circulation owing to the fact that Swiss and Italian token coins were struck at lower finenesses. See Redish (chapter 3 in this volume).

143 This replication mirrored a very strong trade dependence. See *US Monetary Commission* (1876, vol. II, pt. 2, p. 144) and Willis (1901, p. 15).

144 The monetary dependence of Switzerland and Belgium was particularly acute owing to a historically large circulation of French coin within their borders. By the end of the 1850s, for example, most of the metallic transactions in Switzerland were in French gold. In 1860, 87 percent of the coins in circulation in Belgium were French. With respect to trade, the Latin Union satellites were especially dependent given their large trade sectors. Belgium, for example, was consuming only about $\frac{1}{14}$th of its total yearly production in this period.

145 *International Monetary Conference* (1867, p. 45).

146 Helfferich (1927, p. 146).

147 Stolper (1940, p. 32) called the German policy initiative one of "extraordinary significance" in moving the developed world toward a monetary transformation. McCulloch (1879, p. 14) saw it as the pivotal, crucial event urging the world to a gold standard. William Sumner's testimony portrayed the German policy change in similar terms. See *US Monetary Commission* (1876, vol. II, p. 356). See also Friedman (1990b, p. 90).

148 To the extent that this perception drove Germany onto gold, it is not unreasonable to attribute some element of self-fulfilling prophecy onto the scramble for gold itself. It is clear, however, that irrespective of this perception, structural forces and secular conditions in the market for metals were pushing Germany and the Continent to gold. This perception merely increased the urgency to adopt gold. More is said on the role of self-fulfilling prophecy below.

149 The French indemnity was the main cause of the silver inflow given that it was liquidated in such a way as to shift French assets to Germany, thus making

Germany's international creditor position greater. In the second quarter of 1871, for example, Great Britain exported 2 million pounds' worth of silver to Germany. Also of note was the decline in Indian net silver imports in 1870: they had gone from over $36 million in 1869 to less than $5 million in 1870 (see Table 2.1).

Much has been said about the importance of gold transfers from the indemnity in making possible Germany's transition to a gold standard. But in actuality very little gold was transferred. Only 15 percent (742 million out of 5 billion francs) of the indemnity was actually liquidated in money, and only 5 percent (273 million francs) was liquidated in gold. It was principally liquidated in stocks, credits, and bills of exchange. Germany, in fact, experienced no net increase in her gold stocks until she began liquidating her excess silver on the world market in 1873. See US Monetary Commission (1876, vol. I, pt. 2, p. 79); Willis (1901, p. 110); and Russell (1898, p. 107).

150 The net imports of silver into Sweden increased from 3,129 kilograms in 1870 to almost 28,000 in 1872. Sweden coined more than twice as much silver in 1871 than it had in 1870 (4,361 to 9,975 kilograms). Norway imported more than three times as much specie in 1871 (mostly silver) than it had in 1870. See US Monetary Commission (1876, vol. II, pt. 2, pp. 516–528).

151 Helfferich (1927, p. 175).

152 White (1893, p. 23).

153 Estimates of Hector Hay and Ernest Seyd show an increase from $51 million to $61 million. See Laughlin (1886, p. 218).

154 Willis (1901, p. 136).

155 By the Economist's estimates global gold production declined from $108 million in 1871 to $87 million in 1872. See Laughlin (1886, p. 218).

156 Because of relatively smaller endowments of precious metals in monetary use, the transition in Germany's Northern satellites caused less concern. The impact of their conversion was mainly psychological, as the realization of an expected trend that would engulf the developed world. See Helfferich (1927, p. 175).

157 Upton (1884, p. 208) directly attributed the demonetization of silver in Holland and Latin Union nations to the fear of this mass of German silver displacing their gold circulations.

158 International Monetary Conference (1879, p. 57). In actuality, the reality fell somewhat short of the fears. German authorities were careful in liquidating their supply of silver out of fear of depressing the world price of the metal. It was not until 1876 that any significant amount of silver was actually liquidated. Up until 1876 most of the territorial coins called in were used for coining Imperial silver coins. Of the years 1873 to 1876, only in 1874 was more silver liquidated than was assigned to German mints for coinage. Of the estimated 856.7 million marks of silver that Germany needed to dispose of (i.e., that silver stock in monetary use above the subsidiary coin needs of the German population) in 1873, only 204.9 million had been liquidated by 1876. This figure was only 14 percent of the world's total silver production in that four-year period.

See Helfferich (1927, p. 170) and *US Monetary Commission* (1876, vol. II, pt. 2, pp. 77, 78).

159 Laughlin (1886, p. 224).

160 Laughlin (1886, p. 225).

161 Willis (1901, p. 115).

162 Willis (1901, pp. 89, 90, 116, 301–313).

163 Willis (1901, pp. 114–126).

164 Willis (1901, pp. 127, 128).

165 Willis (1901, pp. 137, 138, 143) called the agreement a compromise between bimetallists and gold advocates. Defenders of bimetallism argued that the conditions in the market for metals were cyclical, and it was fully expected that the values of gold and silver would once more gravitate to levels that would allow silver and gold to circulate concurrently as central monetary metals, and therefore definitive long-run commitments to a gold standard were premature.

166 Interestingly, the governments of Belgium, Switzerland, and Italy all used this agreement to strengthen themselves fiscally. They purchased the requisite silver bullion on the open market, coined the entire amount immediately (thus crowding out private citizens), and deposited the sums with their treasuries. See Willis (1901, pp. 150, 151).

167 From May to November 1874, 32 million gulden in silver had been coined.

168 Helfferich (1927, p. 176).

169 In France, net gold imports slightly increased, while net silver imports declined enormously. Substantially more gold was now being coined in both France and Belgium.

170 Willis (1901, pp. 158–160).

171 Up until this year, the Ministry of Finance, erstwhile defender of bimetallism in France, was able to keep it out of the Chambers where gold had resounding support.

172 Also at the basis of France's unilateral move was a pronounced fear of being pre-empted onto gold by the Swiss, who had been requesting a gold Union for some time, and the Belgians whom recent elections had placed under the leadership of Frère-Orban and his pro-gold Liberals. See Willis (1901, pp. 162–165).

173 Except, of course, for Italy which was exempted for one year.

174 Sherman (1895, pp. 541, 615, 617, 618) and Blaine (1884, vol. II, p. 605). See also the various testimonies and letters to the *US Monetary Commission* (1876, vol. I). There is some debate on the magnitude of the influence of these external concerns behind the demonetization of the silver dollar in the Act of 1873. O'Leary (1960) argues that the principal author of the bill, H.R. Linderman, was compelled by critical developments in Europe and the world market for metals. Friedman and Schwartz (1963, p. 115) are somewhat skeptical as to Linderman's principal motivation. It is clear, however, that as early as 1872, Linderman did acknowledge the potential dangers of both the increased supply of silver in the world and the change of standards in Germany. And, in fact, Friedman (1990a, pp. 1165–1167) more recently appears to converge closer to O'Leary's position.

175 Blane (1884, vol. II, p. 606).

176 Linderman suggested that any such unilateral initiative by one nation would lead other nations to think, "Here is a good chance . . . to get rid of our silver." See *US Monetary Commission* (1876, vol. II, p. 198). Pirmez, the Belgian delegate at the International Monetary Conference of 1878, argued that any viable multilateral return to bimetallism must include all important silver nations, otherwise free-riders would use the new union to liquidate their excess silver. See Russell (1898, p. 215).

177 This represented a fairly common response to the US Monetary Commission's question: What would be the consequences of remonetizing silver in the United States? See the testimonies of Fitch, Ropes, and Sumner in *US Monetary Commission* (1876, vol. II, pp. 35, 313, 345).

The severity of the perceived consequences (among monetary authorities) of incurring the "sucker's payoff" (i.e., opening their mints to silver while other nations did not) leads us to question Friedman's (1990a, p. 1174, 1990b, p. 91) contention that a unilateral resumption of bimetallism by the United States in the mid-1870s could have stabilized the bimetallic market ratio. The events in Latin Union nations and the failure of the Dutch resumption in 1874 made nations extremely reluctant to initiate or support any unilateral actions in this direction. And given the propensity of free-riding behavior among core nations, it is likely that a unilateral US initiative would have invited much of the surplus silver from the Continent. It is doubtful that the United States could have withstood this rapid and large flood of silver.

178 In describing this policy, France's Léon Say underscored the threat which was felt from the large pool of excess silver in Germany yet to be liquidated. See *International Monetary Conference* (1879, pp. 55, 56).

179 Quoted in Helfferich (1927, p. 181).

180 Russell (1898, p. 227) identified an element of self-fulfilling prophecy in what he called the "vicious circle" of the 1870s: "states were afraid of employing silver on account of the depreciation, and the depreciation continued because the states refused to employ it."

181 Structural and proximate factors leading to the scramble were inextricably connected. A large component of the nervousness in the 1860s and 1870s were fears of unstable money, fears which were nurtured by shifting structures of political power. (The US Monetary Commission, 1876, vol. I, p. 4, underscored the importance of stable-money interests in bringing about the demonetization of silver in Europe.) The growth in trade and internationalization of finance forged stronger links which bound the monetary chain gang, as did the perception of gold as a political and economic status symbol. And the thought of losing one's gold circulation caused grave concern. All this enhanced the nervousness over the anticipation of changes in foreign monetary practices.

182 Keynes ([1913] 1971, p. 53) noted how the forced circulation of gold in India in 1900–01 failed because the sovereign (owing to its high value) was not suitable for such a poor country.

183 In Portugal's case it appears that both financial and trade dependence on Great Britain overcame some structural impediments in determining their monetary

standard. I am indebted to Jaime Reis for these facts pertaining to the Portuguese case.

184 Schumpeter (1954, p. 770).

185 The ruling oligarchs were trying to arrest the appreciation of their exchange rate. See Ford (1962, pp. 167–169).

186 Interestingly, these factors, too, tended to covary with economic development.

187 Portugal shows some elements of a crucial case.

188 Whatever incongruity was created by cheap gold in the 1850s was quickly eliminated by its relative appreciation in the 1860s.

189 The reference here is specifically to the literature on the political business cycle, which has identified a pro-inflation bias in the politics of representative democracies. See, for example, Nordhaus (1975).

190 Insofar as redundancy of monetary practices at the domestic level had international manifestations, the gold standard was an example of an additive regime: it was the sum of identical parts. Other such additive regimes are conceivable. For example, a group of nations each instituting unilateral free trade would form a free trade bloc. Non-additive regimes would dictate that domestic policies differ: macroeconomic policy-coordination regimes, for example, dictate that nations take different positions on the Phillips curve.

References

Albrecht-Carrié, René, 1950. *Italy From Napoleon to Mussolini*, New York: Columbia University Press.

Barnouw, A.J., 1944. *The Making of Modern Holland: A Short History*, New York: Norton.

Beard, Charles and Mary Beard, 1927. *The Rise of American Civilization*, vol. II, New York: Macmillan.

Birch, J.H.S., 1938. *Denmark in History*, London: John Murray.

Blaine, James G., 1884. *Twenty Years of Congress From Lincoln to Garfield*, 2 vols., Norwich: Henry Bill.

Bordo, Michael, 1987. "Bimetallism," in J. Eatwell, M. Milgate and P. Newman (eds.), *The New Palgrave*, London: Macmillan.

Bordo, Michael and Anna Schwartz (eds.), 1984. *A Retrospective on the Classical Gold Standard: 1821–1931*, Chicago: University of Chicago Press.

Bouvier, Jean, 1970. "The banking mechanism in France in the late 19th century," in Rondo Cameron (ed.), *Essays in French Economic History*, Homewood: Irwin: 341–369.

Cammaerts, Emile, 1921. *A History of Belgium*, New York: Appleton.

Campbell, Colin and William Dougan (eds.), 1986. *Alternative Monetary Systems*, Baltimore: Johns Hopkins University Press.

Cecco, Marcello de, 1974. *Money and Empire: The International Gold Standard, 1890–1914*, Totowa: Rowman & Littlefield.

Chapman, Guy, 1962. *The Third Republic of France: The First Phase 1871–1894*, New York: St. Martin's Press.

Chevalier, Michel, 1859. *On the Probable Fall in the Value of Gold*, trans. Richard Cobden, New York: Appleton.

Clare, George, 1909. *A Money-Market Primer, and Key to the Exchanges*, London: Effingham Wilson.

Clark, Champ, 1920. *My Quarter Century in Politics*, vol. I, New York: Harper & Brothers.

Clough, Shepard and Charles Cole, 1946. *Economic History of Europe*, Boston: Heath.

Dandliker, Karl, 1899. *A Short History of Switzerland*, trans. E. Salisbury, London: Swan Sonnenschein.

Derry, T.K., 1968. *A Short History of Norway*, Westport: Greenwood.

Dorn, James and Anna Schwartz (eds.), 1987. *The Search for Stable Money: Essays in Monetary Reform*, Chicago: University of Chicago Press.

Economist, October 27, 1866.

Eichengreen, Barry (ed.), 1985. *The Gold Standard in Theory and History*, New York: Methuen.

Farmer, E.J. [1886] 1969. *Conspiracy Against Silver or a Plea for Bimetallism in the United States*, New York: Greenwood.

Flotow, Ernst, 1941. "The Congress of German economists, 1858–1885: a study of German unification," Ph.D. dissertation, American University.

Ford, A.G., 1962. *The Gold Standard 1880–1918: Britain and Argentina*, Oxford: Clarendon Press.

Friedman, Milton, 1990a. "The crime of 1873," *Journal of Political Economy*, 93 (December): 1159–1194.

  1990b. "Bimetallism revisited," *Journal of Economic Perspectives*, 4 (Fall): 85–104.

Friedman, Milton and Anna J. Schwartz, 1963. *A Monetary History of the United States*, Princeton: Princeton University Press.

Gallarotti, Giulio, forthcoming. "Centralized versus decentralized international monetary systems: the lessons of the classical gold standard," in James Dorn (ed.), *Alternatives to Government Fiat Money*, Dordrecht: Kluwer.

Gourevitch, Peter, 1978. "The second image reversed: the international sources of domestic politics," *International Organization*, 32 (Autumn): 881–911.

Greenfield, R. and H. Rockoff, 1991. "Gresham's law regained," Rutgers University (ms.).

Hamerow, Theodore, 1958. *Restoration, Revolution, Reaction: Economics and Politics in Germany 1815–1871*, Princeton: Princeton University Press.

  1972. *The Social Foundations of German Unification 1858–1871*, Princeton: Princeton University Press.

Helfferich, Karl, 1927. *Money*, 2 vols, trans. Louis Infield, New York: Adelphi.

Jervis, Robert, 1976. *Perception and Misperception in International Politics*, Princeton: Princeton University Press.

Keohane, Robert, 1984. *After Hegemony: Cooperation and Discord in the World Political Economy*, Princeton: Princeton University Press.

Keynes, John Maynard, [1913] 1971. "Indian currency and finance," in *The Collected Writings of John Maynard Keynes*, vol. I, New York: St. Martin's Press for the Royal Economic Society.

Kindleberger, C., 1975. "The rise of free trade in Western Europe, 1820–1875," *Journal of Economic History*, 35 (March): 20–55.

1984. *A Financial History of Western Europe*, London: George Allen & Unwin.

Krasner, Stephen, 1982. "Structural causes and regime consequences: regimes as intervening variables," *International Organization*, 36 (Spring): 185–205.

Laughlin, J. Laurence, 1886. *The History of Bimetallism in the United States*, New York: Appleton.

Lovett, Clara, 1982. *The Democratic Movement in Italy*, Cambridge, MA: Harvard University Press.

Martin, David, 1973. "1853: the end of bimetallism in the United States," *Journal of Economic History*, 33 (December): 825–844.

McCulloch, Hugh, 1879. *Bimetallism*, New York: G.P. Putnam's Sons.

Milward, Alan and S.B. Saul, 1973. *The Economic Development of Continental Europe 1780–1870*, Totowa: Rowman & Littlefield.

Nielsen, Axel, 1933. "Monetary unions," *Encyclopedia of the Social Sciences*, 10 (June): 595–601.

Nordhaus, William, 1975. "The political business cycle," *Review of Economic Studies*, 42 (April): 169–90.

O'Leary, Paul, 1960. "The scene of the crime of 1873 revisted: a note," *Journal of Political Economy*, 68 (August): 388–392.

Plessis, Alain, 1985. *The Rise and Fall of the Second Empire, 1852–1871*, trans. Jonathan Mandelbaum, Cambridge: Cambridge University Press.

Redish, Angela, 1990a. "Bimetallism in nineteenth century France: a razor's edge," University of British Columbia (ms.).

1990b. "The evolution of the gold standard in England," *Journal of Economic History*, 50(4): 789–805.

Rolnick, A. and W. Weber, 1986. "Gresham's law or Gresham's fallacy?," *Journal of Political Economy*, 94 (February): 185–199.

Rosenberg, Arthur, 1962. *The Birth of the German Republic 1871–1918*, New York: Russell & Russell.

Russell, Henry, 1898. *International Monetary Conferences: Their Purposes, Character and Results*, New York: Harper & Brothers.

Schumpeter, Joseph, 1954. *History of Economic Analysis*, New York: Oxford University Press.

Sherman, John, 1895. *John Sherman's Recollections of Forty Years in the House, Senate and Cabinet*, 2 vols., Chicago: Werner.

Slater, M.H., 1886. *Money. A Brief Treatise on Bimetallism in Plain Words*, Washington: National Bimetallic Coinage Association.

Stern, Clarence, 1964. *Golden Republicanism: The Crusade for Hard Money*, Ann Arbor: Edwards Brothers.

Stern, Fritz, 1977. *Gold and Iron: Bismarck, Bleichröder, and the Building of the German Empire*, New York: Knopf.

Stolper, Gustav, 1940. *German Economy 1870–1940*, New York: Reynal & Hitchcock.

Stromberg, Andrew, 1931. *A History of Sweden*, New York: Macmillan.

Unger, Irwin, 1964. *The Greenback Era: A Social and Political History of American Finance, 1865–1879*, Princeton: Princeton University Press.

Upton, J.K., 1884. *Money in Politics*, Boston: D. Lothrop.

US Congress, House, 1878. *Report of the Commissioners on Behalf of the United States to Attend the International Monetary Conference*, 45th Congress, 3rd Session, October 17.

US Congress, Senate, 1867. *International Monetary Conference of 1867*, 40th Congress, 2nd Session, December 19.

    1868. *Report of the Committee on Finance on Bills, Reports, and Memorials Relating to International Coinage*, 40th Congress, 2nd Session, June 9.

    1876. *US Monetary Commission*, vols. I and II, 44th Congress, 2nd Session, August 15.

    1879. *International Monetary Conference of 1878*, 45th Congress, 3rd Session, February 6.

White, Horace, 1891. "Bimetallism in France," *Political Science Quarterly*, 6 (June): 311–337.

    1893. *The Gold Standard*, New York: *Evening Post* Publishing Co.

Willis, H.P., 1901. *A History of the Latin Monetary Union: A Study of International Monetary Action*, Chicago: University of Chicago Press.

Wolfers, Arnold, 1962. *Discord and Collaboration: Essays on International Politics*, Baltimore: Johns Hopkins University Press.

Young, Oran, 1982. "Regime dynamics: the rise and fall of international regimes," *International Organization*, 36 (Spring): 277–297.

Zeldin, Theodore, 1958. *The Political System of Napoleon III*, London: Macmillan.

Zucker, Stanley, 1975. *Ludwig Bamberger: German Liberal Politician and Social Critic*, Pittsburgh: University of Pittsburgh Press.

3 The Latin Monetary Union and the emergence of the international gold standard

ANGELA REDISH

In 1865 France, Switzerland, Italy, and Belgium agreed to coordinate their monetary systems under the rubric of the Latin Monetary Union. Although pervasively mentioned in monetary histories of Europe, the rationale for the establishment of the Latin Monetary Union is not well known, and its role in the development of European monetary systems has not been correctly understood. It is most frequently viewed as an attempt to establish a bimetallic standard in Europe, and is therefore seen as a failure or dead end in the evolution of the European monetary system.

In this chapter I show that rather than being a bastion of bimetallism the Union was formed because the member countries were on a *de facto* gold standard. It is no coincidence that the Union was established after the rapid decrease in the price of gold in the 1850s drove silver out of the circulation of each of the four countries. This caused a dramatic shortage of small-denomination coins and prompted the introduction of token coins. However, although each of the four nations had the same full-bodied coins, they introduced different token coinages. Efficient management of the token coinage required cooperation amongst the four countries. The Union established a common token currency: it stated the type of token, the quantity that would be issued, and the conditions for convertibility.

The Union should be viewed as a step on the path to gold monometallism – not as a dead end attachment to bimetallism. It would have been equally necessary if the four countries had been on a *de jure* gold standard as it was with their *de jure* bimetallic standards. Indeed, when the price of gold rose in the 1870s, and the *de jure* bimetallic standard would have restored a *de facto* silver standard, the Union countries quickly abandoned bimetallism.[1] They terminated the free coinage of silver, although they did not remove the legal tender status of the silver coins, creating a system subsequently known as the "limping gold standard."

The most frequently cited cause of the institution of the Union was a desire to expand the bimetallic currency area. For example, Yeager (1976, p. 296) states that the Union was established "in hopes of promoting an international standardization of currencies on a bimetallic basis." Ken-

68

wood and Lougheed (1971, p. 119) suggest a similar motivation: "In an effort to stabilize the situation and promote an international bimetallic system, France summoned a meeting of the franc-using nations in 1865." Yet, in 1865 the majority of countries were on a bimetallic standard, and the bimetallic area did not need promotion.

An alternative view (Kindleberger, 1984) is that the Union represented an optimal currency area in the Mundell (1961) sense. While I will argue that it did represent an optimal currency area in some ways, it cannot have been so in the Mundell sense. Mundell defines an optimal currency area in terms of the desirability of flexible exchange rates in the absence of labor mobility. Yet in the nineteenth century virtually all exchange rates were fixed and monetary authorities did not make exchange rate choices for their employment consequences.

A more relevant factor in the emergence of the Union was the general climate of economic integration in the mid-nineteenth century. The expansion in international trade is well documented, and reflected transportation improvements, technological and political changes, as well as trade liberalization. Examples of the latter include England's move to free trade, Italian and Swiss unification, the formation of the *Zollverein*, and the 1860 Cobden–Chevalier Treaty. International expositions provided further evidence of the desire for integration, as did attempts to introduce a uniform system of weights, measures and coinage in Western Europe. The latter is particularly relevant in the context of the Union; in 1867 a subcommittee of the International Statistics Congress met in Paris and delegates from 22 countries (including the United States) voted to establish the gold standard and an international unit of account based on the 5-franc coin.[2] Clearly the formation of the Union is consistent with this background of harmonization. The importance of international trade increased the gains from standardizing the token coinage.

The chapter begins by describing the monetary systems of the four countries in the 1850s and the effects of the fall in the price of gold. The following section discusses how the four nations individually responded to the fall in the price of gold. I then outline the terms of the monetary union and discuss the benefits of monetary union for the member countries. Finally I discuss why the Union monetary systems did not return to their status quo ante after the rise in the price of gold in the 1870s, but instead terminated the *de jure* bimetallic regime.

Monetary systems in the 1850s

The basic laws creating the monetary units of France, Belgium, and Switzerland are set out in table 3.1. In each country the legislation centered on the franc "germinal," the monetary standard created by the French

Table 3.1 *The coinage of the Latin countries before the Union*

	France	Belgium	Switzerland	Italy
Dates of legislation	1803	5 June, 1832	7 May, 1850	24 August, 1862
Silver				
Basic coin: value	1 franc	1 franc	1 franc	1 lira
weight	5 gm	5 gm	5 gm	5 gm
fineness	90%	90%	90%	90%
Value/kg fine silver (ME_s)	222.2	222.2	222.2	222.2
Mint price/kg fine silver	220.56			220.5
Denominations	5f, 2f, 1f	5f, 2.5f, 1f	5f, 2f, 1f	5f, 2f
	50c, 20c	50c, 20c	50c	
Gold				
Basic coin: value	20f	20f		
weight	6.45 gm	6.45 gm		
fineness	90%	90%		
Value/kg fine gold (MEg)	3444.4	3444.4		
Mint price				
Denominations	20f, 40f	20f		
Coin ratio: MEg/ME_s	15.5	15.5		

Source: Willis (1901, p. 164).

revolutionary government in 1803. That law created a bimetallic standard in which 1 franc was defined as a 90 percent-fine silver coin weighing 5 grams.[3] A 20-franc coin containing 6.45 grams of 90 percent-fine gold was also established, making the relative value of gold to silver in the French coins 15.5.

The legislation reflected the outcome of considerable debate between 1789 and 1803 over the desirable properties of a monetary system. There was general agreement on the need to eliminate the abuses that had characterized the *ancien régime*. Under the *ancien régime* coins were assigned values in livres tournois (the unit of account) but these were not stamped on the coin. The government could therefore collect a seigniorage tax and alter the standard of value by changing the legal tender value of the coins. The new law required that the coin's value in francs be stamped on the face of the coin (Article 16). Furthermore it stipulated that seigniorage could not be charged on metal sold to the mint, although the expenses of coinage were to be so charged (Article 11).

Most of the debate, however, concerned the problem of adopting a bimetallic standard to provide convenient-size coins of both high and low denominations, while avoiding the instability caused by periodic revaluations of coins in one metal when the relative prices of the two metals changed. The preamble to the Act and the debates preceding its passage make clear that the legislation was not intended to create a pure bimetallic standard. Rather, it was intended that if the market price of gold differed from 15.5 to such an extent that it caused problems for the coinage, gold (and never silver) was to be revalued.[4] Importantly, this asymmetry was not embodied in the legislation.

In 1798 when French armies invaded the Netherlands and briefly (1810–14) incorporated them into the French empire they also imposed the new French monetary system. In 1816 the Dutch gulder was re-established in the Netherlands but when the Belgian provinces revolted and declared independence from the Netherlands in 1830, they reinstituted the French monetary system (see table 3.1).

In 1798 French revolutionary armies also invaded Switzerland, where they established the Helvetic Republic and again instituted a monetary system based on the franc (Carson, 1970). Between 1803 and 1850 the right to mint coins returned to the individual cantons, who created a currency that was "as motley as it was inconvenient" (Lardy, 1878, p. 190). After unification in 1848, the power to mint and define money was reserved to the Federal government, which adopted a silver coinage identical in dimension and composition to that of France and Belgium, although it made no allowance for either minting or giving legal tender status to gold coins. In June 1852 the silver coins of France, Belgium, and some Italian states were made legal tender.

Napoleon had introduced the franc to Italy also, in 1793, but it was suppressed in 1814. Unification in 1861 led to the creation of a national monetary unit, and again led to the adoption of the French system. The lira weighed 5 grams and was 90 percent-fine silver, and the gold–silver ratio was 1:15.5 (Kindleberger, 1984, p. 137). Coins of Belgium, Switzerland, and France were also given legal tender status. The legislation (being passed in 1862, after the fall in the price of gold) also provided for the issue of token silver coins, discussed below. Thus by 1852 the French, Belgian, and Swiss economies all used the same unit of account and gave legal tender status to coins issued by each other.[5]

The fall in the price of gold

Between 1820 and 1848, the relative price of gold exceeded 15.5 times that of silver, and in both France and Belgium silver – the "bad" money – had a tendency to drive gold coins out of circulation. An 1839 report prepared for a government commission by Dumas (a chemist of the Academy of Science)

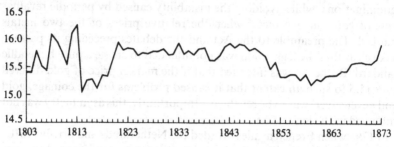

3.1   The relative price of gold to silver

and Colmont (the Inspector-General of the Finance Department) noted that "l'or est en très grande partie sortie de France, et que ce qui nous en reste n'a pas cours dans les transactions ordinaires"[6] (cited in Thuillier, 1983, p. 310).

In 1849 a number of causes interacted – the discoveries of gold in California and Australia, an increase in the use of silver in the "Asian trade" – to generate a fall in the price of gold, which remained below 15.5 times that of silver until 1866 (see Figure 3.1). Gold therefore became the "bad" money and tended to drive silver out of circulation. There is now an extensive literature on the operation of Gresham's Law and while the operation of Gresham's Law when gold is the good money is controversial, it is widely accepted that when silver coin (more accurately, low-denomination coin) is the good money it will tend to be driven from circulation.[7] Define the official value of coins containing 1 kilogram of silver or gold as the mint equivalent of silver (MEs) or gold (MEg) respectively, and the coin ratio (Rc) as the mint equivalent of gold divided by the mint equivalent of silver. Assume that transactions costs are zero, and that mint fees and seigniorage rates are zero so that the mint equivalent is equal to the mint price.[8] Then, if the coin ratio exceeds the relative market price of gold to silver (R), gold is overvalued at the mint and is the "bad" money. It will be profitable to take 1 kilogram of silver coins (MEs in francs), melt them down, trade the silver for R kilograms of gold and sell this to the Mint for R times MEg, since $(MEg/R) > MEs$. (Conversely, if $R < Rc$ silver is overvalued and will drive gold coin out of circulation.)

Consider the following example: A 1-franc coin contained 4.5 grams of pure silver (90 percent of 5 grams) so that the mint equivalent of silver was 222.2. The 20-franc gold coin contained 6.45 grams of 90 percent pure gold and so the mint equivalent of gold was 3445 [20 × 1000/(6.45 × 0.9)]. The coin ratio was therefore $Rc = 3445/222.2 = 15.5$. If the market relative value of gold (R) was 15, then 1 kilogram of silver (contained in coins worth 222.2

francs) could be exchanged for $\frac{1}{15}$ kilograms of gold which could be sold to the mint for 229.7 (3445/15) francs, generating a 7.5-franc profit. The bad money (gold) is brought into the mint and the good money (silver) is exported.

All silver coins had the same mint equivalent on leaving the mint. However, wear and tear would reduce the silver content of coins, raising their mint equivalent, i.e., it would take more coins with a higher aggregate face value to contain 1 kilogram of silver. Coins with a low mint equivalent would be culled (withdrawn from circulation) first. Thus the mint equivalent of a full-bodied 5-franc coin would be 222.2 francs, while a smaller coin whose weight had been reduced 3 percent by wear would have a mint equivalent of 229.1. The coin ratio is 15.5 (3444.4/222.2) for the newly minted coins and 15.04 (3444.4/228.9) for the worn coins. In the absence of transactions costs it would be profitable to export the full-bodied coin when the ratio fell below 15.5, and to export the worn coin when the ratio fell below 15.04.

Since larger coins tended to suffer less from wear the larger silver coins (the 5-franc and 2-franc coins) would be the most profitable to export or melt down. The 5-franc and 2-franc coins were already becoming scarce by 1853–54 when silver was only undervalued by 1.3 percent. By 1859 when the market value of gold was 15.19 times that of silver, (i.e., silver was undervalued by 2.0 percent) the smaller coins were also withdrawn from the circulation.

It is not surprising that similar events occurred in Belgium. What is perhaps more surprising is that Switzerland – which was on a monometallic silver standard – was not exempt from the problem.[9] As stated above, French silver coins were legal tender in Switzerland but no gold coins were. Yet French gold coins circulated in Switzerland in the late 1840s and were accepted at their face value which was close to their market value – where silver is the numeraire. The silver coins disappeared in the same way that they had in France and Belgium: Soetbeer noted that "one can without exaggeration assume that $\frac{9}{10}$ of all transactions in Switzerland are performed by means of gold and especially through the agency of the 20 franc pieces."[10] However, creditors who received payments in gold (since this was the widely available medium of exchange) demanded a premium to reflect the fact that a 20-franc gold coin was worth less than 20 francs in silver.[11]

The essential rationale for bimetallism in the early nineteenth century was that only with gold and silver coins circulating concurrently at par could a country have conveniently-sized coins of both large and small denominations.[12] The fall in the price of gold had created a *de facto* gold standard in Belgium, Switzerland, and France by 1860, which meant that there was no medium of exchange for small-denomination payments. Historically, monetary authorities had resolved such a problem by a general recoinage of silver. The alternative solutions were to increase the mint equivalent of silver or decrease the mint equivalent of gold. The political unpopularity of the latter meant that the former option was typically chosen. The mint equivalent could be raised by increasing the official value of the silver coins or by reducing their silver content. Since silver coins were typically aliquot portions of the unit of account, (e.g., 20 centimes, 50 centimes) a recoinage was usually preferred to calling up the money.

Changes in the relative price of the specie metals had generated *de facto* monometallism before. What was unusual in the 1850s was that the response of the monetary authorities was not to revalue gold or silver, but to issue a token coinage that would provide a small-denomination medium of exchange. Such a coinage was not technologically feasible prior to the nineteenth century.[13]

The individual responses

The value of gold coins minted in France in 1850 exceeded that of every year since 1818 and the French government established a Monetary Commission to examine the causes and consequences of the fall in the price of gold (Willis, 1901, p. 302). No documents remain of that Commission; however, the government did begin issuing a 10-franc coin in that year. Four years later a 5-franc gold coin was created. (This coin weighed only 1.6 grams and was not widely used.) In February 1858 a second Commission was established to study the monetary situation. It concluded that since the price of gold might rise again at any time changes to the structure of the monetary system were unwarranted, but recommended the imposition of an export tax on exports of silver. The recommendation was ignored.

In 1860 Switzerland became the first nation to adjust its monetary system to the fall in the price of gold, and to attempt to provide a small-denomination medium of exchange. Beginning in 1854 the Swiss government had discussed the advisability of making gold coins legal tender. In 1860 French gold coins were given legal tender status and the fineness of the silver coins (excluding the 5-franc coin) was reduced to 80 percent. This made the fractional, and 1-franc coins into tokens (see table 3.2) and raised their mint equivalent to 250. Their export would be unprofitable unless the relative price of gold fell below 13.8. The 5-franc coin was left at a fineness of 0.9 so that the standard remained *de jure* bimetallic; however, by 1860 virtually no 5-franc coins were in circulation in Switzerland. In addition the new legislation ended the free minting of all but the 5-franc coin. The new token coins were all minted on government account.

Table 3.2 *Uncoordinated issues of token coins*

	France	Belgium	Switzerland	Italy
Date of legislation	24 May, 1864		31 Jan., 1860	24 Aug., 1862
Denominations	50c, 20c		2f, 1f, 50c	1f, 50c, 20c
Fineness	83.5%		80%	83.5%
Mint equivalent: ME_t	239.5		250	239.5
Coin Ratio: MEg/ME_s	14.38		13.78	14.38

Source: Willis (1901).

The new Swiss tokens were identical in size and weight to the 1-franc, 2-franc and 50-centimes pieces of France and Belgium, but contained 10 percent less silver. Furthermore Swiss silver coins were legal tender in France and Belgium and were widely accepted prior to 1860. Not surprisingly, entrepreneurs imported the new coins into France, where they were accepted at par.[14]

The scarcity of change continued and worsened, and complaints to the French government increased after Switzerland introduced its token silver coinage. In June 1861 the French Minister of Finance created a third Commission and instructed it to examine the causes of the scarcity of fractional coinage and to suggest measures that would permit the fractional silver coin to "satisfy the needs of the circulation and suffice for the payments of salaries and furnish the small change required in business" (Willis, 1901, p. 36). The commission's recommendations, that the fineness of all the silver coins except the 5-franc coin be reduced, were ignored. However, the government reminted 22 million 5-franc pieces into subsidiary coins on its own account, and insisted that $\frac{1}{40}$ (and later $\frac{1}{20}$) of all silver coined had to be made into subsidiary coins (Costes, 1885, p. 141). These measures had limited effect as private silver coinages were negligible after 1856, and the government's coins were soon culled from the circulation.

Italy, in establishing its uniform currency in 1862, introduced token silver coins that were 83.5 percent fine. By 1863 "the invasion of the French circulation by new Italian coin had already proceeded sufficiently far to be regarded as an additional danger" (Willis, 1901, p. 39).

Finally in 1864 the French government introduced legislation that incorporated the recommendations of the 1861 Commission. It proposed that the fineness of all silver coins other than the 5-franc piece be reduced from 90 percent to 83.5 percent, and contained all the specifications that characterized early token legislation. The fineness was chosen so that export or culling would be unprofitable at all expected silver prices but, given that constraint, it was kept as high as possible to prevent counterfeiting.[15] All tokens would be coined on government account, and to prevent "overissue" the amount was limited to the amount of full-bodied coins withdrawn from the circulation plus 25 million francs "if needed." The tokens would be limited legal tender between private agents but government offices would receive them in unlimited quantities – a restriction that ensured that the tokens would trade at par, i.e., above their intrinsic silver value. The law was passed with a significant modification. Only the 50-centimes and 20-centimes coins would become tokens. The 1-, 2- and 5-franc coins were not reduced since the law of 1803 stated that the franc is 5 grams of 90 percent-fine silver and is the monetary unit. The predictable result – that 5-, 2-, and 1-franc silver coins would not be evident in the circulation – ensued, and contemporaries continued to complain about the inconvenience of making change for 5-franc pieces with 20-centimes and 50-centimes pieces.[16]

By 1865 Belgium was the only country of the four without its own token currency and its circulation was virtually devoid of Belgian coin. The tokens of the other three nations circulated widely but were not legal tender. In 1865 the Belgian government called for a meeting of the four nations in order to find a communal solution to the problem of the small coins.

The Convention of 1865

The delegates to the Convention met six times between November 20 and December 23. De Parieu (Vice-President of the French Council of State) opened the conference and concluded his speech with a list of eight questions the Convention would address. These (listed in the Appendix on p. 82) all concerned the subsidiary coinage and noticeably excluded the question of abandoning the bimetallic standard for the gold standard. Concern from delegates from other nations, who all advocated adoption of the gold standard, compelled de Parieu to add this issue to the agenda.

The delegates quickly resolved most of the issues. There would be free coinage of gold and each member state would receive at par gold coins minted by the other states. All silver coins less than 5 francs were to be token coins. The tokens would be of uniform fineness. Each state could mint up to 6 francs *per capita*, and the tokens would be legal tender amongst private agents only in payments up to 50 francs. The right to mint tokens was reserved to the government. State treasuries would accept up to 100 francs in the tokens of the other states. Each state stood ready to buy at par with gold or 5-franc silver coins, tokens held by Treasuries of other states.

The most controversial issues were whether or not to continue the free minting of the 90 percent-fine 5-franc silver coins – i.e., to maintain the *de jure* bimetallic standard – and what fineness to adopt for the token coins. The delegates of Italy, Belgium, and Switzerland all advocated a *de jure* gold standard, but the French delegation flatly refused such a change.

Prior to 1850 the Union nations had been on a *de facto* silver standard and there had been little debate about the merits of the system. There were (prior to the 1850s) two advantages of the silver standard. Moving to a gold standard would be costly as the silver money stock would have to be replaced with (relatively expensive) gold. Furthermore a gold standard would not provide a small-denomination medium of exchange. By the 1860s these problems had been overcome. The low price of gold had ensured that the majority of the specie money stock was gold, and the token issues, already in use in three of the four nations, showed how a small-denomination medium of exchange could be supplied.

Why then, did the Union not legislate a gold standard? In the first place there was no immediate need: the monetary systems of all the nations were on a *de facto* gold standard. Secondly, the delegates from France flatly refused. Two explanations for French behavior have been proposed: first, that the Bank of France preferred a bimetallic standard, and Napoleon's fiscal needs required him to accommodate the Bank's wishes (Willis, 1901). Secondly, that Napoleon was planning an international monetary conference in 1867 at which he hoped a world monetary standard would be adopted. Napoleon intended to trade his willingness to go from bimetallism to a gold standard in return for that gold standard being based on the French gold coinage (Russell, 1898). The Convention finally agreed to continue the free minting of silver 5-franc coins 90 percent fine, and that they would be received by all the member states.

The fineness of the tokens was an issue because the existing Swiss tokens were 80 percent fine while those of Italy and France were 83.5 percent. It was finally decided that the larger emissions of 83.5 percent-fine coins (of which 116 million francs had been issued in contrast with 10 million francs in 80 percent-fine coins) made a choice of 83.5 percent fineness wiser. The Swiss were given 12 years to retire their 80 percent-fine coins.

The treaty was ratified in July 1866 and went into force on August 1, 1866.

The benefits of an international medium of account

Since Italy, Switzerland, and France had unilaterally issued a token coinage, why was a multilateral response required? Why did Belgium suggest such a response and the other nations so readily agree? While the answer is different for specific countries, the bottom line is that each country realized that there were gains from having a uniform numeraire and unit of account.[17] That is, the usefulness of a unit of account increases with the number of agents/transactions that use it. In 1864 each country (except Belgium) had different denominations of tokens and had different finenesses. Many foreign tokens circulated in each country and yet they were not legal tender and were not convertible into gold at par without the costs of transportation to the country of origin. The issue of token coins generated seigniorage revenue equal to the difference between the official value of the token and the gold costs of its silver content. For example, the Swiss franc of 1860 contained 4 grams of silver which in 1860 had a gold value of 90 centimes.[18] Seigniorage-maximizing behavior would cause a country to increase its issues, which would leak into neighboring countries, exacerbating the problem.[19]

Belgium, Switzerland, and Italy also joined the Union to give themselves a forum to convert France to gold monometallism. While they wished to adopt a gold standard, there were more gains from maintaining a common unit of account with France. Furthermore, in 1865 the point was academic – each country was already on a *de facto* gold standard.

An alternative explanation for the creation of the Union is that it formed an optimal currency area in the Mundell (1961) sense. This literature on optimal currency areas has analyzed the desirability of monetary union (i.e., a fixed exchange rate) in the twentieth century world of fiat money systems. Thus the calculus involves trading off the benefits of a reduction in transactions costs implied by a fixed exchange rate against the cost of losing the ability to run an independent monetary policy. In the nineteenth century world of commodity money standards, the costs and benefits of a monetary union were clearly very different, because under a commodity money standard monetary authorities had virtually no control over monetary policy to give up.

The argument that the Union represented an attempt to institute international bimetallism is, I think, inappropriate or at least anachronistic. The agreement allowed for and encouraged other nations to join, as Greece did in 1867. However, only France of the four countries wished to maintain a *de jure* bimetallic standard, and there is considerable evidence that her stance (which the *de facto* gold standard made costless) represented a bargaining chip to be surrendered later, rather than a hard-line philosophical position.

Finally, we can turn to the accomplishments of the Union. It did institute a token coinage, which was reasonably successful. It did not encourage bimetallism. As shown above, in the early 1860s the Union countries were on a *de facto* gold standard. As shown below, when the *de jure* bimetallic standard might have affected the monetary systems of the member countries they all abrogated the bimetallic standard.

The limping gold standard

The adverse consequences of the fall in the relative price of gold provided the impetus for the Convention of 1865, and the object and accomplishment of the Convention was to provide a uniform small-denomination coinage (i.e., token silver). Ironically, the price of gold rose shortly after the Convention. However, this did not end the Union because the partner countries decided not to return to a *de facto* silver standard, and because in the interim both France and Italy had made bank notes legal tender.

In France the Suspension of Convertibility (*cours forcé*) began in 1870 as a reaction to the Franco–Prussian War. Although the Bank of France did not formally resume convertibility until 1878, the depreciation of the franc was limited especially after the Bank began redeeming its 20-franc notes in gold in 1873 (Willis, 1901, p. 148). The Italian experience was very different. With brief exceptions the notes of the Banca Nazionale were legal tender between 1866 and 1884, as a result of war and unification-related fiscal problems. By 1868 the lira had depreciated by 12 percent. This meant that the Italian token coins that were accepted as legal tender in the Union countries were driven out of domestic circulation and used to pay foreign debts. The Italian government agreed only to redeem repatriated tokens in their paper currency. Termination of the 1866 treaty would have left the other nations with stocks of these depreciated tokens, providing a strong motivation for the other three countries to maintain the treaty.

The other reason for the prolongation of the treaty was the unwillingness of the Union nations to return to a *de facto* silver standard. Since all four countries had been on a *de facto* gold standard in 1865, the question of the standard had been academic. When the increase in the price of gold in the 1870s threatened to impose a *de facto* silver standard in the bimetallic Union nations, immediate action was taken to prevent silver driving the gold coin out of circulation. A series of expedient measures by individual countries and the Union created a mixed standard, subsequently known as the "limping gold standard," under which only gold was freely minted but the existing silver 5-franc coins were unlimited legal tender

In January 1870 the Italian mint lowered its mint price of silver from 220.5 to 218.8 (Willis, 1901, p. 130). In September 1873, the French government imposed a daily limit of 250,000 francs for silver coinage, a limit that was reduced to 150,000 francs in November. In October 1873 the Belgian government suspended the free coinage of silver. In November 1873 Switzerland asked France to convene a meeting of the Union nations so that uniform measures could be taken. The French government agreed to call a Convention.

Table 3.3 *Silver coinage limits, million francs*

	France	Belgium	Switzerland	Italy	Greece[a]
Tokens					
Dec. 1865	239	32	17	141	9
Oct. 1878	240	33	18	170	10.5
5-franc piece					
Jan. 1874	60	12	8	40[b]	
Feb. 1875	75	15	10	50	5
Feb. 1876	54	10.8	7.2	36	12
Feb. 1877	27	5.5	3.6	18	6
Feb. 1878					
Nov. 1878	Coinage of 5f pieces suspended				

Notes:
[a] Greece joined the union in 1868.
[b] Italy was given an additional 20 million lire limit.
Source: Willis (1901).

At this Conference in January 1874 the Belgian delegates clearly stated the need for a cooperative response. Although Belgium had suspended domestic silver coinages, foreign silver would displace the gold coin unless a multilateral response was undertaken. The Swiss delegates agreed and suggested formal adoption of the gold standard. The French and Italian delegates preferred to maintain the status quo with the addition of limits to silver coinage. While there was a desire to limit the moneyness of silver coin, the large quantities of 5-franc coins, minted between 1867 and 1873 represented a potential liability to the various governments. That is, the value in gold of these coins was less than 5-francs; if the coins were to be "tokens" the government would have to stand ready to redeem them at 5-francs in gold. The problem was exacerbated by the large holdings in Switzerland, Belgium, and France of Italian 5-lire coins. If Italy were not included in the new arrangements these countries would take a loss.

On January 31, 1874 the four nations undertook to limit the quantity of silver 5-franc pieces each would coin that year (see table 3.3). The four countries took different paths in creating this coinage. The Belgian, Swiss, and Italian governments bought the silver bullion and had it coined on government account, receiving the difference between the market price (in gold) and 5 francs as revenue (Willis, 1901, p. 151). The French continued to permit free coinage until June 1875 (Willis, 1901, p. 159), when the Treasury also sold silver to the mint. However, private sales were continued. In

February 1876, the waiting period was approximately two years and the interest cost (20 francs) eliminated the difference between the market price (200.6 francs) and the mint price (222.56 francs). In August 1876 the government proclaimed a law suspending the coinage of silver 5-franc coins, and the reception of bullion for minting. (The law was subsequently continued by a law of January 5, 1878.) In December 1876, the Belgian government similarly suspended its coinage of the 5-franc piece. The countries then agreed that the annual meetings had served little purpose and readily agreed to coinage limits for 1877 of half those of the previous year. In late 1877 similar restrictions were agreed on for 1878.

In 1878 the Union countries reconvened. The Convention of 1865 expired in 1880 but while the *raison d'être* of the Convention – the problem of subsidiary coinage – had gone, it had left an awkward legacy: the smaller countries could not afford to redeem the large French holdings of their overvalued silver coin. The Convention of 1878 slightly increased the limits of the token silver coinage (see table 3.3) and finally suspended the coinage of the 5-franc silver coin. Thus the "limping gold standard" was inaugurated: only gold was freely minted, but the existing 5-franc silver coins were still unlimited legal tender.[20]

Conclusion

It [bimetallism] is to our conception, less a theory than the result of the primitive inability of the legislators to combine together the two precious metals otherwise than by way of an unlimited concurrence – metals, both of which are destined to enter into the monetary system, but which recent legislators have learned to co-ordinate by leaving the unlimited function to gold alone and reducing silver to the role of divisional money.
Léon Say, *Exposé des motifs*, Bill of 21 March, 1876, cited in Shaw (1896, p. 196).

Between 1800 and 1900 the Western world moved from a bimetallic standard to a gold standard. This had several important effects not the least of which was the establishment of relatively fixed exchange rates and a standard of value. The process by which this change occurred took the better part of a century, and the change proceeded at different rates in different countries. An understanding of the process would require analysis of social, political, and economic factors and this chapter represents only a very small part of such a larger study.[21]

The Latin Monetary Union has been interpreted as a monetary union dedicated to bimetallism. If this were the case it would stand out as a dead end in the path to the gold standard. In fact the Union, to the extent that it was about monetary matters, should be seen as a step toward, not away from, the gold standard. As Say put it, the adoption of the gold standard required that legislators learn how to issue a token currency, and this was the *raison d'être* of the Union.

The issue of tokens was more complex in the Union countries than in Britain and the United States because (1) countries were contiguous and therefore international trade in coins could be virtually costless, and (2) the countries had identical full-bodied coins and a history of granting legal tender to each other's currency. These conditions meant that cooperation would generate a superior coinage at relatively low cost.

Appendix: Agenda of the Convention of 1865

1. What inconveniences have arisen from the different subsidiary moneys of the countries?
2. Would it be useful to establish a monetary union to facilitate reciprocal circulation of subsidiary money?
3. Should such a union have identical subsidiary coins or just less diversity than now? What fineness should be adopted in either case?
4. Should the union prescribe the fineness of all coins less than or equal to 4 francs?
5. Should these coins be limited legal tender amongst private agents?
6. Should the governments state a maximum account of wear before coins must be reminted?
7. What should determine the quantities of issue?
8. Would it be advisable to state that gold coins would be accepted by Public Treasuries?
9. With respect to the 5f piece, would it be advisable to reconsider the bimetallic standard?
   Source: Chausserie-Laprée (1911, pp. 17–19)

Notes

The author would like to thank the editors of this volume, seminar participants at Rutgers University and MacMaster University, and Ann Carlos for useful suggestions and comments. Any remaining errors or incoherences are her own.

1 Gallarotti (chapter 2 in this volume) argues that the adoption of the gold standard in the 1870s reflected both the changes in the value of gold in the 1870s and such structural factors as the rise in political power of urban capitalists, economic growth, and a "gold ideology."

2 However, a commission established in Britain to consider adoption of the new unit argued that although the benefits of uniformity were significant, they were outweighed by the high costs of establishing a new numeraire and adjusting all contracts written on the basis of the old numeraire. By the 1870s the prospects of an international monetary standard had been eliminated by the Franco–Prussian War and subsequent German monetary reform.

3 In 1794, the revolutionary government introducd the decimal system based on the silver franc, although only a 5-franc piece was coined.

4 See Chevalier (1857) for a detailed history of the legislation.

5 Interestingly, the granting of legal tender status to foreign coins was widespread even amongst countries using different units of account. Thus gold coins of France, Spain and Great Britain were legal tender in the United States until 1857.

6 "Gold has for the most part left France and that which remains isn't used in ordinary transactions."

7 Rolnick and Weber (1986) argue that the high cost of computing premia exceed the benefits of a correct valuation for low-denomination coins, but not for high-denomination coins. Thus high-denomination coins circulate at a premium but are not driven out of circulation, while small-denomination coins are driven out of circulation. Greenfield and Rockoff (1991) argue that the premium is simply the necessary profits to pay for costs of culling and that a premium did not mean that coins were not driven from circulation. The issue is not resolved.

8 Redish (1990) explicitly considers positive transactions costs and mint fees.

9 A contemporary report noted that "The silver 5 franc piece disappeared first, and soon the fractional coins were in turn attracted away" (*Journal des économistes*, t2, ser3, no. 5, 1866).

10 Cited in Willis (1901, p. 30).

11 Chausserie-Laprée (1911, p. 13).

12 In 1803 the French government had contemplated establishing a silver mono-metallic standard, but decided that the inconvenience of dealing with large volumes of silver coins made such a scheme inefficient. They also discussed permitting the issue of gold coins without any fixed legal tender value. However, it was argued that silver for large payments, although inconvenient, would frequently dominate the risky use of gold and thus the inconvenience would not be avoided.

13 See Redish (1990) for a detailed discussion of the technological constraints on the issue of token coins before 1800.

14 In April 1864, the French Treasury prohibited its public offices accepting the Swiss tokens (Fould, 1864, p. 782).

15 Chausserie-Laprée (1911, p. 14) quotes the authorities as selecting "une valeur nominale supérieure à sa valeur réelle, de manière à la garantir de toute exportation, et sans que sa valeur nominale puisse offrir une prime suffisante pour en provoquer la contrefaçon." The counterfeiting of concern may be individuals making coins of the same fineness as official coins but making private profits from the difference between the cost of the metal content and the face value of the coin. Counterfeiters could also make coins with a lower silver content for more gain. The lower the silver content the harder it is to establish the silver content, and therefore as fineness decreased both sorts of counterfeiting became more prevalent.

16 Fould (1864, p. 784) in a report to the Emperor Napoleon.

17 Niehans (1978) distinguishes between the numeraire, e.g., silver, and the unit of account, e.g., 5 grams of 90 percent fine silver. The Union countries in 1864 already had the same numeraire and the same unit of account.

18 Since $R = 15.29$ and $MEg = 3444$, the gold value of the token 80 percent-fine franc $= ((5 \times 0.8)/15.29) \times (3444/100) = 0.9$.
19 A similar problem was common in the seventeenth-century, see Van der Wee (1977).
20 Willis (1901, p. 183) argues that the real focus of the Convention was not the continuation of the token coins or the question of the 5-franc coin, but the measures to be taken with respect to Italy.
21 Mertens (1944) provides a history of the move toward the gold standard. Redish (1990) argues that Britain adopted the gold standard in 1816 because she had learned how to issue token silver coins. Friedman (1990) disagrees with this, and argues that the adoption of the gold standard in Britain was a result of happenstance: an accident that was the major factor causing Germany and the United States subsequently to join the gold standard. See also Gallarotti (chapter 2 in this volume).

References

Carson, R.A.G., 1970. "Coins of Europe," in *Coin: Ancient, Mediaeval and Modern*, vol. 2, London: Hutchinson.

Chausserie-Laprée, P., 1911. *L'Union monétaire latine*, Paris: Arthur Rousseau.

Chevalier, M., 1857. *Sur la Cause probable de la baisse de la valeur d'or*, Paris: Capelle Libraire edn.

Costes, H., 1885. *Les institutions monétaires de la France*, Paris: Guillaumin et Cie.

Fould, A., 1864. "Origins of the monetary union called Latin – A report to the Emperor by the Minister of Finance;" reprinted in the Appendix to "Proceedings of the International Monetary Conference of 1878," US Congress House, misc. doc. no 396, 49th Congress, 1st Session (US serial set 2430): 782–786.

Fratianni, M. and F. Spinelli, 1984. "Italy in the gold standard period 1861–1914," in M. Bordo and A. Schwarz (eds.), *A Retrospective on the Classical Gold Standard: 1821–1931*, Chicago: University of Chicago Press.

Friedman, M., 1990. "Bimetallism revisited," *Journal of Economic Perspectives*, 4 (Fall): 85–104.

Great Britain, Parliamentary Papers, 1867–8. "Report of the International Conference on Weights, Measures and Coin," British Parliament Papers, 1867–8 [4021] XXVII.801.

Greenfield, R. and H. Rockoff, 1991. "Gresham's law regained," Rutgers University (ms.).

Kenwood, A. and A. Lougheed, 1971. *The Growth of the International Economy, 1820–1960*, London: George Allen & Unwin.

Kindleberger, C., 1984. *A Financial History of Western Europe*, London: George Allen & Unwin.

Lardy, D. 1878. "'Statement of the Monetary legislation and coinage in Switzerland' presented to the International Monetary Conference of 1878, August 29, 1878," reprinted in "Proceedings of the International Monetary Conference of

1878," US Congress, House, misc. doc. no. 396, 49th Congress, 1st Session (US serial set 2430): 190–191.

McKinnon, R., 1963. "Optimum currency areas," *American Economic Review*, 53: 717–725.

Mertens, J., 1944. *La naissance et le développement de l'étalon-or*, Paris: Presses universitaires de France.

Mundell, R.A., 1961. "A theory of optimal currency areas," *American Economic Review*, 51: 637–665.

Niehans, J., 1978. *The Theory of Money*, Baltimore: Johns Hopkins University Press.

Redish, A., 1990. "The evolution of the gold standard in England," *Journal of Economic History*, 50(4): 789–805.

Rolnick, A. and W. Weber, 1986. "Gresham's law or Gresham's fallacy?," *Journal of Political Economy*, 94 (February): 185–199.

Russell, H., 1898. *International Monetary Conferences. Their Purposes, Character and Results*, London: Harper & Brothers.

Shaw, W.A., 1896. *The History of Currency*, reprinted 1967, New York: Augustus M. Kelly.

Thuillier, G., 1983. *La monnaie en France au début du XIX siècle*, Geneva: Librairie Droz.

Van der Wee, H., 1977. "Monetary, credit and banking systems," in E.E. Rich and C.H. Wilson (eds.), *The Cambridge Economic History of Europe*, vol. 5, Cambridge: Cambridge University Press: 290–393.

Willis, H.P., 1901, *A History of the Latin Monetary Union: A study of International Monetary Action*, Chicago: University of Chicago Press.

Yeager, L., 1976. *International Monetary Relations. Theory, History and Policy*, New York: Harper & Row.

4 Greenback resumption and silver risk: the economics and politics of monetary regime change in the United States, 1862–1900

CHARLES W. CALOMIRIS

Introduction

An enduring contribution of macroeconomic theory in the 1970s and 1980s was its emphasis on the role of expectations of future behavior in causing current movements in asset and commodity prices. While this approach had been applied to the valuation of stocks and bonds, the contribution of recent macroeconomics has been to translate the asset-pricing approach to the problems of understanding movements in exchange rates and price levels by taking explicit account of policy processes and agents' expectations (Muth, 1961; Sargent, 1973; Dornbusch, 1976; Krugman, 1979; Sargent and Wallace, 1981; Flood and Garber, 1983, 1984; Obstfeld and Rogoff, 1983; Obstfeld, 1986; Grilli, 1986, 1990). In particular, these models showed that a complete analysis of the price and exchange rate processes requires an explicit description of the money-supply process, and explicit modeling of anticipations of possible switches in monetary regimes. In a fixed exchange rate regime, promises of convertibility will be convincing only if government reserve holdings and long-run fiscal policy make those promises credible.

Uncertainty regarding future monetary regimes was a central feature of American political and economic life in the second half of the nineteenth century. From 1862 to 1879 the United States operated on a greenback standard with no convertibility maintained between the greenback and gold. Following a decade of bitter political struggle over resumption of convertibility, the greenback became convertible into gold in January 1879. But after resumption of convertibility, a new threat to the dollar emerged in the form of the "free-silver" movement. The goal of this movement was to re-establish a bimetallic standard, which would have led to a *de facto* switch to a depreciated silver dollar standard. These struggles were the defining characteristics of party platforms and national political campaigns. The soft- and hard-money wings of the Democratic party were described in terms of their positions on greenback resumption in the 1870s and free coining of silver during the years of silver controversy from 1876 to 1896. President Grant's most controversial actions included his resistance to greenback supply increases, and his veto of inflationist legislation in 1874 (Unger, 1964). William J. Bryan's famous speech at the Democratic Convention in 1896 decried the "cross of gold" that threatened the crucifixion of America. Massive outflows of gold from the Treasury in the mid-1890s threatened to exhaust Treasury gold holdings and led President Cleveland to call Congress back into session to deal with the problem.

Economists and historians have emphasized the potential depressive effects of currency risk through its effects on interest rates and international capital flows during the 1890s. Friedman and Schwartz (1963, 1982) and Garber (1986) argue that silver risk increased *ex post* costs of borrowing, because anticipated possible increases in the price level (reflected in high nominal interest rates *ex ante*) were not realized (that is, the United States stayed on the gold standard). Conversely, other research has stressed how the credibility of the maintenance of, or likely return to, the gold standard at other times has been beneficial in lowering the costs of private and public finance (Bordo and Kydland, 1989; Calomiris, 1988a, 1988b, 1991).

Despite the importance of greenback and silver regime risks for American financial history, there have been only a few attempts to quantify the importance of the political events of this period using the tools of the recent rational expectations literature. In this chapter, I will analyse the role that anticipations of possible regime switches played in determining nominal variables during the greenback suspension of convertibility and the silver crisis; use financial data to provide evidence of regime-specific inflation expectations; and argue that accounting for monetary regime expectations and risk are important for measuring *ex ante* real interest rates and for understanding some apparent departures from the normal pro-cyclicality of the price level during this period.

With respect to the era of greenback suspension, I argue that anticipations of future resumption set current prices and exchange rates, and that nominal money was endogenous to these expectations. Moreover, institutional constraints on the money-supply process imposed important dynamic restrictions on the price process. While the supply of greenbacks was restricted, national bank notes were the marginal component of the supply of paper currency. The real supply of national bank notes was an increasing function of expected inflation. In equilibrium, the zero-profit condition for national bank currency issues required expected deflation. Thus current prices reflected not only long-run expectations of the price level, but also expected deflation.

I then analyze the struggle over silver during the last decades of the nineteenth century. Silver risk ultimately concerned the maintenance of the token status of silver currency, which was threatened by the (unlikely) possibility of a return to "free silver" after 1878. Building on the model developed in the previous section, I argue that the run on the dollar in 1893 reflected a relatively high probability of a return to a suspension of convertibility. This, rather than the possibility of immediate conversion to a silver standard, was the main risk underlying forward premia and depletions of the Treasury gold reserve. I provide evidence that the probability of a switch to silver was never substantial in the 1890s, even though it caused large increases in nominal interest rates and *ex post* real interest rates.

This analysis suggests possible pitfalls for econometric studies of the nineteenth century US economy that fail to take account of regime changes and regime risk, which are explored in the following section. The nineteenth century US experience included episodes of substantial expected deflation and inflation. These expectations were sometimes realized, and sometimes not. Average expected inflation varied importantly over time, as did the relationship between money and price, and the autocorrelations of either series. Nominal interest rates provide an underestimate of *ex ante* real rates of return during the greenback suspension, and an overestimate of *ex ante* real rates of return for some episodes in the early 1890s. At the same time, *ex post* real interest rates were higher than *ex ante* rates during the early 1890s because of unrealized expected inflation. Ironically, debtors, who had led the free-silver movement, suffered most from the uncertainty and high costs of credit it created.

Macroeconometric models that assume unchanging money and price processes over the nineteenth century are misspecified. Financial returns data from the analysis on pp. 88–119 can be useful to distinguish between periods of expected and unexpected price change. To illustrate the potential importance of taking account of regime change, I show that controlling for expected deflation during the 1870s helps to explain the weak pro-cyclicality of prices during the late nineteenth century. Once one adjusts for shifts in expectations of price level change, prices and output exhibit much stronger comovement.

Greenback issues and their valuation under suspension

The laws authorizing the creation of legal tender notes (or "greenbacks") beginning in April 1862 were novel in three important respects. First, prior to this date no Treasury securities had been given private legal tender status, although Treasury notes were sometimes receivable in payment of government dues. Second, unlike previous federal currency issues (the Treasury notes of 1814 and the "demand notes" of 1861), the legal tender notes were neither convertible into gold upon demand, nor useful for extinguishing gold-denominated liabilities like tariffs. Third, in contrast to earlier Treasury issues, vast amounts of greenbacks were issued, and the Treasury had authority (and later would be required) to reissue any greenbacks it received. This made greenbacks an important permanent component of the money supply. The 1862 legislation thus marked three important precedents of lasting importance for US monetary history: government encroachment in determining the numeraire for private debts; a departure from specie-based government note issues; and a permanent government role in providing a medium of exchange.[1]

During the greenback suspension domestic transactions were performed almost exclusively in paper currency and paper-denominated deposits, and gold was driven from domestic circulation. The exceptions to this rule were the Pacific states, where specific provisions were made to remain on a gold standard (Lester, 1939). Until January 1875, there was no legislation establishing a timetable for returning to convertibility into gold on demand. Convertibility was achieved, as promised, on January 1, 1879, at which point specie and paper currencies once again circulated side by side.

Price and exchange rate determination

The value of greenbacks relative to gold (or other commodities) varied greatly from 1862 until the resumption of convertibility in January 1879. At their nadir, in July 1864, greenbacks were valued in the New York gold market at less than 37 percent of their face value. Calomiris (1988b) reviews the literature on the valuation of greenbacks. The primary controversy in this literature has been whether the current supply of greenbacks, or news relevant for future government policy in support of greenbacks, was the most important determinant of their value. I argue that the latter view (espoused by Mitchell, 1903, 1908) seems to conform better to economic theory and available empirical evidence.

There are three central components in my model of the price process under greenback suspension. The first is expectation formation about the long-run future greenback value of gold (and the price level). The second is the institutional arrangement whereby the government licensed national banks to provide money, along with related regulations relevant for the money-supply process. The third is a money-demand equation.

The United States was on an inconvertible paper-money (greenback) standard from 1862 through the end of 1878. Throughout that period the government promised eventual resumption of convertibility at the gold-parity exchange rate, but it was not until 1875 that the Resumption Act made the timing of that commitment explicit. That is not to say that expectations of resumption were constant prior to, or after, the Resumption Act. Throughout the period other actions by the government influenced the perceived probability of resumption. In particular, the greater the government's reliance on greenback-denominated (as opposed to specie-denominated) debt, the less credible its commitment to resumption was perceived to be (as shown in Calomiris, 1988b). And after the Resumption Act, markets reacted during the 1876 election to the risk of a reversal of the commitment to resume on January 1, 1879.

Resumption was a policy that would not have happened suddenly. Thus resumption expectations concerned the price level at a distant point in the future. The relationship between resumption expectations and the future price level can be summarized by expression (4.1) (which assumes, for convenience, an equivalence between the greenback price of gold and the price level):[2]

$$E_t P_{t+u} = a_t(1) + (1 - a)_t(P'),$$
(4.1)

where a is the probability of resumption having occurred by time $t + u$, and $P' > 1$ is the expected price level at $t + u$ contingent on resumption not having occurred. For simplicity, I will think of P' as predetermined.

The second ingredient in the model is the money-supply process, which was set, in part, by government regulation. I assume that demand fixed the ratios of deposits and gold holdings relative to paper currency. Gold was used primarily for foreign trade and for domestic transactions on the West Coast (Lester, 1939). With regard to deposits, there were no legal restrictions or greenback reserve requirements, and the assumption of a fixed ratio of paper money to deposits is defensible empirically for this period.[3] Under these assumptions it is sufficient to model the demand and supply for paper currency to determine the equilibrium time-path of prices.

Paper currency consisted of two components, which were perfect substitutes: greenbacks and national bank notes.[4] The supply of greenbacks was exogenously set by policy, and was unresponsive to changes in prices (see Calomiris, 1988b, for a detailed discussion). National bank notes were issued by national banks, but were fully backed and guaranteed by the federal government. National banks, in essence, were licensed to issue government paper money under strict regulations. National banks held greenbacks and government bonds as required reserves against notes issued. National bank notes were the marginal (endogenous) component of the paper money supply, and were issued according to their profitability for national banks.[5] In essence, national bank note issues were a separable activity from the rest of banking. On the margin banks equated the profit from diverting capital toward the creation of notes, or toward commercial lending (and deposit creation).

The costs of issuing notes consisted of the opportunity cost from diverting capital to (possibly) lower-interest required government bond investments and zero-interest required greenback reserves,[6] and a 1 percent tax on notes issued. Calomiris (1988b, pp. 218–219) shows that, for a given *real* marginal profit rate on alternative use of bank capital (s), we can write the zero-profit condition of national bank note supply as:

$$s = L\{i_b - [(0.9q)i_l + 0.009]\} - n^e, \tag{4.2}$$

where $L > 1$ is Cagan's (1965) leverage ratio on the use of bank capital for the creation of national bank notes, i_b and i_l are the nominal interest rates on government bonds and loans (for the marginal bank), q is the marginal bank's greenback reserve ratio (which varied by location), 0.009 reflects the simple tax on bank note issues, and n^e is expected inflation.

Under risk-neutrality and fully integrated capital markets, s and the real rates of return on government bonds and all banks' loans are equal, and expected inflation (deflation) is determined by rearranging the terms in (4.2). This solution for expected inflation implies constant expected *deflation* in equilibrium. Intuitively, the potential profitability of issuing national bank notes limits the equilibrium rate of seigniorage (or inflation tax) and hence requires a negative rate of expected inflation.

More generally, bank loan interest rates can vary across regions due to limitations on capital mobility, and there is much evidence to suggest that such variation was important in the US unit banking system (for reviews see Binder and Brown, 1991; Calomiris, 1992). James (1976) argued that the regional composition of national bank note issues reflected such differences in bank lending opportunity costs. Under the assumption of different given real lending rates across banks, the supply of notes will be an increasing function of the rate of inflation, and the equilibrium rate of inflation will be determined jointly by (4.2) and the demand function for currency (4.3).

$$(B/P)_t = b(Y_t, r_t + n_t^e), b_1 > 0, b_2 < 0, \tag{4.3}$$

where B is nominal paper currency (greenbacks plus national bank notes during the suspension), P is the price level, b is the money-demand function, Y is real output, and r is the real rate of interest on alternative assets.[7] For simplicity, I follow the classical assumptions of predetermined real output and real interest rates. The note-supply function is determined by summing across all banks. Banks with high loan interest rate opportunities will be the last to devote capital to note issuing.

Conditions (4.2) and (4.3) solve for the equilibrium values of the rate of inflation (deflation), the real stock of currency, and its components. We derive the time-path of the expected price process by beginning with $E_t P_{t+u}$ from (4.1), and solving recursively for the previous periods' prices using the

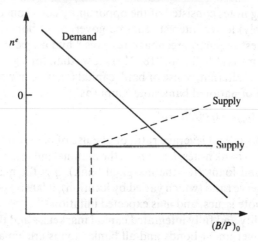

4.1   Equilibrium in the currency market

equilibrium rate of inflation (deflation). Given solutions for expected
inflation (deflation), real currency, and the price level over time, the money-
demand equation implies the equilibrium nominal amount of paper money
holdings of the public, which consists of a predetermined amount of
greenbacks and an endogenous supply of national bank notes.

Figure 4.1 depicts the equilibrium in the currency market under two
alternative specifications of national bank note supply. Under integrated
capital markets, all rates of return are equal and the supply schedule is flat
at the equilibrium rate of deflation. Under imperfectly integrated capital
markets, $i_b < i_l$ and $i_b < s + n^e$, and the supply schedule will be upward
sloping in expected inflation. The kinks in the supply functions reflect the
real value of predetermined greenback balances. If the supply schedule is
sufficiently steep, it is possible for the equilibrium to entail expected
inflation rather than deflation. Positive equilibrium expected inflation
requires sufficiently large rates of return on bank stock and loans relative to
government bonds for the marginal bank, and is unlikely if there are
substantial additional costs associated with note issue (in addition to the 1
percent tax), as argued by Champ, Wallace and Weber (1992). For this
reason, and because of empirical evidence for expected deflation discussed
below, it seems reasonable to characterize equilibrium price expectations as
deflationary during the suspension.

We can also use this model to understand the determination of the
equilibrium amount of real national bank notes issued under the post-1879
specie standard. In this case, either the supply of government-issued
currency in the hands of the public or gold will be the marginal component

of currency supply. In practice after 1879, gold coin and certificates were the marginal component, as the supply of greenbacks remained fixed by law. Under the gold standard, the rate of inflation was mainly determined exogenously by world markets for gold and other commodities, and the expected rate of inflation under the gold standard was essentially zero (Klein, 1975; Shiller and Siegel, 1976; Rockoff, 1984; Barsky, 1987). Now the zero-profit condition (4.2) alone will determine the amount of national bank notes issued, such that the marginal issuer earns zero profits when the expected inflation rate is zero. Thus the amount of national bank note issues should rise, *ceteris paribus*, when moving from a regime with expected deflation to a regime with a zero expected inflation rate.

Our model of money and prices under the greenback suspension has some interesting testable implications. The price of gold (and price level) processes should have followed a random walk with negative drift; individuals should have expected predictable deflation; news about the probability and timing of resumption should have been an important determinant of innovations in the price of gold and price level; and (contrary to Friedman and Schwartz, 1963) the supply of greenbacks – an inframarginal component of the money supply – should have been relatively unimportant for price movements.[8]

Calomiris (1988b) provides evidence supporting each of these implications of the model, including evidence of deflationary expectations, of the importance of fiscal-policy news, and of the differential pricing of greenbacks and demand notes,[9] which is consistent with the asset-pricing approach. On the causal role of greenbacks in determining other variables I presented results from a vector autoregression among monetary aggregates, commodity prices, the price of gold, output, fiscal news proxies and the interest rate which supported the statistical irrelevance of greenbacks for gold and commodity price determination. News regarding the government's choice of numeraire for its debt, however, was an important determinant of gold price movements – presumably because it contained information about future government resumption policy.

For present purposes I wish to stress the empirical findings in favor of expected deflation, and the measures of anticipated movements in prices. For mid-1869 through 1878 data are available on gold- and greenback-denominated securities from which one can extract precise measures of expected deflation only if one knows each period's default risk premium on railroad bonds. Column (4) of table 4.1 compares the actual annual rate of greenback appreciation at each point in time to the implied forecast of the rate of appreciation assuming no variation in the risk premium. At each date shown in the table I compare the actual rate of appreciation of greenbacks from that date to 1881 with the forecasted rate of appreciation

Table 4.1 Bond yield differentials and long-run appreciation

Period	Average differential between gold and greenbacks yield[a] (1)	Expected appreciation (Current differential less differential for July–December 1878) (2)	Average actual rate of greenbacks appreciation to 1881[b] (3)	Appreciation forecast error (2)–(3) (4)	Appreciation forecast error allowing time-varying risk premium[c] (5)
January–June 1869	1.33	3.53	2.00	1.53	0.43
July–December 1869	0.49	2.69	1.85	0.84	−0.26
January–June 1870	−0.52	1.68	0.93	0.75	−0.35
July–December 1870	−0.42	1.78	0.93	0.85	−0.15
January–June 1871	−1.01	1.19	1.09	0.10	−1.00
July–December 1871	−0.95	1.25	1.10	0.15	−0.95
January–June 1872	−0.02	2.18	1.26	0.92	−0.18
July–December 1872	0.01	2.21	1.40	0.81	−0.29
January–June 1873	−0.09	2.11	1.90	0.21	−0.89
July–December 1873	−0.26	1.94	1.39	0.55	−0.55
January–June 1874	−0.65	1.55	1.60	−0.05	−0.05
July–December 1874	−0.45	1.75	1.50	0.25	0.25
January–June 1875	0.07	2.27	2.36	−0.09	−0.09
July–December 1875	0.09	2.29	2.30	−0.01	−0.01
January–June 1876	−1.19	1.01	2.50	−1.49	−1.49
July–December 1876	−1.07	1.13	1.76	−0.63	−0.63
January–June 1877	−1.22	0.98	1.36	−0.38	−0.38

July–December 1877	−1.21	0.99	0.84	0.15	0.15
January–June 1878	−1.32	0.88	0.40	0.48	0.48
July–December 1878	−2.20	0.00	0.10	0.10	0.10

Notes:

[a] $\frac{1}{6}\sum_{j=1}^{6}[i_{sp}(j) - i_{gr}(j)] = d$.

[b] The average of monthly exchange rate closings for the period was used to measure the current gold price of greenbacks. The 6s of 1881 were redeemable on June 1, 1881.

[c] This calculation sets the risk premium equal to 1.10 for 1869–73, and 2.20 for 1874–78.

Source: Calomiris (1988b).

implied by the yield differential between greenback- and gold-denominated bonds with that maturity.

There is clearly positive serial correlation in the measured forecast errors, which may reflect either time variation in the risk premium, or coincidentally serially correlated news. Positive measured forecast errors suggest a time varying risk premium, since it is not reasonable to suppose that people expected resumption at greater than the parity level. The measured forecast errors are consistent with the view that agents had been sanguine of a timely resumption in the early 1870s. The positive values of the forecast errors for the period prior to 1873 probably reflect a rising default premium on railroad bonds after the Panic of 1873.[10] Column (5) provides an alternative rough measure of the appreciation forecast error under the assumption that the risk premium doubled (rose from 1.1 to 2.2) after the Panic of 1873.

The estimated forecast errors in column (5) indicate that there were changes in expectations regarding a timely resumption. Times of relative pessimism include 1871, 1873–early 1874, and early 1876. In all three cases qualitative historical accounts support the view that these were times when resumption policy was questioned. 1871 saw a change in Treasury policy which was perceived as a signal of a possible significant increase in the supply of greenbacks and was regarded as a threat to a timely resumption. This policy was promptly reversed to restore confidence (see Dewey, 1903, pp. 360–361). The controversy wore on until Grant's veto of April 1874, which Dewey (1903, p. 361) describes as "a turning point in the agitation for an increased volume of treasury legal tender notes." The estimates in column (5) support the view that resumption expectations rose after the veto.

The brief pessimism regarding resumption in early 1876 coincided with the political struggle over resumption prior to the election of 1876. The Democrats were divided between "hard"- and "soft"-money advocates. The desire to maintain unity and to attract soft-money independents led to a tolerance of the soft-money minority in the Democrat-controlled Congress, and the possibility of a swing toward repeal of the Resumption Act. Repeated attempts by soft-money Democrats to force consideration of the repeal of the Act prior to the election were thwarted by procedural rules and then finally by the nomination of the hard-money candidate, Tilden, in July. The repeal movement failed to force the issue prior to the election in an attempt to extract a price for party unity. Tilden's empty promises to postpone resumption and a party platform pledging the same were not viewed as credible commitments. The nomination of Tilden in July had effectively put to rest any true threat of a postponement of resumption. Even the House bill calling for postponement which passed on August 5,

1876 was nothing more than a political ploy; it was deliberately kept vague and passed with a vote of 106 to 86, with 93 abstentions.

In summary, table 4.1 indicates that much of the deflation of the 1870s was anticipated. Furthermore, changes in estimated resumption expectations coincide with some political events that historians have pointed to as turning points in resumption expectations, particularly the election of 1876.

Modeling silver standard risk and expected inflation

Legislation demonetizing silver (the "Crime of '73") occurred in the midst of the controversy over resumption of greenback convertibility. In response to fears of a decline in the value of silver due to new silver discoveries, Congress discontinued the free coining of silver, and thereby prevented a *de facto* inflation in the dollar numeraire (i.e., a change from a gold standard to a silver standard).

The "Crime" was first identified by the Greenbackers during the election of 1876 as evidence of a creditor conspiracy to lower prices. The demise of the greenback inflationist movement after 1876 ushered in the free-silver movement as a substitute means for inflationist debtors (especially farmers) to achieve an increase in the price level. Until that time, complaints about the end of free coining of silver in 1873 were absent, and there was no political movement to speak of favoring the free coining of silver (see Laughlin, 1886, pp. 209–214, Russell, 1898, pp. 150–191). According to Russell (1898), worried Congressmen during the election of 1876 even claimed (disingenuously) to be unaware of the abrogation in 1873 of free-silver coining. From that point on, gold standard conservatives and inflationist pro-silver advocates struggled intermittently for 20 years over the possible conversion from a gold to a silver standard.

The only pro-silver legislation to pass Congress during this period were two compromise measures, the Bland–Allison Act of 1878 and the Sherman Purchase Act of 1890. Both provided for the limited issue (not free coining) of silver coins or silver-related paper currency (i.e., currency issued for government purchase of silver bullion). These acts were viewed as temporary measures by silver advocates. The central goal of the pro-silver lobby remained the return to free silver. To mitigate the inflationary consequences of a return to free silver (and thus make it more politically attractive to hard-money advocates) Congress sponsored several international conferences from 1878 to 1892 (see Russell, 1898, for detailed discussion of each), which were designed to persuade all countries to adopt a uniform bimetallic standard. It was argued that if this could be achieved, then the value of silver would be increased, and the return to free coining of silver could be accomplished with little effect on prices. All of these conferences were unsuccessful, owing in part to the lack of agreement over the form of the new bimetallic standard (limited or unlimited coining of silver) and which silver–gold ratio should be adopted (Russell, 1898).

Beginning in the spring and summer of 1893, there was growing apprehension that the continuing minting of silver in compliance with the Sherman Act, along with continuing net outflows of resources from the Treasury owing to the decline in tariff revenues relative to expenditures, might lead to a cessation of gold convertibility at the Treasury. These fears produced additional strain on the Treasury through a dramatic increase in demands for conversion of paper currency (as shown in table 4.2). The continuing decline in the Treasury's reserves led to the repeal of the Sherman Act in November 1893, which halted the increase in paper currency supply and helped the Treasury shore up its stock of gold.

Free-silver advocates continued to call for a repeal of the "Crime of '73." William Jennings Bryan's Presidential campaign in 1896 saw a resurgence of a movement to permit the free coining of silver, but Bryan's defeat marked the end of the pro-silver movement. The Gold Standard Act of 1900, and the gold price inflation of the late 1890s (which reduced debt burdens of pro-silver farmers) ensured that the pro-silver platform would never return.[11]

The risk of a return to free silver associated with Bryan's election campaign is easy to understand, but the potential risk to the gold standard in the aftermath of the Sherman Act, and the emergence of a perceived increase in numeraire risk in 1893 can be understood only within the context of the specific political struggle that gave rise to the minting of silver coins and the issuing of silver certificates from 1878 to 1893, and the economic constraints that affected the value of these token currencies.

Legislative history

Several pieces of silver-coining legislation were proposed and struck down in Congress. The Act of 1878 was a compromise between the inflationist forces who advocated free coining of silver, and those who fought any potential threat to the gold standard. According to the provisions of the Act, the Treasury would purchase between $2 and $4 million worth of silver (in market value) on the open market. Thus as the gold price of silver declined, more silver dollars would be coined for any given value of silver purchased. The silver would be coined and placed into circulation by the Treasury through government purchases. Silver coin would be returned to the Treasury in one of two ways: either in payment of any dues to the

Table 4.2 *Gold redemptions and the gold reserve (000)*

Year	Redemptions in gold during each month			Net gold in Treasury, coin and bullion ($)
	United States notes ($)	Treasury notes of 1890 ($)	Total ($)	
January, 1892	152	160	312	119,575
February	206	270	476	122,122
March	476	256	733	125,815
April	438	259	697	119,910
May	335	287	622	114,232
June	568	1,854	2,423	114,342
July	4,086	5,149	9,235	110,444
August	1,049	5,091	6,141	114,156
September	2,264	1,824	4,088	119,396
October	283	316	599	124,006
November	406	292	698	124,410
December	5,700	4,538	10,238	121,267
	15,964	20,297	36,261	
January, 1893	6,359	5,137	11,497	108,182
February	5,811	8,017	13,829	103,284
March	1,642	3,285	4,926	106,892
April	12,569	7,483	20,052	97,011
May	12,077	4,471	16,548	95,049
June	3,073	1,178	4,251	95,485
July	772	264	1,036	99,203
August	1,190	1,158	2,348	96,009
September	144	197	341	93,582
October	263	433	695	84,385
November	299	217	516	82,959
December	296	222	517	80,892
	44,494	32,063	76,556	
January, 1894	119	238	356	65,650
February	10,983	8,211	19,193	106,527
March	2,266	1,195	3,461	106,149
April	6,072	1,594	7,666	100,202
May	25,131	1,410	26,541	78,693
June	20,708	1,461	22,170	64,873
July	13,368	556	13,923	54,976
August	4,210	532	4,741	55,217
September	636	300	937	58,875
October	2,543	505	3,048	61,362

Table 4.2 (*cont.*)

	Redemptions in gold during each month			Net gold in
Year	United States notes ($)	Treasury notes of 1890 ($)	Total ($)	Treasury, coin and bullion ($)
November	7,085	715	7,800	105,425
December	30,820	1,088	31,907	86,244
	123,941	17,803	141,744	
January, 1895	43,415	1,702	45,118	44,706
February	4,785	776	5,561	87,086
March	809	280	1,089	90,643
April	734	284	1,018	91,247
May	735	432	1,166	99,151
June	645	402	1,046	107,512
July	3,123	704	3,827	107,236
August	16,219	345	16,564	100,330
September	17,120	258	17,377	92,912
October	1,849	318	2,167	92,943
November	15,616	418	16,035	79,334
December	19,788	425	20,213	63,262
	124,837	6,344	131,181	
January, 1896	15,686	762	16,449	49,846
February	21,081	656	21,737	123,963
March	6,381	475	6,857	128,646
April	6,755	376	7,131	125,394
May	21,727	313	22,040	108,345
June	7,964	297	8,261	101,700
July	16,275	1,010	17,285	110,719
August	11,389	981	12,370	100,958
September	3,437	1,225	4,661	124,035
October	9,907	2,167	12,074	117,127
November	3,137	925	4,062	131,510
December	858	273	1,132	137,317
	124,597	9,461	134,058	
January, 1897	594	352	946	144,800
February	521	403	924	148,661
March	679	570	1,249	151,786
April	6,935	567	7,502	153,341
May	8,045	838	8,883	144,320
June	6,595	519	7,113	140,791

Table 4.2 (*cont.*)

	Redemptions in gold during each month			Net gold in
	United States notes	Treasury notes of 1890	Total	Treasury, coin and bullion
Year	($)	($)	($)	($)
July	5,072	203	5,275	140,818
August	2,876	241	3,116	144,216
September	2,598	144	2,742	147,663
October	2,505	191	2,696	153,573
November	1,787	324	2.110	157,364
December	1,816	204	2,019	160,912
	40,023	4,554	44,577	

Source: Burke (1899, p.24).

government, for which the coins would be received at their face (not intrinsic) value; or through exchanges of coins for silver certificates, which would be backed 100 percent by the silver so deposited with the Treasury. In addition to new issues of coins and certificates, coins and silver certificates previously returned to the government in payment of taxes, tariffs, or other dues could be returned to circulation through the regular course of government purchases.

Under the Bland–Allison Act, silver coins were not convertible directly into gold. Yet silver currency issued under the Bland–Allison Act always traded at its face value. As Laughlin (1886) recognized, and as discussed in detail below, tax payment parity can be as good as a convertibility option for maintaining a token's value if tax payments are large enough relative to token currency.[12]

The Sherman Act of 1890 was essentially a continuation of the Bland–Allison Act, but required larger monthly purchases of silver – $4.5 million (in coin produced). The Sherman Act differed from the Bland–Allison Act in three other respects. First, the amount purchased each month was not a fixed amount of silver in dollar units of bullion purchased, but a fixed amount of silver in face value of currency produced. Thus the amount minted did not fluctuate with the gold value of silver, as before. Second, rather than issue silver coin which was convertible into silver certificates, the Treasury would use newly authorized Treasury notes to buy the silver bullion. Third, the policy of the Secretary of the Treasury was to redeem these notes on demand in gold.[13] The only substantive differences between the Sherman Act and the Bland–Allison Act were the amount of token currency issued, and the Treasury's voluntary commitment to redeem

Treasury notes in gold on demand. The other differences were neutral with respect to their effect on the currency issued and the potential threat to the gold standard.

Modeling the potential collapse of the gold standard

The collapse of the gold standard did not occur in the 1890s, although I will show that the discussion of contemporaries and evidence from market indicators are consistent with moments of significant concern regarding short-run convertibility, and a small implied probability of a long-run switch to silver. Modeling the risk of dollar depreciation entails imagining a possible, but unrealized (counterfactual) world. The goal is to construct a coherent model of the possible suspension or collapse of the gold standard for the 1890s which is consistent with a variety of observed data, and with the fears voiced by sophisticated financial observers of the time.

Perhaps surprisingly, despite the importance of the silver crisis years of the 1890s for American financial history, there has been only one attempt to construct a formal model of the potential threat to the gold standard posed by silver, namely Grilli (1990). Grilli proposes a "speculative-attack" model in which the amount of gold currently in the Treasury is positively related, and the amount of outstanding paper currency negatively related, to the probability of maintaining the gold standard. Short-run reductions in the gold reserve, or increases in the currency supply, increase the risk of a collapse of the gold standard because, by assumption, the long-run money-supply growth process is assumed to be an extrapolation of the short-run process. Not surprisingly, the period of recession and low tariff revenues (partly due to the revised schedule of duties under the McKinley Tariff) was one of high deficits, short-run decumulation of gold in the Treasury, and – under the provisions of the Sherman Act – increase in outstanding silver-related currency (shown in table 4.3). These facts, combined with Grilli's method for estimating the long-run money supply, explain the run on the dollar in 1893 as a rational expectation of an inconsistency between the pledge to maintain the gold standard and the long-run expected money supply.

Despite some attractive features of this model, the treatment of the money-supply and deficit processes is an important weakness. As Grilli's framework recognizes, what matters most for fixed exchange rate credibility is the long-run viability of the gold standard. One necessary condition for maintenance of the gold standard is the "transversality condition" for the government's ability to maintain gold convertibility in the future, which he argues depends on the long-run factors governing deficits and the supply of currency. But government credibility, and post-suspension dollar prices, do not always depend exclusively on predetermined changes in the government supply of money, or on government deficits.

Consider what would have happened to the price level if during the 1890s *current* gold convertibility had been suspended, but it remained a certainty that the government would eventually control deficit-driven expansion of money and return to gold convertibility. The post-suspension price level would be determined using the model developed on pp. 89–92 above. Dollar depreciation at the time of suspension would be a function of the expected duration of the suspension and the equilibrium expected deflation implied by the zero-profit condition governing the marginal supply of money (national bank notes), as in (4.2) above. As before, the money supply would be endogenous to the price level. Suspensions anticipated to be short-lived would have little effect on the price level.

If the government's ultimate commitment to gold were uncertain, and if the only other possibility were the adoption of a silver standard (by Act of Congress), then the price level at the time of the suspension of convertibility would be determined by the expected duration of suspension and the equilibrium rate of deflation, and by the probability-weighted future price levels under either the gold or silver standard (as in (4.1) above).

Grilli's model of the 1890s differs from mine in three important respects. First, Grilli envisions a range of long-run outcomes for the value of the dollar other than the two alternative specie standards (silver or gold) that were at the focal point of the debates in the 1890s. Second, Grilli views the money-supply process as the driving force of long-run price determination. In contrast, my model stresses the endogeneity of money supply through national bank note issues, and stresses long-run expectations of government support for gold. Third, Grilli argues that short-run increases in deficits in the 1890s threatened the long-run viability of the gold standard. I am convinced by Bohn's (1991) evidence that short-run deficits never constituted a long-run threat to gold during this period.

Bohn's study of deficit processes in the United States from 1792 to 1988 argues that increases in deficits elicited reductions in expenditures and increases in taxes that prevented deficits from threatening the money-supply process. Bohn employs an error-correction framework to show that the government responded to deficits as if it were preventing the violation of its intertemporal budget constraint. Deficits eventually hit "reflecting barriers" and triggered government policies to prevent continuing deficits and monetization of debt. Thus the high deficits of the 1890s (see table 4.4) were probably not expected to persist, and thus they would not be expected to influence long-run money-supply growth.

Grilli's model also equates a change in government currency with a

Table 4.3 Currency in circulation, 1876–1900[a], ($ million)

Year	Gold	Silver dollars	Silver certificates	Treasury notes of 1890	U.S. notes (greenbacks)	National bank notes	Other[b]	Total
1876	25.0	NA	0	0	331.4	316.1	55.1	727.6
1877	25.0	NA	0	0	337.9	301.3	58.1	722.3
1878	25.0	NA	0	0	320.9	311.7	71.5	729.1
1879	110.5	NA	0.4	0	301.6	321.4	84.7	818.6
1880	220.6	18.9	6.0	0	315.8	336.2	75.9	973.4
1881	312.6	28.4	38.8	0	319.8	346.4	79.8	1,115.8
1882	355.9	32.2	57.2	0	314.7	352.5	69.8	1,182.3
1883	347.1	36.0	71.7	0	313.2	349.8	24.1	1,241.9
1884	340.7	40.4	97.4	0	307.9	333.5	116.5	1,236.4
1885	342.8	39.3	105.1	0	296.3	309.1	198.6	1,291.2
1886	360.4	52.9	89.2	0	306.4	306.9	140.3	1,256.1
1887	377.8	55.4	139.1	0	315.9	278.4	148.6	1,315.2
1888	396.4	56.5	196.6	0	300.5	249.1	172.3	1,371.4
1889	377.0	54.8	255.5	0	302.7	210.8	196.7	1,397.5
1890	375.2	56.5	294.7	0	326.9	183.3	194.6	1,431.2
1891	406.7	59.9	310.5	38.1	327.3	164.0	197.8	1,504.3
1892	408.9	57.1	327.3	87.1	318.5	167.4	253.7	1,620.0
1893	407.9	58.1	322.1	132.5	319.0	171.9	184.7	1,596.2
1894	496.8	52.0	330.0	140.1	270.6	199.7	186.5	1,675.7
1895	483.8	52.8	321.6	118.0	266.9	206.6	156.5	1,606.2

1896	455.9	52.7	336.3	98.1	225.6	215.3	137.7	1,521.6
1897	520.2	53.0	362.8	86.6	248.8	224.8	163.5	1,659.7
1898	649.6	57.6	391.2	100.2	290.2	224.6	126.5	1,839.9
1899	724.3	63.4	401.3	93.1	311.1	238.1	124.2	1,955.5
1900	618.6	67.6	408.5	78.6	322.8	294.1	284.5	2,074.7

Notes:

[a] Dates for June.

[b] Includes gold certificates, subsidiary silver and currency certificates of 1872.

NA Not available.

Source: National Monetary Commission (1910, pp. 158–163).

Table 4.4 *Government receipts and outstanding debt, 1876–1900*

Year	Ordinary receipts		Public debt less cash in Treasury	
	Total ($ million)	Per capita ($)	Total ($ million)	Per capita ($)
1876	281	6.2	2,061	45.7
1877	279	6.0	2,019	43.6
1878	262	5.5	1,999	42.0
1879	292	6.0	1,996	40.9
1880	357	7.1	1,919	38.3
1881	382	7.5	1,820	35.5
1882	409	7.8	1,675	31.9
1883	370	6.9	1,539	28.7
1884	334	6.1	1,439	26.2
1885	337	6.0	1,375	24.5
1886	351	6.1	1,282	22.3
1887	383	6.5	1,175	20.0
1888	378	6.3	1,063	17.7
1889	391	6.4	976	15.9
1890	420	6.7	891	14.2
1891	356	5.6	852	13.3
1892	374	5.7	842	12.9
1893	343	5.2	839	12.6
1894	306	4.5	899	13.3
1895	322	4.7	902	13.1
1896	315	4.5	955	13.6
1897	399	5.6	987	13.8
1898	442	6.1	1,027	14.1
1899	555	7.5	1,155	15.6
1900	574	7.5	1,108	14.5

Source: National Monetary Commission (1910, pp. 253–255).

change in total currency outstanding, ignoring the important role of national bank notes as the marginal component of currency supply under suspension of convertibility. As noted above, the presence of national bank notes has important implications for the determination of the price process. Consider, for example, what would happen if the government credibly announced a future switch to a silver standard and an immediate suspension of greenback convertibility, but constrained the growth of greenbanks to zero and refused to mint silver freely in the interim. The money supply would adjust immediately to the new policy through an increase in national bank notes, and the dollar would depreciate immediately to a level consistent with long-run establishment of free-silver minting and interim expected deflation. This example illustrates the pitfalls of viewing the money supply as predetermined, and the importance of incorporating long-run expectations of silver conversion and the supply function for national bank notes into a model of price determination and speculative attack during the period of silver risk.

Token silver issues and the maintenance of the gold standard

If, as Bohn (1991) argues, the short-run deficits of the 1890s posed no significant threat to the long-run maintenance of the gold standard, what about the token currency Acts themselves? Did the Bland–Allison or Sherman Acts, *per se*, threaten the gold standard through their effects on the money supply, or in some other way? An investigation of the possible role of the silver Acts requires a detailed analysis of the various components of currency and the factors governing their supply during the 1890s.

By the 1890s the supply of currency in the United States consisted of full-valued gold coins and gold certificates, paper currency in the form of greenbacks and national bank notes (direct and indirect obligations of the government to redeem in *either* gold or silver on demand, depending on which served as the specie numeraire for the monetary system), and silver token currency (silver coins, silver certificates, and Treasury notes of 1890).

Assume for simplicity that all forms of token and full-valued currency trading at par are perfect substitutes in a physical sense for transactions and storage purposes, and that there is an exogenous (growing) real demand for currency, M_t (expressed in gold units). Furthermore, consistent with the provisions in both silver Acts, assume that silver currency is receivable in payment of taxes at par with gold.

The silver token currency-supply process implied by the two Acts can be summarized by:

$$S_t = xt - \sum_{w=0}^{t} (T_s - G_s)_w, \tag{4.4}$$

where S_t is the stock of silver token currency in circulation at time t, x is the constant amount of new token currency issued per year (roughly \$2 million per month under the Bland–Allison Act and \$4.5 million per month under the Sherman Act), T_s are the annual tax payments made in silver, and G_s are the government purchases made with token currency previously received in taxes.[14] The S_t process is bounded from above by xt because, by definition, the sum of the G_s terms must be less than or equal to the sum of the T_s terms.

An attack on the currency could have occurred as a result of token currency issues if either of two conditions regarding expectations of the long run were violated. First, if people believed that the supply of government-issued token currency in the hands of the public (silver tokens plus greenbacks) expected to prevail in the future would eventually overtake the total real demand for currency, then gold would disappear and token currency would cease to be an inframarginal component of the money supply. In this case, the tax transversality condition would be violated. The prices of gold and commodities would eventually be determined by the intrinsic value of the silver dollar. Given the real demand for money and the exogenous-supply component of money (greenbacks, a limited supply of token silver and Treasury notes), national bank notes would increase endogenously to equalize total supply and demand of currency at a depreciated value of the dollar. Expected deflation would characterize the transition to the long-run establishment of free coining in silver.

A second possible violation of the tax transversality condition might occur even if the total stock of token money were not expected to overtake the total real demand for money. If the ratio of the stock of token currency to the flow of tax payments were expected to become sufficiently high permanently then individuals would eventually be able to avoid using gold for tax payments forever. In this case, the tax transversality condition would again be violated, and tax receivability would not ensure current parity of the two currencies.[15] If this were expected to occur and the government were not expected to act to support the currency through maintenance of convertibility into gold on demand, then there would be an immediate collapse of the gold standard.

In both these scenarios, the collapse of the gold standard is immediate. An expectation of a future violation of a transversality condition leads to an immediate run because there can be no forecastable excessive capital losses on token currency in equilibrium, and because the supply of national bank notes is endogenous (thus nominal government currency does not determine the current value of the dollar).

These theoretical possibilities of a collapse of the gold standard through expectations of the increasing supply of the exogenous component of token currency, however, do not appear to be relevant empirically. One cannot reasonably argue that a permanent continuation of the Sherman Act, and other government policies in place in the 1890s, would have led to token currency overtaking total currency demand, either in terms of money stock holdings or tax payment flows. Under existing law, the supply of greenbacks was fixed at $346.7 million.[16] Thus any indefinite continued expansion of token currency under existing law would have had to come from the silver Acts themselves. Money demand and taxes are both tied to the real economy, would be reasonably expected to grow at some rate over time, and could never be permanently overtaken by a linear function like xt. That is, in comparing the long-run growth of money demand and token currency.

$$\lim_{t \to \infty} (M_0 e^{gt})/(xt + N) = \infty \qquad (4.5)$$

where g is the rate of increase of money demand, and N is the constant ceiling on other paper currency supplied.

Empirical evidence suggests that the exogenous component of nominal token currency would never have exceeded the total demand for currency in gold units, and thus there was no real risk of token currency displacing gold. The total amount of currency in circulation (currency outside the Treasury) grew at roughly 4 percent from 1878 to 1898, from $729 million to $1,840. These were not extraordinary years with respect to the business cycle, and therefore serve as useful benchmarks for long-run money-demand growth. From 1878 to 1890 $351 million in silver currency was created under the Bland–Allison Act, while total money demand increased by $702 million. Gold in circulation rose substantially (by $350 million), while national bank notes fell $129 million, as table 4.3 shows.[17] Clearly, an indefinite continuation of the Bland–Allison Act could not have displaced full-valued currency at any time.

By mid-1890 total currency in circulation was $1,431 million. The Sherman Act implied an annual issue of $54 million in Treasury notes. An expected 4 percent annual growth rate for money demand, however, implies that total money demand would be expected to increase each year by upwards of $56 million. In fact, from 1890 to 1893 gold in circulation actually increased $33 million, while total currency holdings increased $165 million (consistent with a roughly 4 percent growth rate).[18] Thus even the larger increases in silver currency due to the Sherman Act never threatened to displace gold by overtaking total money demand (see the related discussion in Friedman and Schwartz, 1963, pp. 128–134).

In summary, I have argued that in the absence of some other change in policy affecting the long-run credibility of the gold standard, the currency emissions from the Sherman Act of 1890 could not have threatened the gold standard.

Free-silver risk and the run on the dollar

Notwithstanding the above arguments regarding the irrelevance of deficits and token currency supply for long-run maintenance of the gold standard and the token status of silver and paper currency, there clearly was substantial concern in 1893 and thereafter regarding the maintenance of the gold standard, which is visible in the financial press, the actions of Congress and President Cleveland, and the data on redemptions of paper currency at the Treasury (see table 4.2).

Moreover, the focus of much of this concern was the Treasury's gold holdings, and the threat deficits and silver currency issues posed for the short-term maintenance of the reserve.[19] How can this evidence be reconciled with the above arguments regarding the irrelevance of token currency growth and deficits for the long-run viability of the gold standard?

Irrelevance of token currency and deficits for the *long-run* viability of the gold standard does *not* imply their irrelevance for *short-run* convertibility. In the model presented on p. 103, even departures from convertibility that are known to be temporary may still result in depreciation of the dollar (and expected appreciation during the suspension, which returns the currency to par). Moreover, return to gold after suspension would not have been certain since there remained a strong constituency for free silver until Bryan's defeat in 1896. Even though suspension itself would have no obvious effect on the probability of victory for free silver,[20] suspension of convertibility implied that current and subsequent perceptions of free-silver risk would be reflected in varying rates of discount of the currency during suspension rather than a contraction of its supply (which, under convertibility, would have maintained parity).

An additional necessary condition for suspension to result in depreciation is that tax receivability would not provide an alternative form of *short-run* backing for the currency. Imagine, contingent on suspension, that the public were able to return all paper currency to the government (say, at the beginning of each month) in partial payment of tax obligations. That is, each period the public pays in paper currency *and gold*, and the government immediately spends the currency it receives. In this case, there would be virtually no depreciation in the currency, since it would effectively be "redeemed" each period at par in gold. This is only true, however, if the public must pay some taxes each period in gold as well as in paper. If it were feasible to pay all taxes in token currency, then taxes would not provide short-run support to the currency. Figure 4.2 plots the proportion of tax payments made in gold (or gold certificates). These data indicate that at several times from 1878 to 1896, and practically for the entire interval from 1892 to 1897, taxes were paid almost exclusively in token currency. It seems reasonable to suppose that if suspension had occurred – increasing the incentive to pay taxes in tokens – people would have been able in the short run to avoid paying taxes in gold, and therefore tax receivability would not have provided an alternative means of short-run support for the currency.

To sum up, it seems that the main threat to the gold standard in the 1890s was a temporary suspension of convertibility that would have allowed the

Customs receipts and means of payment

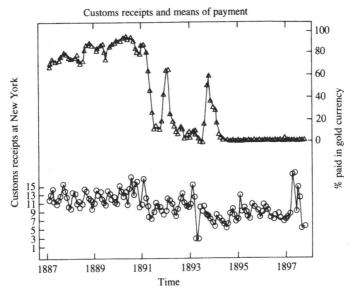

4.2   Percentages of each kind of currency received from customs at
      New York, 1878–98

dollar to fall to a small discount. This discount would have reflected three
separate influences: the probability of the passage of free-silver legislation
during the period of expected suspension, the relative value of silver and
gold in the market, and the duration of the expected suspension. The higher
the risk of free silver, the lower the value of silver, and the higher the
duration of suspension, the greater the potential post-suspension
depreciation of the currency.

The discount would not be influenced by the (inframarginal) supply of
greenbacks and Treasury notes. Unlike models of speculative attack in fiat-
money regimes (e.g., Grilli, 1990), the money supply would not be the
exogenous forcing process determining the dollar's value in a post-collapse
state. As during the greenback suspension, national bank notes would have
become the marginal component of currency supply, and the total nominal
supply of money would have been endogenous along with the price level.
While the probability of an attack would be influenced by short-run paper
(and other token) currency outstanding relative to reserves, the post-
collapse value of the dollar would be determined by the combined influence
of the risk of free-silver victory, the relative value of silver, the equilibrium
rate of inflation/deflation, and the expected duration of the suspension.

The following informal model captures the essence of the problem.
Consider a holder of government paper currency. Assuming a shoe-leather
cost to redeeming currency in gold (alternatively, a convenience service to

paper as opposed to gold currency) the currency holder will "run" the Treasury only if the expected capital loss of not doing so is sufficiently large. Depreciation will occur only if reserves at the Treasury are exhausted (i.e., if there is a successful "attack"). The holder of greenbacks contemplating whether to run the Treasury must determine: (1) whether his information sources indicate that the depreciation contingent on an attack is large enough to provide an incentive for running the Treasury; (2) whether suspension is likely – that is whether *other holders* of government currency are likely to agree with his assessment of the possibility of a run on the Treasury; and (3) whether his decision to run the Treasury today, rather than postpone his decision until tomorrow, will result in a change in the chance of his receiving gold if he does run (i.e., whether he is likely to be one of the first in line today but not tomorrow). Given that individuals may disagree on the fundamental risks affecting the long-run value of the currency, they will try to infer each other's decisions by observing the depletion in the government's reserve. Furthermore, they will have the incentive to act quickly as that depletion accelerates in order to avoid being last in line. Thus as reserves fall, the possibility of a run increases for any given amount of expected post-attack depreciation. Furthermore, for given levels of currency outstanding and reserves in the Treasury, increases in expected post-attack depreciation will prompt action by increasing numbers of currency holders (with diverse views regarding fundamental risk and possibly diverse shoe-leather costs).[21]

One can write the probability of an attack as:

$$A_t = v(R_t, N + S_t, P'_t, a_t, u), \quad v_1 < 0, \; v_2, v_3, v_4, v_5 > 0, \tag{4.6}$$

where R is the level of reserves, $N + S$ is the supply of outstanding paper (and other token) currency, P' is the silver price of gold, a is the probability of victory for free silver at time $t + u$, and u is the expected duration of the suspension (and delay in legislative decision making regarding free silver conditional on suspension). For simplicity, assume that suspension is expected to last for a fixed duration, and let P' follow a random walk (thus at any time the value of P' is expected to remain constant).[22]

If suspension did occur, then the price level would be determined by:

$$e_t = z(n^e, Q_t, a_t, u), \quad z_1, z_2, z_3, z_4 > 0. \tag{4.7}$$

As on pp. 89–92, n^e would be determined by (4.2) and (4.3). The expected future price level at $t + u$ is determined by P' and a (as in condition (4.1)), and the current price level is determined by the expected future price level and the rate of expected deflation.

The unconditional expectation of the one-period ahead future price of gold at any time prior to the occurrence of suspension is given by:

$$E_{t-1} e_t = (1 - A_{t-1}) 1 + A_{t-1} z(n^e, P'_{t-1}, a_{t-1}). \tag{4.8}$$

Each period agents construct estimates of a, observe R, P', and $N+S$, and decide whether to expend resources to demand redemption of their paper currency from the government. If enough agents demand redemption, suspension of convertibility will occur.

Once suspension has occurred, agents know that suspension will end u periods after it begins. At that time, either the government will successfully return to par convertibility in gold, or it will announce a policy of "free-silver" coining, implying that the dollar price of gold will be equal to P'. a is the probability of the success of free silver. At the time of suspension, the price level expected for u periods later is $(1 - a)1 + aP'$. The current price level is derived from the price level expected at $t + u$ and the expected rate of dollar appreciation, which is given by (4.2) and (4.3).

Each period agents form expectations of the probability a suspension will occur, based in part on their expectation of the "shadow exchange rate" – the price of gold that would prevail immediately after a suspension. The shadow exchange rate is an increasing function of P' and a, and A is an increasing function of the shadow exchange rate.

The discounts on the demand notes of 1861 after the suspension of convertibility in December 1861 provide an example of the counterfactual small depreciation that could have occurred in the 1890s if the Treasury had suspended convertibility. As already noted, the demand notes were useful for extinguishing tax liabilities denominated in gold. From December 1861 to March 1863 the demand notes circulated at a discount relative to gold, and a premium relative to greenbacks. By March 1863 they had disappeared from circulation, having been "redeemed" in the interim through tariff payments. The average discount rate on demand notes was roughly 4 percent during this period, and discounts ranged from 0.5 percent (in late February 1863) to 9.2 percent (in late July 1862). By late February 1863 the comparable discount rate on greenbacks had risen to greater than 40 percent. Clearly, the difference between the gold value of greenbacks and demand notes reflected the duration of their effective suspension periods, and the different risks associated with their long-run convertibility. For demand notes, the risk was that tariff receivability would be discontinued prior to the paying in of all demand notes. For greenbacks, the risk was that the promised long-run return to gold would not occur.

Evidence on depreciation expectations due to silver risk

How can one verify that silver risk during the 1890s involved expectations of a small depreciation, rather than the possibility of an immediate move to a silver standard? Abstracting from risk premia, the interest rate differential between otherwise identical dollar- and gold-denominated securities provides an estimate of the expected rate of currency depreciation. Short-term interest rate data for choice two-name commercial paper in New York provide a short-run nominal interest rate series for a default risk-free instrument. Greef (1938, p. 56) claims that one New York bank's losses on commercial paper during the troubled years 1891–95 amounted to a trivial 0.05 percent. A riskless gold-denominated interest rate for New York can be derived from prices of bills of exchange (of New York banks) on London banks under the assumption that the pound faced no exchange rate risk during this period. There were no references in the *Economist* to imminent collapse of the pound or British exchange rate risk during this period, despite British promotion of the international conferences on bimetallism. Indeed, British investors repatriated their capital investments in America in response to silver risk, especially in 1893.[23]

Data from the National Monetary Commission (1910) on 60-day and "sight" bills of exchange prices can be used to construct a measure of the gold-denominated interest rate in New York as follows. Assuming "sight" bills were redeemable in 10 days (i.e., that it took 10 days to travel to London from New York), then the ratio of the price of sight and 60-day bills traded in New York today implies an interest rate in gold units over the 50-day period beginning 10 days hence. This can be converted into a rough measure of the 60-day rate by multiplying by 6/5.

Table 4.5 reports 60 day nominal and real interest rates for the last week and day, respectively, of each month from 1893 through 1896, and calculates expected depreciation (n_{60}^e) as the difference between the two rates. These data indicate that at no point during the period did markets anticipate any significant risk of a change from a gold to a silver standard in the near term, which is consistent with the political history of the silver movement's uphill battle. Moreover, even a successful campaign in Congress to switch to a silver standard would have taken much longer than 60 days to complete. Rather than view the 2 percent 60-day expected depreciation of the dollar in June 1893 as a 2.7 percent chance of an imminent conversion to the silver standard (using P' as the post-attack price level, given in table 4.5), one should view expected depreciation as the product of the probabilities of a temporary suspension of convertibility and the expected immediate depreciation contingent on suspension. For example, a 2 percent expected depreciation is consistent with a 20 percent chance of suspension and a 10 percent post-attack expected depreciation. Of course, there is a wide range of probabilities whose product equals 2 percent, so it is not possible to estimate separately the probability of suspension or the expected depreciation of the currency contingent on

Table 4.5 *Expectations of depreciation*

Year		Nominal 60-day rate, two-name choice 60-day commercial paper in New York[a]	Gold 60-day rate, derived from exchange markets in New York on London[b]	n^e_{60}	P'^c
1893	1	0.75	0.49	0.26	1.54
	2	0.92	0.49	0.43	1.54
	3	1.33	0.49	0.84	1.55
	4	1.00	0.74	0.26	1.54
	5	1.33	0.86	0.47	1.55
	6	2.50	0.49	2.01	1.70
	7	2.50	0.62	1.88	1.76
	8	2.50	1.12	1.38	1.74
	9	1.33	0.49	0.84	1.72
	10	0.92	0.74	0.18	1.79
	11	0.80	0.62	0.18	1.84
	12	0.63	0.62	0.01	1.89
1894	1	0.58	0.62	−0.04	2.02
	2	0.58	0.49	0.09	2.15
	3	0.50	0.37	0.13	2.01
	4	0.50	0.37	0.13	2.05
	5	0.50	0.37	0.13	2.05
	6	0.50	0.37	0.13	2.04
	7	0.50	0.25	0.25	1.99
	8	0.54	0.37	0.17	1.98
	9	0.58	0.37	0.21	2.01
	10	0.46	0.25	0.21	2.04
	11	0.50	0.37	0.13	2.12
	12	0.50	0.25	0.25	2.15
1895	1	0.50	0.25	0.25	2.14
	2	0.67	0.37	0.30	2.05
	3	0.67	0.37	0.30	1.94
	4	0.63	0.37	0.26	1.93
	5	0.46	0.25	0.19	1.94
	6	0.46	0.25	0.19	1.94
	7	0.50	0.25	0.25	1.94
	8	0.63	0.25	0.38	1.93
	9	0.83	0.25	0.58	1.90
	10	0.83	0.25	0.58	1.91
	11	0.67	0.37	0.30	1.94
	12	1.00	0.37	0.63	1.91
1896	1	1.00	0.25	0.75	1.93
	2	0.83	0.25	0.58	1.96

Table 4.5 (*cont.*)

Year	Nominal 60-day rate, two-name choice 60-day commercial paper in New York[a]	Gold 60-day rate, derived from exchange markets in New York on London[b]	n_{60}^e	P'^c
3	0.92	0.25	0.67	1.94
4	0.83	0.25	0.58	1.94
5	0.75	0.25	0.50	1.94
6	0.75	0.25	0.50	1.96
7	1.00	0.25	0.75	1.96
8	1.67	0.50	1.17	1.94
9	1.17	0.62	0.55	1.91
10	1.67	0.75	0.92	1.87
11	0.92	0.81	0.11	1.86
12	0.67	0.62	0.05	1.86

Notes:
[a] Two-name, choice commercial paper is the highest rate reported for the last week of each month, as given in National Monetary Commission (1910), pp. 122–125.
[b] The gold rate is constructed from 60-day and sight bills of exchange traded on the last day of each month, from National Monetary Commission (1910, pp. 192–195.
[c] P', The silver price of gold, is from Laughlin (1886, Appendix II, Tables F and G) and for 1896, the continuation of the same series in the *Economist*.

suspension. If, as argued before, the depreciation of the demand notes in 1862 and 1863 is an indication of the likely post-attack depreciation of the dollar in the 1890s, then the range of reasonable estimates of the probability of suspension in June 1893 can be narrowed to, say 10–30 percent.

The estimates of expected depreciation reported in table 4.5 should be viewed as upper bounds on true expected depreciation for two reasons. First, I assume a zero depreciation risk premium; second, I use the highest rate quoted for choice commercial paper as the definition of the nominal interest rate.[24]

The timing of the run on the dollar in 1893, evident both in the high interest rate differentials observed for March through September and the redemptions of greenbacks and Treasury notes during the same period, can be understood within the context of the model developed above. Two important events increased currency risk during late 1892 and early 1893: the election of Cleveland and the failure of the International Conference on bimetallism. While Cleveland's hard-money views figured prominently in his inaugural speech in March 1893, his plan for supporting the gold standard and issuing debt remained unclear, and there was fear that he would wait too long to raise the necessary resources (see the *Economist*, March 4, 1893, pp. 265–266, and March 11, pp. 289–290), making suspension more likely. There was also concern that, as a Democrat, Cleveland might be more prone to compromise with the soft-money wing of his party.

The increasing pessimism over the adoption of an international bimetallic currency policy during 1892, and the indefinite recess of the International Monetary Conference in December 1892 – which would never reconvene – led to a fall in the value of silver relative to gold, as people became pessimistic of any future monetary role for silver as an international currency (see the *Economist*, December 10, p. 1544, December 17, p. 1577, and December 24, p. 1615). From January 1892 to July 1893 the gold value of silver $(1/Q)$ fell some 30 percent (Laughlin, 1886, p. 294). The collapse of the Convention also led to renewed pressure from the pro-silver lobby in Washington, as there was no more reason to postpone unilateral action by the United States in anticipation of a joint international bimetallic policy. While Grilli (1990) is correct to point to increased pressure on the gold standard from increased currency supply and declining reserves, prior political news may have precipitated much of the subsequent decline in the reserve position through its effect on expectations and silver's value (i.e., an increase in a and P′).

Cleveland's vigorous opposition to the Sherman Act, his success in convincing commercial banks of the need to help shore up the Treasury's reserve, and increasing Congressional support for his views – culminating in the repeal of the Sherman Act on October 30 – signalled Cleveland's commitment to maintain parity and his skill in protecting the gold standard. Furthermore, the repeal of the Sherman Act removed a major source of short-term pressure on the reserve.

One interesting feature of the data in table 4.5 is the absence of any significant short-term depreciation risk from November 1893 until late 1895. In particular, the data provide little support for Garber and Grilli's (1986) and Grilli's (1990) view that the Belmont–Morgan syndicate (of February 1895) saved the gold standard. Instead they indicate that Bryan's candidacy was the only substantial threat to the gold standard after the crisis of 1893. Weekly data on interest rates reported in National Monetary Commission (1910, pp. 123–124) do not alter this conclusion. Indeed, from November 1894 through February 1895 interest rates on top-quality two-name paper in New York never exceeded 4 percent and did not vary much from week to week. There is no evidence from interest rate differentials of any significant expected depreciation in the dollar during this period.

Garber and Grilli (1986) and Grilli (1990) echoed earlier historians of the Belmont–Morgan syndicate (Burke, 1899) in arguing that there was substantial concern over the Treasury gold reserve in 1894 and 1895. The Resumption Act of 1875 gave the Treasury the power to raise funds through any of the bonds authorized in the Refunding Act of 1870 so long as the bonds were sold at a price greater than or equal to par.[25] Effectively, this meant that bonds could be sold at yields less than or equal to 5 percent. The Secretary of the Treasury used this power in January and November 1894.[26] But, as shown in table 4.2, the depletion of the gold reserve accelerated in late 1894 and early 1895. Garber and Grilli (1986) describe this as a run on the dollar, and argue that the Belmont–Morgan syndicate of February 1895 ended the run.

The agreement with the syndicate gave the government an option to buy gold with bonds in the future on demand, and required that at least half of the gold would be shipped from Europe. The reason for this latter provision was that preceding bond issues were not deemed entirely successful in shoring up the government's reserve, in part because domestic bond holders (who were required to purchase bonds with gold) obtained much of their gold by redeeming paper currency at the Treasury (Burke, 1899, p. 27). Alternatively, bond purchasers who used their own gold holdings to buy bonds replenished their gold holdings by converting domestic currency into gold after buying the bonds. Banks continued to provide gold to the Treasury in exchange for paper currency in 1894, but could not compensate for the large private withdrawals by bond purchasers (Burke, 1899, pp. 27–29).

While the gold-purchase option clearly was of use to the government in 1895, it is not clear that it was crucial to maintaining convertibility. On the one hand, it does seem that the very rapid daily withdrawals of gold from the Treasury in late January (averaging more than $3 million per day for the last seven days of the month) represented a lack of confidence in the gold standard. Furthermore, this was reversed after the deal with the syndicate was announced in February. On the other hand, however, the withdrawals in January seemed to reflect concern over the Administration's willingness to continue to use its powers of bond issue. Burke (1899, p. 28) writes of the period prior to the government's resort to the banking syndicate:

The first indications of a general withdrawal of gold for hoarding seems to have been noticed on January 17. Eight days after the movement culminated in the total withdrawal of over seven million in a single day. Three days later the President sent his special message to Congress and as nothing was done to allay public fears, withdrawals continued to be heavy. Negotiations [with Congress] for a new bond issue [in a form other than that allowed by the Act of 1870, which the Administration viewed as desirable] were begun on January 30th and withdrawals at once fell off and reached a minimum of $63,374 on February 4th. Delay and rumors over some difficulty in negotiations caused the withdrawals to increase to $390,302 on February 5th and to $729,479 on the next day. Denial of the rumor again caused a falling off in the withdrawals.

Once these plans failed, withdrawals began anew, and the government was forced to resort to the syndicate as a backup measure. Thus without the collapse of the earlier negotiations, and the fears that Congress or the Administration might not act swiftly enough to issue bonds to protect the gold standard, the syndicate might have been entirely unnecessary.

How can one reconcile the large withdrawals from the Treasury in December through February 1895 and the concern over the Treasury's reserve with the small interest rate differential in table 4.5? One possible explanation is that the procrastination of the Administration in issuing bonds in early 1895 raised the possibility of a very brief suspension of convertibility, which would have been expected to prompt immediate large issues of government bonds to replenish the reserve (bonds could have been placed in foreign markets to avoid reserve depletion by domestic bond holders).[27] One can imagine that importers and exporters anticipating the possibility of a brief suspension may have feared a postponement of immediate access to gold for international transactions. This would explain the hoarding of gold from December 1894 through February 1895, without implying a significant expectation of currency depreciation.

Inflation expectations and the pro-cyclicality of prices

The preceding sections indicate that the 1870s and the 1890s saw periods of unusual regime-specific inflation expectations, due in the first instance to expectations of resumption, and in the second instance to the perceived possibility of the collapse of the gold standard. One important implication of these findings is that "Phillips-Curve" modeling of the nineteenth and twentieth centuries as a single epoch, which implicitly assumes unchanging expected and actual price processes, may introduce error into the measured relationship between output and price movements.

Since the seminal work of Friedman (1968), Phelps (1968), Phelps et al. (1970), and Lucas (1972, 1973), researchers have emphasized the import-ance of expectations in modeling the relationship between price and output comovements. Interpretations of the price–output relationship can be usefully grouped into three categories: models of wage and price rigidity (as in Blanchard, 1987; Fischer, 1977; Gordon, 1980, 1982, 1990; Lucas, 1990; Taylor, 1980), models of imperfect information about monetary distur-bances (Lucas, 1972, 1973), or models of the allocative effects of unantici-pated price changes under nominal financial contracting (Bernanke, 1983;

Bernanke and Gertler, 1990; Calomiris, Hubbard, and Stock, 1986; Calomiris and Hubbard, 1989a, 1990; Fisher, 1933). Despite important differences, these three modeling strategies agree that anticipated and unanticipated changes in prices will be associated differently with output movements. In particular, anticipated inflationary (or deflationary) disturbances will not be as strongly associated with output growth (or decline) as unanticipated inflationary (or deflationary) disturbances.

The evidence for expected deflation in the 1870s and expected inflation in the 1890s leads one to expect weak or perverse association between output and price movements during these periods. The predictions are clearer for the 1870s. During the 1870s expected deflation should not have been associated with decline in output.

The effect of silver risk on the relationship between price and output in 1893 and 1896 is harder to predict. On the one hand, the realized flat time-path of prices was deflationary compared to the expected price level (which incorporated the possibility of a switch to silver), and thus little deflation could be consistent with large output declines. On the other hand, devaluation expectations led to a flight to gold, which was deflationary (given some domestic autonomy in price determination). For example, mid-1893 witnessed large declines in prices (see Calomiris and Hubbard, 1989a). Furthermore, because expectations of devaluation were not uniform within 1893 or 1896, annual data on GNP and the GNP deflator (used below) may mask important short-run effects.

Any discussion of the pattern of association between price and output must acknowledge the disagreement that currently exists over the proper measures of these variables for the mid-to-late nineteenth century. Three commonly used annual series now exist: the Gallman–Kendrick series (Gallman, 1966), the Balke–Gordon (1989) series, and the Romer (1989) series. Table 4.6 provides annual data for real output and the price level from the two most recent sources.

Visual inspection of table 4.6 shows that during the 1870s and 1890s the normal pro-cyclical pattern of association between growth in real output and growth in the price level is not immediately visible. Nor does it seem to be consistent across subperiods.[28] The distinction between expected and unexpected price change seems to be relevant for the pattern of association between output and price. During the 1870s substantial deflation was associated with positive growth, particularly from 1875 to 1879. From 1892 to 1896 prices were essentially flat (in annual data), while output growth was exceptionally slow. The output–price correlation (in log differences) increases substantially when the 1870s are excluded from the sample. Using Romer's data the correlation rises from 0.056 to 0.387. Using Balke and Gordon's data the correlation rises from 0.103 to 0.231.

Table 4.6 *Real GNP and the GNP deflator, 1869–1913*

Year	Romer (1989) estimates		Balke and Gordon (1989) estimates	
	GNP (billion 1982 dollars)	Implicit price deflator (1982 = 100)	Real GNP (billion 1982 dollars)	Implicit GNP deflator (1982 = 100)
1869	75.609	10.244	78.2	10.49
1870	75.464	9.661	84.2	9.98
1871	76.952	9.769	88.1	9.86
1872	89.605	9.423	91.7	9.60
1873	94.863	9.329	96.3	9.51
1874	96.205	9.169	95.7	9.25
1875	97.684	8.945	100.7	8.85
1876	104.628	8.539	101.9	8.51
1877	110.797	8.207	105.2	8.38
1878	118.906	7.627	109.6	7.87
1879	127.675	7.378	123.1	7.64
1880	139.990	8.166	137.6	8.03
1881	143.580	7.998	142.5	7.99
1882	149.307	8.267	151.6	8.16
1883	152.097	8.141	155.3	7.88
1884	155.684	7.730	158.1	7.53
1885	157.789	7.260	159.3	7.35
1886	164.375	7.173	164.1	7.35
1887	169.453	7.240	171.5	7.35
1888	168.940	7.352	170.7	7.47
1889	175.030	7.402	181.3	7.48
1890	182.964	7.256	183.9	7.30
1891	191.757	7.166	189.9	7.30
1892	204.279	6.893	198.8	7.21
1893	202.616	7.036	198.7	7.23
1894	200.819	6.603	192.9	6.85
1895	215.668	6.513	215.5	6.74
1896	221.438	6.342	210.6	6.76
1897	233.655	6.383	227.8	6.66
1898	241.459	6.572	233.2	6.75
1899	254.728	6.799	260.3	6.86
1900	264.540	7.136	265.4	7.00
1901	284.908	7.086	297.9	7.04
1902	291.572	7.335	303.0	7.14
1903	306.239	7.420	311.7	7.33
1904	307.127	7.502	323.5	7.39
1905	323.162	7.676	353.2	7.40

Table 4.6 (*cont.*)

	Romer (1989) estimates		Balke and Gordon (1989) estimates	
Year	GNP (billion 1982 dollars)	Implicit price deflator (1982 = 100)	Real GNP (billion 1982 dollars)	Implicit GNP deflator (1982 = 100)
1906	351.499	7.873	367.7	7.64
1907	361.920	8.206	362.0	7.98
1908	346.800	8.145	342.2	7.81
1909	368.872	8.422	382.1	7.82
1910	383.888	8.645	383.8	8.14
1911	391.858	8.603	396.0	8.12
1912	407.112	8.944	418.9	8.32
1913	424.492	9.009	435.4	8.40

Table 4.7 provides a rough means for quantifying the importance of expected price changes in modeling the association between output and price. I regress price growth on output growth, with and without separate dummies for the 1870s and 1893/1896.[29] These dummies should be thought of as price expectations-shift variables. The R^2 in the regressions rises markedly when the dummies are included (from 0.011 and 0.003 to 0.327 and 0.239, respectively for the Balke–Gordon and Romer data sets). The size of the coefficient linking price and output movements increases by a factor of two using Balke and Gordon's data, and a factor of three using Romer's data. Consistent with Klein (1975) and Barsky (1987), the constant term is essentially zero in all the regressions.

The dummy variable for the 1870s is of the predicted sign and large in both regressions, and is statistically significant. It is also interesting to note that the Durbin–Watson statistic improves in both cases in the presence of the dummy variables. As I have argued, the 1870s were unusual in that there was persistent predictable deflation. This accounts for the reduction in serial correlation of inflation disturbances once the mean rate of deflation in the 1870s is controlled for.

The sign of the dummy for 1893/1896 is different in the two regressions, its size is small, and it is statistically insignificant. As noted above, the marginal effects of anticipated inflation in prices in the 1890s are difficult to predict, and difficult to measure in annual data.

This evidence suggests that future work on cyclical patterns in price change for other times and places in which monetary regime changes

Table 4.7 *Price change regressions, 1869–1913*

Dependent variable	Data source	Constant[a]	Coefficient $d \ln$ (real GNP)[a]	1870s dummy[a]	1893/96 dummy[a]	R^2	Durbin–Watson
$d \ln$ (GNP deflator)	Ba ke and Gcrdon (1989)	−0.0077 (0.0056)	0.0671 (0.1002)	—	—	0.011	1.33
$d \ln$ (GNP deflator)	Ba ke and Gcrdon (1989)	−0.0016 (0.0053)	0.1069 (0.0883)	−0.0349 (0.0082)	0.0063 (0.0171)	0.327	1.70
$d \ln$ (GNP deflator)	Romer (1989)	−0.0053 (0.0086)	0.0611 (0.1693)	—	—	0.003	1.54
$d \ln$ (GNP deflator)	Romer (1989)	−0.0001 (0.0082)	0.1777 (0.1581)	−0.0420 (0.0119)	−0.0045 (0.0239)	0.239	1.85

Notes:
[a] Standard errors in parent neses.
— not available.

occurred, or might have occurred, could benefit by using financial returns data to distinguish between anticipated and unanticipated changes in the price level. The importance of taking account of regime switching in analyzing the pro-cyclicality of prices is supportive of Lucas' (1976) exhortation that econometricians take account of changes in individuals' decision rules that follow from changes in policy regimes.[30]

Conclusion

This chapter has argued that modeling the money-supply process and the effects of expectations of monetary regime changes yields important insights for macroeconomic historians. During the expected deflation of the 1870s, nominal rates were lower than real rates, and substantial expected deflation was accompanied by modest economic growth. During episodes of suspension risk during the silver controversy of the mid-1890s, nominal rates were much greater than real rates. At their maximum, in June 1893, annualized nominal rates were more than 12 percentage points above real rates. The effect of silver risk on dollar depreciation expectations and nominal interest rates was due in large part to the effect of long-term silver risk and short-term silver currency issues on the depletion of the gold reserve of the Treasury, which increased the possibility of an attack on the dollar and a suspension of convertibility.

In addition to the implications of our results for measuring *ex ante* and *ex post* real costs of borrowing, and for the debate over the Phillips Curve and the pro-cyclicality of prices, these results have implications for the international integration of capital markets and the operation of the "Atlantic economy." In particular, real rates of interest between London and New York were much closer than nominal interest rate differentials would suggest. Comparisons of long-term government bond yields in Calomiris (1991) – possible only after the elimination of numeraire risk on US specie bonds in 1869 – and comparisons of short-term real interest rates (Calomiris and Hubbard, 1989b) show that real interest rate differentials between London and New York were small. Interest rate differentials typically were less than 2 percent, and remained within a band width of 3 percent.

Notes

I thank Jeremy Atack, Michael Bordo, Karen Lewis, Larry Neal, Hugh Rockoff, and seminar participants at the Wharton School, the University of Illinois, and the NBER Summer Institute on the Development of the American Economy for helpful comments.

1 The perceived need for an inconvertible paper currency in early 1862 must be understood within the context of the policies and events of 1861. The first government currency issue of the Civil War was the demand notes of 1861. These were convertible into gold upon demand, and useful for extinguishing government tariff liabilities at par with gold. Like the Treasury notes issued during the War of 1812, these notes retained nearly their entire par value by virtue of their receivability for duties even when, at the end of 1861, they were made inconvertible into gold on demand. The government suspension of convertibility followed the suspension of the banking system in the face of adverse news about government finances in December 1861 (the surprisingly bleak annual report of the Secretary of the Treasury, and the threat of war with Britain over the Trent Affair).

Banks held large amounts of government securities in December 1861, and were unusually at risk of a deterioration in government credit. When government credibility declined, banks were threatened with insolvency, and were forced to suspend. Indeed, Hammond (1970) argues that private legal tender authority for a depreciated paper currency in 1862 was a disguised means for bailing out troubled banks, which had suffered from the decline in the value of government securities. By linking all bank liabilities as well as assets to the government currency numeraire, the government insulated banks from the declining value of their holdings of government debt.

2 Calomiris (1988b) shows that, in fact, the price level and exchange rate were closely related at short and long frequencies during the years of greenback suspension.

3 See Calomiris (1988b, table 1 and n. 2).

4 National bank notes were backed 111 percent by government bonds deposited at the Treasury and, redundantly, by the full faith and credit of the federal government.

5 All national banks had an incentive to issue some national bank notes because they were required to hold a minimum amount of government bonds, which were used as collateral for the notes (Hetherington, 1990). On the margin, however, national banks chose whether to buy bonds in order to supply notes. Changes in the real supply of national bank notes reflected changes in bank opportunity costs and changes in the price of government bonds, and were limited by a variety of possible ceilings. See Calomiris (1988b, nn. 3, 5, and 9); Friedman and Schwartz (1963, p. 23); Cagan (1965); James (1976); Laughlin (1886, p. 249).

6 For simplicity, I assume risk-neutrality, so there is no partially offsetting benefit to holding government bonds, and in equilibrium real rates of return on bonds and loans are equal.

7 I assume that the demands for currency and bank deposits are in fixed proportions, and hence that bank deposits can be excluded from the model. Calomiris (1988b) argues that, empirically, the demand for currency is quite stable as a function of interest rates and income. Bordo (1989, p. 51) correctly points out that there is much evidence for money-multiplier stability (and hence stability of

the currency:deposit ratio), but he incorrectly criticizes my model for assuming that the money multiplier was unstable.

8 The predetermined supply of greenbacks might still matter for prices for two reasons: first, as a signal of government resumption intentions, and second, if the supply function for bank notes is upward sloping, through its effect on the location of the kink in figure 4.1. A higher predetermined supply of greenbacks will lower equilibrium expected inflation and increase the price level at each date prior to expected resumption. Such an effect would be significant economically only if the supply schedule were implausibly steep.

9 Demand notes were redeemable at par in payment of duties, but not convertible on demand into gold. Expected continuing parity in tax payments kept demand notes trading nearly at par relative to gold, until all demand notes were replaced by greenbacks. See Mitchell (1903) for a detailed discussion.

10 In Calomiris (1988b, n. 18) I incorrectly argued against Fels' (1959) conjecture that railroad risk had risen after 1873. I miscalculated that a rise in railroad risk implied an increase over time in the numbers in column (4). In fact, the opposite is true, and the data provide some support for Fels' position.

11 For a discussion of the link between agrarian unrest and financial distress during this period see Stock (1984).

12 Laughlin later ignored the potential importance of gross tax backing in his discussion of the threat to silver (pp. 272–273), and focused instead on the level of gold reserves, arguing that "to mean anything, redemption must redeem on any and all occasions. Anything short of that is a sham" (p. 277). While this statement is not correct as a general proposition, my subsequent discussion will be in agreement with Laughlin's emphasis on the gold reserve during this period, given that taxes provide little means of immediate redemption for token currency after 1890.

13 The notes were redeemable in either gold or silver, at the discretion of the Treasury. But the Treasury was charged in the Act with maintaining the various currencies on a parity with each other in accordance with their legally defined ratio.

14 In this analysis, I treat the silver Acts of 1878 and 1890 as expected to be permanent changes. This is not to say there was no possibility of repeal. Clearly, from the beginning there was a possibility of repeal, especially if the Acts were found to threaten the gold standard. Ultimately, repeal occurred in 1893 in response to just such a threat. Nevertheless, for purposes of argument, it is useful to ask whether a permanent continuation of the Acts by themselves could have threatened the gold standard.

15 This "tax transversality condition" was well understood by contemporaries as an important source of support for token (or paper) currencies, and was employed to explain different relative prices between token currencies with different tax backing. For example, Laughlin (1886, pp. 238, 253–258) emphasized the role that tax arbitrage played in maintaining the currency issued under the 1878 Act at par (p. 253):

This [tax receivability] is a species of daily redemption of the silver dollar; for as gold has hitherto been required . . . in payment of customs, now that silver dollars are receivable equally with gold for that purpose, they must remain at par with gold until there is forced upon the circulation more than is necessary for such uses . . . In brief we have unconsciously created a system of quasi-redemption of silver in gold by accepting silver at the customs when otherwise gold would be demanded.

Laughlin also noted that the silver trade dollar, created by the Act of 1873, which was not receivable in payment of taxes after its value fell in 1876, circulated at its intrinsic value and below the value of the silver dollars created under the 1878 Act. The trade dollar continued to trade at a discount until legislation in 1887 provided for its redemption at par in order to remove it from circulation.

Mitchell (1903) had referred to the tax-parity constraint to explain the relative price of greenbacks and the old demand notes of 1861. Demand notes were receivable at par with gold for customs, while greenbacks were not. Otherwise they were equivalent – neither was redeemable on demand in gold, and the two were physically similar. Demand notes maintained nearly their entire face value while greenbacks fell to two-thirds of their face value. By early 1863 all demand notes had disappeared from circulation, having been used in the interim almost exclusively to pay for customs duties (Mitchell, 1903, p. 196). During 1862 and early 1863 demand notes received a higher valuation because of their *expected* usefulness for redeeming tariff obligations in future months.

16 The Act of May 31, 1878 forbade further retirement of greenbacks; thus all greenbacks redeemed at the Treasury had to be reissued to maintain a fixed amount in circulation. National bank notes were demand-determined under the gold standard. Unlike the pre-1879 period, expected long-run inflation was near zero (see Barsky, 1987).

17 Data are from National Monetary Commission (1910, pp. 157–158).

18 National Monetary Commission (1910, pp. 157–158).

19 For examples, see Ford (1895); Warner (1895); Burke (1899); and the following entries in the *Economist*: December 10, 1892, p. 1544; March 4, 1893, pp. 265–266; March 11, 1893, pp. 289–290; April 15, 1893, pp. 441–442; June 3, 1893, p. 656; June 10, 1893, pp. 690–691; July 22, 1893, p. 873; September 9, 1893, pp. 1081–1082; October 14, 1893, pp. 1225–1226; October 28, 1893, pp. 1281–1282.

20 Some observers argued that President Cleveland deliberately postponed shoring up the gold reserve in 1893 to create an atmosphere of crisis to galvanize anti-silver support (the *Economist*, June 3, 1893, p. 656). Similarly, one can argue that allowing suspension might have worked against the passage of free-silver legislation.

21 This model shares common features with information-based models of bank runs (Jacklin and Bhattacharya, 1988; Chari and Jagannathan, 1988; Calomiris and Kahn, 1991; Calomiris, Kahn and Krasa, 1992).

22 See Roll (1972) and Calomiris (1988b) for supporting evidence during the greenback suspension.

23 Evidence for this view that capital was scarce during the early-mid 1890s comes from Wilkins (1989, pp. 151–152, 580–581) and from contemporary chroniclers. The *Economist* of London provided weekly analysis of US capital markets, which often took the form of lengthy discussions of problems of capital flight,

which it linked to the risk of the switch to silver. See especially the columns of March 4, 1893, p. 265; March 11, 1893, pp. 289–290; April 15, 1893, p. 442; and June 3, 1893, p. 656. In the March 11 issue, for example (p. 290), the foreign correspondent writes: "it would appear, therefore, that for some time longer doubts as to the ability of the Treasury to maintain the parity of silver and gold will continue to act as a drag upon business in the States, to depreciate the value of American securities, and to cause a certain uneasiness and want of stability in the European money market."

24 In modern data for fiat-currency regimes the observed risk premium may be large, and the forward rate may not be closely linked to the expected future spot rate. In the 1890s, however, the risk premium was probably a much smaller part of the forward premium. If potential depreciation over short intervals was bounded by, say, 10 percent, then exchange rate risk would be relatively small compared to the exchange rate risk in a fiat-money regime where money follows a random walk. My model of potential depreciation, and the data in table 4.5, imply small depreciation conditional on a collapse of fixed parity.

25 The January and November issues of 5 percent coupon bonds were sold at substantial premia, with respective yields to maturity of 3 and 2.88 percent (Burke, 1899, p. 32).

26 In February 1893 the Secretary had received assistance from New York banks. Six banks voluntarily exchanged $8.25 million in gold for legal tender notes to support the gold reserve.

27 According to the *Economist* (March 11, 1893, p. 290):

Some doubts have been expressed as to the possibility of placing any large amount of such bonds here, because of the possible disturbance to the money market which would result from the shipment of gold to the States in payment for them. No consideration of that kind, however, would deter investors from subscribing if reasonable terms were offered. If they thought about the money market at all, they would leave it to take care of itself, and a Government of the high credit of that of the United States is about as independent of the goodwill of intermediaries as is our own. The ability of the States to borrow here, and, as a consequence, to draw gold hence, need not, therefore, be questioned.

28 Of course, the formulation of the price–output relation varies, and need not take the form of a consistent contemporaneous association between output and price growth. For example, Gordon (1990) associates price and wage change with deviations of output from its potential level, which is calculated using peak-to-peak benchmarks. It is beyond the scope of this chapter to join the ongoing debate over the form of the Phillips Curve, or to provide new estimates of it. Instead, I am interested in pointing out the relevance of expectations for simple correlations between output and price growth.

29 There is no good reason to treat prices as endogenous to output changes, as these regressions (and most similar regressions in the Phillips Curve literature) assume. Indeed, Calomiris and Hubbard (1989a, 1989b) show that, in monthly data, price growth predicts output growth in Granger causality tests, and not vice versa. Furthermore, chroniclers of business-cycle conditions tended to view prices as leading indicators and economic causes of boom or decline, which is consistent with the debt-deflation view of the pro-cyclicality of prices.

30 In a related vein, in a recent study of wage adjustment in the United States and the United Kingdom, Alogoskoufis and Smith (1991) found important differences in Phillips Curves (the response of wages to cyclical changes in employment and inflation) between the post-Second World War and the pre-First World War periods, and related these to the different exchange rate regimes (price processes) governing these eras.

References

Alogoskoufis, George S. and Ron Smith, 1991. "The Phillips Curve, the persistence of inflation, and the Lucas critique: evidence from exchange rate regimes," *American Economic Review* (December): 1254–1275.

Balke, Nathan and Robert J. Gordon, 1989. "The estimation of prewar GNP: methodology and new results," *Journal of Political Economy* (February): 38–92.

Barsky, R.B., 1987. "The Fisher hypothesis and the forecastability and persistence of inflation," *Journal of Monetary Economics*, 19 (January): 3–24.

Bernanke, Ben S., 1983. "Nonmonetary effects of the financial crisis in the propagation of the Great Depression," *American Economic Review* (June): 257–276.

Bernanke, Ben S. and Mark Gertler, 1990. "Financial fragility and economic performance," *Quarterly Journal of Economics* (February): 87–114.

Binder, John J. and Anthony T. Brown, 1991. "Bank rates of return and entry restrictions, 1869–1914," *Journal of Economic History* (March): 47–66.

Blanchard, Olivier J., 1987. "Aggregate and individual price adjustment," *Brookings Papers on Economic Activity*, 1: 57–122.

Bohn, Henning, 1991. "Budget balance through revenue or spending adjustments? Some historical evidence for the United States," *Journal of Monetary Economics* (June): 333–360.

Bordo, Michael D., 1989. "The contribution of *A Monetary History of the United States, 1867–1960* to monetary history," in Michael D. Bordo (ed.), *Money, History, and International Finance: Essays in Honor of Anna J. Schwartz*, Chicago: University of Chicago Press: 15–78.

Bordo, M.D. and F.E. Kydland, 1992. "The gold standard as a rule," Federal Reserve Bank of Cleveland, *Working Paper*, 9205 (March).

Burke, W.M., 1899. "Bond issues and the gold reserve," *Sound Currency* (February): 17–32.

Cagan, Phillip, 1965. *Determinants and Effects of Changes in the Stock of Money, 1875–1960*, New York: Columbia University Press.

Calomiris, Charles, W., 1988a. "Institutional failure, monetary scarcity, and the depreciation of the continental," *Journal of Economic History* (March): 47–68.

1988b. "Price and exchange rate determination during the greenback suspension," *Oxford Economic Papers* (December): 189–220.

1991. "The motives of U.S. debt management policy, 1790–1880," *Research in Economic History*, 13: 67–105.

1992. "Regulation, industrial structure and stability in U.S. banking: an historical perspective," in Michael Klausner and Lawrence J. White (eds.), *Structural Change in Banking*, New York: Business One Irwin.

Calomiris, Charles W. and R. Glenn Hubbard, 1989a. "Price flexibility, credit availability, and economic fluctuations: evidence from the United States, 1894–1909." *Quarterly Journal of Economics* (August): 430–452.

1989b. "International adjustment under the classical gold standard: evidence for the U.S. and Britain, 1879–1914" (mimeo).

1990. "Firm heterogeneity, internal finance, and 'credit rationing,'" *The Economic Journal* (March): 90–104.

Calomiris, Charles W. and Charles M. Kahn, 1991. "The role of demandable debt in structuring optimal banking arrangements," *American Economic Review* (June): 497–513.

Calomiris, Charles W., R. Glenn Hubbard and James Stock, 1986. "The farm debt crisis and public policy," *Brookings Papers on Economic Activity*, 2: 441–479.

Calomiris, Charles W., Charles M. Kahn and Stefan Krasa, 1992. "Optimal contingent bank liquidation under moral hazard" (mimeo).

Champ, Bruce, Neil Wallace and Warren E. Weber, 1992. "Resolving the national bank note paradox," *Quarterly Review*, Federal Reserve Bank of Minneapolis (Spring): 13–21.

Chari, V.V. and Ravi Jagannathan, 1988. "Banking panics, information, and rational expectations equilibrium, *Journal of Finance* (July): 749–763.

Dewey, Davis R., 1903. *Financial History of the United States*, London: Longmans, Green & Co.

Dornbusch, Rudiger, 1976. "Expectations and exchange rate dynamics," *Journal of Political Economy* (December): 1161–1176.

Fels, Rendigs, 1959. *American Business Cycles, 1865–1897*, Chapel Hill: University of North Carolina Press.

Fischer, Stanley, 1977. "Long-term contracts, rational expectations, and the optimal money supply rule," *Journal of Political Economy* (February): 191–206.

Fisher, Irving, 1933. "The debt-deflation theory of Great Depressions," *Econometrica* (October): 337–357.

Flood, Robert and Peter M. Garber, 1983. "A model of stochastic process switching," *Econometrica* (May): 537–551.

1984. "Collapsing exchange rate regimes: some linear examples," *Journal of International Economics* (August): 1–13.

Ford, Worthington C., 1895. "Foreign exchanges and gold movement in 1894 and 1895," *Sound Currency* (October): 421–436.

Friedman, Milton, 1968. "The role of monetary policy," *American Economic Review* (March): 1–17.

Friedman, Milton and Anna J. Schwartz, 1963. *A Monetary History of the United States, 1867–1960*, Princeton: Princeton University Press.

1982. *Monetary Trends in the United States and the United Kingdom*, Chicago: University of Chicago Press for the NBER.

Gallman, Robert E., 1966. "Gross National Product in the United States, 1834–1909," in Robert E. Gallman (ed.), *Output, Employment, and Productivity in the United States after 1800*, New York: Columbia University Press.

Garber, Peter M., 1986. "Nominal contracts in a bimetallic standard," *American Economic Review* (December): 1012–1030.

Garber, Peter M. and Vittorio Grilli, 1986. "The Belmont–Morgan syndicate as an optimal investment banking contract," *European Economic Review* (June): 649–677.

Gordon, Robert J., 1980. "A consistent characterization of a near-century of price behavior," *American Economic Review Papers and Proceedings* (May): 243–249.

1982. "Price inertia and policy ineffectiveness in the United States, 1890–1980," *Journal of Political Economy* (December): 1087–1117.

1990. "What is new-Keynesian economics?," *Journal of Economic Literature* (September): 1115–1171.

Greef, Albert O., 1938. *The Commercial Paper House in the United States*, Cambridge, MA: Harvard University Press.

Grilli, Vittorio U., 1986. "Buying and selling attacks on fixed rate systems," *Journal of International Economics* (February): 143–456.

1990. "Managing exchange rate crises: evidence from the 1890s," *Journal of International Money and Finance*, June, 258–275.

Hammond, Bray, 1970. *Sovereignty and an Empty Purse: Banks and Politics in the Civil War*, Princeton: Princeton University Press.

Hetherington, Bruce W., 1990. "Bank entry and the low issue of national bank notes: a re-examination," *Journal of Economic History* (September): 669–676.

Jacklin, Charles J. and Sudipto Bhattacharya, 1988. "Distinguishing panics and information-based bank runs: welfare and policy implications," *Journal of Political Economy* (June): 568–592.

James, John A., 1976. "The conundrum of the low issue of national bank notes," *Journal of Political Economy* (April): 359–367.

1985. "Shifts in the nineteenth-century Phillips Curve relationship," National Bureau of Economic Research Working Paper, no. 1587.

Klein, Benjamin, 1975. "Our new monetary standard: the measurement and effects of price uncertainty," *Economic Inquiry*, December: 461–483.

Krugman, Paul, 1979. "A model of balance of payment crises," *Journal of Money, Credit and Banking* (August): 311–325.

Laughlin, J. Laurence, 1886. *The History of Bimetallism in the United States*, New York: Appleton.

Lester, Richard A., 1939. "Retention of the gold standard in California and Oregon during the greenback inflation," chapter 7, in Richard A. Lester (ed.) *Monetary Experiments: Early American and Recent Scandinavian*, Princeton: Princeton University Press: 161–174.

Lucas, Robert E., 1972. "Expectations and the neutrality of money," *Journal of Economic Theory* (April): 103–124.

1973. "Some international evidence on the output–inflation tradeoff," *American Economic Review* (June): 326–334.

1976. "Econometric policy evaluation: a critique," in K. Brunner and A. Meltzer (eds.), *The Phillips Curve and Labor Markets*, Carnegie-Rochester Series on Public Policy: 19–46.

1990. "The effect of monetary shocks when price is set in advance" (mimeo).

Mitchell, Wesley Clair, 1903. *A History of the Greenbacks*, Chicago: University of Chicago Press.

  1908. *Gold, Prices and Wages Under the Greenback Standard*, Berkeley: University of California.

Muth, John F., 1961. "Rational expectations and the theory of price movements," *Econometrica* (July): 315–335.

National Monetary Commission, 1910. *Statistics for the United States, 1867–1909*, Washington, DC: Government Printing Office.

Obstfeld, Maurice, 1986. "Rational and self-fulfilling balance of payments crises," *American Economic Review* (March): 72–81.

Obstfeld, Maurice and Kenneth Rogoff, 1983. "Speculative hyperinflations in maximizing models: can we rule them out?," *Journal of Political Economy* (August): 675–689.

Phelps, Edmund S., 1968. "Money wage dynamics and labor market equilibrium," *Journal of Political Economy* (August): 678–711.

Phelps, Edmund S. *et al.*, 1970. *The New Microeconomics in Employment and Inflation Theory*, New York: Norton.

Rockoff, Hugh, 1984. "Some evidence on the real price of gold, its cost of production and commodity prices," in Michael D. Bordo and Anna Schwartz (eds.), *A Retrospective on the Classical Gold Standard, 1821–1931*, Chicago: University of Chicago Press: 613–650.

Roll, Richard, 1972. "Interest rates and price expectations during the Civil War," *Journal of Economic History* (June): 476–498.

Romer, Christina D., 1989. "The prewar business cycle reconsidered: new estimates of Gross National Product, 1869–1908," *Journal of Political Economy* (February): 1–37.

Russell, H.B., 1898. *International Monetary Conferences: Their Purposes, Character, and Results*, New York: Harper & Brothers.

Sargent, Thomas J., 1973. "Rational expectations, the real rate of interest, and the natural rate of unemployment," *Brookings Papers on Economic Activity*, 2: 429–480.

Sargent, Thomas J. and Neil Wallace, 1981. "Some unpleasant monetarist arithmetic," *Quarterly Review*, Federal Reserve Bank of Minneapolis (Fall): 1–17.

Shiller, Robert and Jeremy J. Siegel, 1976. "The Gibson paradox and historical movements in real interest rates," *Journal of Political Economy* (August): 891–907.

Stock, James H. 1984. "Real estate mortgages, foreclosures, and Midwestern agrarian unrest, 1865–1920," *Journal of Economic History* (March): 89–106.

Taylor, John, 1980. "Aggregate dynamics and staggered contracts," *Journal of Political Economy* (February): 1–24.

Unger, Irwin, 1964. *The Greenback Era: A Social and Political History of American Finance, 1865–1879*, Princeton: Princeton University Press.

Warner, John D., 1895. "The currency famine of 1893," *Sound Currency* (February): 337–345.

Wilkins, Mira, 1989. *The History of Foreign Investment in the United States to 1914*, Cambridge, MA: Harvard University Press.

Part II

Successful and unsuccessful adherence to the gold standard

5 Spain during the classical gold standard years, 1880–1914

PABLO MARTÍN-ACEÑA

Introduction

The last quarter of the nineteenth century saw the spread of an international monetary system based on gold, linking the economy of the major countries of the world with fixed exchange rates for their domestic currencies. The gold standard offered a common solution to the monetary problems of the period and provided a relatively stable financial framework for economic growth. As Eichengreen (1985) put it, the appeal of the system can be traced to the belief that it provided price, income and exchange stability and an automatic mechanism to correct balance of payments disequilibria. The gold standard would reduce the risks associated with international trade and investment and would promote domestic specialization and long-term planning, thus contributing to the attainment of higher growth rates. The adherence of almost all countries of the international economy could be taken as the most apparent proof that the system had some considerable virtues. To remain outside the gold standard was at least unwise, unless major forces had proved that its adoption would have been catastrophic for the development of the national economy, or that policy makers had tried to avoid the presumed burden of the system and decided to manage an independent monetary policy in order to promote economic growth. To be off the gold standard meant implicitly to opt for a certain isolation and a loose intergration with the international economy.[1]

The Spanish case appears in striking contrast with the international experience. Spain never adopted the gold standard. Convertibility of paper money into gold and/or silver was maintained until 1883, when eventually it was suspended. Resumption never took place, neither before 1914 nor after. Contrary to most European currencies, the peseta thus remained inconvertible and its exchange rate fluctuated in terms of gold throughout.[2] In this chapter we offer a brief historical account of the Spanish monetary experience between 1880 and 1914. In the first section we look at the situation before 1883 and describe the events that led to the suspension of convertibility; next we examine closely the behavior of the exchange rate and try to explain its fluctuations both in the short and in the long run. We then study how monetary policy was actually conducted between 1880 and 1914: we look to the money-supply process and also to both the gold reserve and the discount rate policies. The two concluding sections discuss why Spain did not adhere to the gold standard and what consequences this had for the economy as a whole. We argue that to remain formally out of the gold standard regime, although not exceedingly damaging, was certainly inconvenient. Spain could, and should, have joined the international monetary system. Spain did not fully exploit either the advantages of international specialization or the facilities of the integrated European capital markets. Inconvertibility and exchange rate variability introduced a higher risk in Spain's international transactions, both on trade and on capital accounts, and the country faced greater difficulties in balance of payments adjustment. By being off the gold standard, the Spanish monetary regime was partly detached from the international system and the Spanish economy remained to a large extent isolated from the world economy.[3]

From bimetallism to inconvertibility, 1868–1883

In 1868 the Spanish authorities approved a currency reform introducing a bimetallic standard and establishing the peseta as the monetary unit.[4] The official rate of exchange between gold and silver was set at the ratio of 1:15.5, similar to that adopted by the countries which in 1865 formed the Latin Monetary Union.[5] In 1874 the Bank of Spain was granted the monopoly of issue in the entire country, although the government retained the power to establish a limit on the quantity of bank notes in circulation and the rules regulating the relationship between the note issue and reserve requirements. At the official ratio, notes were freely convertible into both gold and silver.[6]

After 1873 the price of silver in international markets began to fall, and by 1876 the market exchange ratio of silver for gold had risen to 18:1. To cope with the *de facto* undervaluation of gold, two options were open to the authorities: to defend bimetallism with successive and continuous devaluations of the official silver price, trying to adjust it to its market value; or to demonetize silver, suspend the minting of new silver coins and adopt the gold standard. The latter was the course followed by the majority of the European countries, including the signatories of the Union, which in 1878 suspended the free coinage of silver and eventually deserted the bimetallic standard.[7]

In Spain there was an attempt to follow the example of the Union; in 1876 the government discontinued the free coinage of silver on private account and gold coinage was resumed after having been suspended in 1873. Furthermore, the Junta Consultiva de la Moneda (the Committee on Currency Reform) recommended the interruption of the minting of silver and the adoption of the gold standard.[8] The government, however, ignored the recommendations of the Junta. But as the market price of silver fell, the unaltered official ratio undervalued gold relative to the market and, as predicted by Gresham's Law, silver eventually drove gold out of circulation and the gold reserves of the Bank of Spain dwindled (table 5.1). Convertibility of notes into gold was maintained until the middle of 1883 thanks to successive trade surpluses and a constant stream of capital imports.[9] The suspension took place in the summer of 1883 and the decision came, in Sardá's opinion, after a contraction in foreign investment associated with the Paris stock market crash of January 1882.[10] The measure was taken, so the argument goes, to defend the metallic reserves of the Bank of Spain and to check the disappearance of gold from circulation and the export of gold.[11] However, the suspension did not bring the desired effects and gold coins in fact went out of circulation.

At this point it is convenient to follow the events that led to the suspension of convertibility and to examine the subsequent developments in order to understand the decision and to appreciate the alternatives open to the authorities.[12] Presumably the winds of the international economic crisis had already been felt in Spain by the middle of 1882.[13] The trade surplus of 1881 had been reduced by half by the end of 1882 and the deficit in the current account must have been fairly large; given the prevailing climate in the international capital market, it is also reasonable to assume that the inflow of capital imports was severely curtailed. The impact of the external disequilibrium was felt in official gold holdings, which dropped dramatically to reach their lowest level since 1874. Hence, with a reduction of gold reserves of 75.3 million pesetas (60 percent of total gold holdings in 1881), lack of confidence in the ability of the Bank to preserve convertibility must have been widespread. The crisis also coincided with an operation undertaken by the Treasury to reduce the outstanding debt and to alter its maturity. The conversion had been initiated in December 1881 and was therefore in full swing by the end of 1882. Since the conversion implied a partial default on the foreign debt, the conditions of international markets for Spanish borrowing sharply deteriorated. The operation itself probably provoked a prompt outflow of capital to buy external bonds held by non-residents who refused to accept the conversion of the old bonds; since both the interest and principal of the external debt were paid in gold, Spanish investors were willing to hold the new government debt rather than to hold

Table 5.1 *The Spanish stock of gold, in million pesetas*

Year	Gold in circulation	Gold in the Bank of Spain
1874	1,131	18
1875	1,057	36
1876	1,002	46
1877	966	45
1878	915	53
1879	793	101
1880	753	105
1881	685	125
1882	774	50
1883	736	51
1884	670	70
1885	619	80
1886	541	110
1887	534	91
1888	480	105
1889	384	153
1890	333	168
1891	263	201
1892	186	243
1893	151	250
1894	117	257
1895	106	241
1896	67	241
1897	—	274
1898	—	342
1899	—	406
1900	—	395
1901	—	370
1902	—	395
1903	—	410
1904	—	419
1905	—	453
1906	—	471
1907	—	453
1908	—	472
1909	—	535
1910	—	554
1911	—	561
1912	—	641
1913	—	674
1914	—	720

Note:
— not available.
Sources: Tortella (1974b, Tables Doc. IV-4–Doc. IV-9).

pesetas or assets denominated in pesetas, given the uncertainty of preserving convertibility.[14]

Confronted with the fall in the volume of official foreign assets, the Bank rate was raised one percentage point in an attempt to close the gap between the desired and the actual stock of gold and, simultaneously, the Bank also engaged in foreign exchange purchases to defend its position.[15] Nevertheless, a discount rate of 5 percent was insufficient to attract capital since the official rate had been increased simultaneously in the main foreign financial centers that were also trying to weather the crisis. In addition to raising the discount rate, the authorities tightened monetary conditions. High-powered money hardly varied and the budget period which ended in June 1882 closed with an unprecedented surplus after large deficits in previous fiscal years.

Despite these measures, the situation did not improve. The external disequilibrium deteriorated in 1883; the trade balance registered the worst results of the decade and the outflow of gold continued.[16] This was sufficient to undermine the resistance of the authorities who, probably by the middle of 1883, began to see the official gold reserves falling even more. The government finally suspended convertibility of notes into gold and the exchange rate was left free to move out of its gold points. The immediate result of the decision was to check the loss of Bank reserves, which by the end of the year showed signs of having been replenished.

The suspension of 1883 has been considered "inevitable" and "indispensable," if a heavy contraction in economic activity was to be avoided. The burden of adjustment to the external shock was left to the exchange rate. And yet, the decision to suspend the conversion of bank notes into gold was not the only alternative available. The authorities could have raised the official price of gold to the market price and demonetized the stock of silver, as the Junta had recommended. Furthermore, adjustment could have proceeded by allowing the stock of money to contract as reserves were dwindling and by imposing higher interest rates than those enforced. Fiscal restraint would also have been needed. Short-term capital imports might not have been attracted but outflows would have been checked. Full adjustment would have doubtless required a decline in internal prices and nominal income; neither employment nor real output should have been affected provided money wages and prices adapted frictionlessly. But even if we assume some degree of inflexibility, the resulting unemployment might not have been entirely undesirable. Perhaps it would have proved to be efficient enough to bring domestic costs to international levels and thereby increase the competitive position of the Spanish economy. Marginal business would have been eliminated and allocation of resources brought on to more competitive lines. Certainly, inconvertibility avoided deflation but disengaged the Spanish economy from the international financial system.

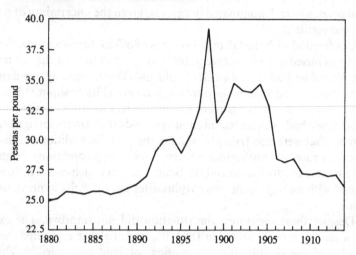

5.1   Peseta–pound sterling nominal exchange rate, 1880–1914

The evolution of the peseta exchange rate, 1883–1914

After the suspension of convertibility, the authorities allowed the Spanish currency to float freely on the exchange market but, contrary to what one would have expected, there was no immediate decline in its international value. The price of the peseta in terms of pounds hardly varied and for a few years remained at the rate that it had reached at the beginning of the decade (figure 5.1). Various factors could explain this stability. First, a positive balance of trade might have eased pressure on the market. Secondly, the public deficit remained within reasonable limits (at an average of about 43 million pesetas, a mere 0.7 percent of national income) and the capital market did not receive new issues of short-term Treasury bills.[17] Between 1883 and 1887 the monetary base hardly increased, and neither did the money supply, since the deposit–currency ratio was reduced, reflecting the general lack of confidence that prevailed at the beginning of the decade. In addition, as shown in figure 5.4, Spanish interest rates were consistently higher than international interest rates. Finally, it can be argued that speculators, who had witnessed the quick recovery of Bank of Spain reserves, expected a swift resumption of specie payments at par. Accordingly, they sold gold against pesetas hoping to make profits once the exchange rate appreciated.

At the end of the decade, especially after 1890, the situation changed. The value of the peseta fell mildly but continuously between 1890 and 1896. The decline started in 1888. At first it was slow and then it accelerated, with the

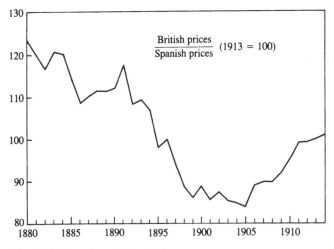

5.2   Relative prices, 1880–1914

result that between 1888 and 1895 there was a depreciation of the exchange rate from 25.6 to 28.9 pesetas to the pound. After 1895 the exchange rate rose sharply till it attained a maximum in 1898, when the pound was valued at almost 40 pesetas, which represented a 50 percent depreciation relative to parity. There can be no doubt that the non-adoption of the gold standard caused speculators to change their expectations and begin to lose faith in the Spanish currency, reselling their stocks of pesetas. Furthermore, apart from 1894 and 1895, years of surplus, the public budget deficit persisted, and the fact that Spanish prices and international prices evolved differently (figure 5.2) also contributed to the rise in foreign rates.[18] The slight negative growth in the money supply in this same period probably prevented a more pronounced depreciation of the peseta. But after 1896, public spending increased rapidly and the budget deficit widened, especially in 1898 and 1899, when large extraordinary expenditures were approved to finance the war in Cuba. To cover the deficit the Treasury was forced to borrow heavily from the public and the Bank. Almost 2,000 million pesetas of short-term bills were floated; part of this amount was taken by the private non-banking sector, part by the financial system which increased its liquidity considerably, and part was placed in the portfolio of the central bank; furthermore, the Treasury also asked for advances from the Bank of Spain.[19] The result was a substantial increase in the money supply which experienced an unprecedented rate of growth of almost 7.9 percent. The Treasury also secured a significant reduction in the Bank of Spain's discount rate, from 5 to 3.5 percent, a measure which was aimed at reducing the cost of the debt.

Domestic prices increased quickly and sharply, widening the gap relative to foreign prices. Simultaneously interest rates fell and the peseta depreciated rapidly in relation to the pound, to such an extent that at the turn of the century the Spanish currency had lost about 30 percent of its 1880 value.

The end of the Spanish American War, in which Spain lost its last overseas colonies, permitted the return to financial orthodoxy and monetary stability and signaled a marked downward tendency in the exchange rate. At first there was a quick fall, followed by a temporary rise and eventually, between 1900 and 1914, a constant appreciation. In these 14 years the peseta managed to recover almost all of its previous value, by 1914 reaching a rate of 26.1 pesetas to the pound, a mere 4.6 percent below its 1880 value.

After 1900 the authorities introduced a deflationary policy aimed at stabilizing the exchange rate.[20] During the following five years and until 1905, the stock of money contracted and 275 million pesetas were withdrawn from circulation, while the Ministry of Finance carried out a massive policy of conversion of 1,900 million pesetas of Treasury bonds outstanding. Besides, a fiscal reform approved in 1900 provided for successive budget surpluses until 1909.[21] Prices were stabilized and within a few years there was a process of conversion towards international levels; thereby the difference between Spanish domestic prices and international prices narrowed quite appreciably (figure 5.2).

At the same time the end of the war and the consequent independence of the colonies brought about a substantial repatriation of capital, which reached its maximum level in the first years of the new century. The Bank of Spain also bought up important quantities of gold in order to strengthen foreign reserves. Parallel to this, imports of foreign capital resumed after 1906. Presumably after this year foreign investors looked at the Spanish currency with more confidence, and they might again have anticipated a speedy re-establishment of the convertibility of the peseta. They therefore reconsidered their investment plans in Spanish assets and, after two decades of retreat channelled resources to newly-developed sectors such as the chemical and the electrical industries as well as to public utilities. The exchange rate immediately mirrored the impact of the re-establishment of the old pattern of the balance of payments equilibrium: its appreciation was as quick and as spectacular as its previous decline had been. The revaluation and subsequent stabilization of the exchange rate (and prices) brought about a fall in interest rates, pushing them closer to European levels. All these developments led the authorities to reconsider the adoption of the gold standard, although no definite decision was taken.

In the long run, it could be expected that, according to the theory of purchasing power parity (PPP), the nominal exchange rate should reflect

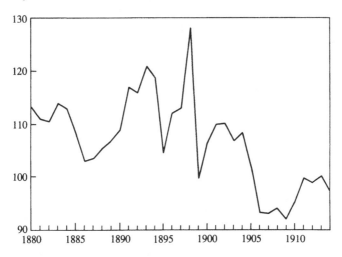

5.3   Peseta–pound sterling real exchange rate (1913 = 100)

the differences between the level of domestic and foreign prices. Figure 5.3, which shows the course followed by the real exchange rate, suggests, however, that there were important deviations with respect to the parity line.[22] We see that on the whole, for most of the period, the peseta was undervalued with respect to PPP. On the other hand, after 1904 the opposite is the case, since the peseta is overvalued with respect to PPP. Finally, between 1910 and 1914 it approached the level of its theoretical parity.[23] Table 5.2 shows the result of regressing the variations of the logarithm of the exchange rate on the variations of the logarithm of prices. The value of the correlation coefficient (R^2), as well as the value of the estimated parameters show that PPP does not adequately explain the fluctuations in the exchange rate.

Fratianni and Spinelli arrived at a similar conclusion when they tried to explain the divergence of the lira with respect to its line of parity over a period similar to the one we are looking at here. In their opinion, the factor which explains such divergences in the real exchange rate with respect to its theoretical parity is what they called "country risk." That is to say:

whenever financial markets perceived that the Italian government was not following prudent fiscal and monetary policies, the markets rated Italian debt instruments as less than risk-free assets. Potential owners of Italian debt instruments demanded a premium for the nonzero probability of a complete or partial default.

Hence, the authors found that "large and persistent deviations from PPP were associated with Italian financial assets carrying a higher yield, inclusive of exchange-rate appreciation, than French financial assets."[24]

Table 5.2 *The peseta–pound sterling exchange rate: a test of the PPP hypothesis*

Sample period	Constant	Domestic prices	Foreign prices
1880–1914	−0.002	0.635	−0.340
	(−0.141)	(1.893)	(−0.989)
$R^2 = 0.10$			
DW = 2.47			
SER = 0.06			

Notes:
t-statistics in parentheses.
Sources: Peseta–pound exchange rate: Appendix 2, p. 162; Spanish prices: Appendix 2, p. 162; British prices: Mitchell and Deane (1962).

This kind of argument can also be applied in our case. As can be seen in figure 5.4, the returns of Spanish financial assets were consistently maintained above British, French, and even Italian yields. The evolution of the Spanish yields also exhibits certain parallels with the trend of the exchange rate and with the behavior of financial policy. In the 1890s, the persistent budget deficit and the subsequent monetary expansion until 1900, plus the memory of the unfavorable conversion of the public debt of 1882–83, was perceived and interpreted by investors as an increase in the level of "country risk," which in turn reflected an increase in the returns from bonds. On the contrary, after 1900 the adoption of a more prudent fiscal and monetary policy justified a reassessment of previous expectations, thereby reducing the probability of default, which was then translated into an appreciation in Spanish debt titles, which in turn resulted in a reduction in interest rates, bringing them closer to European level.

The non-adoption of the gold standard was then associated with the existence of a marked instability in the value of the peseta. The Spanish currency, like the ruble, the Austrian crown, and the lira during the period of inconvertibility, was subject to many strong fluctuations;[25] its price in terms of pounds oscillated between 25.6 pesetas in 1883 and 39.2 pesetas in 1898, and then back to the exchange rate established in 1865. During the periods in which the monetary authorities followed a somewhat unorthodox financial policy, the exchange rate experienced a strong depreciation. When, on the other hand, the authorities opted for fiscal and monetary discipline, as if they had adhered to gold, the exchange rate tended to appreciate and to follow a path of greater stability. Interest rates were consistently higher in Spain than in those countries which adhered to gold,

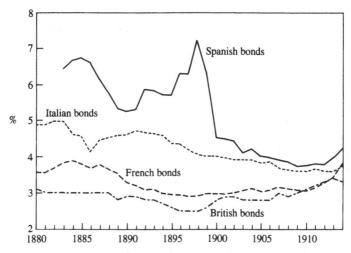

5.4   Yields on long-term government bonds

and even higher than in those countries which, although not formally on gold, adopted an orthodox financial policy and pegged their currencies to gold. Only when the Spanish authorities imposed fiscal and monetary discipline did the exchange rate improve and interest rates tend to move towards European levels. Finally, the nominal depreciation of the exchange rate was greater than the deterioration in relative prices; the real depreciation of the peseta that ensued therefore allowed the balance of trade to close with positive and increasing surpluses between 1883 and 1900. However, the rate of growth of exports, in real terms, was much lower between 1883 and 1900 and between 1900 and 1914 than previously, and the share of the foreign sector in national income diminished.[26]

Monetary policy and the stock of money

The Spanish financial system in the period 1874–1914 was composed basically of three groups of institutions: the Bank of Spain, which received the monopoly of issue in 1874, the private commercial banks, and the savings companies.[27] Together they supplied the total amount of bank notes and bank money outstanding. On the other hand, the Treasury furnished the metallic (gold and silver coins) in circulation. Table 5.3 shows the composition of the stock of money for selected years; the main component was currency in the hands of the public (bank notes and gold and silver coins), which in 1874 represented 91 percent of the total money supply; furthermore, specie dominated over bank notes. After this year the share of

Table 5.3 *The quantity of money and its components, in million pesetas*

Year	Currency held by the public (1)	Demand deposits (2)	Time deposits (3)	Money supply (4)
1874	1,605	133	31	1,769
1880	1,513	367	97	1,977
1890	1,769	518	175	2.462
1900	2,204	908	259	3,371
1914	2,344	928	624	3,896

Source: Martín-Aceña (1990, Appendix, tables 1–4).

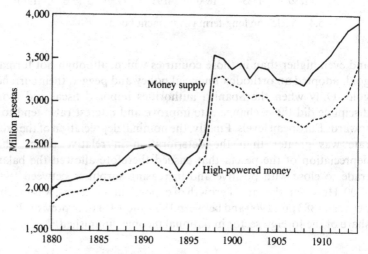

5.5   Money supply and high-powered money, 1880–1914

both bank notes and bank deposits increased; and by 1913 commercial bank deposits represented nearly 40 percent of the stock of money.

In figure 5.5 we can follow the evolution of both the money supply and high-powered money for the entire period.[28] The money stock increased secularly, although it exhibited substantial cyclical fluctuations. Between 1874 and 1914 the money supply multiplied by 2.2, which means that it grew at an annual rate of 2.0 percent. During the years when bimetallism was enforced (from 1874–82), the growth rate was nearly 2.0 percent; this same rate was recorded between 1883 and 1890. Afterwards the money supply

Table 5.4 *The money supply process, 1874–1914*

	Absolute rate of growth (%)			Relative contribution (%)		
Period	M	MB	m	M	MB	m
1874–1914	2.0	1.7	0.3	—	85.0	15.0
1874–1882	2.0	1.4	0.6	—	70.0	30.0
1883–1900	2.8	2.8	0.0	—	100.0	0.0
1900–1914	1.0	0.4	0.6	—	40.0	60.0

Notes:
 M = money supply
MB = monetary base
 m = money multiplier
Source: Appendix 1.

followed two opposite cycles: from 1890–94 it hardly increased, but later from 1895–1900 its growth accelerated notably. Finally two other cycles can be distinguished between 1900 and 1914: from 1901–09 the quantity of money declined at a average rate of -0.4 percent, while in the second cycle, from 1909–14, it increased at a rate of nearly 2.7 percent.

The contributions of the three proximate determinants to the secular growth rate of the Spanish money stock for the whole period and two subperiods are shown in table 5.4. We confirm the large contribution of the monetary base, which in absolute terms contributed 1.7 percent to the growth of the money stock, while the deposit–currency and the deposit–reserve ratios combined contributed 0.3 percent. The relative share of the monetary base was thus 85 percent, while the base money multiplier accounted for the remaining 15 percent. Basically, it was the secular rise in the deposit–currency ratio that produced the positive contribution of the asset ratio (see Appendix 1, p. 161). Thus, while the deposit–currency ratio increased from 0.31 in 1880 to 0.66 in 1914, the corresponding figures for the deposit–reserve ratio were 1.57 and 1.50, respectively

As we have seen, the monetary base accounted for the major share of the secular expansion of the Spanish money stock. We may now ask what factors determined its evolution. We may first inquire whether the Spanish authorities ran their monetary system as if they were on the gold standard. Nurkse (1944) and Bloomfield (1959) investigated central bank practices following the rules of the gold standard game. They argued that if a country is managing its monetary system in accordance with the gold standard rules, it is likely to increase the money supply when gold flows in and decrease it when gold flows out. As Nurkse put it:

Whenever gold flowed in, the central bank was expected to increase the national currency supply not only through the purchase of that gold but also through the acquisition of additional domestic assets; and, similarly, when gold flowed out, the central bank was supposed to contract its domestic assets also.

To test if they followed this rule, we have reproduced Nurkse's and Bloomfield's exercise by examining year-to-year changes in the Bank of Spain's domestic income-earning assets and its international reserves. The results for Spain (table 5.5) are somewhat unclear but not different from those obtained for other countries by Bloomfield and others.[29] In 20 out of 34 instances we find changes in the same direction in the international and domestic assets of the Bank of Spain; by contrast, there are 14 instances in which they move in opposite directions. This evidence would indicate, according to Nurkse and Bloomfield, that the Bank of issue did not systematically follow the rules of the game.

We cannot therefore explain the movements of the Spanish money supply by consulting only the rules of the gold standard game. In fact since Spain had not adhered to the system, these results are not unexpected. Like many other national monetary authorities of the period, the Spanish authorities followed their own rules, if any, and they ran the system in accordance with them. But they may have not followed any rule whatsoever, and money supply may have not been the result of policy, but endogenously determined.[30] In fact, table 5.6 seems to suggest that there were no rules. The most that can be said is that changes in base money reflected changes in total credit to the Treasury, since the variations in both series exhibit the same sign in seven periods. The monetary base expanded and contracted according to the position of the Treasury in the Bank, which in turn depended on the size of the budget deficit. The combined change in international reserves and in credit to the private sector simply reinforced the effects of government financing through the central bank. The volume of Bank of Spain credit was thus essentially determined by Treasury needs and by the demand for bank accommodation at whatever interest rates happened to exist.

We might also expect the central bank of a gold standard country to raise its discount rate when it lost gold, and to lower this rate when it gained gold. Despite being off the gold standard, the Spanish authorities might have taken the movements in the level of international reserves as a guide for action to manage the official discount rate. Hence, the Bank of Spain would raise its rediscount rate when it lost gold and lower it when it gained gold. To test this hypothesis, we have also performed Bloomfield's exercise, plotting the Bank's rate of discount against the reserve ratio. As can be observed in figure 5.6 no clear inverse correlation is found between the movements of the international reserves, mainly gold, and the rediscount

Table 5.5 *Annual changes in Bank of Spain net foreign reserves and net domestic assets, 1880–1914, million pesetas*

Year	Change in domestic assets (1)	Change in foreign reserves (2)	Sign of correlation (3)
1880	84	40	+
1881	134	20	+
1882	52	− 75	−
1883	55	1	+
1884	48	19	+
1885	131	10	+
1886	28	30	+
1887	44	− 19	−
1888	109	14	+
1889	129	48	+
1890	35	15	+
1891	1	33	+
1892	− 36	42	−
1893	− 29	7	−
1894	− 179	7	−
1895	166	− 16	−
1896	105	—	0
1897	206	33	+
1898	608	68	+
1899	− 205	64	−
1900	− 15	− 11	+
1901	22	− 25	−
1902	− 204	25	−
1903	35	15	+
1904	− 119	9	−
1905	− 129	34	−
1906	− 86	18	−
1907	− 13	− 18	+
1908	− 135	19	−
1909	62	63	+
1910	− 3	19	−
1911	36	7	+
1912	54	80	+
1913	61	33	+
1914	119	46	+

Source: Anes (1974b); Tortella (1974b).

Table 5.6 *Changes in money supply, high-powered money, and its major factors*

Period	M	HPM	IR	T	PS
1880–85	△	△	–	+	+
1885–90	△	△	+	+	+
1890–95	▽	△	+	+	–
1895–1900	△	△	+	+	+
1900–05	∨	▽	+	–	+
1905–10	△	▽	+	–	+
1910–15	△	△	+	+	+

Notes:
M Money supply;   HPM High-powered money;   IR International reverses;   T Treasury;   PS Private sector.
△ (increase);   ▽ (decrease);   + (increase;   – (decrease).
Sources: Anes (1974b, 1974c); Tortella (1974a); Martín-Aceña (1985).

rate, except for the early 1880s and late 1890s. From 1900–10, when the reserve ratio was increasing, the rate failed to decline. Again, the empirical evidence for Spain tends to confirm Bloomfield's results for other European central banks. The Bank of Spain discount rate moved relatively infrequently, and when reserves accumulated the rate was, more often than not, kept unaltered.

Now we may also like to know by what criteria, if any, the bank manipulated its discount rate. Consider first the possibility that the authorities, keeping an eye on the conditions of major financial centers, moved its rate accordingly, but fixed it at a higher level, either to attract capital or to prevent undesirable outflows. This argument, however, faces some difficulties. We find cases where rates are falling in London, Paris, and Berlin, while they are rising in Madrid: quite clearly this seems to have been the case in 1881. On the contrary, by the end of the decade, European central banks were pushing rates upward, while the Spanish central bank approved substantial reductions between 1898 and 1900. After 1900 the criterion may have some explanation; if Spain's central bank guide was the Bank of France, movements in the former's rate are a mirror of what happened to the latter's discount rate. In France the rate was not altered during the first decade of the present century and then it was increased in 1910; our evidence for Spain shows a similar policy.

But we may also argue that the Bank of Spain had no particular criteria, or that the discount rate policy was at the Treasury's service; that is to say, it

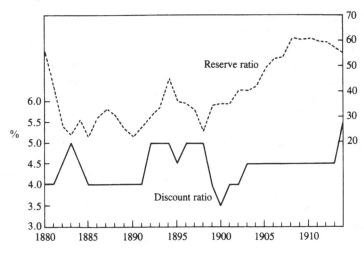

5.6   The reserve ratio and the discount ratio

was used to secure the success of public debt issues. This argument does not lack support. The increases adopted at the beginning of the 1880s were made, undoubtedly, to persuade holders of government paper to accept the 1882–83 consolidation of the short-term bonds outstanding into long-term debt. At the close of the century, the new wave of Treasury bills that appeared in the market as a consequence of war financing were accompanied by convenient reductions in an attempt to keep debt interest charges as low as possible.

In short, the evidence suggests that there was not one single criterion guiding the Bank's discount rate policy. Treasury needs, movements in gold reserves, and conditions in foreign markets, all combined to dictate the rather infrequent changes in the rediscount rate. What we find is an ad hoc policy rather than a management consciously oriented to regulating the economic business cycle and the volume of credit.[31] Furthermore, the relative rigidity and high level of the Bank of Spain discount rate also implies the maintenance of relatively large excess reserves of gold and foreign exchange, which at no time constrained the note issue. To protect these excess reserves, it was helpful to hold Spanish interest rates above Western European rates.[32]

But the non-commitment to the gold standard and the introduction of a floating exchange rate removed any requirement to hold reserves for international payments. The suspension of convertibility made it theoretically unnecessary to hold reserves to back up the note circulation; however, the Bank of Spain retained a large volume of gold reserves and, in fact, the metallic guarantee was reinforced several times.[33] In part, this can be explained by the conservative reserve policy of the authorities as far as legal requirements were concerned, and it reiterated the power of the gold standard rule. When in 1883 convertibility into gold was suspended the legal requirement to maintain gold reserves against the note issue was not removed. On the contrary, the authorities kept a 25 percent metallic guarantee (gold and silver) as the legal minimum of the total paper in circulation. As indicated in table 5.7, this forced the Bank of Spain to hold a yearly average of 141.7 million pesetas in reserves between 1883 and 1890. In addition, the Bank held excess gold reserves on average of 96.9 million pesetas during the same period. Legal requirements were increased in 1891. The Bank had to keep 16.5 percent of the total notes in circulation in gold and the same percentage in silver. This represented yearly average holdings of gold of 159.5 million pesetas between 1891 and 1898. The Bank also maintained excess reserves over and above that percentage that amounted on average to 85 million pesetas. In 1898, and again in 1902, gold reserve requirements were increased. This forced the Bank to hold on average 272 million pesetas between 1898 and 1901, and on average 403.4 million pesetas until 1913. Excess reserves were also increased: 117.3 million pesetas for the first period and 99.7 million pesetas for the second. For the entire period, 1891–1913, the Bank held yearly average excess reserves in gold of 100 million pesetas and an average of 278 million pesetas as legal requirements (4 percent of national income in 1901). Being off the gold standard, this represented a severe and unnecessary burden on the Bank and on the economy as a whole. The reserves undoubtedly represented a net loss in terms of goods and services foregone. To maintain reserves could have been justified only if the authorities were always contemplating, as was the case, the possibility of reintroducing the gold standard and the convertibility of paper money.[34]

The gold standard and the Spanish balance of payments

Modern literature has seen in Spain's balance of payments problems the key reason that explains both the suspension and the country's subsequent isolation from the international monetary system. It was above all the country's inability to earn the required foreign exchange, or gold, to preserve convertibility that led to suspension.[35] It is argued that to have remained in the system after 1883 would have implied a tremendous contraction in the domestic economy in order to protect reserves and demonetize the silver stock. It is also argued that the gold standard was not suitable for "poor and uncompetitive" countries like Spain. Furthermore,

Table 5.7 *Metallic reserves requirements, million pesetas*

Year	Bank note	Guarantee		Excess reserves
		Legal	Actual	
1880	243.1	61	236.0	175.0
1881	346.2	87	252.2	165.9
1882	333.6	83	124.7	41.7
1883	350.9	88	111.0	23.0
1884	383.3	96	167.9	71.9
1885	409.0	117	152.0	35.0
1886	526.6	132	238.2	106.2
1887	612.1	153	309.9	156.2
1888	719.7	180	324.1	144.1
1889	735.5	184	275.1	91.1
1890	734.1	184	247.5	63.5
1891[a]	811.7	133.9	201.1	67.2
1892	884.1	145.9	243.3	97.4
1893	927.7	153.1	249.8	96.7
1894	909.7	150.1	256.7	106.6
1895	994.4	164.1	240.5	76.4
1896	1,031.4	170.2	240.8	70.6
1897	1,206.3	199.0	278.9	79.9
1898	1,444.0	238.3	341.6	103.3
1899	1,517.9	252.0	405.7	153.7
1900	1,591.6	270.4	395.0	124.6
1901	1,638.3	282.2	369.7	87.5
1902	1,623.3	379.6	394.6	15.0
1903	1,608.7	372.4	409.8	37.4
1904	1,599.4	367.5	419.1	51.6
1905	1,550.1	343.1	453.0	109.9
1906	1,524.8	330.4	471.0	140.6
1907	1,557.1	346.6	453.4	106.8
1908	1,642.8	309.4	472.3	82.9
1909	1,671.0	403.5	534.8	131.3
1910	1,715.2	425.6	553.5	127.9
1911	1,762.8	449.9	560.7	111.3
1912	1,862.8	499.9	640.9	141.5
1913	1,931.3	533.7	674.1	140.4

Note:
[a] Since 1891 only gold.
Sources: Anes (1974a); Tortella (1974a).

the country, within the gold standard, would have been subject to an intolerable and unnecessary discipline given the problems of the balance of payments. Hence, the best policy was to adopt a floating paper standard that in theory eliminated altogether the need for official reserves for international payments, get rid of the discipline and postpone the adjustment to more favorable times.[36]

Yet, one may ask whether the balance of payments problems, if they did in fact exist, were of such magnitude that they prevented the country from entering the gold standard. We may also inquire if the Spanish level of official reserves, compared with that of other countries, can tell us anything about the ability of the authorities to preserve convertibility.

Data collected by Prados (1982) show that Spain's balance of trade exhibited a series of continuous surpluses after 1873. However annual outpayments for "invisibles" were significantly high, so that the overall current account balance may have been negative, particularly in the 1880s.[37] Nevertheless, the balance on current account alone does not tell us the whole story. From an economic point of view what matters is the overall balance of payments, and an accounting disequilibrium is measured by the difference between the totals of "above-the-line" credits and debits which are made up of current account and capital account items, which are not independently determined. A surplus in the capital account balance,

is almost inevitably accompanied by a deficit in the country's current account . . . This current account deficit, far from being grounds for alarm, is the way in which capital in real terms comes into the country as the counterpart of the financial transfer. The rise in the country's goods-and-service imports relative to its exports is how additional amounts of real resources become available to the borrowing government units and business and even consumers.[38]

Given the situation on the current account side, a deficit in the balance of payments will arise as a result of the country's inability to obtain a capital account surplus. For a growing economy with limited domestic resources, one can perfectly define a problem in the balance of payments as the country's inability to absorb financial resources from abroad.[39]

With this in mind we can now look at the limited evidence that we have for Spain. Between 1876 and 1882 Spain received large amounts of long-term capital that roughly came to balance the deficits in the current account.[40] If some gold was siphoned off from circulation it must be attributed to the relentless action of Gresham's Law. During these years conditions were excellent for the adoption of the gold standard. In fact, after 1876 the government discontinued the free coinage of silver on private account and the Junta Consultiva de la Moneda (the Committee on

Currency Reform) recommended gold monometallism.[41] Bank reserves, on the other hand, increased from 36.6 million pesetas in 1876 to 152.2 million pesetas in 1883. During these years the deficit was kept within reasonable limits; but, as has been mentioned already, the government ignored the recommendation of the Junta and no final decision to adopt the gold standard was taken.

After 1883 the Spanish currency was detached from the international monetary system, and capital mobility was seriously hampered. One may argue that the suspension came to disrupt the pattern of external adjustment of the previous period, and as a result difficulties in the balance of payments situation emerged. From 1883 until the turn of the century foreign investment ceased and, therefore, the economy lost the ability to earn the required surplus on capital account.[42] Certainly it could be argued that even if the government had not suspended convertibility in 1883 the developments of the late 1890s would have forced it to do so. But this, however, is an *ex post* argument which neither helps greatly to justify that decision nor explains why the gold standard was not adopted, say, between 1884 and 1895. If we turn briefly to this last point we see no reason why Spain could not have joined the gold standard some time between these two years. If we assume that the resumption of specie payments had to be done at the parity which prevailed before 1883, a successful attempt would have had to have been made to bring down prices in order to avoid a shortage of foreign exchange. Resumption, say, in 1885, would have required a price level 8 percent lower than the prevailing level that year. If resumption had taken place in the early 1890s, prices would first have to have fallen by about 15 percent.

So far, the assumption has been that the attempt would have been at the pre-suspension parity, but this need not have been so. Questions of prestige apart, the authorities could have chosen the most "adequate" parity. A reasonable exchange rate might have been that indicated by PPP at the time of the resumption.[43] Since there is no *a priori* reason to believe that capital imports would not have resumed, the old pattern of the balance of payments settlement could have been restored. Besides, several developments favoured the approach to the international monetary system: (1) an increase in the level of Bank reserves after 1884; (2) the maintenace of the Bank discount rate above the rate prevailing in Paris, London, and other European financial centers; (3) the reduction of the servicing of the foreign debt after 1883; and (4) the introduction of a new protective tariff in 1891.

Let us assume, however, that the decision taken in 1883 was the best or the only possible one given the international crisis, the gold losses of the Bank of Spain, and the precarious financial situation of the Treasury. Let us also assume that the period 1883–1900 presented "unsolvable" problems and that a fluctuating exchange rate offered the best available alternative. Yet, the country could have also gone into the gold standard after 1900. External and internal developments made a decision in favor of connecting the Spanish monetary system with the international one propitious. Between 1902 and 1913 the capital account surplus in the balance of payments reappeared. Sardá estimates that in this period the annual current account deficits might have been slightly over 200 million pesetas, but they were compensated by important receipts of capital imports from different sources.[44] The war years and the final independence of the colonies provoked a repatriation of capital into the country that reached its peak in the first two years of the twentieth century. Foreign capital imports also resumed after 1906, following the stabilizing policy initiated by Villaverde in 1900 and continued by his successors in the Ministry of Finance. As we have already seen, the objective of the policy was to bring monetary order to the dislocated Spanish financial situation after the war. The program was very much the same as Count Witte's in Russia before resumption. Supposedly, the intention was to introduce the gold standard.[45]

External factors also favored a resumption of specie payments, among others, the new trends in the world production and price of gold that had from the late 1890s been facilitating the entrance of new members (Russia, India, Japan, Italy, Austria–Hungary, Greece, Romania) into the "club." Those who had left the system (Argentina) also returned to it after 1900. The gold standard in the first 14 years of the twentieth century therefore became universal and provided the framework for a period of spectacular economic growth. The Spanish economy was prepared to join the international monetary system; nevertheless, the decision was never reached. This was a repetition of what had happened between 1868 and 1876, when the country approached the Latin Monetary Union, but the decision to join it was never adopted.

A measure of the ability to adhere to the gold standard: the level of reserves

We can now turn briefly to another argument which presumably influenced the authorities' choice: the existence of an adequate level of reserves. Disregarding the awkward question of what is meant by "adequate" and the different motives for holding international reserves,[46] we can try to see how the Spanish level of gold reserves compares with that of other countries.

Table 5.8 serves our purposes well. It offers for selected years the ratio of

Table 5.8 *Ratios of reserves to imports*

	(A) Ratio of gold reserves to imports			(B) Ratio of total reserves to imports		
	1890	1900	1913	1890	1900	1913
Austria–Hungary	—	54.2	36.5	—	57.8	38.2
Belgium	3.5	4.1	4.9	13.4	16.0	12.9
Denmark	19.0	17.7	19.9	23.4	18.3	22.4
France	25.4	49.7	41.7	25.4	49.7	42.0
Germany	13.8	8.6	10.8	13.9	10.1	12.8
Italy	13.5	23.7	47.4	13.5	30.5	52.8
Netherlands	3.0	2.9	3.8	3.7	3.5	4.2
Norway	12.0	9.4	8.0	17.0	12.5	14.1
Russia	94.6	109.9	111.2	94.6	109.9	154.5
Spain	18.9	41.8	51.5	18.9	41.8	51.1
Sweden	5.1	8.9	12.0	14.4	24.6	31.2
Switzerland	6.4	9.0	8.3	6.4	9.0	11.1
United Kingdom	5.5	—	4.3	—	—	—

Note:
— not available.
Sources: The underlying figures for gold, silver, and foreign exchange holdings have been taken from Haupt (1892); Leong (1933); Lindert (1969); Bloomfield (1963). All import figures are from Mitchell (1975).

reserves (official holdings of gold and foreign exchange) to imports in different countries.[47] The conclusion that can be drawn from table 5.8 is clear. Whether we consider only the holdings of gold or also include foreign exchange holdings, Spain does not seem to fare unfavorably in international comparison. The Spanish ratio fell among the highest in 1890 and, as matter of fact, both in 1900 and 1913 it is remarkably high. If one had to pass a judgment only on the basis of this ratio, it would be difficult to affirm that the country was in an uncomfortable position. On the contrary, this ratio indicates that Spain had no problems of international liquidity: compared with other European countries, Spain had a larger margin of reserves to face temporary balance of payments deficits.

Spain during the gold standard period

So far, we have argued that Spain could have joined the gold standard "club" at any time; also implicit in our argument is the view that it not only

Table 5.9 *Aggregate behavior of the Spanish economy, 1874–1914*

(A) Real per capita income in Western European countries (PPP)

Year	Spain (1800 = 100)	Spain's income as percentage of income in			
		Great Britain(%)	France (%)	Germany (%)	Italy (%)
1800	100	68	89	—	—
1830	98	57	77	82	78
1860	109	41	59	71	67
1890	169	45	68	79	103
1910	194	45	59	64	89

Note:
— not available.
Source: Prados (1990, table 1).

(B) Selected Spanish economic indicators (average annual rate of growth, %)

Year	GNP (1)	Industrial production (2)	Exports (3)
1874–83	1.9	3.3	7.0
1883–1900	1.1	1.8	1.8
1900–14	1.1	1.5	2.6

Source: Estadísticas Históricas de España (1989).

could, but that it should, have been part of the international monetary system.

Table 5.9 despicts the aggregate behavior of the Spanish economy between 1874 and 1914. From this we can draw two conclusions: first, that Spain performed relatively poorly in comparison with other European countries; secondly, that the rate of growth for the three indexes in table 5.9 decelerated after 1883.[48] In my opinion this slower growth can be partly attributed to the fact that Spain after 1883 lost contact with the international economic community. The Spanish economy did not enjoy the benefits of the growing interdependence of the European financial system that resulted from the world-wide adoption of the gold standard. Spain did not participate in the new wave of international capital investment of the 1880s and 1890s[49] and the Spanish economy remained relatively isolated from the expanding European short-term capital market.[50] Foreign capital ceased coming in the last twenty years of the century because the country went off the gold standard.

Haim Barkai (1973), studying the effects of the adoption of the gold standard in Tsarist Russia, made an attempt to evaluate the costs and benefits of its introduction. His method involved the calculation of the so-called "absorption ratio," estimated as the ratio of external inflow of real resources to national income. An increase in the ratio would suggest that the country gained as a consequence of the adoption of the gold standard, and the larger the increase the greater the benefit. On the other hand, a decrease in the ratio would suggest that the establishment of the gold standard affected the economy negatively.

Since I found Barkai's approach quite imaginative and attractive I have tried to repeat his test with Spanish data. Then the question is: what would have been the level of national income in 1913 had Spain adhered to the gold standard? To answer this question I have used Barkai's procedure, computing the ratio of current account deficit to national income in different years.

The pre-suspension period (1876–80) has been taken as the base period for comparison. From the balance of trade figures and from Sardá's (1948) estimates of outpayments for invisibles we have come to the conclusion that the annual deficit on current account for these years might have been, on average, around 200 million pesetas. The national income in 1873, as estimated by Tortella (1974a), amounted to approximately 6,200 million pesetas. In consequence, the economy, according to this rough calculation, may have been absorbing resources from abroad that represented 3.2 percent of total GNP. If instead of Tortella's national income estimates we make use of the more recent calculation by Prados (1990) for 1880, the result is very similar. Repeating this same calculation for other years we obtain the fact that the absorption ratio fell to 1.1 percent in 1890, was 1.9 percent in 1900 and then rose to 2.4 percent in 1913. After 1883 the economy was, therefore, on the whole, absorbing external resources at a lower rate than before. According to this calculation the loss in terms of inflows of resources foregone could have been in the order of 1–2 percent of GNP per year between 1883 and 1900, and slightly less thereafter. If we assume that Spain, within the gold standard, would have been able to maintain at least the same absorption ratio as before 1883, it is not unreasonable to suppose that larger inflows of resources would have induced higher rates of growth of total GNP. How much higher it is impossible to tell at this stage, but it would surely have brought the Spanish rate of growth closer to the European average.

It is my view that the Spanish monetary and financial authorities adopted the wrong course of action at a crucial time. The only way to benefit fully from the expansion of world trade and international investment that took place in the 30 years before 1914 was to be on the gold standard, formally or informally. Because Spain remained off the gold standard, the country was partially detached from the international business community and the result was one of the lowest rates of industrialization in Western Europe.

Whether the gold standard worked as expected by the theory or whether it performed all the functions that the traditional approach has attributed to it, is to some extent irrelevant. Here the critical issue is that for various reasons the center countries of the international economy adopted gold convertibility and fixed exchange rates for their national currencies. The rest of the nations followed suit one after the other. No choice was left to small and poor countries but to adopt the gold standard.

As Wieser (1892–93) indicated when examining the process of the resumption of specie payments in Austria–Hungary:

our monetary policy was by implication decided for us in the decision taken by Western Europe, with which we could not but agree . . . If Europe errs in adopting gold, we must still, for good or evil, join her error, and we shall thus receive less injury than if we insist on being "rational" all by ourselves.[51]

Probably the Spanish authorities did not foresee the consequences of the decision of 1883. In that year, when the countries of the Latin Monetary Union had not yet decided to leave bimetallism, one can understand why it was so: in 1883 the system was far from universal. But the government became aware of the virtues of the system and of its growing importance. Besides, the Spanish authorities did not contemplate unconvertibility as definite; as a matter of fact, they disliked a regime of floating exchange rates for the peseta and they never attempted to conduct an independent monetary policy. Particularly after 1900, the authorities' aim was to join the gold standard and policy was designed to introduce it. Yet the formal decision to resume convertibility was never taken.

The non-adoption of the gold standard must not be seen as the only cause of the Spanish economic backwardness, but as a contributory factor in widening the difference between Spain and the rest of the Western European countries. This chapter has tried to show that the adoption of the gold standard was both possible and advisable. To be out of the international monetary system implied a choice for autarkic development; it meant partial isolation. Both autarky and isolation exacted a burdensome cost.

Appendix 1

Table 5A.1 *The money stock, 1880–1914, million pesetas*

Year	Money supply (1)	High-powered money (2)	Deposit– currency ratio (3)	Deposit– reserve ratio (4)
1880	1,977	1,808	0.31	1.57
1881	2,065	1,909	0.30	1.48
1882	2,076	1,941	0.23	1.54
1883	2,112	1,959	0.22	1.66
1884	2,128	1,981	0.26	1.50
1885	2,247	2,093	0.29	1.48
1886	2,245	2,080	0.32	1.44
1887	2,253	2,103	0.37	1.33
1888	2,354	2,185	0.38	1.36
1889	2,443	2,222	0.41	1.46
1890	2,462	2,283	0.39	1.35
1891	2,498	2,334	0.43	1.28
1892	2,406	2,227	0.39	1.36
1893	2,363	2,189	0.38	1.36
1894	2,190	1,987	0.36	1.53
1895	2,346	2,143	0.43	1.40
1896	2,419	2,259	0.45	1.27
1897	2,625	2,384	0.48	1.40
1898	3,538	3,271	0.59	1.25
1899	3,500	3,299	0.54	1.20
1900	3,371	3,195	0.53	1.18
1901	3,444	3,154	0.51	1.33
1902	3,272	3,042	0.48	1.28
1903	3,401	3,083	0.52	1.38
1904	3,377	3,045	0.53	1.40
1905	3,259	2,884	0.55	1.48
1906	3,239	2,796	0.59	1.59
1907	3,242	2,777	0.59	1.64
1908	3,118	2,705	0.63	1.64
1909	3,340	2,800	0.65	1.70
1910	3,427	2,818	0.66	1.81
1911	3,533	2,871	0.66	1.89
1912	3,692	3,007	0.65	1.90
1913	3,827	3,105	0.66	1.91
1914	3,896	3,378	0.66	1.50

Source: Martín-Aceña (1990, Appendix, tables 1–5).

Appendix 2

Table 5A.2 *Prices and exchange rates, 1880–1914*

Year	Spanish wholesale price index 1913 = 100 (1)	British wholesale price index 1913 = 100 (2)	Nominal exchange rate (pesetas per pound sterling) (3)	Real exchange rate[a] (pesetas per pound sterling) (4)
1880	90.0	110.7	24.9	30.7
1881	90.6	108.7	25.1	30.1
1882	93.9	109.6	25.7	29.9
1883	89.5	108.1	25.6	30.9
1884	81.5	97.9	25.5	30.6
1885	80.5	91.8	25.7	29.3
1886	79.9	86.7	25.7	27.9
1887	77.0	84.8	25.5	28.0
1888	78.4	87.4	25.6	28.6
1889	79.7	88.8	26.0	28.9
1890	79.1	88.7	26.3	29.5
1891	78.0	91.8	26.9	31.7
1892	80.2	86.8	29.0	31.4
1893	78.1	85.3	30.0	32.7
1894	75.2	80.3	30.1	32.1
1895	79.5	77.9	28.9	28.3
1896	75.8	75.7	30.4	30.4
1897	82.4	77.3	32.6	30.6
1898	90.5	80.0	39.2	34.7
1899	92.1	79.1	31.4	27.0
1900	96.7	85.8	32.6	28.9
1901	96.9	83.0	34.8	29.8
1902	94.7	82.7	34.1	29.8
1903	97.7	83.2	34.0	28.9
1904	99.5	84.3	34.7	29.4
1905	100.0	83.8	32.9	27.6
1906	97.3	86.5	28.4	25.3
1907	101.4	91.0	28.1	25.2
1908	98.6	88.4	28.4	25.5
1909	97.3	89.4	27.2	24.9
1910	98.2	93.4	27.1	25.8
1911	94.7	93.9	27.2	27.0
1912	99.4	98.6	27.0	26.8
1913	100.0	100.0	27.1	27.1

Table 5A.2 (*cont.*)

Year	Spanish wholesale price index 1913 = 100 (1)	British wholesale price index 1913 = 100 (2)	Nominal exchange rate (pesetas per pound sterling) (3)	Real exchange rate[a] (pesetas per pound sterling) (4)
1914	99.7	100.6	26.1	26.3

Note:

[a] The real exchange rate (*ER*) in column (4) has been computed

$$E_R = \frac{E_N \cdot P_F}{P_D}$$

where E_F = the nominal exchange rate; P_F = the foreign (British) wholesale price index (1913 = 100); and P_D = the domestic (Spanish) wholesale price index (1913 = 100).

Sources: Estadísticas Históricas de España (1989); Mitchell and Deane (1962).

Appendix 3

Table 5A.3 *Yield on long-term government bonds, 1880–1914, % per year*

Year	Spanish deuda (1)	British consol (2)	French bonds (3)	Italian bonds (4)
1880	—	3.10	3.56	4.88
1881	—	3.00	3.54	4.87
1882	—	3.00	3.67	4.97
1883	6.42	3.00	3.83	4.97
1884	6.66	3.00	3.88	4.61
1885	7.73	3.00	3.79	4.56
1886	6.61	3.00	3.66	4.14
1887	6.14	3.00	3.78	4.46
1888	5.76	3.00	3.63	4.52
1889	5.33	2.80	3.51	4.58
1890	5.24	2.90	3.26	4.60
1891	5.30	2.90	3.18	4.71
1892	5.87	2.80	3.07	4.66
1893	5.84	2.80	3.10	4.63
1894	5.72	2.70	2.98	4.59
1895	5.71	2.60	2.96	4.37
1896	6.31	2.50	2.94	4.35
1897	6.29	2.50	2.90	4.18
1898	7.21	2.50	2.92	4.06

Table 5A.3 (*cont.*)

Year	Spanish deuda (1)	British consol (2)	French bonds (3)	Italian bonds (4)
1899	6.33	2.60	2.98	4.01
1900	4.51	2.80	2.98	4.02
1901	4.48	2.90	2.96	3.97
1902	4.42	2.90	2.99	3.91
1903	4.10	2.80	3.06	3.91
1904	4.21	2.80	3.11	3.90
1905	4.00	2.80	3.03	3.82
1906	3.97	2.80	3.08	3.87
1907	3.91	3.00	3.16	3.69
1908	3.86	2.90	3.13	3.63
1909	3.74	3.00	3.07	3.61
1910	3.76	3.10	3.06	3.60
1911	3.81	3.20	3.14	3.67
1912	3.79	3.20	3.27	3.60
1913	3.98	3.40	3.44	3.58
1914	4.22	3.30	3.78	3.75

Note:
— not available
Sources: column (1) Martín-Aceña (1985).
   column (2) Mitchell and Deane (1962).
   column (3) and column 4 Fratianni and Spinelli (1984).

Appendix 4

Table 5A.4 *Budget deficit and trade balance, 1875–1914, million pesetas*

Year	Budget deficit (1)	Trade balance (2)
1875	− 10.2	62.7
1876	− 111.3	− 76.9
1877	5.8	73.4
1878	− 13.0	53.2
1879	− 29.7	22.0
1880	− 77.7	122.9
1881	− 58.4	184.7
1882	− 1.2	60.5
1883	31.2	0.0

Table 5A.4 (*cont.*)

Year	Budget deficit (1)	Trade balance (2)
1884	− 45.4	20.4
1885	− 28.3	70.6
1886	− 81.6	97.5
1887	− 15.4	70.5
1888	− 72.7	141.1
1889	− 121.8	23.8
1890	− 67.5	31.5
1891	− 49.7	220.4
1892	− 53.4	354.6
1893	− 19.0	291.2
1894	74.8	149.9
1895	5.7	207.7
1896	− 26.0	437.7
1897	9.5	447.3
1898	− 146.2	488.1
1899	− 80.4	63.5
1900	35.5	133.2
1901	37.8	15.3
1902	71.0	52.8
1903	23.0	16.0
1904	53.4	73.6
1905	72.2	73.3
1906	102.9	296.7
1907	65.4	297.6
1908	56.5	151.0
1909	− 50.9	178.1
1910	− 5.8	163.1
1911	6.5	176.7
1912	− 62.4	160.1
1913	− 70.7	− 28.3
1914	− 166.2	− 213.3

Sources: Estadísticas Históricas de España (1989); Martín-Aceña (1985).

Notes

This chapter has benefited from generous comments by a large number of scholars. I wish to acknowledge the helpful remarks and suggestions of Michael Bordo, Jon Cohen, Francisco Comín, Roberto Cortés Conde, Scot Eddie, Barry Eichengreen, Leandro Prados, Jaime Reis, Pedro Tedde, Peter Temin, Gianni Toniolo, Gabriel Tortella, Jeffrey Williamson and participants at seminars at the University of

Toronto, Harvard University, the University of Chicago, the University of Illinois at Urbana, Indiana University at Bloomington, Rutgers University and the Conference on the "Gold Standard in the Countries of the Periphery," Universidade Nova de Lisboa. However, I alone must take responsibility for resisting their efforts to keep me on the straight and narrow.

1 Three recent and excellent surveys of the international gold standard are Ford (1989) for the period 1870–1914, Moggridge (1989) for the interwar years, and Drummond (1987) for the period 1900–1939. For a discussion of the myths and realities of the gold standard and main debates raised by the literature, see Bordo (1984, pp. 23–119); Bordo (1986); Eichengreen (1985, pp. 1–35). Still valuable also is the classical paper by Triffin (1964).

2 Only China, among the major countries, remained on a silver standard, as well as various Latin American countries whose currencies were inconvertible for extended periods.

3 I have already developed some of these arguments in Martín-Aceña (1981).

4 The reform of 1868 has been studied thoroughly by Fernández Pulgar and Anes (1970).

5 The peseta was thereby made equal to the French franc and the exchange rate with the pound sterling was fixed at 25.22 pesetas. Nevertheless Spain did not join the Union. Although this is a topic that deserves further examination, it can be suggested that one possible reason was that the Spanish authorities did not like to accept the commitments implied by the new monetary agreement. See also chapters 2 and 3 in this volume.

6 Anes (1974a, pp. 125 et seq.).

7 A short account of the history of the Latin Monetary Union may be found in Dam (1982) and De Cecco (1984); see also chapter 3 in this volume.

8 Sardá (1948, p. 178).

9 Sardá (1948, pp. 266–267). See Appendix 4, p. 164 for figures on the trade balance.

10 Sardá (1948, pp. 183–184).

11 Tortella (1974a, p. 480).

12 The quantitative information used for the reconstruction of the economic events described in this section is included in Appendixes 1–4.

13 Some aspects of this crisis have been studied by Tedde (1974, pp. 276 et seq.).

14 Solé Villalonga (1964, pp. 36–39); and more recently Anes and Tedde (1976, pp. 35–50). Barthe (1905) estimated the outflow of capital as a direct consequence of the debt conversion at 25 million pesetas.

15 Sardá (1948, p. 184). The conversion might have prevented a further and larger rise of the central bank rate, since it would have endangered the success of the new issue which was offered at a nominal interest of 4 percent.

16 In any event, gold would have disappeared since the metallic ratio defined in 1868 remained unaltered.

17 For a full and comprehensive study of Spanish public finance during these years, see Comín (1988, pp. 575–644).

18 While international prices fell by 15 percent between 1885 and 1895, Spanish

prices did not decline at all. For English prices we have taken the index of Sauerbeck, as reproduced in Mitchell and Deane (1962).

19 Tallada (1946, p. 118); Solé Villalonga (1964, p. 38); Anes and Tedde (1976, pp. 46 *et seq*); Martín-Aceña (1985, pp. 270 *et seq*.).

20 Tallada (1946, pp. 144–166; Sardá (1948, p. 235); Solé Villalonga (1967); Anes (1974a, pp. 172–182).

21 Comín (1988, pp. 580–587 and 645–668).

22 By assumption, the 1913 exchange rate is at PPP. Sizeable upward divergences from 100 imply a real depreciation of the peseta; downward divergences, a real appreciation.

23 The evolution of the real exchange rate is compatible with the results registered by the balance of trade. Thus, the systematic depreciation of the real exchange rate explains the improvements in the balance of trade, particularly during the 1890s; the appreciation of the following decade was reflected in a deterioration of the surplus, which in fact vanished in the last two years of the century. On the other hand, the figures show that both the nominal and the real exchange rate were subject to frequent and substantial fluctuations which most probably increased the level of uncertainty and risk for all international transactions, both on current and on capital account.

24 Fratianni and Spinelli (1984, p. 427).

25 See Crisp (1953–54); Yeager (1969); Fratianni and Spinelli (1984).

26 The rate of growth of exports for 1865–83, 1883–1900 and 1900–14 was, respectively, 5.7 percent, 1.8 percent and 0.4 percent.

27 A study of Spanish banking between 1874 and 1914 is found in Tedde (1974); for the evolution of the financial system compared with other European countries, see Martín-Aceña (1987).

28 The evolution of the stock of money has been studied by Tortella (1974a), and more recently by Martín-Aceña (1990).

29 See the original paper by Whale (1937); also Drummond (1976) for Russia, Jonung (1984) for Sweden, and McGouldrick (1984) for Germany. For French financial and monetary policy during the classical gold standard years the most useful is still White (1933). For a review and a summary of the evidence, see Michaely (1968); Drummond (1987); Ford (1989).

30 In fact if one adheres to the monetary approach to the balance of payments, as McCloskey and Zecher (1976) do, the stock of money is always endogenous. According to this theory, prices of traded commodities and assets, as well as interest rates are determined in world markets. The law of one price in goods and assets markets prevails and it is assured by perfect arbitrage. Under this assumption, to follow the rules of the game is irrelevant; the central bank lacks the power to determine the domestic money supply (it only can affect its composition) and gold flows lose their importance as a source of variations of the money stock.

31 Olariaga (1977, p. 133).

32 Concerning this issue of a "monetary rule," Bordo and Kydland (1992) state that time-series analysis of the persistence of inflation for various countries

across extensive periods of suspension and adherence to gold before 1914 suggests that the gold standard rule was prominent. Hence, it could possibly be argued that the fact that the peseta exchange rate, before 1890 and after 1900, did not depart from parity suggests that the Spanish financial authorities did follow the gold standard rule.

33 Anes (1974a, p. 183).

34 It should be added that the rules regulating the relationship between the note issue of the Bank of Spain and its gold reserves did not restrict the supply of bank notes during this period. The Bank normally kept its currency issue far below the legal maximum that the law permitted. The link was loose due to the flexibility of the reserve rules, which were modified several times.

35 Sardá (1948, chapter VIII and IX).

36 For this argument, see Tortella (1974a, pp. 480–481).

37 Sardá (1948, pp. 205–206, 219–223, 238–240) has estimated that payments for invisibles may have amounted to an average of 110 million pesetas between 1883 and 1901 and to an average of 131 million pesetas for the period 1902–13. Barthe (1905) estimated that outpayments in this same account reached an annual average of 131 million pesetas between 1892 and 1895 and 108 million pesetas between 1896 and 1902.

38 Yeager (1976, p. 48).

39 Mundell (1968, pp. 134–139).

40 Sardá (1948, pp. 186–187) estimated that between 1876 and 1881 the current account deficit may have amounted to 1,000 million pesetas, which was covered by capital imports of the same magnitude. For foreign investment in Spain during the nineteenth century, see Broder (1976).

41 Sardá (1948, pp. 178–179).

42 Sardá (1948, p. 200) estimated that between 1883 and 1891 the deficit on current account was near 2,000 million pesetas and between 1892 and 1901 close to 1,000 million pesetas. Capital imports during the first period reached only 150 million pesetas according to Sardá, while Barthe (1905) offers a sum of 675 million pesetas for the whole period (1883–1902).

43 Certainly, one must bear in mind that restoring gold convertibility at a devalued parity would have involved a loss of credibility in the pre-1914 world, and might have led market agents to doubt the reliability of Spain's future commitments to gold, since they would expect a new devaluation when economic conditions deteriorated. I owe this valuable point to Michael Bordo.

44 Sardá (1948, pp. 241–242 and 268–275).

45 Sardá (1948, p. 235); Anes (1974a, pp. 172–182).

46 On this issue see, for example, the discussion in Machlup (1976, pp. 260–276); and also IMF (1958).

47 These same ratios have been explained and calculated by Bloomfield (1963, pp. 30–31).

48 For an overview of the performance of the Spanish economy in a comparative perspective, see Prados (1990).

49 Thomas (1967); Bloomfield (1968); Cottrell (1975); Edelstein (1982).

50 Bloomfield (1963), Cottrell (1975), and Yeager (1976) argue that currency depreciation and flexible exchange rates may have discouraged foreign investment. The uncertainty associated with exchange rate instability and lack of convertibility negatively influenced the flow of capital to peripheral non-gold standard countries.
51 Wieser (1892–93, pp. 388–389).

References

Anes Alvarez, R., 1974a. "El Banco de España (1874–1914): Un Banco nacional," in G. Tortella and P. Schwartz (eds.), *La Banca Española en la Restauración* (vol. II), Madrid: Banco de España.

1974b. "Una serie de base monetaria (1874–1919)," in G. Tortella and P. Schwartz (eds.), *La Banca Española en la Restauración* (vol. II), Madrid: Banco de España.

1974c. "Balances sectorizados del Banco de España (1874–1915)," in G. Tortella and P. Schwartz (eds.), *La Banca Española en la Restauración* (vol. II), Madrid: Banco de España.

Anes Alvarez, R. and P. Tedde, 1976. "La deuda pública y el Banco de España (1874–1900)," *Hacienda Pública Española*, 38.

Barkai H., 1973. "The Macroeconomics of Tsarist Russia in the Industrialization Era," *Journal of Economic History*, 33.

Barthe y Barthe, A., 1905. *Estudio crítico de la crisis monetaria*, Madrid.

Bloomfield, A., 1959. *Monetary Policy under the International Gold Standard, 1880–1914*, New York: Federal Reserve Bank of New York.

1963. "Short-term capital movements under the pre-1914 gold standard," *Princeton Studies in International Finance*, Princeton: Princeton University Press.

1968. "Patterns of fluctuations in international investment before 1914," *Princeton Studies in International Finance*, Princeton: Princeton University Press.

Bordo, M.D., 1984. "The gold standard: the traditional approach," in M.D. Bordo and A. Schwartz (eds.), *A Retrospective on the Classical Gold Standard: 1821–1931*, Chicago: University of Chicago Press.

1986. "Explorations in monetary history: a survey of the literature," *Explorations in Economic History*, 23.

Bordo, M.D. and F.E. Kydland, 1992. "The gold standard as a rule," Federal Bank of Cleveland, *Working Paper*, 9205 (March).

Bordo, M.D. and A. Schwartz (eds.), 1984. *A Retrospective on the Classical Gold Standard: 1821–1931*, Chicago: University of Chicago Press.

Broder, A., 1976. "Les investissements étranger en Espagne au XIXème siècle: méthodologie et quantification," *Revue d'Histoire Economique et Social*, 54 (1).

Cecco, M. de, 1984. *International Gold Standard: Money and the Empire*, New York: St. Martin's Press.

Comín, F., 1988. *Hacienda y economía en la España contemporánea (1800–1936)*, Madrid: Instituto de Estudios Fiscales.

Cottrell, P.L., 1975. *British Overseas Investment in the Nineteenth Century*, London: Macmillan.

Crisp, O., 1953–54. "Russian financial policy and the gold standard at the end of the nineteenth century," *Economic History Review*, 6.

Dam, K.W., 1982. *The Rules of the Game. Reform and Evolution in the International Monetary System*, Chicago: University of Chicago Press.

Drummond, I., 1976. "The Russian gold standard 1897–1914," *Journal of Economic History*, 36.

1987. *The Gold Standard and the International Monetary System, 1900–1939*, Studies in Economic and Social History, London: Macmillan.

Edelstein, M., 1982. *Overseas Investment in the Age of High Imperialism: The United Kingdom, 1850–1914*, New York: Columbia University Press.

Eichengreen, B. (ed.), 1985. *The Gold Standard in Theory and History*, New York: Methuen.

Estadísticas Históricas de España, 1989. Siglos XIX–XX (A. Carreras, director), Madrid: Fundación Banco Exterior.

Fernández Pulgar, C. and R. Anes Alvarez, 1970. "La creación de la peseta en la evolución del sistema monetaria de 1847 a 1868," *Ensayos sobre la economía española a mediados del siglo XIX*, Madrid: Ariel.

Ford, A.G., 1962. *The Gold Standard 1880–1918: Britain and Argentina*, Oxford: Clarendon Press.

1989. "International financial policy and the gold standard, 1870–1914," P. Mathias and S. Pollard (eds.), *The Cambridge Economic History of Europe*, vol. VIII, Cambridge: Cambridge University Press.

Fratianni, M. and F. Spinelli, 1984. "Italy in the gold standard period, 1861–1914," in M.D. Bordo and A.J. Schwartz (eds.), *A Retrospective on the Classical Gold Standard: 1821–1931*, Chicago: University of Chicago Press.

Haupt, O., 1892. *The Monetary Question in 1892*, London: Wilson.

IMF, 1958. *International Reserves and Liquidity*, Washington, DC: IMF.

Jonung, L, 1984. "Swedish Experience under the Classical Gold Standard, 1873–1914," in M.D. Bordo and A. Schwartz (eds.), *A Retrospective on the Classical Gold Standard, 1821–1931*, Chicago: University of Chicago Press.

Leong, Y.S., 1933. *Silver. An Analysis of Factors Affecting its Price*, Washington DC: The Brooking Institution.

Lindert, P.H., 1969. "Key currencies and gold, 1900–1913," *Princeton Studies in International Finance*, Princeton: Princeton University Press.

Machlup, F., 1976. "Further reflections on the demand for foreign reserves," in M. Machlup (ed.), *International Payments, Debts and Gold*, New York: New York University Press.

Martín-Aceña, P. 1981. "España y el patrón-oro, 1880–1913," *Hacienda Pública Española*, 69.

1985. "Déficit público y política monetaria en la Restauración, 1874–1923," in P. Martín-Aceña and L. Prados de la Escosura (eds.), *La Nueva Historia Económica en España*, Madrid: Tecnos.

1987. "Development and modernization of the financial system, 1844–1935," in

N. Sánchez Albornoz (ed.), *The Economic Modernization of Spain, 1830–1930*, New York: New York University Press.

1990. "The Spanish money supply, 1874–1935," *Journal of European Economic History*, 19 (1).

McCloskey, D.N. and Zecher, J.R., 1976. "How the gold standard worked, 1880–1913," in J.A. Frenkel and H.G. Johnson (eds.), *The Monetary Approach to the Balance of Payments*, London: Allen & Unwin.

McGouldrick, P., 1984. "Operations of the German central bank and the rules of the game, 1987–1913," in M.D. Bordo and A. Schwartz (eds.), *A Retrospective on the Classical Gold Standard, 1821–1931*, Chicago: University of Chicago Press.

Michaely, M., 1968. *Balance of Payments Adjustment Policies*, New York: Columbia University Press for the NBER.

Mitchell, B.R., 1975. *European Historical Statistics, 1750–1970*, London: MacMillan.

Mitchell, B.R. and P. Deane. 1962 *Abstract of British Historical Statistics*, Cambridge: Cambridge University Press.

Moggridge, D., 1989. "The gold standard and national financial policies, 1913–39," in P. Mathias and S. Pollard (eds.), *The Cambridge Economic History of Europe*, vol. VIII, Cambridge: Cambridge University Press.

Mundell, R.A., 1968. "Growth and the balance of payments", in R.A. Mundell (ed.), *International Economics*, New York: Macmillan.

Nurkse, R., 1947. *International Currency Experience: Lessons of the Inter-war Period*, Geneva: League of Nations, 1944; reprinted by United Nations.

Olariaga, L., 1977. *La política monetaria en España*, 2nd edn., Barcelona: Banca Mas Sarda.

Prados de la Escosura, L., 1982, *Comercio exterior y crecimiento económico en España, 1826–1913: Tendencias a largo plazo*, Servicio de Estudios del Banco de España, *Estudios de Historia Económica*, 7, Madrid.

1990. "El desarrollo económico español en el contexto europeo, 1800–1930," in P. Martín-Aceña and F. Comín (eds.), *Empresa pública e industrialzación en España*, Madrid: Alianza Editorial.

Sardá, J., 1948. *La política monetaria y las fluctuaciones de la economía española en el siglo XIX*, Madrid: Consejo Superior de Investigaciones Científicas.

Solé Villalonga, G., 1964. *La deuda pública y el mercado de capitales*, Madrid: Instituto de Estudios Fiscales.

1967. *La reforma fiscal de Villaverde, 1899–1900*, Madrid: Ed. de Derecho Financiero.

Tallada Pauli, J.M., 1946. *Historia de las Finanzas españolas en el siglo XIX*, Madrid: Espasa Calpe.

Tedde, P., 1974. "La banca privada española durante la Restauración," in G. Tortella and P. Schwartz (eds.), *La Banca española en la Restauración*, vol. I, Madrid: Banco de España.

Thomas, B., 1967. "The historical record of international capital movements to 1913," in J. Adler (ed.), *Capital Movement and Economic Development*, London: Macmillan and New York: St Martin's Press.

Tortella, G., 1974a. "Las magnitudes monetarias y sus determinantes," in G. Tortella and P. Schwartz (eds.), *La banca española en la Restauración*, vol. I, Madrid: Banco de España.

1974b. "Estimación del stock de oro en España (1874–1914)," in G. Tortella and P. Schwartz (eds.), *La banca española en la Restauración*, vol. II, Madrid: Banco de España.

Triffin, R., 1964. "The evolution of the international monetary system: Historical reappraisal and future perspectives," *Princeton Studies in International Finance*, Princeton: Princeton University Press.

Whale, P.B., 1937. "The working of the pre-war gold standard," *Economica*, 14 February: 18–32.

White, H.D., 1933. *The French International Accounts, 1880–1913*, Cambridge, MA: Harvard University Press.

Wieser, F., 1892–93. "Resumption of specie payment in Austria–Hungary," *Journal of Political Economy*, 1.

Yeager, L., 1969. "Fluctuating exchange rates in the nineteenth century: the experience of Austria and Russia," in R.A. Mundell and A.K. Swoboda (eds.), *Monetary Problems of the International Economy*, Chicago: University of Chicago Press.

1976. *International Monetary Relations: Theory, History and Policy*, New York: Harper & Row.

6 Canada and the gold standard, 1871–1914: a durable monetary regime

TREVOR J.O. DICK AND JOHN E. FLOYD

The gold standard era that lasted from 1821 to 1931 was remarkable for the prevailing widespread confidence in the ability of gold and fixed exchange rates to facilitate a smooth adjustment to disturbances in the balance of payments.[1] The durability of this monetary regime varied widely from country to country. Canada provides an example of a country that survived on the gold standard with minimal government intervention from 1870 to 1914.[2] Why did the gold standard work so well for Canadian balance of payments adjustment, and what was the nature of the adjustment process?

In this chapter we argue that the central feature of the Canadian case was the international mobility of capital. Capital flowed freely into the country over the entire growth period, aided by a set of banking institutions that were well suited to service these flows. Capital mobility presents a new challenge to theorists of balance of payments adjustment. The important distinction between balance of payments and balance of trade adjustment is not easily accommodated within the traditional price-specie-flow mechanism. In fact, this traditional view is both logically and empirically unacceptable as an interpretation of the Canadian evidence. Capital mobility raises new questions about the origin of price adjustments and their significance for maintaining balance of payments equilibria. A modern portfolio theory of balance of payments adjustment, we argue, best accommodates the realities of capital and commodity flows. This theory explains the performance of the gold standard in the Canadian case very well. It radically alters the way balance of payments adjustment should be viewed.

In the following sections we first review the place of Canada in the international economy before the First World War and the role of the Canadian banking system. We then explore the theory of balance of payments adjustment, dealing with the implications of capital mobility, with Canadian price-level determination, and with asset equilibrium. We then present the Canadian evidence that supports our revised theory of adjustment. We sketch a reinterpretation of the process of balance of payments adjustment to each of the main shocks that occurred during the

173

period, and in the final section, we conclude, as did Viner (1924), that the Canadian experience offers a fine example of the smooth operation of the gold standard wherein the balance of payments has to adjust to massive shocks caused by long-term capital inflow. But we also conclude, unlike Viner (1924), that this smooth operation was the result of the unrestricted accommodating behavior of government and banking institutions that had the confidence of the financial community, rather than the necessary outcome of the operation of the classical price-specie-flow mechanism.

Canada and the international economy

The period 1870–1914 is a critical and controversial one in Canadian economic growth. National income estimates suggest that the economy reached a turning point near the beginning of the twentieth century when urbanization, industrialization, and net capital inflows began to accelerate (Urquhart, 1986). The later nineteenth century, in contrast, was a period of general deflation that may have entailed some output sacrifices (Dick, 1990). These observations are superficially in accord with long-standing traditional interpretations (Easterbrook and Aitken, 1958; Rostow, 1978).

   The association of early twentieth century growth with the settlement of the prairie West has led to major controversy over the importance of staple-led growth (Chambers and Gordon, 1966; Caves, 1971). The economy grew relatively slowly after Confederation while wheat and forest products contributed about equally to untrending levels of exports that accounted for 15–20 percent of GNP. After the turn of the century the picture is more complicated; while exports of wheat grew much faster, they did not do so until after 1910. An investment boom in which manufacturing and non-farm investment played a large role characterized the first decade of the century (Innis, 1936; Ankli, 1980; Buckley, 1955).

   Whatever the outcome of these controversies, there is now strong quantitative evidence to suggest some acceleration in both intensive and extensive growth by the turn of the century and a persistent pattern in international settlements over the entire period (Urquhart, 1986). The current account balance was virtually always negative, implying persistent net capital inflow. Domestic savings fell short of investment demand, particularly after 1900 (Edelstein, 1982). During the three periods of investment boom, the early 1870s, 1880–85, and 1900–14, the ratios of gross total fixed capital formation to GNP were respectively 20 percent, 20 percent, and 25–30 percent while the ratios of domestic savings to GNP were only 12.8 percent, 13.5 percent, and 19 percent (Urquhart, 1986). Canada, in company with other developing areas having high ratios of land to other resources, such as Argentina, Australia, and the United States, absorbed surplus labor and capital from England and other European countries (Field, 1912; Paterson, 1976). Investment and capital flows occurred as part of long swings of the Atlantic economy in which Canada participated. Trade and investment boomed alternately in Europe and North America in response to shifting comparative advantage and investment opportunities (Buckley, 1952, 1963; Cairncross, 1953; Thomas, 1973; Lewis, 1978).

The benefits of Canada's participation in the international economy were evident not only in the rate of economic growth but also in the structural change that occurred. Capital formation included massive transcontinental railroad construction that linked all parts of the country together for the first time. The relative importance of manufacturing as compared to agriculture altered permanently in favor of the former (Green and Urquhart, 1987). The average annual rate of growth of secondary manufacturing was about 5 percent between 1870 and 1890, 2 percent in the 1890s, and 6 percent from 1900 to 1910. The output of iron and steel and transportation equipment grew at 12.4 percent per year. Whatever impetus staples may have had for these changes, the national economy by 1914 was certainly more complex than a simple leading-sector model of staple production could accommodate.

Canadian banks and the migration of capital

The Canadian banking system was unique among capital-importing countries. Relatively few large banks, each with multiple branches throughout the country, were chartered and permitted to issue their own notes subject only to a limitation based on the amount of paid up capital stock. Banks were not required to keep reserves. The government did not guarantee to redeem bank notes. Bank notes were not made legal tender.

The security of bank note issue was nonetheless assured by several special features of the system. Bank stock holders were subject to double liability. Bank notes were made the first lien against banks' assets. All banks were required to redeem their own notes both at head office and at major centers across the country: "On account of the ease with which notes are redeemed, every bank accepts at par the notes of all other banks exactly as if they were legal tender, and then sends them to the nearest redemption center to be exchanged for gold coin or Dominion notes, or to be used as a credit offset in the redemption of its own notes" (Johnson, 1910, pp. 62–63). There were remarkably few bank failures before 1914 compared to the record of many other systems, particularly that of the United States (Beckhart, 1929, pp. 480–483). Of the 26 Canadian banks that failed before 1923, one-half of them were able to pay their depositors in full upon liquidation (Beckhart, 1929, p. 479). Failure seems to have been the result of head office corruption rather than of some underlying widespread financial crisis that Canadian banks were unable to withstand.

The note issue of banks was particularly well tuned to the requirements of business. The capital requirement caused banks to increase their capitalization with the growth of their business, and redemption worked to make the supply of bank money highly elastic to the demands of business. Their portfolios were conservative in comparison to those of US banks. Branches, particularly foreign branches, expanded rapidly after 1890 (Beckhart, 1929, pp. 362–375; Rich, 1988, Appendix B). Branch banking appeared to permit loans to be made at lower interest rates than otherwise despite increasing concentration in the banking industry toward the end of the nineteenth century. The ability of the system to shift funds rapidly as required was exemplified in the crop-moving season, particularly in 1907 when some Canadian banks became lenders of last resort in New York (Rich, 1989).

After Confederation the government introduced and expanded the use of Dominion notes, redeemable in gold, in an effort to recapture the seigniorage the commercial banking system had pre-empted during its early growth. In 1881, for example, bank notes were restricted to denominations of 5 dollars and over, and 40 percent of banks' primary reserves had to be in Dominion notes. In 1891, a Circulation Redemption Fund was established, into which banks were required to deposit gold and/or Dominion notes to an amount equal to 5 percent of their average circulation – a measure also designed to prevent the notes of failed banks from being quoted at a discount.

Despite the absence of formal reserve requirements, banks kept reserves as a normal business practice, and their habits in this regard were particularly sensitive to world capital market conditions. Reserves usually consisted of gold and assets that could be quickly turned into gold – cash, call loans, and securities. Little gold and only modest amounts of cash, about 10 percent to 12 percent of bank liabilities, were commonly kept as primary reserves. Call loans, highly liquid and mostly held in New York and London as secondary reserves were at least as important (Viner, 1924). Other security placements were considered less liquid and less likely to be drawn down when a bank was pressed. Altogether, these forms of reserve constituted 30–40 percent of net bank liabilities before 1914 (Beckhart, 1929, p. 434).

The participation of Canadian banks in the call loan and security markets of New York and London was partly the result of the absence in our period of a domestic short-term money and call loan market in Canada. Only in Montreal after 1900 is there evidence of a domestic call loan market, but the nature and functioning of this market is unclear and there is controversy over whether the loans were really short-term (Rich, 1988, chapter 5; Goodhart, 1969, p. 142; Morrison, 1966, p. 66; Dick and Floyd, 1991, 1992). The participation in foreign markets provided a direct link between financial conditions at home and in the United States and England. Although the deposit–reserve ratio declined significantly in Canada during the external financial crises of 1877–78 and 1894–95, there were no banking panics (Bordo, 1985, p. 61). This is credited to the risk pooling possible under a system of branch banking and to the role played by the Canadian Bankers' Association, a unique organization that supervised note issue, regulated clearing houses, and took charge of suspended banks. Apart from regulating the conditions under which banks could be chartered and promoting the circulation of Dominion notes, the government made little attempt at intervention before the passage of the Finance Act in 1914. Given the evidence of the pro-cyclical behavior of the Canadian money supply (Hay, 1966, 1967; Rich, 1988) and the monetary transmission process of the international business cycle operating under the gold standard (Bordo, 1985), it is remarkable that Canadian banks turned in such a stable performance.

Notwithstanding the concentration in banking and the popular criticism this elicited toward the end of the nineteenth century, there can be no doubt that the expansion of branches both at home and abroad was dramatic testimony to the large role they played in accommodating the overall economic expansion after the mid-1890s. A relatively few banks quickly penetrated all areas of new settlement with branches. Abroad, foreign branches accumulated the gold and foreign exchange that accompanied the massive capital inflow and made these available to finance the trade deficit. Sterling derived from the net inflow of capital from England before 1914 was transformed into United States dollars in New York largely to pay for a surplus of Canadian imports from the United States. According to McIvor (1958, p. 81), "the banks' exchange purchases, from exporters and borrowers, roughly offset the rising demands of importers for foreign funds." The smoothness with which these transactions were accomplished under the gold standard regime underlines the mobility of capital promoted by the operation of the banking system and the role this played in helping to maintain balance of payments equilibrium.

It should be recognized that while banks played a major role by collaborating with the government in its commitment to the gold standard, their role was largely one of a passive facilitator. This is seen in the pro-cyclical behavior of the money supply and in the close correspondence between the business cycle at home and abroad (Chambers, 1964).[3] Indeed, it will be argued below that within the gold standard context neither the government nor the banks had much scope for active monetary policy. Control of the money supply through sterilization was not possible. The greater elasticity of the money supply under branch banking also permitted greater volatility of prices (Williamson, 1989).

This chapter maintains that these institutions of banking, taken in conjunction with the government's precommitment to the gold standard and unrestricted international capital flows, were uniquely appropriate to facilitate Canada's growth experience in 1870–1914. Given the premium placed by the National Policy on growth relative to other economic goals such as stability and distribution, the gold standard was a durable monetary regime that smoothly accommodated growth within this institutional context. The key to this accommodation, to which we now turn, is the mechanism by which the balance of payments adjusted to the major disturbances caused by net capital inflow.

Capital mobility and balance of payments adjustment

Capital flows introduce a new element into the gold standard literature on balance of payments adjustment that had hitherto focused mainly on adjustment dominated by trade flows in an environment where the balance of payments was virtually synonymous with the balance of trade. According to the classical view, long-term capital flows are exogenous and short-term flows are driven by interest rate differentials. The inflow of long-term capital caused a balance of payments surplus that resulted in an inflow of gold and secondary reserves. This expansion of the monetary base led to an expansion of notes and deposits and to an increase in the nominal money supply, which led in turn to a rise in the Canadian price level. The higher price level raised the costs of exports relative to imports, deteriorating the trade balance enough to finance the inflow of capital. In the short run, inflows of long-term capital should have driven short-term interest rates in Canada down, pushing short-term capital abroad and temporarily relieving some of the pressure on money and prices. Most inflows of reserves and variation in them through time fell upon call loans and deposits in New York and London, with gold reserves representing a small, stable, and declining fraction of primary and total reserves (Viner, 1924).

The classical treatment of international short-term capital flows, however, involves a fallacy of composition. Individual wealth holders may shift their portfolios toward securities whose interest rates are rising and away from securities whose interest rates are falling. But when all wealth owners behave in this way, excess demand is created for securities whose rates are rising and excess supply for securities whose rates are falling. The higher rates fall and the lower rates rise until wealth holders are prepared to hold the outstanding stocks of securities. Remaining differences among interest rates in a well-functioning capital market result from the risk evaluations of investors.

Without addressing this basic problem with the theory, subsequent generations of economists have modified Viner's interpretation to emphasize the interdependence between the growth and investment process and the net capital inflow by allowing for foreign trade multipliers (e.g., Meier, 1953; Ingram, 1957; Stovel, 1959; Cairncross, 1968). Nevertheless, the basic problem did not go unnoticed. Angell (1925a, 1925b, 1925c), for example, noted that the data show no clear sequence from the gold and secondary reserves of the banks to the Canadian money supply and price level. Even Viner (1924, p. 171) had noticed that it seemed as though the banks were adjusting their reserves to their note and deposit liabilities rather than vice versa. And Taussig (1927), Viner's teacher, had serious doubts about the price-specie-flow mechanism applied to the American case (Flanders, 1989, pp. 233–236).

The missing link in the historical literature about the adjustment process in a world of international capital mobility generally, and in the Canadian case in particular, is the determination of asset equilibrium in a multinational context. The present chapter offers a model that overcomes the shortcomings of the simple price-specie-flow model by viewing the balance of payments as a monetary phenomenon operating within a framework of international capital mobility.[4] Building on earlier work (Johnson, 1958a; Fleming, 1962; Mundell, 1963; Harkness, 1969; Floyd, 1969, 1985; Mussa, 1982), we present a portfolio model of balance of payments adjustment that assumes interest rate arbitrage and leads to international price linkages without requiring strict purchasing power parity (McCloskey and Zecher, 1976, 1984).

This portfolio model maintains that it was the expansion of investment associated with Canadian growth and financed by capital inflow that increased aggregate demand and raised the price level. The rise in prices had two effects. First, it led to an increase in imports relative to exports creating a balance of trade deficit equal to the net capital inflow. Second, together with the growth of output, it led to an increase in the demand for nominal money holdings by domestic residents. To maintain portfolio equilibrium, these residents exchanged assets for money on the international market at world interest rates. The Canadian banking system was obliged, given convertibility of banknotes and deposits into gold, to provide the desired additions to the money supply, thereby financing the rise in the price level. In the process, banks acquired the observed increases in their holdings of gold and secondary reserves in New York and London.

The portfolio theory of adjustment has two principal parts. The first part explains the determination of the price level and the balance of trade in a world where capital is internationally mobile. The second part explains the significance of asset equilibrium to balance of payments adjustment under capital mobility. A small-country assumption is appropriate.

The determination of the Canadian price level

The long-standing quantity theory view that the price level is determined by the quantity of money does not apply in an unqualified manner to a small open economy where openness includes unrestricted participation in the world capital market and the exchange rate is fixed, as under the gold standard. The world price level is determined by the world money supply but the money supplies of individual countries like Canada are endogenous. The Canadian price level was the outcome of both the real forces that affected non-traded goods' prices relative to the prices of traded goods (for which Canada was a price taker), and the monetary conditions that prevailed in the rest of the world transmitted to Canada through the markets for traded goods in the context of world capital market integration.

The essence of Canadian price-level determination can be captured by a highly simplified model that includes only one internationally traded good and two non-traded goods. Equality of the total payments and receipts of domestic residents in a small open economy is the point of departure.

$$P_U U + P_T T + DSB = P_U U_C + P_T T_C + S, \tag{6.1}$$

where P_U and P_T are the prices of non-traded and traded goods respectively, U and T are the domestic outputs of the respective goods, U_C and T_C are the quantities of them consumed, S is domestic savings, and DSB is net repatriated earnings (interest and dividend receipts from abroad minus the corresponding payments to foreigners), sometimes referred to as the debt service balance. (6.1) says that total earnings from the production of traded and non-traded goods plus net earnings from abroad must be either saved or spent on the consumption of traded and non-traded goods.

Total domestic investment expenditures can be expressed as

$$I = P_U U_I + P_T T_I, \tag{6.2}$$

where U_I and T_I are the quantities of the two goods absorbed into investment. Adding and subtracting the level of investment on the right-hand side of (6.1) yields

$$P_U U + P_T T + DSB = P_U (U_C + U_I) + P_T (T_C + T_I) + S - I. \tag{6.3}$$

Equality of the demand and supply of the non-traded good implies

$$U = U_C + U_I. \tag{6.4}$$

Combining (6.4) and (6.3) yields

$$P_T(T - T_C - T_I) + DSB + I - S = 0 . \tag{6.5}$$

The balance of trade plus the debt service balance plus the net capital inflow must sum to zero as a condition of real goods market equilibrium.

The equilibrium relative price of non-traded goods can be shown to depend on a set of real factors exogenous to the domestic economy. (6.4) and (6.5) can be expanded by imposing some standard behavioral relations (Dick and Floyd, 1991, 1992). Consumption depends on income with the division between traded and non-traded goods depending on the price ratio P_U/P_T. Investment depends on the level of output, the rate of interest, and technological change and natural resource discoveries. Again, the division between non-traded and traded goods-demand depends on relative prices. On the supply side, aggregate output depends on the stocks of labor and capital in the economy and on technology. And the allocation of output between non-traded and traded goods depends on relative prices. Finally, aggregate income depends on aggregate output, the debt service balance, and the exogenously determined terms of trade. The equilibrium relative price of non-traded in terms of traded goods can be obtained by substituting these behavioral relations into (6.4) and rearranging the resulting expression to bring P_U/P_T to the left-hand side.[5] The result is of the form

$$\frac{P_U}{P_T} = Q(N, K, DSB, r, \mu, \Omega) , \tag{6.6}$$

where N and K are the stocks of labor and capital, r is the real rate of interest, μ is the terms of trade, and Ω is a portmanteau variable incorporating technological change and natural resource discoveries.

The effects of changes in N and K on the relative price variable are ambiguous because they shift the demand for non-traded goods and the supply in the same direction. A fall in r increases investment and the demand for the non-traded good, causing P_U/P_T to rise. An improvement in the terms of trade raises income and consumption, again increasing the demand for and relative price of the non-traded good.[6] The effect of the portmanteau variable is positive by construction – technological change permitted the development of new land, leading to an increase in the demand for non-traded goods. A decline in the debt service balance over time resulting from net inflows of capital reduces the income associated with each level of domestic output and results in lower relative prices of non-traded goods than otherwise.

The domestic price level, defined in terms of the prices of goods produced, can be expressed as a geometrically weighted index of traded and non-traded goods' prices. Taken in combination with (6.6), this gives

$$P = P_U^\alpha P_T^{1-\alpha} = \left[\frac{P_U}{P_T}\right]^\alpha P_T = [Q(N,K,DSB,r,\mu,\Omega)]^\alpha P_T, \tag{6.7}$$

where α is the share of the non-traded good in domestic output. The price of traded goods can then be expressed in terms of the price index of goods produced abroad as follows:

$$P_T = \frac{1}{(q^*)^{\alpha^*}} P^*, \tag{6.8}$$

where q^* is the ratio of non-traded to traded goods' prices in the rest of the world, P^* is the index of output prices abroad, and α^* is the share of non-traded goods in the rest of the world's price index. Substitution into (6.7) yields:

$$P = \frac{[Q(N,K,DSB,r,\mu,\Omega)]^\alpha}{(q^*)^{\alpha^*}} P^*. \tag{6.9}$$

Since the Canadian real interest rate equals the foreign rate plus a risk premium, equation (6.9) can be rewritten:

$$P = [Q(N,K,DSB,r^* + \Phi,\mu,\Omega)]^\alpha P_T$$
$$= \frac{[Q(N,K,DSB,r^* + \Phi,\mu,\Omega)]^\alpha}{(q^*)^{\alpha^*}} P^*. \tag{6.10}$$

This reduces to (6.9) when the risk premium Φ is zero.

The domestic economy is too small to have any influence on the price level and interest rate in the rest of the world, so (6.10) is sufficient to determine the domestic price level. Domestic goods are more or less expensive than the rest of the world's goods in accordance with the conditions of their production and the extent of the demand for them on the part of world (including domestic) residents. Whether the price level at home is high or low relative to foreign prices depends therefore on real factors relating to production and consumption. Neither the supply nor demand for money in the *domestic* economy has any influence.

Canadian asset equilibrium under the gold standard

The outstanding feature of the balance of payments adjustment process under the gold standard was the ease with which Canadian bankers and wealth holders in general could adjust their holdings of domestic and foreign securities in the face of disturbances to their portfolio equilibria wrought by the activities of foreign investors. The existence of an international capital market and the telegraphic communication that gave

Canada a presence in important financial centers like London and New York established the type of environment in which the portfolio adjustments necessary to maintain balance of payments equilibrium, given fixed gold parities, could take place with relative ease. Interest rates in Canada and abroad could thus adjust to levels at which wealth holders were content to hold the existing stocks of domestic and foreign securities.

Although capital was internationally transferable in the sense that there was little or no restriction on the compositions of wealth holders' portfolios, it was doubtless the case that capital was less than perfectly mobile internationally in the sense that wealth holders regarded domestic and foreign assets as less than perfect substitutes. Imperfect substitutability was reflected in interest rate differentials that incorporated risk premia. These premia reflected the usual default and political risks as well as the risk of depreciation arising from potential abandonment of the gold standard. International trade in capital assets was not artificially restricted in any important way.

The keys to the portfolio adjustment model are the equations determining the demand for money and the stock of foreign exchange reserves.

$$M = P L(r^*, \Phi, Y) \tag{6.11}$$

$$R = \delta(r^* + \Phi, V, Z) M, \tag{6.12}$$

where M is the nominal stock of money, R is the domestic stock of international reserves, $L(r^*, \Phi, Y)$ is the demand function for money, $\delta(r^* + \Phi, V, Z)$ is the equilibrium ratio of international reserves to the money supply, Z is the real debt service balance ($= DSB/P$), and V is a scale variable representing the size of the banking system.[7] A rise in the real debt service balance increases the reserve ratio – the banking system holds more short-term assets under conditions where the country's long-term indebtedness is high since more international transactions are likely to occur. The level of the function $\delta(r^* + \Phi, V, Z)$ will also depend on the variance of trade flows, held constant here.

The demand for money depends on both domestic and foreign interest rates (or equivalently, on the foreign interest rate and the risk premium), and reduces to the standard form $L(r, Y)$ when capital is perfectly mobile.[8] In either case, the arguments in the function are exogenous and cannot adjust in the face of any excess demand or supply of money as they would in a closed economy. Instead, the nominal money supply must adjust endogenously to changes in demand.

Balance of payments adjustment under the gold standard ensures this endogeneity. Suppose, for example, that the banking system creates through its domestic loan and discount policies less money than domestic residents want to hold. Domestic residents, having insufficient money holdings, will sell assets to acquire them. As this sale of assets spills over into the international capital market, the foreign currency acquired is taken to the banks and converted into domestic currency. The banks thereby acquire international reserves and create money in equal amounts. Similarly, if the banks create more money than domestic residents want to hold the non-banking public will buy assets abroad, forcing the banks to reduce the money supply and lose reserves in equal amounts. The banks can therefore control their reserve levels by expanding and contracting domestic credit. An expansion leads to excess money holdings on the part of the public and an outflow of reserves as money holdings return to their desired level; a contraction leads to deficient money holdings and an expansion of reserves as the public remedies the deficiency. While the banking system controls its reserve levels by appropriately adjusting domestic credit policies, however, it has *no* control over the domestic money supply. The latter always equals whatever domestic residents want to hold. The banks can only control the division of their asset portfolios between domestic loans and discounts and international reserves.

Equations (6.11) and (6.12) show that the country's stock of international reserves depends on the demand for money and the banking system's reserve ratio. In Canada before 1914, the public's desired money holdings determined the banking system's note and deposit liabilities and the outstanding stock of small-denomination Dominion notes. The various factors, such as interest rates, that affect the profit-maximizing reserve ratios of banks, and the government's chosen gold reserve ratio against its Dominion note liabilities translated this demand for money into a demand for international reserves.[9] Changes in the gold stock and the stock of reserves have no causal effect on the domestic price level. Indeed, the opposite is the case. Increases in the price level emanating from real forces of demand and supply and/or monetary developments in the rest of the world cause the public to hold more money, which in turn causes the banks to create that money and hold larger reserves.

The balance of payments surplus is the flow of increases per unit of time in the country's stock of international reserves. Combining (6.11) and (6.12) and differentiating with respect to time holding the risk premium constant yields

$$\frac{dR}{dt} = [\delta(r^*+\Phi,V,Z)\,L(r^*,\Phi,Y)]\frac{dP}{dt} + [\delta(r^*+\Phi,V,Z)\,P\,L_{r^*} + M\,\delta_{r^*}]\frac{dr^*}{dt}$$

$$+ [\delta(r^*+\Phi,V,Z)\,P\,L_y]\frac{dY}{dt} + [M\,\delta_v]\frac{dV}{dt} + [M\,\delta_z]\frac{dZ}{dt}, \qquad (6.13)$$

where δ_j and $L_{j,}$ $(j=r^*,y,v,z)$, are partial derivatives in the functions $\delta(r^*+\Phi,V,Z)$ and $L(r^*,\Phi,Y)$. dP/dt and dY/dt are the derivatives of the equilibrium levels of P and Y with respect to time, dV/dt and dZ/dt are exogenous (but dV/dt could possibly be represented by some function of dY/dt and dM/dt), and dr^*/dt is determined abroad.

A final perspective on the nature and implications of asset equilibrium is provided by observing that aggregate savings in (6.5) can be split into two components – the banking system's accumulation of gold and secondary reserves, denoted by dR/dt, and all other net accumulations of assets by domestic residents on both private and public account, denoted by S'

$$S = \frac{dR}{dt} + S'. \tag{6.14}$$

Since the prices of non-traded and traded goods and the quantities of both goods produced and consumed are unaffected by the change in the level of bank reserves, the flow of reserves has no effect on savings. Thus, S' declines (increases) dollar for dollar with increases (declines) in dR/dt.

Changes in the balance of payments surplus or deficit thus arise solely from changes in the proportion of the economy's savings that takes the form of government gold and gold and secondary reserve accumulations of the chartered banks. If domestic residents want to add to their money balances at an increased rate, they allocate a greater proportion of their savings to the accumulation of bank notes and deposits and a smaller proportion to the accumulation of other assets. The banks are forced to supply this additional money either by accumulating international reserves or by expanding their domestic loan portfolios. The amount of reserves accumulated depends on the banking system's desired ratio of reserves to note and deposit liabilities.[10] In contrast to the standard classical price-specie-flow mechanism, there is no direct causal relationship between the inflow of gold and secondary reserves and the balance of trade. Changes in the balance of trade can affect the gold inflow only if they lead to changes in the private sector's desired rate of monetary growth. These conclusions do not depend on whether capital is perfectly or imperfectly mobile. Even if the risk premium varies through time, imperfection of capital mobility can have no fundamental effect on the process by which balance of payments adjustment occurs.

It is also evident from the above that the existence of Dominion notes does not alter our interpretation of balance of payments adjustment. Subject to the reserve requirement and the prohibition against small-denomination bank notes, the quantity of Dominion notes held was voluntary. As Rich (1988) points out, the government did attempt to increase the outstanding stock of Dominion notes relative to its gold backing in the early days of Confederation and thereby economize on the cost of servicing the public debt. But we regard this as fiscal rather than monetary policy. Although it undoubtedly reduced bank profits, it did not affect the money supply – the public could adjust its money holdings by buying and selling assets abroad, thereby forcing the banks to create whatever money supply it desired. The government could not use Dominion notes as an instrument of monetary policy as the term is usually defined. Changes in reserve requirements and in the size of the gold stock used as backing for Dominion notes would have resulted in net changes in international reserves and in the observed flow balance of payments adjustments, but these changes must have been exogenous as far as the balance of payments adjustment mechanism was concerned.

Canadian evidence and the portfolio theory

The appendices in Dick and Floyd (1992) describe an extensive body of data pertaining to Canadian trade, income, money, prices, and interest rates now available for the 1871–1913 period. This permits a longer-term perspective than was possible for Viner (1924) who began his story with 1900. The statistical relationship among capital flows, relative prices, and the balance of trade, and the connection between monetary equilibrium and bank portfolios does not discriminate between our portfolio theoretic approach and earlier views of the adjustment process. It is the results of tests concerning the determinants of international reserve flows combined with a demonstration that short-term capital flows were not related to domestic/foreign interest rate differentials that offer the principal evidence in support of our reinterpretation of balance of payments adjustment. It can also be shown that the crude classical mechanism of adjustment, in the presence of international capital mobility, is inconsistent with ordinary maximizing behavior (Dick and Floyd, 1992, chapter 9).

In the classical approach, the balance of payments is defined as the sum of two separately determined partial equilibrium components: the balance of trade (determined by domestic and foreign incomes and relative prices) and net capital inflow (with long-term flows determined exogenously and short-term flows determined by interest rate differentials). In the portfolio approach, by contrast, a balance of payments surplus arises from an increase in the desired rates of accumulation of money balances by domestic residents and/or reserves by banks. The determinants of the trade balance are the same in both theories, but the portfolio approach is distinctive in placing the trade balance in a general equilibrium context such that capital inflow determines the trade balance via its effect on aggregate demand and domestic and foreign prices.

To confirm the classical adjustment mechanism when capital mobility is present requires more than a well-fitting trade balance equation. Since net capital flows enter additively in the classical approach, the trade balance determinants should also figure directly in determining the balance of payments surplus. According to that view, the real balance of payments surplus is determined by relative domestic and foreign prices, domestic and foreign incomes, the exogenous real long-term net capital inflow, and the ratio of domestic to foreign interest rates. And since the trade balance and capital flow enter classical balance of payments determination as independent additive components, the coefficients of relative prices and incomes should be the same whether the dependent variable is the balance of trade or the balance of payments surplus. According to the portfolio theory, however, there is no dependency between the balance of trade and the balance of payments surplus. The latter is strictly determined by changes in the demand for money on the part of the public and shifts in the chartered banks' portfolios between international reserves and other assets.

The traditional classical balance of payments adjustment mechanism can be specified as follows:

$$\frac{R_t - R_{t-1}}{P_{t-1}} = \phi_o + \phi_q PR_t + \phi_y Y_t + \phi_y^* Y_t^* + \phi_N LN_t + \phi_r \frac{r_t}{r_t^*} + \phi_z Z_t + u_t,$$

$$(6.15)$$

where R is the gold and secondary reserves of the chartered banks plus the gold reserves of the Government of Canada, PR_t is the ratio of the Canadian to the foreign price level, Y_t and Y_t^* are domestic and foreign incomes, LN_t is the long-term net capital inflow, Z_t is real net repatriated earnings on capital or debt service balance, and u_t is a random error term.

If the classical theory is true, relative prices and incomes have the same effect on the balance of trade as they do on the balance of payments. The balance of trade is determined according to

$$RBT_t = \gamma_o + \gamma_q PR_t + \gamma_y Y_t + \gamma_y^* Y_t^* + \gamma_n LN_t + \gamma_r \frac{r_t}{r_t^*} + \gamma_z Z_t + v_t, \quad (6.16)$$

where RBT_t is the real balance of trade, γ_z equals zero as long as the income variables are properly defined and, under the usual classical assumptions, γ_n and γ_r also equal zero.[11] If the classical specie-flow mechanism is the correct one with which to address the data, then $\phi_q = \gamma_q$, $\phi_y = \gamma_y$, and $\phi_y^* = \gamma_y^*$. And the coefficient ϕ_z should be unity in (6.15). If the portfolio theory is true, the coefficients ϕ_q, ϕ_y, and ϕ_y^* will be insignificantly different from zero in the balance of payments equation (6.15), and significantly negative, negative, and positive, respectively, in the balance of trade equation (6.16). In addition, the portfolio theory predicts that the coefficients of the long-term net capital inflow and the interest rate differential will be insignificantly different from zero in the balance of payments equation. The real balance of payments surplus is determined by the arguments in (6.13) (modified as

(6.17) below) independently of everything except the real debt service balance.

Equations (6.15) and (6.16) are estimated as a system using the seemingly unrelated regression technique.[12] Two sets of cross-equation restrictions are tested. First, the null hypothesis of the classical approach, that $\phi_q = \gamma_q$, $\phi_y = \gamma_y$, and $\phi_y^* = \gamma_y^*$ is soundly rejected with a χ^2 (3) of 39.3 and a tiny P-value.[13] Second, the null hypothesis of the portfolio approach, that all coefficients in the real reserve flow equation (6.15) except the real debt service balance are zero is not rejected. (The χ^2 (5) here is 8.08 and the P-value 0.152.) The portfolio theory outperforms the traditional specie-flow theory.

The two constrained equations are presented in columns (2) and (3) of table 6.1. The real reserve flow equation (column (3)) fits poorly with only the real long-term net capital inflow and domestic income variables significant at less than the 5 percent level and correctly signed. The crucial relative price and interest rate differential variables are insignificant and wrongly signed. The real trade balance equation (column (1)) fits extremely well.

Another comparison of the classical and portfolio approaches can be made by deriving an estimating equation for the portfolio theory from (6.11), (6.12), and (6.13) and comparing the fit with that of equation (6.15):[14]

$$\frac{R_t - R_{t-1}}{P_{t-1}} = \beta_{r*}\left(\frac{R_{t-1}}{P_{t-1}}\right)[r_{t*} - r_{t*-1}] + \beta_y\left(\frac{R_{t-1}}{P_{t-1}}\right)\left[\frac{Y_t - Y_{t-1}}{Y_{t-1}}\right]$$

$$+ \beta_v\left(\frac{R_{t-1}}{P_{t-1}}\right)\left[\frac{V_t - V_{t-1}}{V_{t-1}}\right] + \beta_p\left(\frac{R_{t-1}}{P_{t-1}}\right)\left[\frac{P_t - P_{t-1}}{P_{t-1}}\right] \qquad (6.17)$$

$$+ \beta_z\left(\frac{M_{t-1}}{P_{t-1}}\right)[Z_t - Z_{t-1}] + w_t$$

where

$$\beta_{r*} = \frac{1}{L}\frac{\partial L}{\partial r^*} + \frac{1}{\delta}\frac{\partial \delta}{\partial r^*}, \ \beta_y = \frac{Y}{L}\frac{\partial L}{\partial Y}, \ \beta_v = \frac{V}{L}\frac{\partial L}{\partial V}, \ \beta_z = \delta_z, \ \beta_p = 1.0.$$

The estimates of equation (6.17) are shown in table 6.2. A dummy variable was incorporated to account for shifts in the structure of the banking system around 1890. The standard errors are substantially lower than those of the estimate of (6.15) (given in column (3) of table 6.1). The price-level coefficient is insignificantly different from unity and the debt service coefficient is significantly negative to indicate that an increase in the real deficit on debt service brings an increase in the real reserve inflow.

We now pool the independent variables in (6.15) and (6.17) in a single estimating equation for the real reserve flow and perform two F-tests:[15] (1)

Table 6.1 *The balance of trade, balance of payments, and relative prices*

	OLS Real trade account surplus (1)	SUR Real trade account surplus (2)	SUR Real balance of payments surplus (3)	OLS Non-traded goods' prices: Canada ÷ rest of world (4)
Constant	26.64 (0.506)	75.27 (1.33)	−71.48 (−1.15)	106.4 (69.2)
Canadian price level + rest of world price level	−1.24 (−3.12)	−1.74 (−3.56)	0.506 (0.951)	
Canadian real income	−3.20 (−8.60)	−2.81 (−5.44)	−1.31 (−2.33)	
Rest of world real income	4.30 (7.65)	4.21 (5.94)	1.52 (1.96)	
Long-term net capital inflow		0.111 (0.880)	0.263 (1.92)	
Canadian long-term interest rate ÷ UK long-term interest rate		−0.518 (−0.036)	−10.24 (−0.647)	
Real debt service balance		0.990 (1.764)	−0.339 (−0.554)	
Total real net capital inflow				0.231 (8.69)
Number of observations	42	42	42	42
R^2	0.897	0.906	0.229	0.653
Standard error	16.194	16.171	17.654	8.266
Durbin–Watson	1.77	1.945	2.385	0.488

Note:
The figures in brackets are t ratios.

Table 6.2 *Estimation of the real reserve under the portfolio theory*

	Real balance of payments surplus	
	(1)	(2)[a]
Constant	6.38	6.43
	(2.87)	(2.38)
Price-level variable	1.03	1.0
	(1.62)	
Foreign real interest rate variable	−0.17	−0.17
	(−5.78)	(−5.89)
Canadian real income variable	−1.18	−1.18
	(−2.32)	(−2.41)
Scale of banking system variable	0.734	0.731
	(2.39)	(2.44)
Debt service variable	−0.003	−0.003
	(−4.51)	(−4.78)
Dummy variable	−6.03	−6.08
	(−1.73)	(−1.84)
Number of observations	42	42
R^2	0.780	0.774
Standard error	9.423	9.292
Durbin–Watson	1.979	1.971

Notes:
[a] In calculating this regression, the coefficient of the price-level variable is constrained to equal unity.
The figures in brackets are *t*-ratios.

that the explanatory variables in the classical theory contribute no explanation to real reserve flows beyond what the portfolio theory variables explain; and (2) that the explanatory variables in the portfolio theory contribute no explanation to real reserve flows beyond what the classical theory variables explain. We obtain $F(6,29)=1.84$ for inclusion of the classical variables and $F(6,29)=18.62$ for inclusion of the portfolio variables. Hypothesis (1) can be rejected only at about the 12 percent level, while (2) is soundly rejected with a tiny P-value. The portfolio variables clearly dominate. The portfolio theory hypothesis that the price coefficient in (6.17) is unity and that all the classical variables are zero cannot be rejected – $F(7,29)=1.58$ for these restrictions, resulting in a P-value of 0.179.

In our earlier work (Dick and Floyd, 1991, 1992) we searched for a relationship between short-term capital flows and the differential of Canadian over rest of the world interest rates of the sort postulated by the classical theory. No convincing empirical relationship was found.

The interaction among capital flows, relative prices and the balance of trade is consistent with a portfolio theory of adjustment. Some part of the capital implanted during business expansions consisted of Canadian non-traded goods, thereby increasing domestic aggregate demand. The prices of Canadian non-traded goods were bid up relative to the prices of traded goods and of non-traded goods abroad. Domestic production of exports and consumption of imports fell and the trade balance deteriorated, reducing aggregate demand to make room for the increased domestic production of new capital goods. A trade deficit just sufficient in real terms to finance the inflow of capital emerged. The relationship between relative domestic and foreign non-traded goods' prices and the net capital inflow is clearly shown in regression (4) in table 6.1.[16]

Econometric analysis of the demand for money, the determinants of velocity, the composition of money holdings, and the composition of bank reserves for our period yields regression results that are consistent with our portfolio interpretation and sensitive to structural changes circa 1890 in the environment in which portfolio changes were being made (Dick and Floyd, 1992). It appears that the working of asset markets was undergoing substantial efficiency improvement during the early part of our period.

How Canada absorbed external shocks before 1914

There were three main episodes of net capital importation over the 1871–1913 period corresponding to long swings in the Atlantic economy (Thomas, 1973, pp. 256–258), as well as a number of international business cycles (Thorp, 1926, chapter 12; Chambers, 1964). These were all disturbances to which the balance of payments had to adjust. Here, we address primarily the long swing evidence, proceeding with reference to figure 6.1.

In the early years following Confederation prosperity lasted until 1873 and was accompanied by rising net capital inflows. Gross immigration, railroad capital formation, and residential construction all rose as better investment opportunities were perceived in Canada relative to England, the origin of most of the capital inflow. The relative prices of non-traded goods rose. The production costs of exports and the consumption of imports also rose, leaving a deficit in the trade balance to match the capital inflow. In addition, the terms of trade, exogenous to Canada, began to turn in Canada's favor, a factor that probably helped stimulate the net capital inflow and contributed to the trade deficit. Bank branches, note issue and

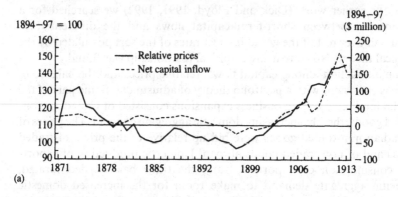

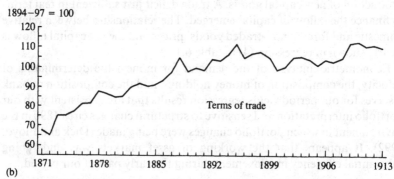

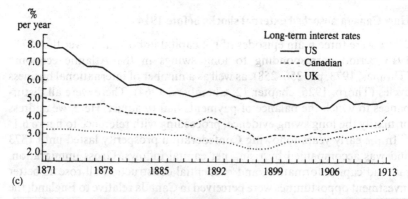

6.1   Canadian relative to foreign prices of all goods, real net capital
        inflows, the terms of trade, and long-term interest rates

the money supply increased in response to the increased demand for money as output and prices rose. While the Bank of England was experiencing a fall in reserves and gold was flowing out of England, gold was not flowing conspicuously into Canada (Viner, 1924; Rich, 1988), so that the mechanism of adjustment cannot have been from the gold flow to money to prices (Thomas, 1973, p. 264).

The above pattern was substantially reversed from 1875 until 1880. While Canada continued to run a current account deficit, this deficit and the associated net capital inflow declined markedly to 1879 and the prices of non-traded goods fell faster than prices in general. Improvement in the terms of trade also slackened. As a result, the rise in the money stock flattened and bank expansion slowed (Bloomfield, 1968, p. 25). Gross immigration, net capital formation and residential construction all declined. A similar slump was occurring in the United States at the same time. Meanwhile, shipbuilding and new construction were booming in England (Thomas, 1973, p. 268). There was little gold loss from Canada, however, as banks moved to adjust their reserve ratios downward (Rich, 1988). Banks were, of course, unable to influence interest rates. The Canadian rate moved more into line with US and UK rates, at least in part because of the increased integration of Canada into world asset markets.

The next long upswing of capital inflow and domestic capital formation occurred in the first half of the 1880s after the US resumption, followed by a downswing into the mid-1890s. Once again pressure on Canadian resources is evident in the rise of Canadian non-traded goods' prices relative to traded goods' prices and to non-traded goods' prices in the rest of the world. All these price movements, as before, helped goods' markets to clear and the current account deficit increased. The capital inflow supported a new round of population-sensitive domestic capital formation in railroads and urban construction. During this expansion the Canadian Pacific Railway was completed. At the same time, new residential construction and shipbuilding in the United Kingdom declined (Thomas, 1973, p. 268). By the late 1880s, however, all of these movements tended to reverse themselves once again. As the pressure on Canadian resources subsided, the prices of non-traded goods in Canada fell faster than elsewhere.

The last episode of capital inflow and expansion was the most dramatic of all with only a minor interruption during the crisis of 1907–08. Net capital inflows rose to unprecedented heights and the pressure on Canadian resources drove non-traded goods' prices strongly upward relative to both traded goods' prices and non-traded goods' prices in the rest of the world. Even though Canadian wheat production and exports rose substantially toward the end of the period, Canada's contribution to world totals was modest and unlikely to have been a factor in moderating the movement in the terms of trade. Overall price movements created a trade deficit to match the capital inflow. Banks grew apace to meet the increase in the demand for money as output and prices rose.

The crisis of 1907 further illustrates the application of our portfolio interpretation of balance of payments adjustment. Research on this crisis demonstrates that there was no significant relationship between seasonal variations in the balance of trade and in the balance of payments surplus and that the rise in world interest rates at the time led to a reduction in the demand for money balances in Canada and downward pressure on chartered bank reserves (Rich, 1989). The banks would have been forced to cut domestic loans to maintain reserve ratios had the government not supplied them with advances in the form of Dominion notes against the collateral of high-grade securities. The banks then redeemed some of these Dominion notes in gold. In effect the chartered banks were allowed to maintain their reserve levels in the face of a decline in the nominal money stock by borrowing from the government rather than reducing their lending to grain exporters in the peak season. Had the banks reduced their loans, exporters would have had borrow abroad, with the conversion of the borrowed funds into Canadian dollars providing the desired inflow of bank reserves. The issue here is not the size of money supply, which is unaffected by how the demand for money is met, but the composition of bank liabilities and the locus of borrowing by domestic exporters. The banks and the government characteristically worked together to supply the needs of business within the framework provided by the gold standard. The Canadian banks did not experience financial stress of the sort experienced abroad largely because of the soundness of the banks themselves – panic conversions of deposits into notes did not occur.

The durability of Canada's gold standard regime

What, then, were the fundamental constituents that made the gold standard so successful in the Canadian case? What distinguished the gold standard as a monetary regime worthy of survival for so long? Canada shared in two features of the gold standard era (Schwartz, 1986, p. 70). This era was one of peace and Canada, like other nations that sustained a long history of adherence to the gold standard, possessed a government that exercised an unshakeable precommitment to gold and pursued a national economic policy that was largely "acquiescent." At no time prior to 1914 did Canada suspend convertibility of bank or Dominion notes into gold. Confidence was maintained throughout. At the same time, Canada paid the price of following the international business cycle rather closely (Chambers, 1964) by forfeiting domestic control over her money supply, allowing the latter to remain endogenous.

Because Canada was a small country and offered no restrictions to the free flow of international capital, however, the gold standard regime was even more likely to be durable. Banks and government could hold whatever stock of gold they wished within reason without having adverse effects on prices and employment (Floyd, 1985, p. 65). The banking system provided the perfect vehicle for asset holders to arrange their portfolios in whatever way necessary to ensure that the demand for money was satisfied.

This regime came to an end only when the government instituted a new means of money creation that enabled the banks to extend credit outside the discipline of the gold standard. Under the Finance Act, passed to help finance Canada's contribution to the First World War, banks could borrow reserves without limit from the government by pledging an equivalent amount of purchases of public debt. Redemption of Dominion notes in gold was suspended. The essential constituent of the gold standard, pre-commitment to gold, had been forsaken.

Notes

The authors would like to thank Anna Schwartz, Michael Bordo and Forrest Capie for their comments and suggestions in preparing this chapter.

1 Britain resumed specie payments in 1821 after the Napoleonic Wars. She and most other countries abandoned gold in 1931. Bordo and Schwartz (1984, p. 1).

2 The currency used in Canada had been fixed in terms of gold since before Confederation (which occurred in 1867). Convertibility essentially ended with the passage of the Finance Act in 1914, at the beginning of the First World War.

3 Canada's business cycle was more closely related to that of the United States than that of the United Kingdom, a fact not inconsistent with alternating long swings on either side of the Atlantic (Lewis, 1978, chapter 1).

4 The monetary nature of balance of payments adjustment in our model arises from the implications of capital mobility and is not imposed by any prior commitment to monetarism. Indeed, controversy still abounds over the application of the so-called "monetary approach" (Mundell, 1968; Frenkel and Johnson, 1976) to the historical gold standard (Bordo and Schwartz, 1984).

5 Identical results are obtained by substituting the behavioral relations into (6.5).

6 When the terms of trade are exogenous exports and imports can be aggregated into a single good, so extension of the model to four goods would complicate it unnecessarily. A change in the terms of trade can be viewed as a change in the export relative to the import price component of the index of traded goods prices without a change in P_T itself.

7 In simple terms, the theory underlying these two equations is as follows. Each country's residents hold the portfolio mix of domestic assets, foreign assets, and money that maximizes utility. Any given portfolio mix in each country generates two marginal rates of substitution – between domestic physical capital assets and money and foreign physical capital assets and money. These two marginal rates of substitution are the reciprocals of the interest rates at which the country's residents are prepared to hold that particular mix of assets in their portfolios. Assets are exchanged among domestic and foreign residents until the interest rate at which both countries' residents hold each country's assets is the same. These levels of domestic and foreign interest rates are determined simultaneously with the equilibrium portfolio mixes of the residents of the two countries. The excess of the domestic over the foreign interest rate is the risk premium on domestic assets in the world capital market.

8 Zero expected inflation and full employment are assumed. It is well known that there was virtually no correlation between interest rates and inflation rates under the gold standard (Barsky and Summers, 1988). Sargent (1973) also found evidence of very long adjustment lags in United States data symptomatic of nearly static expectations. The time-path of price adjustment, however, remains controversial. Relaxing these assumptions would complicate, though not significantly alter, the conclusions of the present analysis (Dick, 1990).

9 The chartered banks' gold holdings as a proportion of their total reserves also depended on interest rates and profit considerations.

10 Substitution of (6.13) into (6.5) yields

$$dR/dt = P_T(T - T_C - T_I) + DSB + I - S'$$

which is the balance of payments surplus stated in the traditional manner as the trade surplus plus the debt service balance plus the autonomous net capital inflow. The interpretation of this equation differs from that of the traditional one, however, in that dR/dt is affected only by S', and not by either the balance of trade or DSB.

11 More sophisticated versions of the traditional approach would postulate, via the transfer mechanism, a negative relationship between the real long-term net capital inflow and the real trade balance, and (normally) a positive relationship between the real long-term net capital inflow and the balance of payments surplus. An inflow of capital would increase spending and imports at home and reduce spending and imports abroad, but the total balance of trade effect would normally be less than the capital inflow itself (Johnson, 1958b). The portfolio approach views the overall net capital inflow as the critical determinant of the trade balance, requiring relative price (real exchange rate) adjustments to bring the latter into line with it. There is no reason why the division of that total net capital flow into its short-term and long-term components should have any effect on the demand for domestic relative to foreign goods and the balance of trade.

It might also be argued that domestic/foreign interest rate differentials might also affect the trade balance. Higher domestic interest rates will reduce domestic investment, and with it the level of imports.

12 We would like to thank Gordon Anderson, Alan Hynes, Greg Jump, Angelo Melino, and Rick Simes for suggesting this particular approach, and Angelo Melino and Dwayne Benjamin for helpful discussions regarding interpretation of the results.
13 If the restrictions are broadened to include $\phi_z = 1$ and $\gamma_z = 0$, rejection occurs with a χ^2 (5) value of 60.4.
14 First differences of (6.13) are divided by the price level at time $t - 1$ and translated into elasticities using (6.11) and (6.12).
15 For further non-nested tests, namely J-tests and complete parameter encompassing tests, see Dick and Floyd (1991, 1992).
16 For further details, see Dick and Floyd (1991, 1992).

References

Angell, J.W., 1925a. "The effects of international payments in the past," in *The Inter-ally Debts and the United States*, National Industrial Conference Board, New York: NICB: 138–189.
    1925b. "Review of Canada's balance of international indebtedness 1900–1913," *Political Science Quarterly*, 40: 320–322.
    1925c. *The Theory of International Prices: History, Criticism and Restatement*, Cambridge, MA: Harvard University Press.
Ankli, Robert E., 1980. "The growth of the Canadian economy, 1896–1920. Export led and/or neoclassical growth," *Explorations in Economic History*, 17 (July): 251–274.
Barsky, Robert B. and Lawrence H. Summers, 1988. "Gibson's paradox and the gold standard," *Journal of Political Economy*, 96 (June): 528–550.
Beckhart, Benjamin Haggott, 1929. *The Banking System of Canada*, New York: Henry Holt.
Bloomfield, Arthur I., 1968. "Patterns of Fluctuation in International Investment Before 1914," *Princeton Studies in International Finance*, Princeton: Princeton University Press.
    1986. "Financial crises, banking crises, stock market crashes and the money supply: some international evidence, 1870–1933," in F. Capie and G.E. Wood (eds.), *Financial Crises and the World Banking System*, New York: St. Martin's Press: 190–248.
Bordo, Michael D., 1985. "The impact and international transmission of financial crises: some historical evidence, 1870–1933," *Revista Di Storia Economica*, 2: 41–78.
Bordo, Michael D. and Anna Schwartz (eds.), 1984. *A Retrospective on the Classical Gold Standard: 1821–1931*, Chicago: University of Chicago Press.
Breckenridge, Roeliff Morton, 1910. National Monetary Commission, United States, Congress, and Senate, *The History of Banking in Canada*, doc. no. 332, 2nd session, 61st Congress, Washington, DC: Government Printing Office.
Buckley, K.A.H., 1952. "Urban building and real estate fluctuations in Canada," *Canadian Journal of Economics and Political Science*, 18 (February): 41–62.

1955. *Capital Formation in Canada 1896–1930*, Toronto: University of Toronto Press.

1963. "Working paper on population, labour force and economic growth," Banff Business Policies Conference on Canadian Economic Survival, Banff Advanced School of Advanced Management and the Universities of Alberta, Manitoba and Saskatchewan.

Cairncross, A.K., 1953. *Home and Foreign Investment 1890–1913*, Cambridge: Cambridge University Press.

1968. "Investment in Canada," in A.R. Hall (ed.), *The Export of Capital from Great Britain, 1870–1914*, London: Methuen.

Caves, Richard E., 1971. "Export-led growth and the new economic history," in J.N. Bhagwati, R.W. Jones, R.A. Mundell and J. Vanek (eds.), *Trade, Balance of Payments and Growth*, Amsterdam: North-Holland: 403–442.

Chambers, E.J., 1964. "Late nineteenth century business cycles in Canada," *Canadian Journal of Economics and Political Science*, 38 (August): 391–412.

Chambers, E.J. and D.F. Gordon, 1966. "Primary products and economic growth: an empirical measurement," *Journal of Political Economy*, 74 (August): 315–332.

Dick, Trevor J.O., 1990. "Price flexibility and economic instability in Canada: a preliminary investigation of 1870–1914," *Working Paper*, Berkeley: Department of Economics, University of California.

Dick, Trevor J.O. and J.E. Floyd, 1991. "Balance of payments adjustment under the international gold standard: Canada, 1871–1913," *Explorations in Economic History*, 28: 209–238.

1992. *Canada and the Gold Standard: Canada 1871–1913*, New York: Cambridge University Press.

Easterbrook, W.T. and H.G.J. Aitken, 1958. *Canadian Economic History*, Toronto: Macmillan.

Edelstein, M., 1982. *Overseas Investment in the Age of High Imperialism: The United Kingdom 1850–1914*, New York: Columbia University Press.

Field, Fred W., 1912. *Capital Investments in Canada*, Toronto: *Monetary Times of Canada*.

Flanders, M. June, 1989. *International Monetary Economics, 1870–1960*, Cambridge: Cambridge University Press.

Fleming, J.M., 1962. "Domestic financial policies under fixed and flexible exchange rates," *IMF Staff Papers*, 9 (November): 369–379.

Floyd, J.E., 1969. "International capital movements and monetary equilibrium," *American Economic Review*, 49 (September): 503–517.

1985. *World Monetary Equilibrium*, Philadelphia: University of Pennsylvania Press.

Frenkel, Jacob A. and Harry G. Johnson (eds.), 1976. *The Monetary Approach to the Balance of Payments*, Toronto: University of Toronto Press.

Goodhart, C.A.E., 1969. *The New York Money Market and the Finance of Trade, 1900–1913*, Cambridge, MA: Harvard University Press.

Green, Alan and M.C. Urquhart, 1987. "New estimates of output growth in

Canada: measurement and interpretation," in D. McCalla (ed.), *Perspectives on Canadian Economic History*, Toronto: Copp, Clark, Pitman: 182–199.

Harkness, Jon, 1969. *Monetary and Fiscal Policies in Closed and Open Economies: The Portfolio Approach*, Ph.D. dissertation, Queen's University.

Hay, K.A.J., 1966. "Early twentieth century business cycles in Canada," *Canadian Journal of Economics and Political Science*, 32 (August): 354–365.

1967. "Money and cycles in post Confederation Canada," *Journal of Political Economy*, 75: 263–273.

Ingram, J.C., 1957. "Growth and capacity in Canada's balance of payments," *American Economic Review*, 48 (March): 93–104.

Innis, H.A., 1936. "Significant factors in Canadian economic development," *Canadian Historical Review*, 18: 374–384.

Johnson, Harry G., 1958a. "Towards a general theory of the balance of payments," in H.G. Johnson (ed.), *International Trade and Economic Growth*, London: Allen & Unwin: 153–168.

1958b. "The transfer problem and exchange stability," in H.G. Johnson (ed.), *International Trade and Economic Growth*, London: Allen & Unwin: 169–195.

Johnson, Joseph French, 1910. National Monetary Commission, US, Congress, and Senate, *The Canadian Banking System*, Doc. no. 583, 2nd Session, 61st Congress, Washington, DC: Government Printing Office.

Lewis, W. Arthur, 1978. *Growth and Fluctuations, 1870–1913*, London: Allen & Unwin.

McCloskey, D.N. and J.R. Zecher, 1976. "How the gold standard worked, 1880–1913," in J.A. Frenkel and H.G. Johnson (eds.), *The Monetary Approach to the Balance of Payments*, London: Allen & Unwin: 357–385.

1984. "The success of Purchasing Power Parity: historical evidence and implications for macroeconomics," in M.D. Bordo and A. Schwartz (eds.), *A Retrospective on the Classical Gold Standard: 1821–1931*, Chicago: University of Chicago Press.

McIvor, R.C., 1958. *Canadian Monetary, Banking and Fiscal Development*, Toronto: Macmillan.

Meier, G.M., 1953. "Economic development and the transfer mechanism," *Canadian Journal of Economics and Political Science*, 19 (February): 1–19.

Morrison, G.R., 1966. *Liquidity Preferences of Commercial Banks*, Chicago: University of Chicago Press.

Mundell, Robert A., 1963. "Capital mobility and stabilization under fixed and flexible exchange rates," *Canadian Journal of Economics and Political Science*, 27 (November): 475–485.

1968. *International Economics*, New York: Macmillan.

Mussa, Michael, 1982. "A model of exchange rate dynamics," *Journal of Political Economy*, 90 (February): 74–104.

Paterson, D.G., 1976. *British Direct Investment in Canada, 1890–1914*, Toronto: University of Toronto Press.

Rich, George, 1988. *The Cross of Gold, Money and the Canadian Business Cycle, 1867–1913*, Ottawa: Carleton University Press.

1989. "Canadian banks, gold and the crisis of 1907," *Explorations in Economic History*, 26 (April): 135–160.

Rostow, W.W., 1978. *The World Economy, History and Prospect*, Austin: University of Texas Press.

Sargent, Thomas J., 1973. "Interest rates and prices in the long run," *Journal of Money, Credit and Banking*, 5 (February): 385–449.

Schwartz, Anna J., 1986. "Alternative monetary regimes: the gold standard," in C.D. Campbell and W.R. Dougan (eds.), *Alternative Monetary Regimes*, Baltimore: Johns Hopkins University Press: 44–72.

Stovel, John A., 1959. *Canada in the World Economy*, Cambridge, MA: Harvard University Press.

Taussig, Frank W., 1927. *International Trade*, New York: Macmillan.

Thomas, Brinley, 1973. *Migration and Economic Growth*, Cambridge: Cambridge University Press.

Thorp, Willard Long, 1926. *Business Annals*, New York: National Bureau of Economic Research.

Urquhart, M.C., 1986. "New estimates of Gross National Product, Canada, 1870–1926: some implications for Canadian development," in R. Gallman and S.L. Engermann (eds.), *Long-term Factors in American Economic Growth, NBER Studies in Income and Wealth*, Chicago: University of Chicago Press: 9–94.

Viner, Jacob, 1924. *Canada's Balance of International Indebtedness, 1900–1913*, Cambridge, MA: Harvard University Press.

Williamson, Stephen D., 1989. "Restrictions on financial intermediaries and implications for aggregate fluctuations: Canada and the United States 1870–1913," in O. Blanchard and S. Fischer (eds.), *NBER Macroeconomics Annual*, Cambridge, MA: MIT Press: 803–340.

7 Australia's payments adjustment and capital flows under the international gold standard, 1870–1913

DAVID POPE

Introduction

While much has been written about the international gold standard and how it functioned for major economies in the five decades or so before 1914, little detailed work has been done on the so-called "peripheral" countries like Australia. A study of Australia presents some interesting contrasts to the "core" countries, in that she was a major gold producer and continued on gold in the face of internal disequilibrium of gigantic proportions (20–25 percent of Australia's workforce being unemployed in the 1890s). This chapter examines how the exchange rate was determined and the role of automatic adjustments to the balance of payments through capital flows.

Australian economists in the 1920s and 1930s (and economic historians since) dismissed specie movements as the equilibrator of payments because these depended on bankers' need for coin, rather than the exchange rate. Instead, Australian writers espoused a regulatory mechanism in which bankers played the crucial role. Under this "managed exchange standard," external disequilibrium was corrected by banks altering their (domestic) credit and permitting their foreign reserves to fluctuate in accord with the balance of payments. There has been no attempt empirically to verify such assertions, or to test old and modern theories of payments adjustment.

This chapter examines the adjustment process through an intercountry portfolio equilibrium model founded on the monetary approach to the balance of payment (MABP), as well as through the traditional Humean dynamics of the classical price-specie-flow mechanism (PSF). The role of Australia's bankers is also appraised.

The first section describes Australia's historical record of development, factor flows, balance of payments, and monetary regime. The latter involved a fixed rate of exchange (quoted in relation to sterling, the key currency of the era). It is clear that Australia remained solvent with regard to her external accounts – though suffering deeply from internal disequilibrium in the 1890s – and that specie flows were motivated more by the

201

fortunes of gold production than by the trade balance. The next section sets out the main conjectures of these features, and is followed by the formal modeling of these views (involving what we describe as augmented MABP and PSF models of capital movements) and our econometric results. The final section provides interpretation and conclusions.

Australia's economy, balance of payments, and monetary regime

Australian contours

Australia was, and today remains, a small rich open economy. By 1860 Australia had attained a world pinnacle of *per capita* real income, a position achieved through pastoral expansion and gold mining and facilitated by particularly high workforce participation rates. The 30 years following 1860 saw a prodigious effort by both the private and public sectors to achieve a real physical control of the continent. In this period the central thrust of public policy was to establish the main arterial communications systems – railways and the telegraph. The bulk of private sector investment funds went into the pastoral industry and residential construction (particularly in the 1880s), the need of the latter reflecting rapid population growth and demographic patterns dating back to the gold rushes (Hall, 1963; Kelley, 1965). These years were characterized by rapid urbanization. By 1890 two-thirds of the population lived in cities and towns, a fraction matched by the United States only by 1920 and by Canada not until 1950. Associated with this urban growth manufacturing's share in GDP rose from some 6 percent in the 1860s to 13 percent in the 1880s (the rural sector's share stood at 26 percent in the 1880s, the construction sector, 16 percent, trade and transport, 20 percent) (N.G. Butlin, 1970).[1]

The boom of the 1880s and the subsequent downturn of the 1890s is clearly shown in figure 7.1. In terms of average growth rates, real GDP expanded vigorously at 4.8 percent per annum between 1861 and the end of the 1880s. Growth then collapsed to 0.8 percent in the years 1889–1905 (recovery from the depression was delayed by severe and protracted drought), before renewed rapid growth at 5.2 percent per annum from the mid-1900s to the outbreak of war in 1914. These high growth rates of real product before and after the 1890s did not translate into similarly high *per capita* performance, at least arithmetically, because of the rapid growth of Australia's population (figure 7.1).[2] Australia represented a very different set of circumstances to those of Britain where rises in product *per capita* generally came through modest rises in real product in association with limited growth in numbers.

The Australian mode of development emphasized extensive growth.

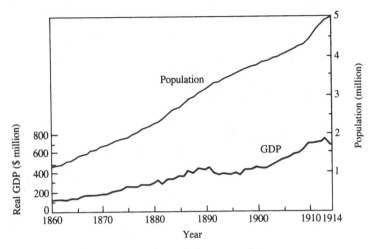

7.1   Australia's product and population expansion

Central to this were the transfer of population (labor, consumers, tax-payers) and capital from Britain to Australia and the furthering of overseas trade, exporting those goods for which her climate and estate afforded a comparative advantage. However, development was *not* simply a matter of export-led growth. Non-primary activities and the non-traded goods sector, primarily construction and services, were sizeable, if not dominant, in the Australian economy.

Figures 7.2 and 7.3 show Australia's trade balance and balance of payments. Australia exported around 20 percent of her GDP; the ratio of exports and imports combined to GDP was typically double this. Three-quarters of the exports were shipped to Britain, the balance mostly to France, Germany and the United States (wool being the principal good, accounting for usually one-half or more of the value of exports). The biggest source of imports was similarly Britain, comprising clothing, textiles, and producer goods. For all but a comparatively short span of time Australia ran a current account deficit. Yet this was not a problem so long as British investors were prepared to lend their savings to Australians.

Net apparent capital inflow shown in figures 7.2 and 7.3 has been derived by the indirect method, deducted as the residual in the balance of payments.[3] International reserves necessary for the calculation have been derived as the first difference of the sum of the commercial banks' holdings of external cash (cash outside Australia) plus their total gold holdings.[4] Prior to 1876 this series was interpolated on the basis of the change in the commercial banks' net assets in London. The correspondence between our series and that of N.G. Butlin's direct estimates of total net capital inflow

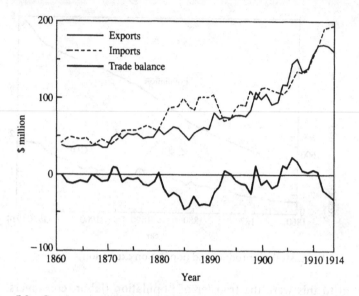

7.2   Components of the trade balance

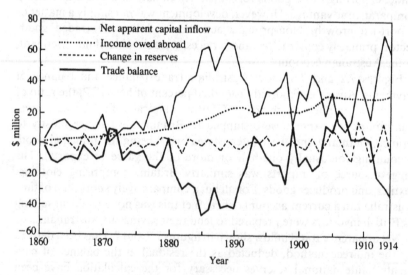

7.3   Australia's balance of payments

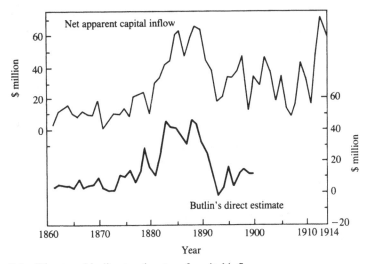

7.4   Direct and indirect estimates of capital inflow

(based on the balance sheets of private institutions, to which were added government net borrowings and immigrants' funds) is remarkably close (see figure 7.4). The correlation between the two series is 0.83.

Virtually all the inflow represented portfolio investment in public and private enterprise. The principal private borrowers in the years before the 1890s' depression were the banks.[5] These funds were drawn from English and Scottish lenders, and placed in interest-bearing deposits of 6 and 12 months.[6]

Figure 7.5 plots the factor transfers. Two points can be briefly made. First, taking the period after 1870 (which is the focus of our subsequent empirical study), a strong correspondence is apparent between the size of the international capital movements and the net migration rate. Second, these patterns reflected both private and public decisions. Australian colonial governments raised capital in London for their railways and allied programs and they also actively promoted immigration from the United Kingdom, the most direct way of doing this being by reducing the cost of transport (Pope, 1981). More roundabout means of quickening the pace of immigration included tariff increases, used in some states, and public works.

The developments in the Australian economy just described took place with a monetary regime of fixed exchange rates. The exchange of Australian pounds per pound sterling (described as the "rate on London") varied little after the turbulent first years of the gold rushes, as seen in figure 7.6. The fixed exchange rate tethered the Australian economy closely to Britain's

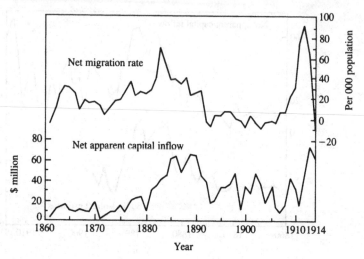

7.5   Factor migration

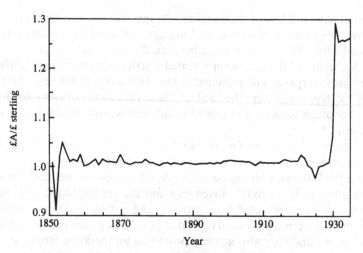

7.6   Exchange rate, 1851–1935, per pound sterling

and through her to the other economies of the world. It removed the possibility of changes in relative prices of traded goods solely owing to currency revaluations (devaluations); and it largely eliminated destabilizing currency speculation and capital movements. There was, perhaps, a cost. At its peak in 1893 unemployment reached 20 percent of Australia's workforce. This compared with just 7.5 percent in Britain. Altering the exchange rate was never considered an option, though devaluation against sterling was chosen by the next generation of Australia's bankers in 1931. Australia in the 1890s thus appears not to fit the usual argument that countries before 1914 observed the gold standard orthodoxy when it made no difference to the domestic economy, but abandoned it as soon as it did (Lindert, 1984, p. 403). This raises the question as to why Australia devalued in 1931, but not in, say, 1891. What forces prevented a switch in monetary regimes in the earlier period, and why was there a switch in 1931?

Why was there no switch in the monetary regime in 1891?

A number of explanations can be entertained. The first might be called the "gold standard solidarity" hypothesis. The records of debate of colonial legislatures, newspapers at the time, and the extant files of the private banks, are silent on the possibility of transforming the monetary regime in the early 1890s. Australia was solidly part of Britain's political and monetary system; to depart seems to have simply been unthinkable. It is not true, however, that detaching from the monetary regime was without precedent, Argentina had halted the convertibility of notes for gold at par after 1884 for the same reasons that Australia might have done in 1891. Yet subsequent developments – internal revolution in Argentina, default, and the Baring crisis – would have hardly recommended the Argentinian experiment to the Australians.

So, to Australians in the late nineteenth century gold standard solidarity meant a commitment to sterling and to things British. Whilst Empire loyalty was still the abiding sentiment in 1931, economic nationalism, economic independence, was by then probably stronger (Tsokhas, 1990). Yet, swings in politics and stronger Australian nationalism, though modifying the mood, tell us little about the economic calculus of the major actors in the decisions to devalue or not devalue. Had the net benefits to different players – sectional interests – changed between 1891 and 1931? Our second hypothesis could be termed the "public choice view." A number of potential gainers and losers can be identified: rural exporters and local manufacturers; governments in servicing their loan debt in the London capital market; banks' management and shareholders.

The decline in export prices and the terms of trade shock were much more severe at the beginning of the 1930s than the 1890s, see table 7.1. But it is quite clear from contemporary journals and newspapers that rural exporters, in particular the sheep farmers, were unpersuaded by the wisdom of devaluation until some time *after* the event, in 1930–31; the issue never arose in 1891.

Similarly, the chronicles of manufacturers' associations reveal no discus-

Table 7.1 *Terms of trade shocks, average annual percentage growth rates*

Period	Export Prices	Terms of trade
1889–91	− 3.68	− 3.30
1929–31	− 18.28	− 16.93

Sources: For 1888–91: Wilson (1931); for 1928–31: Vamplew (1987).

sion of the devaluation in either 1891 or 1931. Significantly higher levels of tariff protection for manufacturers in the 1920s and early 1930s may have blurred their focus on devaluation, making it a less compelling policy requirement. (Rural producers, too, focused on compensating subsidies of one sort or another which, along with uncertainty in their minds of the effects of a move in the exchange rate, deflected their gaze.)

In the early 1890s Australian colonial governments were concerned with their London debt commitments denominated in sterling. While this gave a reason for not devaluing, the possibility of a devaluation appears never to have been discussed. Instead, the issue was one of possible loan conversions on more favorable terms to their government. In any event, in the early 1890s there was no ready apparatus, no government bank, to effect a change. In December 1931, the Commonwealth Bank, established in 1911, assumed control, fixed the rate at £125 per £100 sterling, and bought and sold freely. Moreover, in the 1890s there was no federal government, but six separate colonial parliaments who could not even agree on a standard gauge for their railroad tracks.

The scale of the difference in the terms of trade shocks in the two periods may also be important. Whilst London-domiciled public debt was high in both, the gains from devaluation (via the boost to export income in Australian currency), hence defense against, or amelioration of, a government budget blow-out, was considerably greater in the 1930s. Certainly, at the beginning of the 1930s the federal government explicitly acknowledged its concern with the erosion of its tax earnings and made this clear to the commercial banks – who were the principal players in the exchange market until December 1931.

Two of the three largest banks in Australia in both periods were multinationals, with boards in London and substantial shareholding in Britain. The biggest Australian bank was the Bank of New South Wales. For British-based boards and their shareholders devaluating against sterling spelled lower dividend income on bank profits. Again, there is no discussion of these issues in 1891; there is considerable resistance, however, at the beginning of the 1930s. In converting resistance to support for a devaluation A.C. Davidson, chief executive of the Bank of New South Wales, is usually given the key role.

This suggests a third argument or hypothesis: it was not the weight of pressure groups, special interests, that secured devaluation in 1931, but the spirited and powerful drive of one particular personality. In the Australian representation of events, this was Davidson. He courted, and intelligently imbibed, the views of Professors Shann and Copland (the former an adviser to the Bank of New South Wales), both of whom espoused devaluation as a way of lifting exporters' income. He brought devaluation onto the agenda at interbank meetings and clearly fought hard for it as a strategy for recovery. He threatened that the Bank of New South Wales would go it alone, that is, devalue. British and local banks came to accept this, and followed.

There can be no doubt that Davidson was a remarkable figure in banking circles of his times. But what drove his views, and had the same factors or influences been present four decades before, in the early 1890s? Was it simply a case of the strong individual leaving his imprint on a country's financial history? Davidson had two things on his mind – the good of the national economy (principally, exporters' income) and the good of his bank, and the two were closely related. The former he derived, at least in part, from academic economists. The second had to do with the liquidity of bank customers and especially with his bank's grip on foreign exchange business. The banks had little competition in the exchange market in the early 1890s. At the beginning of the 1930s an "outside" market (that is, outside the banks) had sprung up, and it was this challenge that he sought to match.

Until the end of the 1920s, the banks were responsible for most gold shipments – the federal government mobilized these in 1929 – and con- ducted nearly all exchange business. The banks colluded as they saw it in "setting" the exchange rate. An "outside" market existed in the late nineteenth century but by comparison with the 1930s was tiny in its share. The essential prerequisites for an operator were balances with banks or branches in both London and Australia and, of course, financial resources to indulge in exchange transactions. This limited competition to companies linked with the export trade, namely wool brokers, such as Dalgety, Elder Smith, the AML&F Company, and some English-based companies. Two in this last group included Reuter's Telegram Company and Samuel Monta- gue (the London bullion merchants). In the 1890s the pressure on the exchange rate through the terms of trade shock was less than the early 1930s and the growth of players was contained by the banks. In the late 1880s and early 1890s they offered concessional rates to big customers who were consistent buyers and sellers of exchange and whose bills and business were especially valued. Positive action was also taken to chop back the growth of an "outside" market in the early 1890s. This at times involved price-cutting (to the South Australian government) to block a quote from Elder Smith, as well as refusing to provide colonial banking services to Samuel Montague. The removal of all banking services to Reuter's was also considered at one time.

At the end of the 1920s and the beginning of the 1930s there were more "outside" players and their effect on bank exchange business was far greater. Davidson, the first among commercial bankers to recognize this, took the initiative. He gave an ultimatum that the Bank of New South Wales would depreciate. The chief executive in Australia of the British-based Union Bank recorded Davidson's arguments and cabled London thus in late December 1930 (Union Bank records, U38):

Bank of New South Wales notified Victoria Banks that owing to volume out-side exchange discrepancy in rates and political pressure deficit [blow-out] they may be compelled quote on and after 6th January Telegraphic Transfer buying rate on London £115 selling rate £115.5. – with usual protective concession own customers thus altering rates and margin Chairman Victoria Banks urges withhold pending Conference in January I support Victoria Chairman.

The other banks followed. The manager of the Union Bank wrote in the middle of January 1931 (Union Bank records, U37):

As intimated by the Bank of New South Wales, it carried out its intention of breaking away from the Bank exchange agreement. The other Banks in self defence were compelled to follow suit, and since then the rates have been increasing every few days, in pursuit of the Bank of New South Wales' quotations. All efforts to catch up with the outside seller.

Subsequently, the Commonwealth Bank set the rate. While Davidson was formally the instigator, the leader, the development of an "outside" market, importantly not present in 1891, might be seen as the driving force among the banks generally.

In asking the question why Australia did not alter its exchange regime in the early 1890s, there is one further consideration. This might be called the "institutional constraint" hypothesis. In essence, an institutional constraint had been removed by 1930–31. At the beginning of the 1890s the commercial banks issued their own notes, there was no federal government note issue. Private notes were redeemable in sterling (gold sovereigns). These were retired by a federal tax in the 1910s. By the mid-1920s federal notes could not be exchanged for gold at the Treasury. Thus, any dispute between commercial banks (British-based and locals) on devaluation against sterling might see the initiator's vaults drained of gold, as it devalued against Britain and other banks operating in Australia. The risks in the 1890s for an individual bank to devalue were great.

The above arguments are not mutually exclusive: for a variety of reasons the 1890s were far less conducive to a regime change than the early 1930s.

The object in the remaining sections of this chapter is to explore the years *before* 1914, specifically, the adjustment system under the gold standard in Australia's case, and in this context, the role of commercial banks in "setting" rates down to the First World War. How did the exchange standard really work in its golden age? What were the possible links between the prevailing international monetary standard and the balance of payments adjustment mechanism? To what extent might payments' balance be restored automatically? To what extent was it a matter of manipulation of economic and commercial policy? And, in particular, what was the role of Australia's bankers?

The adjustment process: conjectures

The gold standard

Under the gold standard a country kept the value of its monetary unit and the value of a defined weight of gold at equality by standing ready to buy and sell gold at a constant price in unlimited amounts. Gold coins of fixed weight (sovereigns in the case of Britain and Australia, and dollars in the case of the United States) circulated, though this was not critical so long as fiduciary money issued by private banks or by the government could be freely converted. Bullion might be converted into coin at the mint for a small fee and coin and bullion freely imported and exported in any amount. As all countries on the standard fixed their currency values in gold this created fixed rates between members, or nearly so, depending on the costs of shipping gold. The bounds within which currency rates between "club" members could vary were called the gold import and export points, the price of exchange between the points being determined by demand and supply. Beyond these points gold flows were deemed to produce a short-run balancing of supply and demand for foreign exchange.

England was the most important member prior to 1914. She had adopted a *de facto* gold standard in 1717 after Sir Isaac Newton overvalued silver at the mint. Between then and 1914 the price of gold was fixed at £4.44 per ounce with only one break, 1797–1821, sparked by a run on the Bank of England's gold holdings with the threat of a French invasion (see also chapter 8 in this volume). No other country held to the rule of free convertibility of domestic currency into gold for so long a period (1821–1914), but in the four decades or so before the First World War most major countries joined, albeit with some variation of legal requirements and institutional practice (Ford, 1962). At the same time, the pound sterling occupied the position of the "key" currency, its popularity no doubt reflecting the sheer volume of Britain's trade (up eightfold between 1850 and 1914) and capital exports. Possibly Britain's leadership role and mystique of success encouraged countries to adhere to the gold standard which otherwise would not have (Bordo and Kydland, 1992; Gallarotti, 1989).

Did Australia belong to the gold standard directly or, rather, indirectly through its association with the pound sterling? Australia certainly exhibited many features characteristic of "club" members. The first was a fixed price for gold. This followed the establishment of a branch of the British Mint at Sydney in May 1855, which fixed the local price for gold identical with that in London. Previously, the diggers' gold had been shipped to London where it was minted or exchanged for coin and partly remitted back to Australia, the double journey across the oceans taking more than six months. The mint in Sydney was a short cut, essential in view of the rapid increase in population and expansion of trade expected as a consequence of the rushes. Also, attention could be drawn to the state of monetary matters in California following 1849, especially so far as the British government was concerned, the establishment of private mints for profit (S.J. Butlin, 1986). In popular thinking, too, a mint would stop the exploitation of diggers by the gold buyers. The establishment of the Sydney Mint with the mint price for gold set equal to that in England appears to have reduced exchange fluctuations to within extremely modest limits (figure 7.6). Except for its special design, the Sydney-minted gold sovereign was of the same weight and fineness (22 carats) as that produced in London.[7] Sydney sovereigns and half-sovereigns became legal tender throughout the Empire in 1863. Other branches of the Royal Mint were opened in Melbourne and Perth.

There were other features of Australia's monetary system which would seem to warrant it full membership of the gold standard. Until 1914 gold coin was the chief form of currency. In Australia, the commercial banks' cash and reserves included gold. Also, before 1914 trading bank notes, and Australian notes, first issued in 1910, were freely convertible into gold. Nor were there any restrictions on the import of gold. There was no limit to the gold bought at the mints at £3.17.10½ per ounce, nor restrictions on its export. As with any foreign exchange market, the gold points for Australia on London exchange rates were never precisely defined. The cost of freight, insurance and interest foregone varied over time and differed at any point,

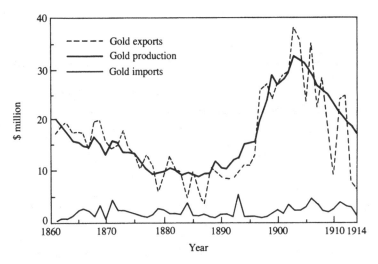

7.7   Gold movements in and out of Australia

depending upon the party undertaking the shipment of gold. Shipping companies, for instance, could carry gold at small cost especially where excess capacity existed. But generally, for the ordinary merchant, the cost of moving gold from Australia to London was around 2½ percent of its value in 1860, 2 percent in the mid-1880s and 1½–1¾ percent on the eve of the First World War.

Despite all these features of the Australian monetary system, it may not have fully encompassed the gold standard. Accounts were mostly settled in sterling, not gold. Moreover, that Australia's gold exports (figure 7.7) largely followed her gold production obscures their role in balance of payments adjustment, and the fact that changes in Australian banks' foreign reserves seem to have substituted for monetary gold movements (discussed later), raises questions of how the classical gold standard results of exchange rate constancy and external solvency over long periods were really achieved.

Humean dynamics

David Hume's essay "Of the Balance of Trade" ([1752] 1955) is generally thought to contain the first statement of the traditional or classical balance of payments adjustment mechanism of an international species standard (see Bordo, 1984). Through the price-specie-flow mechanism an excess of imports leads to gold exports in the short run. This loss of gold reduces the amount of money in the country, since either gold is money or the banking system keeps the supply of money adjusted to the quantity of gold reserves. A fall in the money supply of the country will lead to a decline in prices, according to the quantity theory of money, which holds that, with less money, people spend less, and less spending with unchanged output requires lower prices.

This reduction in prices as a result of the gold outflow is critical to the long-run adjustment mechanism. For lower prices encourage exports as foreigners find the country a cheaper place to shop, and with lower goods prices more foreign exchange will be forthcoming at every foreign exchange rate. Lower prices also reduce imports as locals turn to cheaper domestic goods, so less foreign exchange is demanded and hence the flow of specie corrects the trade imbalance (as well as bringing the foreign exchange market back to mint parity). Hume's theory was buttressed by later classical economists such as Ricardo, Thornton, and Mill.

The classical school's position on capital movements in the balance of payments adjustment was that short-term flows were a response to interest rate differentials triggered by gold flows, and that the gold movements necessary to correct trade balances were more moderate on account of them. Thus Goschen ([1892] 1978, p. 127, as quoted in Bordo, 1984, p. 44) wrote:

money will be dear and scarce in the country which owes much to foreign creditors, and plentiful in that which has exported much; and, high interest will be attracting money to that quarter whence specie is flowing out in payment of foreign debts . . . [an] adverse balance of trade will . . . render the bills on the country which is most in debt difficult of sale, and tend to compel it to export specie; whereas the high rate of interest, which is generally contemporaneous with a drain . . . of specie, will revive a demand for bills on this same country, and enhance their value in other quarters, for there will be a general desire to procure the means of remitting capital to that market where it commands the highest value.

This meant that "where a considerable efflux of specie is taking place, the rate of interest will rise in the natural course of things. The abstraction caused by the bullion shipments will of itself tend to raise that rate" (Bordo, 1984, p. 45; Goschen, [1892] 1978, p. 132). A country could also sustain a temporary balance of trade deficit by borrowing overseas. Long-term capital inflow, however, was ignored or treated as exogenous in the adjustment mechanism. Its role was to catch the focus of later writers.

Antipodean critics

Australian and New Zealand economists developed a number of criticisms of the "pure" classical tradition of Hume. The first was A.H. Tocker who published his paper "The Monetary Standards of New Zealand and

Australia" in the *Economic Journal* in 1924, the year of Jacob Viner's restatement of the specie-flow mechanism in his *Canada's Balance of International Indebtedness*.[8] Tocker, like Viner, was not satisfied that gold movements ever restored external balance, arguing (p. 555) that:

Note issues [in New Zealand and Australia] are not governed by gold reserves . . . Trade and banking statistics show that bankers habitually maintain gold reserves sufficiently large to free them from limitations of legal restriction; the movements of specie depend on the bankers' needs for coin rather than on the exchange rates.

How, then, did the system function? The answer was that international trade and payments were conducted through the commercial banks which kept foreign reserves in London for this purpose. A rise, say, in exports swelled the banks' London funds and their deposits back home. For exporters received payments in the form of deposits credited to their accounts while the banks' sterling balances rose by the same amount. Increased imports had exactly the opposite effect, hence bank deposits and foreign reserves were jointly determined by the net balance of payments. Changes in the net balance of payments affected the money supply through increasing deposits, an increase in net exports causing money to rise, which set in motion equilibrating movements in relative prices (domestic to foreign), which worked to repair external balance and narrow exchange rates. "Like every other method of monetary regulation," Tocker (p. 566) wrote:

this plan postulates the Quantity Theory, and depends for its effect on influencing the amount of monetary media available. Variations in this amount react upon the volume of business, and through business, upon the trade balance, which in turn exerts the chief control over the exchange rates.

Gold flowed but little. What in practice substituted for specie movements were changes in international reserves of the banks.

This downplaying of the role of gold by economists in the early 1920s was to be expected in that the exchange rates on London remained stable during the war when gold movements had been prohibited. As Copland (1925, p. 23) noted: "Thus, in the absence of gold movements, Australian currency was regulated largely in a normal way by the actions of the banks." Acknowledging Tocker's paper, Copland argued that reserves in London and "spending power in Australia which may be roughly measured by excess of deposits over advances" showed similar movements, concluding (p. 22) that "it is our banking system that maintains so close a relation between English and Australian currency."

Subsequent writers returned to the question of the role of foreign reserves in credit creation, Wilson (1935, p. 98) observing that: "London funds, whether we are on the gold standard, the sterling exchange standard, or no standard at all, are closely associated with internal banking and credit policy."

The most detailed statement came from Davidson before the 1936 Royal Commission into Monetary and Banking Systems (Bank of New South Wales, 1936). Davidson took the view that gold movements must be regarded as merchandise trade, "no way different from wheat exports" (p. 54), and that the key to exchange stability was exchange management executed by the Australian trading banks. "The key to exchange management in Australia," Davidson (p. 54) wrote,

has been the attention the individual trading banks have traditionally given to the ratio of advances to deposits . . . [Exports] either increase the bank's deposits or reduce its advances according to whether the exporter is in credit or overdrawn . . . when London funds are increasing, the ratio of advances to deposits tends to decline. Therefore, any action by the banks to restore it to its customary level would expand credit in Australia, with the result that money incomes would be raised tending to force up costs and prices. From the higher money incomes a greater volume of imports would be bought, and by the increase in costs exports would be discouraged, so that by the operation of both factors the growth of London funds would be checked.

In this model of the international adjustment mechanism it is money income as well as relative prices and costs that explain the adjustment. The money supply is somewhat downplayed, while the role of bankers in managing adjustment is elevated.

There were other critics in the interwar years of the classical explanation of how the gold standard worked. The Cunliffe Report of 1918 restated the stylized facts of automatic adjustment in the balance of payments, but this was challenged by those who argued that the prewar standard had been successful because it was a *managed* standard, managed by the Bank of England and the City of London (Smit, 1934; Cassell, 1935). Davidson's evidence before the 1936 Royal Commission was an extreme Australian variant of this theme of management – namely, management by Australian bankers. Other critics of the times included Whale (1937), who challenged the price-specie-flow mechanism (price levels between regions were correlated and adjustment to shocks fast, suggesting arbitrage, not adjustment to gold) and the supposed obedience of central banks to the "rules of the game."

The notion that London managed the gold standard has also been discussed by Sayers (1951), Lindert (1969), and Goodhart (1972). Also in the postwar period Keynesian analysis has been incorporated into textbook treatments of the adjustment mechanism and the open economy multiplier approach adopted to explain the transfer of capital (Meier, 1953; Stovel, 1959; Ford, 1962). According to Ford, capital exports to Argentina were transferred directly through changes in the receiver's income which permitted increased imports.[9] Moreover, any shock to the balance of payments such as a decline in exports reduced income and imports without any significant change in relative prices. But undoubtedly the most novel views of the adjustment mechanism to appear in the last two decades or so are those embodied in the monetary approach to the balance of payments.

The monetary approach to the balance of payments

In this approach, monetary aspects are regarded as the core and essence of the adjustment mechanism (Kreinin and Officer, 1978). In an open economy with fixed rates of exchange the national stock of money, not prices, adjusts to changes in the public's demand for money (Frenkel, 1971; Mundell, 1971; Johnson, 1976). The balance of payments is the means by which open economies adjust their national money stocks to the stocks they desire to hold.

The crucial decisions of individuals and institutions relate to the adequacy of their money balances. Demand for money balances relative to supply determines their expenditure on goods and securities. An increase in the demand for money reduces the public's demand for goods and securities. This leads to reduced imports and expanded exports in goods and capital inflow until the demand for money is met. In the process the trade and/or the capital account move into surplus. In the context of the Australian monetary system of the nineteenth and early twentieth centuries, the flow of goods and money fed external reserves, London funds, which generated an equal rise in domestic deposits, satisfying the Australian demand for money balances.

More generally, a once and for all increase in money in one country and the opposite in another would produce a balance of payments deficit in the first, a surplus in the second, and a flow of money from the first to the second. For the world as a whole the balance of payments will redistribute the world money stock across nations consistent with monetary equilibrium in the constituent national economies. The closer the links among world commodity markets, the higher the degree of capital mobility.

Though not acknowledged in Kreinin and Officer (1978), Williamson (1961, 1963, 1964) was a precursor of the monetarist line, delineating a process of (US) growth (1961, p. 382) in which:

Rapid growth has a tendency to generate excess demands for money (gold) and goods (trade balance deficit), as well as excess supplies of securities (net capital inflow). No one of these elements should be treated with more importance than another, and the equilibrium solution must be general. Gold inflows do not necessarily reflect disequilibrium in the balance of payments, but may simply reflect a tendency towards excess demands for money in a rapidly growing economy.

In the most extreme version of the monetary approach, prices around the world, traded and non-traded, are the same because of instant arbitrage, internationally and domestically. McCloskey and Zecher (1976) tested this assumption by examining price movements between and within regions. Correlations (especially of traded goods) led them to conclude (pp. 379–380) that: "There appears to be little reason to treat ... two countries on the gold standard differently in their monetary transactions from any two regions within each country." The tenor of this result is also expressed in McCloskey and Zecher (1984). They identify purchasing power parity (PPP) with the law of one price. Prices (interest rates) cannot diverge between countries (except for transport costs, tariffs, and transaction costs) because of arbitrage by rational agents. Hence there is no logic to the gold flows predicted in Humean dynamics.[10]

Dick and Floyd (1987) in their study of Canada on the gold standard, 1871–1913, produce results (pp. 161–162) which they conclude:

fully support the view that balance of payments disequilibria are monetary pheno- mena. But they are inconsistent with the purchasing power parity theory frequently used to support that view. Balance of payments disequilibria are monetary pheno- mena because they are the mechanism by which the demand and supply of money are equilibrated ... The ratios of different countries' price levels defined in a single currency are not [however] constant even though price levels are interdependent.[11]

Interdependence of price levels in their analysis (p. 163) is a consequence of "free international trade in capital assets." The parallelism in prices arises because the adjustment mechanism works through "one-shot" portfolio adjustments and not through relative price effects on the balance of trade as the classical theory predicted. Similarly, interest rates are determined by conditions of world portfolio equilibrium.

Most empirical work on the monetary approach to the balance of payments takes the change in foreign reserves as the variable to be explained in regression analysis. However, the balance of payments identity can be rearranged making net apparent capital inflow the dependent variable (see n. 3 below). This approach originated with Kouri and Porter (1974). As in the more conventional foreign reserves-flow equation (where the change in reserves is the dependent variable), the independent variables in a capital-flow equation are the determinants of changes in the demand for and supply of money.

Models and results

Models

Modeling the adjustment mechanism under fixed exchange rates with capital inflow as the dependent variable in the equation has an important advantage. We wish to integrate the real historical experience of Australia's economic development mode – extensive growth through capital and population transfers – with banking and, more broadly, world monetary conditions. In this context capital inflow is the primary variable to focus on in a monetary approach to balance of payments questions. In the first part of this section we specify the models of adjustment, the second part offers our econometric estimates. We begin with a monetarist augmented model of capital movements, then proceed to a classical augmented model.

As defined previously the balance of payments can be considered essentially as a monetary phenomenon. Capital inflow is then a function of changes in the supply of and demand for money; that is:

$$KI = KI(\Delta\mathbf{x}, \Delta\mathbf{y}), \tag{7.1}$$

where

KI is the net apparent capital inflow into Australia

$\mathbf{x}$ is a vector of reduced-form demand determinants of the nominal money stock desired by Australian residents

$\mathbf{y}$ is a vector of reduced-form supply determinants of the nominal Australian money stock

Δ is a change operator

The nominal money stock is the high-powered money multiplier times (the base) foreign reserves; this is

$$M^S = \frac{1}{\delta^A} FR, \tag{7.2}$$

where

δ^A is the inverse of Australia's high-powered money multiplier

FR is foreign reserves.

Equilibrium implies

$$M^S = M^d \tag{7.3}$$

thus

$$\frac{1}{\delta^A} FR = M^d. \tag{7.4}$$

Now capital inflows equate M^s and M^d by altering the monetary base, FR, and thereby indirectly altering the money stock, M, in response to $\Delta\mathbf{x}$ and $\Delta\mathbf{y}$, the changes in the (reduced-form) determinants of demand and supply for money.

We hypothesize that

$$\mathbf{x} = [y^A, P^A, i^F, y^F, P^F, NMR^A]^{12} \tag{7.5}$$

and

$$y = [\delta^A, J^A, NPI^A, X^A], \tag{7.6}$$

where

δ is the inverse of the high-powered money multiplier
y is real income
P is price level
i is interest rate
NPI is net property income owed abroad
NMR is net migration rate
J is imports
X is exports
A is Australia
F is the weighted sum of foreign countries.

The classical model posits capital movements as a function of differences in interest rates. Augmenting the model by the net migration rate (NMR) yields,

$$KI^A = KI^A(i^A, i^F, NMR^A), \tag{7.7}$$

where variables are as previously defined.

The functional forms in which the MABP and PSF models are estimated are indicated in table 7.2.

In table 7.2, from column (1), the low t-value for the difference between the interest rate in Australia and elsewhere (that is, the foreign interest rate), the low Durbin–Watson (D–W) statistic and low $\bar{R}^2$ suggest the wrong functional form, or the more serious error of misspecification. From column (2) in table 7.2, expressing the difference between the Australian and foreign interest rates as a ratio instead of a difference, if anything, there seems to be a worse specification. Taking column (3), lagging the interest rate difference improves its t-value (in brackets), but not the $\bar{R}^2$ and D–W. From columns (4) and (5), introducing the lagged dependent variable to capture slow adjustment or other omitted autoregressive variables yields a more satisfactory, but still low, $\bar{R}^2$ and a satisfactory D–W and h-statistic. However, the interest rate differential is statistically insignificant. The traditional model clearly does not tell the whole story.

An augmented monetarist model and a mixed "monetarist-traditional" model are explored in tables 7.3–7.5. In (A1) (table 7.3) Australian real income and prices are significant "demand for money" determinants of capital flows, as are, on the supply side, lagged income owed abroad and imports combined, and exports. The net migration rate, included as a wealthy entity in the demand for money, just fails the significance test at the

Table 7.2 *Classical augmented model of capital inflow*

Variables	OLS-regression coefficients on variables				
Equation number	(1)	(2)	(3)	(4)	(5)
Aust.–foreign interest difference $(i^A - i^F)$	2.28 (0.87)				
Aust.–foreign interest differential (i^A / i^F)		5.01 (0.43)		2.96 (0.33)	
Lagged Aust.–foreign interest difference $(i^A - i^F)_{t-1}$			5.01 (1.98)**		1.53 (0.72)
Lagged net migration rate $(NMR^A)_{t-1}$	0.89$^{\times 6}$ (2.27)**	0.96$^{\times 6}$ (2.48)**	0.77$^{\times 6}$ (2.08)**	0.65$^{\times 6}$ (2.16)**	0.62$^{\times 6}$ (2.10)**
Lagged capital inflow $(KI^A)_{t-1}$				0.65 (5.48)***	0.62 (4.99)***
Constant	26.12 (6.31)***	20.01 (1.84)*	27.82 (7.13)***	4.40 (0.50)	8.78 (1.79)*
$\bar{R}^2$	0.14	0.12	0.20	0.49	0.50
D–W	0.70	0.67	0.70	2.00††	1.95††
Durbin's h	—	—	—	$-0.12^{\times -2}$††	0.27††
SEE	17.08	17.20	16.46	13.09	13.02

Notes:
t-statistics in parentheses; asterisks indicate degrees of significance:
   *** significant at 1 percent level.
   ** significant at 5 percent level.
   * significant at 10 percent level.
   †† reject hypothesis of serial dependence of residuals at 5 percent level.

10 percent level while the world interest rate is clearly statistically insignificant, the standard error of the estimate being twice the size of the estimated coefficient. The inverse of the high-powered money multiplier also has a very low t-value.

In (A2) (table 7.3) the world interest rate is replaced by the difference between Australian and world rates. The model therefore amalgamates the monetarist approach and the core of the classical model. Put differently, it permits interest differences to intrude into the money-demand determi-

Table 7.3 *Monetarist augmented model of capital inflow (variant A)*

Variables Equation number	OLS-regression coefficients on variables		
	(A1)	(A2)	(A3)
Money demand			
Aust. real income $\Delta(y^A)$	0.20 (3.36)***	0.19 (3.60)***	0.20 (3.71)***
Australian prices $\Delta(P^A)$	117.10 (2.94)***	112.76 (3.23)***	113.20 (3.24)***
Foreign interest rate $\Delta(i^F)$	−0.04 (−0.03)		
Lagged Aust.–foreign interest difference $(i^A-i^F)_{t-1}$		2.09 (1.63)	2.39 (1.81)*
Lagged net migration rate $\Delta(NMR^A)_{t-1}$	$0.30^{\times 6}$ (1.63)	$0.25^{\times 6}$ (1.43)	$0.23^{\times 6}$ (1.31)
Money supply			
Lagged Aust. imports and income owed abroad $(J^A+NPI^A)_{t-1}$	0.89 (12.79)***	0.86 (12.31)***	0.93 (8.99)***
Aust. exports (X^A)	−0.86 (−10.58)***	−0.81 (−9.76)***	−0.88 (−8.02)***
Inverse of high-powered money multiplier $(\Delta\delta^A)$	46.92 (1.34)	26.17 (0.74)	27.00 (0.77)
Lagged capital inflow $(KI^A)_{t-1}$			−0.10 (−0.95)
Constant	−0.19 (−0.05)	0.42 (0.12)	1.26 (0.34)
$\bar{R}^2$	0.83	0.84	0.84
$D-W$	2.39	2.52	2.39
Durbin's h			−1.81
SEE	7.55	7.28	7.29

Note:
See notes to table 7.2.

Table 7.4 *Monetarist augmented model of capital inflow (variant B)*

Variables Equation number	OLS-regression coefficients on variables			
	(B1)	(B2)	(B3)	(B4)
Money demand				
Lagged net migration rate $\Delta(NMR^A)_{t-1}$	$7.01^{\times 3}$ (0.07)	$5.47^{\times 4}$ (0.56)	$-9.40^{\times 3}$ (0.10)	$3.22^{\times 4}$ (0.35)
Aust. real income $\Delta(y^A)$	0.03 (1.27)			
Aust. prices $\Delta(P^A)$	3.74 (0.22)			
Aust. to foreign real income $\Delta(y^A/y^F)$		$-0.85^{\times -2}$ (-1.08)		
Aust. to foreign prices $\Delta(P^A/P^F)$		-5.12 (-0.55)		
Aust. nominal income $\Delta(Y^A)$			0.04 (1.40)	
Aust. to foreign nominal income $\Delta(Y^A/Y^F)$				-2.79 (-1.29)
Lagged Aust.–foreign interest difference $(i^A-i^F)_{t-1}$	0.38 (0.57)	0.07 (0.09)	0.38 (0.58)	0.13 (0.19)
Money supply				
Aust. imports and income owed abroad $(JA+NPI^A)$	1.00 (25.84)***	0.98 (24.39)***	1.00 (26.35)***	0.98 (25.20)***
Aust. exports (X^A)	-0.99 (-21.31)***	-0.97 (-20.64)***	-1.00 (-21.64)***	0.97 (-21.16)***
Foreign base money supply $\Delta(M^F)$		-16.86 (-0.96)		-11.99 (-0.73)
Inverse of high-powered money multiplier $(\Delta\delta^A)$	119.62 (6.25)***	134.87 (6.26)***	120.83 (6.44)***	135.82 (6.42)***
Constant	-0.06 (-0.03)	0.39 (0.21)	1.45 (0.24)	0.27 (0.15)

Table 7.4 (*cont.*)

| Variables | OLS-regression coefficients on variables | | | |
Equation number	(B1)	(B2)	(B3)	(B4)
$\bar{R}^2$	0.96	0.96	0.96	0.96
D–W	1.96††	2.00††	1.94††	2.07††
SEE	3.75	3.76	3.68	3.69

Note:
See notes to table 7.2.

nants of capital movements. This interest rate variable, however, is insignificant and the value of *D–W* high, suggesting negative serially correlated residuals. Adding the lagged dependent variable, $(KI^4)_{t-1}$, to the equation does not alter our previous conclusions on the statistical significance of variables other than for the interest difference, which is significant at the 10 percent level. Negative serial correlation remains a problem, suggesting some degree of misspecification.

Further experimentation, reported in (B1) (table 7.4), reveals that to remove the negative serial correlation and satisfactorily reduce the *D–W* toward 2, it was necessary to enter imports and net property income paid abroad unlagged (with the attendant risk of simultaneity bias). The inverse of the high-powered money multiplier is now also highly significant. The demand for money variables and the interest difference variable remain statistically insignificant. In (B2) (table 7.4) the interest difference variable is retained and Australian real income and prices are replaced by *relative* (Australian to world) real income and prices. World conditions are also represented on the supply side with the inclusion of world base money supply. The use of *relative* prices perhaps needs elaboration. In its strictest form the MABP asserts instant arbitrage for both the prices of tradeables and non-tradeables. In (B2) we assume, following Dick and Floyd (1987), that the former holds (albeit with a minimal lag), but that the prices of non-tradeables in different countries need not equalize even after a substantial passage of time. The divergent prices of non-tradeables cause changes in domestic to foreign prices, of which they are a component.

However, the variables capturing *relative* prices and real income as "demand" determinants of capital movements are both statistically insignificant in (B2) (table 7.4), as on the supply side is the foreign money supply.

Equation (B3) deletes this last variable and reinstates a wholly Australian

Table 7.5 *Monetarist augmented model of capital inflow (variant C)*

Variables	OLS-regression coefficients on variables	
Equation number	(C1)	(C2)
Money demand		
Aust. nominal income $\Delta\delta^A/(Y^A)$	0.52 (24.27)***	
Aust. to foreign nominal income $\Delta\delta^A/(Y^A/Y^F)$		34.52 (2.41)**
Lagged Aust.–foreign interest difference $(i^A-i^F)_{t-1}$	−1.01 (−0.67)	7.44 (1.23)
Lagged net migration rate $\Delta\delta^A/(NMR^A)_{t-1}$	$9.90^{\times 3}$ (0.02)	$1.45^{\times 4}$ $(0.93^{\times -2})$
Money supply		
Aust. imports and income owed abroad (JA^A+NPI^A)	1.01 (80.82)***	0.97 (18.97)***
Aust. exports (X^A)	−1.01 (−71.87)***	−0.95 (−16.86)***
Foreign money supply $\Delta(M^F)$		−212.43 (−1.00)
Constant	0.13 (0.17)	0.69 (0.22)
$\bar{R}^2$	0.99	0.92
$D-W$	2.15	2.06††
SEE	1.34	5.16

Note:
See notes to table 7.2.

dimension to income and prices, but in multiplicative form – namely $\Delta(P^A.y^A)=\Delta Y^A$, nominal income replacing the two variables, real income and prices. In this specification the value of $D-W$ is satisfactory; the supply-side determinants are all highly significant; those on the demand side are not. A number of alternative model specifications were tried, one reported in equation (B4), involving the inclusion of relative nominal incomes and world money supply. In equation (B4) and in others not reported, the supply-side variables, $(J^A + NPI^A)$, X^A and δ^A, were consistently highly significant, the demand variables insignificant.

The two models reported as variant C in table 7.5 explore a different functional form in which money demand, M^d, is converted to base-money demand, FR^d, by premultiplying M^d by the inverse of Australia's high-powered money multiplier, δ^A; that is:

$$FR^d = \delta^A M^d. \tag{7.8}$$

The determinants of FR^d may then be obtained by premultiplying the determinants of M^d listed in (7.5) above by δ^A. Correspondingly, the determinants of base-money supply, FR^d, may be obtained by deleting δ^A from the determinants of M^s listed in (7.6) above.

If capital flows really equate FR^d and FR^s, then the equations reported as variant C can be deemed to be superior functional forms to our earlier representations.

In both equations (C1) and (C2), Australian imports and net income paid abroad combined, and Australian exports, are highly significant, as is Australian nominal income, $\Delta\delta^A Y^A$, in (C1) and relative nominal incomes, $\Delta\delta^A(Y^A/Y^F)$, at the 5 percent level, in (C2).

What can be concluded from the results reported in tables 7.3–7.5 taken as a whole? The results lend little support to the traditional view that interest differences play a major role in capital flows. Our augmented classical model (augmented by the net migration rate) performed poorly. While the net migration rate was a consistently significant determinant of capital movements (presumably through its effect on the rate of return) intercountry interest rates, either differences or in ratio form, were not. Moreover, the degree of variation in capital movements explained by the model was low: the highest value for R^2, as for $\bar{R}^2$, was 0.5.

To explain the other 50 percent of the variance in capital inflow it is necessary to consider the monetarist hypothesis that capital flows equate the demand for and supply of money. The results using a monetarist specification, again augmented by the net migration rate, strongly endorse this hypothesis.

Interpretation and conclusions

The price-specie-flow mechanism is an inadequate description of Australia's gold movements, trade and capital flows. For the most part, gold movements followed a trend driven by production, probably with an inventory lag (figure 7.7). Most of the gold involved merchandise exports to

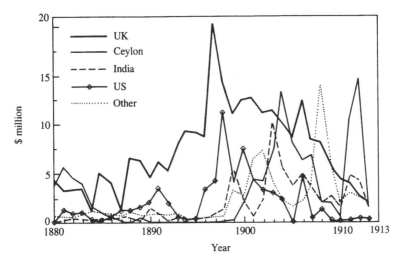

7.8   Major destinations of gold exports

the United Kingdom (figure 7.8), but not all of it. Some fraction represented the banks' shipments to bolster their London balances (Kennett, 1972). Moreover, destinations other than London became increasingly important, principally the United States, India, and Ceylon, and in some cases gold movements were intimately related to the settlement of overseas trade debt. According to Kennett (p. 90) shipments to San Francisco, for instance, were an example of multilateral settlement of debts between the United States, Britain and Australia. Nonetheless, gold exports from Australia had far more in common with the fortunes of production than with trade deficits.

Turning from gold to capital movements, the classical model predicts capital flows on the basis of intercountry differences in interest rates. We augmented this model (and our monetarist models) by adding the net migration rate (essentially as a wealth variable). Whether augmented in this way or not, the classical model explains little: interest rate variables were nearly always insignificant and $\bar{R}^2$ pitifully low.

An alternative view of the determination of capital movements is presented in the monetarists' approach to the balance of payments. To catch the essence of this, suppose the Australian economy suffers an exogenous shock in the form of God-sent pre-harvest weather, such that yields rise markedly. What happens? The increased yields generate the process set out below in figure 7.9, where Δ represents change (in the case of weather, to perfect pre-harvest conditions).

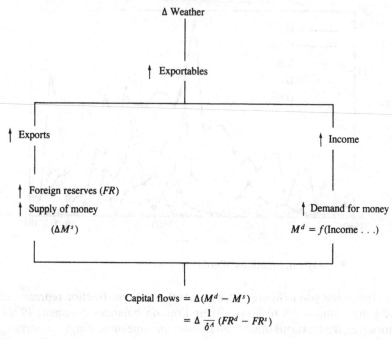

$$\text{Capital flows} = \Delta(M^d - M^s)$$
$$= \Delta \frac{1}{\delta^A} (FR^d - FR^s)$$

7.9 Weather and capital flows

In the monetary approach, capital inflow is a monetary phenomenon produced from changes in the demand for and supply of money. But the basic question is the same for all schools of thought: how did the gold standard cope with exogenous shocks to member countries' current account balances (in the notation of this chapter to their exports, X, imports and net property income owed abroad, $(J + NPI)$)? How did "club" members remain solvent in the presence of exogenous shocks? The monetarists' answer, given on the bottom line of figure 7.9, is that capital movements between member countries equilibrated changes in the money supply and the demand for money. Put simply, the world money stock was redistributed through capital movements in a way that *tended* to equilibrate the constituents' demands and supplies of money (with their currencies being fixed in relation to one another through gold).

What is the evidence for Australia? While many of our estimated equations tend to confirm the demand-side effects of changes in income on capital flows, it is the supply-side determinants operating through the current account balance that are consistently statistically significant (the left-hand side of figure 7.9). On the side of the money-supply determination of international capital movements, and in terms of the debate on how the gold standard operated, our results suggest that capital flows directly offset autonomous changes in exports, imports and net property transfers. Thus in this regard our results indicate that maintenance of the gold standard was easier and more automatic, and certainly different from that suggested by the traditional classical view of capital inflows.

What role did Australia's bankers play in exchange management? Tocker, and especially Davidson, drew attention to the nature of gold exports as merchandise trade, hence Australia's rather different status as a member of the gold standard.[13] Gold movements did not simply reflect the state of a country's trade balance. Yet it is also clear that the banks were responsible for most of the gold shipments out of Australia and conducted nearly all the exchange business. They also colluded in "setting" exchange rates. Yet, the case for a bank-managed gold standard requires qualification. Davidson's interpretation of adjustment turns out to be little more than a description of the money multiplier. While he was certainly perceptive for his times, there were larger monetary forces at work, many of which are encapsulated in the monetary approach to the balance of payments.

Appendix 1: foreign reserves and capital inflow

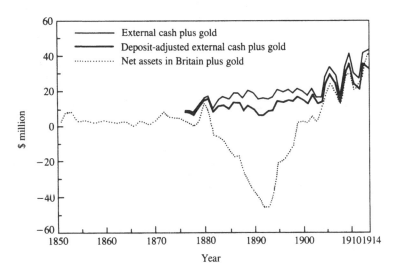

7A.1   Foreign reserves

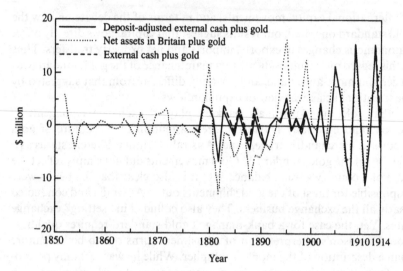

7A.2   Change in foreign reserves

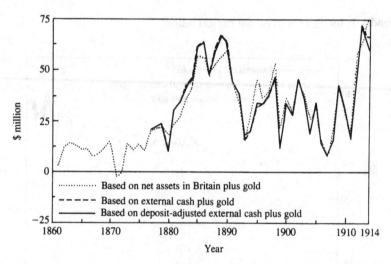

7A.3   Alternative measures of capital inflow

Appendix 2: data in the model

Australian prices (P^A): N.G. Butlin (1962, pp. 33–34).

Australian nominal GDP (Y^A): N.G. Butlin (1987, Table ANA 50–64, col. 64, p. 133).

Australian population: Australia, CBCS (1951, p. 155).

Australian net migration rate (NMR^A): Price (1987, Table IEO 33–41, col. 41, p. 6).

Australian net apparent capital inflow (KI^A) (estimated by components of n. 3, p. 232):

exports (X^A): N.G. Butlin (1962, Table 247, pp. 410–411; Table 262, p. 441; Table 256, p. 436).

imports (J^A): N.G. Butlin (1962, Table 248, pp. 413–414; Table 262, p. 441; Table 257, p. 437).

net property income paid abroad (NPI^A), consisting of income due abroad (total): N.G. Butlin (1962, Table 249, p. 416; Table 262, p. 441; Table 257, p. 437); and income earned abroad: N.G. Butlin (1962, Table 256, p. 436).

net government borrowings (GB): N.G. Butlin (1962, Table 251, p. 424); M. Butlin (1977, Table IV.17, p. 108).

adjusted external cash plus gold (FR^A), consisting of adjusted foreign cash balances: Sheppard (1971, Table (A) 1.1, pp. 116–117) and Butlin, Hall, and White (1971, Table 1, pp. 112–115, Table 2(i), pp. 116–117, Table 2(ii), pp. 120–121); and bullion (gold in Australia): S.J. Butlin Database.

Australian interest rate (i^A): Pope (1987, Table PF 1–5, col. 1, p. 240).

Australian money supply (M^A): Pope (1987, Table PF 75–63, col. 63, p. 247; Table PF 64–71, col. 71, p. 248).

Australian exports (X^A): *see* (KI^A).

Australian imports (J^A): *see* (KI^A).

Australian net property income owed (NPI^A): *see* (KI^A).

Australian foreign reserves (FR^A): *see* adjusted external cash plus gold under (KI^A).

Australian gold exports: N.G. Butlin (1962, Table 247, pp. 410–411; Table 262, p. 441; Table 258, p. 438).

Australian gold production: N.G. Butlin (1962, Table 247, pp. 410–411; Table 262, p. 441; Table 258, p. 438).

Australian gold imports: N.G. Butlin (1962, Table 248, pp. 413–414; Table 262, p. 441; Table 258, p. 438).

Butlin's direct estimate of capital inflow: Lougheed (1987, Table ITFC 14, p. 186).

Foreign interest rate (i^F): weighted short-term rates in United States and United Kingdom from Bordo and Jonung (1987, p. 159, p. 162). Weights are the country shares in the combined real GNP, measured in United States dollars at 1913 rates of exchange.

Foreign prices (P^F): weighted combination of prices from Friedman and Schwartz (1982 – the United Kingdom, Table 4.9, pp. 130–137, and the United States, Table 4.8, pp. 122–129). Weights are as for interest rates.

Foreign money supply (M^F): weighted combination of the United Kingdom, United States, France, Germany, Italy, Norway and Sweden, from Dick and Floyd (1987, p. 176).

Foreign real income (y^r): weighted combination of the United Kingdom, United States, France, Germany, Italy, Norway, and Sweden, from Dick and Floyd (1987, p. 177).

Notes

I thank Robin Pope for considerable assistance with the model and detailed criticism of the chapter. I also thank Jonathan Pincus, Graeme Snooks, Noel Butlin, and participants at the Sydney Economic History Conference (July 1990), particularly Boris Schedvin and Alan Lougheed, for insights and comments. Wayne Naughton provided the computer graphics. Raha Roggero and Barry Howarth are thanked for research assistance and Lorraine Lewis, Ann Howarth, Barbara Trewin, and Jeannie Haxell for the chapter's layout and production.

1 The causes of urbanization and the extent to which industrial expansion stimulated urbanization and vice versa are discussed in N.G. Butlin (1962, pp. 182–214). Rapid urbanization occurred in other countries at this time. However, what is unique in Australia's case is that the process of urbanization did not depend, at least before 1890, on a slackening in growth of numbers occupied in the rural industries.

2 For the three periods above real GDP *per capita* growth rates were 1.3, -0.8, and 2.9 percent per annum. Population growth rates were 3.5, 1.7, and 2.3 respectively (Maddock and McLean, 1987, p. 14).

3 That is,

$$\Delta FR = (X - J) - NPI + (PKI + GB)$$

thus

$$KI = (PKI + GB) = (J - X) + NPI + \Delta FR,$$

where

ΔFR: change in Australian foreign reserves
X: value of exports
J: value of imports
NPI: net property income paid abroad
PIK: private net capital inflow
GB: net government borrowings
KI: net apparent capital inflow

4 The banks did not publish their holdings of foreign reserves, and so this must be estimated. The more conventional measure of London funds, net assets in Britain, was not chosen as this series is heavily affected by rising deposit liabilities in the 1880s. This causes the severe trough in the series shown in Appendix 1, figure 7A.1. I have used external cash holdings of the banks adjusted by the British banks' reserves ratio. Also shown in Appendix 1 is the unadjusted series. Changes in all three series are, in fact, highly correlated, as is the resulting capital inflow series (figure 7A.3).

5 The shares of sectoral borrowers in the private inflow were as follows:

Shares of financial institutions in private capital inflow

Period	Banks	Pastoral	Finance	Insurance
1870–1879	46.7	31.5	4.9	1.2
1880–1889	38.1	22.6	13.6	8.7
1890–1899	− 63.6	− 17.2	− 12.9	6.4

Note:
Residual attributed to mining and miscellaneous companies.
Source: Calculated from N.G. Butlin (1962, p. 424).

6 Sources were diverse. Australian bank managers actively recruited funds directly. Edinburgh had many intermediaries for banks and other financial institutions. There were also many investment trusts and solicitors who simply placed funds into various financial companies in Scotland and London, not knowing, nor really caring, where their funds were ultimately headed.

7 Even the special design was abandoned in 1871.

8 The traditional view was certainly expressed to Tocker. J. Russell Butchart in his Joseph Fisher Lecture in Commerce, *Money, Credit and Exchange* (1923), recorded (p. 14) that: "Prior to August, 1914, the moneys of Great Britain and Australia were kept from varying in value beyond the cost of shipping gold by the principle of ready convertibility of credit [money] into gold and by the facility of shipment of gold from one country to the other. The great service rendered by gold in thus stabilizing the values of the moneys of Great Britain and Australia was of immense value to the peoples of the two countries trading on a great scale with one another."

9 Investment in the borrowing country produced with a lag a rise in exportables and income to service the debt, at least in theory.

10 That is, prices in two countries could not be out of line for considerable periods inducing gold flows, monetary change, followed by adjustment in prices (and interest rates), to correct the imbalance.

11 The law of one price holds for each commodity in each market, they argue, but this does not mean one price level throughout the world.

12 Note that i^A is omitted since x comprises reduced-form determinants. See Kouri and Porter (1974).

13 In fact, gold flows have *not* been treated as merchandise trade in Australia's trade accounts. Wilson, who served as Australia's Statistician (1946–51), was instrumental in producing *The Australian Balance of Payments, 1918–29 to 1948–49* (Australia, CBCS, 1950), and in this and subsequent accounts actual gold exports and imports are excluded from the current account. Instead, gold production less industrial absorption was (and continued to be) entered "irrespective of whether it is physically imported or exported" (Australia, CBCS, 1950, p. 16). In the capital account the gold production less absorption figure found a counterpart in "monetary gold holdings" and, where gold was sold, in

"foreign exchange holdings." The balance of trade calculations contained in this chapter follow this custom. This in no way implies that Wilson, or others since, endorsed the PSF *mechanism*. It merely expresses the view that once out of the ground gold (less absorption) is an offset to trade deficits. From the 1930s the Australian government compulsorily acquired all gold.

References

Australia, Commonwealth Bureau of Census and Statistics (CBCS) 1950. *The Australian Balance of Payments 1928–29 to 1948–49*, Canberra: CBCS.

1951. *Demography 1949, Bulletin*, no. 67, Canberra: CBCS.

Bank of New South Wales, 1936. *Royal Commission on Monetary and Banking Systems 1936: Replies by A.C. Davidson, General Manager, to Questionnaire to Trading Banks*, Sydney: Bank of New South Wales.

Bordo, Michael D., 1984. "The gold standard: the traditional approach," in M.D. Bordo and A. Schwartz (eds.), *A Retrospective on the Classical Gold Standard: 1821–1931*, Chicago: University of Chicago Press: 23–113.

Bordo, Michael D. and Lars Jonung, 1987. *The Long-Run Behaviour of the Velocity of Circulation: The International Evidence*, Cambridge: Cambridge University Press.

Bordo, Michael D. and Finn E. Kydland, 1992. "The gold standard as a rule," Federal Reserve Bank of Cleveland, *Working Paper*, 9205 (March).

Bordo, Michael D. and Anna J. Schwartz (eds.), 1984. *A Retrospective on the Classical Gold Standard: 1821–1931*, Chicago: University of Chicago Press.

Butchart, J. Russell, 1923. *Money, Credit and Exchange* (the Joseph Fisher Lecture in Commerce), Adelaide: Hassell Press.

Butlin, M., 1977. "A preliminary annual data base 1900/1 to 1973/74," *Research Discussion Paper*, 7701, (May), Department of Economic History, RSSS, Australian National University.

Butlin, N.G., 1962. *Australian Domestic Product, Investment and Foreign Borrowing, 1861–1938/9*, Cambridge: Cambridge University Press.

1964. *Investment in Australian Economic Development, 1861–1900*, Cambridge: Cambridge University Press.

1970. "Some perspectives of Australian economic development, 1890–1965," in Colin Forster (ed.), *Australian Economic Development in the Twentieth Century*, Sydney: Australasian Publishing Co. and London: George Allen & Unwin: 266–327.

1987. "Australian national accounts," in Wray Vamplew (ed.), *Australians: Historical Statistics*, Sydney: Fairfax, Syme & Weldon Associates: 126–144.

Butlin, S.J., 1986. *The Australian Monetary System 1851–1914*, Sydney: Reserve Bank of Australia.

Butlin, S.J., A.R. Hall and R.C. White, 1971. *Australian Banking and Monetary Statistics 1817–1945*, Reserve Bank of Australia, *Occasional Paper*, no. 4A, Sydney: Reserve Bank of Australia.

Cassell, Gustav, 1935. *The Downfall of the Gold Standard*, Oxford: Clarendon Press.

Copland, D.B., 1925. "Australian banking and exchange," *Economic Record*, 1 (1) (November): 17–28.

Dick, T.J. and J. Floyd, 1987. "Canada and the gold standard 1871–1913," (ms.); now published as *Canada and the Gold Standard: Canada 1871–1913* (New York: Cambridge University Press, 1992).

Edelstein, Michael, 1982. *Overseas Investment in the Age of High Imperialism: The United Kingdom, 1850–1914*, New York: Columbia University Press.

Ford, A.G., 1962. *The Gold Standard, 1880–1918: Britain and Argentina*, Oxford: Clarendon Press.

Frenkel, J.A., 1971. "A theory of money trade and the balance of payments in a model of accumulation," *Journal of International Economics*, 1 (May): 159–187.

Frenkel, J.A. and H.G. Johnson (eds.), 1976. *The Monetary Approach to the Balance of Payments*, London: George Allen & Unwin.

Friedman, Milton and Anna J. Schwartz, 1982. *Monetary Trends in the United States and the United Kingdom: Their Relation to Income, Prices, and Interest Rates, 1867–1975*, Chicago: University of Chicago Press.

Gallarotti, G.M., 1989. "The classical Gold Standard as a spontaneous order (centralized versus decentralized international monetary systems: the lessons of the classical Gold Standard)," Cato Conference (February) (mimeo).

Goodhart, C.A.E., 1972. *The Business of Banking, 1891–1914*, London: Weidenfield & Nicolson.

Goschen, G.J. [1892] 1978. *The Theory of the Foreign Exchanges*, reprint, New York: Arno Press.

Hall, A.R., 1963. "Some long period effects of the kinked age distribution of the population of Australia 1861–1961," *Economic Record*, 39 (85) (March): 43–52.

Hume, D., [1792] 1955. "Of the Balance of Trade," in E. Rotwein (ed.), *David Hume: Writings on Economics*, London: Nelson: 60–77.

Johnson, H.G., 1976. "The monetary approach to balance-of-payments theory," in J.A. Frenkel and H.G. Johnson (eds.), *The Monetary Approach to the Balance of Payments*, London: George Allen & Unwin: 147–167.

Kelley, Allen C., 1965. "International migration and economic growth: Australia 1865–1935," *Journal of Economic History*, 25 (3) (September): 333–354.

1968. "Demographic change and economic growth: Australia 1861 1911," *Explorations in Economic History*, 5 (3) (Spring/Summer): 207–277.

Kennett, J.A., 1972. "The Australian commercial bank managed gold exchange standard: 1880–1913," Economic History IV, thesis, University of Sydney.

Kouri, Pentti L.K. and Michael G. Porter, 1974. "International capital flows and portfolio equilibrium," *Journal of Political Economy*, 82 (May/June): 443–467.

Kreinin, Mordechai E. and Lawrence H. Officer, 1978. "The monetary approach to the balance of payments: a survey," *Princeton Studies in International Finance*, Princeton: Princeton University Press.

Lindert, Peter H., 1969. "Key currencies and gold, 1900–1913," *Princeton Studies in*

236   David Pope

   International Finance, Princeton: Princeton University Press.

1984. "'Comment' on L. Jonung, 'Swedish experience under the Classical Gold Standard, 1873–1913'," in M.D. Bordo and A. Schwartz (eds.), *A Retrospective on the Classical Gold Standard: 1821–1931*, Chicago: University of Chicago Press: 399–404.

Lougheed, Alan, 1987. "International transactions and foreign commerce," in Wray Vamplew (ed.), *Australians: Historical Statistics*, Sydney: Fairfax, Syme & Weldon Associates: 183–205.

McCloskey, Donald, N. and J. Richard Zecher, 1976. "How the gold standard worked, 1880–1913," in J.A. Frenkel and H.G. Johnson (eds.), *The Monetary Approach to the Balance of Payments*, London: George Allen & Unwin: 357–385.

1984. "The success of Purchasing Power Parity: historical evidence and its implications for macroeconomics," in M.D. Bordo and A. Schwartz (eds.), *A Retrospective on the Classical Gold Standard: 1821–1931*, Chicago: University of Chicago. Press: 121–150.

Maddock, Rodney and Ian W. McLean, 1987. *The Australian Economy in the Long Run*, Cambridge: Cambridge University Press.

Meier, Gerald M., 1953. "Economic development and the transfer mechanism: Canada, 1895–1913," *Canadian Journal of Economics and Political Science*, 19 (February): 1–19.

Mundell, R., 1971. *Monetary Theory*, Pacific Palisades, CA: Goodyear.

Pope, David, 1981. "Modelling the peopling of Australia," *Australian Economic Papers*, 20 (37) (December): 258–282.

1986. "Australian capital inflow, sectional prices and the terms of trade: 1870–1939," *Australian Economic Papers*, 25 (46) (June): 67–82.

1987. "Private Finance," in Wray Vamplew (ed.), *Australians: Historical Statistics*, Sydney: Fairfax, Syme & Weldon Associates: 238–253.

1989. "Free banking in Australia before World War I," *Working Papers in Economic History*, no. 129 (December), Canberra: Australian National University.

Price, Charles, 1987. "Immigration and ethnic origin," in Wray Vamplew (ed.), *Australians: Historical Statistics*, Sydney: Fairfax, Syme & Weldon Associates: 2–22.

Sayers, R.S., 1951. "The development of central banking after Bagehot," *Economic History Review*, 2nd ser., 4 (1): 109–116.

1957. *Central Banking after Bagehot*, Oxford: Clarendon Press.

Sheppard, David K., 1971. *The Growth and Role of UK Financial Institutions 1880–1962*, London: Methuen.

Smit, J.C., 1934. "The pre-war gold standard," *Proceedings of the Academy of Political Science*, 13 (April): 53–61.

Stovel, John A., 1959. *Canada in the World Economy*, Cambridge, MA: Harvard University Press.

Tocker, A.M., 1924. "The monetary standards of New Zealand and Australia," *Economic Journal* (December): 556–575.

Tsokhas, K., 1990. *Markets, Money and Empire: The Political Economy of the Australian Wool Industry*, Melbourne: Melbourne University Press.

Union Bank records, U37 and U38, Archives of Business and Labour, ANU, Canberra.

Vamplew, Wray (ed.), 1987. *Australians: Historical Statistics*, Sydney: Fairfax, Syme & Weldon Associates.

Viner, Jacob, 1924. *Canada's Balance of International Indebtedness, 1900–1913*, Cambridge, MA: Harvard University Press.

Whale, P.B., 1937. "The working of the pre-war gold standard," *Economica*, 4 (February): 18–32.

Williamson, Jeffrey G., 1961. "International trade and U.S. economic development 1827–1843," *Journal of Economic History*, 21 (September): 372–383.

1963. "Real growth, monetary disturbances, and the transfer process: the U.S., 1879–1900," *Southern Economic Journal*, 29 January: 167–180.

1964. *American Growth and the Balance of Payments, 1820–1913*, Chapel Hill: University of North Carolina Press.

Wilson, R., 1931. *Capital Imports and the Terms of Trade Examined in the Light of Sixty Years of Australian Borrowings*, Melbourne: Melbourne University Press.

1935. "London Funds and the Australian Economy," *Economic Record*, 11, Supplement (March): 97–121.

Part III

Wartime upheaval and postwar stabilization

8 British and French finance during the Napoleonic Wars

MICHAEL D. BORDO AND EUGENE N. WHITE

The Napoleonic Wars offer an experiment unique in the history of wartime finance. While Britain was forced off the gold standard and endured a sustained inflation, France remained on a bimetallic standard for the war's duration. For wars of comparable length and intensity in the nineteenth and twentieth centuries, Napoleonic war finance stands out. As Friedman (1990) pointed out, the French experience is a puzzle. Under the *ancien régime* and the revolutionary governments, France's credit was far inferior to Great Britain's; yet, in the years of bitter struggle after 1796, it was the British who used inflationary finance, not the French.

This apparent paradox may be explained by drawing upon the new literatures on tax smoothing, time consistency, and credibility in macroeconomics. Before the Revolution, French fiscal policy strongly resembled the British practice where large temporary increases in wartime expenditures were paid for by increased borrowing, leaving taxes relatively unchanged.[1] This was a relatively efficient strategy for war finance, but its success hinged critically on the credibility of the government to repay its accumulated and enlarged debt after the war. If the government was perceived by the public to be pursuing a time inconsistent policy, that is, a policy likely to produce default once the debt is acquired, this avenue of war finance would have been closed.[2] The French monarchy was not as credible a borrower as the British parliament and consequently was forced to borrow at higher interest rates for the same program of war finance.

Nevertheless, the French were much better creditors than traditionally perceived by historians, and it was only the failure of the *ancien régime* to return to a policy of peacetime balanced budgets after the American War for Independence that brought on the fiscal crisis that led to the Revolution (White, 1989). The revolutionaries frequently and publicly announced their commitment to honor the national debt. In the process of economic reform, they issued paper money, the *assignats*, to cover current deficits and retire the short-term debt. The public willingly held the *assignats* because they regarded the government's promise to redeem the paper money and reorganize the nation's finances as credible. However, the continued decline in tax revenues and increases in expenditures forced the government to issue more money. The resulting hyperinflation ruined what remained of France's financial reputation.

This left the French government with no opportunities to borrow or use inflationary finance. The only means of finance remaining was taxation in France or its conquered territories. In 1797, the government admitted that it could not service the debt and decreed a reduction in the value of the outstanding debt by two-thirds. After this hurdle, the government began the slow and painful process of re-establishing its credibility by deed and by creating institutions signaling its good intentions. In 1800, the new government under Napoleon resumed interest payments on the debt in specie and established the Banque de France and a Sinking Fund. By bringing the budget into balance, paying interest, and retiring the long-term debt, Napoleon was able to bring yields on the government debt down and engage in some very limited borrowing.

Across the channel, at the same time as France was returning to specie convertibility, the Bank of England was forced to suspend convertibility in February 1797. The suspension, initially supposed to end in June 1797, lasted until 1821. Thus, Britain gave the appearance of traveling down the same dangerous road that France had almost a decade before. However, although it was freed from the gold standard constraint, Britain financed most of its expenditures by taxation and borrowing, with a limited use of inconvertible paper. Although there was a modest wartime inflation, Britain managed to ensure that its promise of resumption remained credible. The British government's commitment was credible because, unlike France, its tax system did not collapse and indeed taxes were raised substantially. Moreover, operation of the Sinking Fund of 1786 throughout the war served as a further signal of the government's intention of ultimate redemption. Belief that ultimate budget balance would be restored meant that money creation, like borrowing, was a temporary measure. Hence the British public did not, as in the French case from 1794 to 1796, sharply reduce their holdings of real cash balances and erode the inflation tax base. Britain was thus able to follow a flexible program of war finance.

A tarnished reputation did not allow Napoleon to follow a similar policy. Lacking strong credibility, he was forced to keep the franc convertible. Borrowing was limited and the French were pressed to cover the extra wartime expenditures by raising domestic taxes and imposing heavy levies on the rest of the Empire. The apparent puzzle of French war finance is resolved with a twist: it was the nation's weakness as a borrower, not its strength, that kept it on a specie standard.

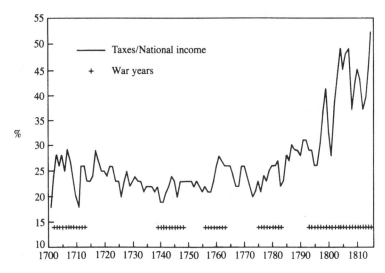

Sources: Gayer, Rostow and Schwartz (1953); Mitchell and Deane
(1982); Mathias and O'Brien (1976)
8.1   Great Britain, tax receipts as a percentage of commodity output

Avant la révolution: **British and French fiscal policy before 1789**

Although the eighteenth century French monarchy has traditionally been
regarded as an unworthy debtor, French fiscal policy resembled the British
practice of keeping the level of aggregate taxation relatively smooth while
borrowing to finance wars. Although neither nation started the century
auspiciously, the British gradually built a reputation as a superior creditor.

Britain's movement towards tax smoothing – financing of wartime
expenditures by borrowing and then servicing and amortizing the debt by
taxation in peacetime – began after the Glorious Revolution of 1688. This
political victory for parliamentary government led to improvements in tax
collection and administration and the development of more modern capital
markets (Dickson, 1967; Brewer, 1989). By the War of the Spanish Succes-
sion (1702–13), Britain's new fiscal program was in place. Taxes as a
percentage of national income in figure 8.1 and as a percentage of commodity output in figure 8.2 did not rise substantially in wartime periods until
the very end of the eighteenth century. Holding taxes relatively stable, the
boom in wartime spending produced very large deficits, as seen in figure 8.3.
These deficits accounted for a very substantial fraction of national income,
as indicated in figure 8.4.

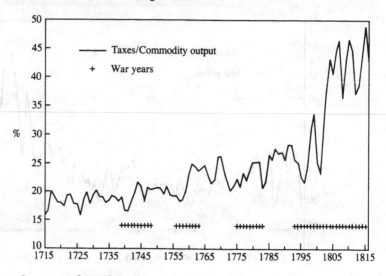

Sources: as figure 8.1
8.2   Great Britain, taxes as a percentage of commodity output

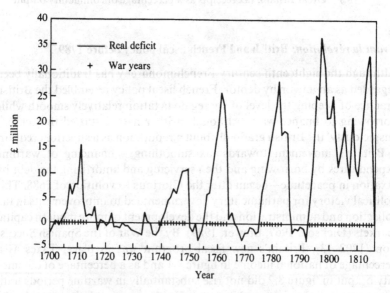

Sources: as figure 8.1
8.3   Great Britain, real deficit (surplus)

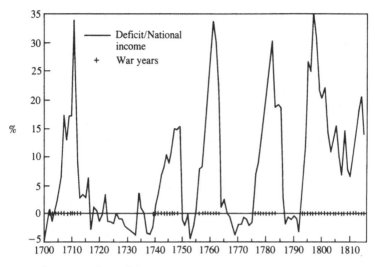

8.4   Great Britain, deficit as a percentage of national income

British wartime expenditures were primarily financed by the issue of "unfunded debt," a variety of short-term obligations that included Army, Navy, and Ordnance bills and increasingly Exchequer bills. The "funded debt" or long-term securities were mostly used during and after the war to retire the more costly unfunded debt. The funded debt was secured by specially earmarked indirect taxes. Before 1713, the funded debt consisted of irredeemable annuities issued at high interest rates (up to 14 percent). Afterwards, the government attempted to reduce both the principal and servicing costs of this outstanding debt by establishing a Sinking Fund (to be supplied by budget surpluses) in 1717 and carrying out a number of conversions of the annuities and other irredeemable debt into redeemable perpetuities.

The most famous conversion plan was the South Sea promotion, which allowed annuitants to convert their annuities into South Sea or government stock. Although the operation of this plan produced the South Sea Bubble with considerable losses for the public, it did convert virtually all of the irredeemable debt and reduce the interest bill (Neal, 1990b). While the collapse of the Bubble temporarily discredited the government, it did ensure that public finance would be divorced from narrow political and private interests, improving over the longer term the credibility of government's fiscal and debt-management policies. The capstone on this development was the final conversion of most of the redeemable debt from 5 percent to 3 percent consols between 1749 and 1757 (Brewer, 1989, p. 124).

Reduction of the debt and of its servicing costs during periods of peace then allowed the government to resume borrowing in ever larger amounts in the succeeding wars, as may be seen in figure 8.3. The shares of wartime expenditure financed by borrowing increased from 51 percent in the Nine Years War (1689–97) to 81 percent in the American War for Independence (O'Brien, 1988, table 3). However, the rise in debt during the Seven Years War (1756–63) and especially the American War, from £130 milion to £243 million, increased fears of national bankruptcy and crippling levels of peacetime taxation to service the debt. As a consequence in 1786, Pitt, the Chancellor of the Exchequer, re-established the Sinking Fund, which during the seven succeeding years of peace used budget surpluses to reduce the debt. The Sinking Fund was viewed by contemporaries as a way of showing the public that taxes would eventually be reduced and hence could be viewed as an investment in sovereign credibility and future borrowing power.

The monthly yield on the 3 percent consols (Brit 3%) from 1770 to 1821 is depicted in figure 8.5.[3] During the American Revolution and the Napoleonic Wars, the interest rate rose sharply.[4] This pattern is consistent with recent developments in the theory of fiscal policy (Barro, 1989). To marshal scarce resources for the war effort, real interest rates should rise in wartime to reduce both present consumption and leisure in favor of saving and labor effort. The nominal interest rate displayed here should be a good proxy for the real interest rate, since up to 1797, Britain adhered to a specie standard, under which the price level was remarkably stable.[5]

France's national finances at the beginning of the century were not greatly inferior to Britain's. John Law's unsuccessful attempt to reorganize the government's finances ended in 1721 with another massive write-down of the debt (Murphy, 1986). The annual interest payments on the *rentes perpétuelles*, or consols were, for example, cut in half (Riley, 1986). Although the collapse of Law's schemes had allowed the government to write down the debt, the French were unable to follow the British and improve their fiscal management, leaving the state's finances relatively precarious. In 1759, in the midst of the Seven Years War, the Crown was forced to suspend repayment of the capital on a variety of short-term debts (Marion, 1914). The continuing financial crisis after the war eventually led to the partial bankruptcy of 1770 when reimbursement of the capital of maturing securities was again suspended and the interest payments on securities were reduced. After this last crisis, the Crown made a new commitment to fiscal stability. Finance ministers successfully balanced the budget or ran surpluses up to the American war, as shown in the budgets

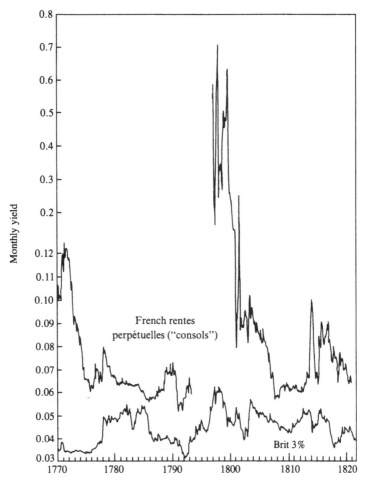

Sources: Neal (1990a); *Gazette de France*; *Ancien Moniteur*; Courtois (1877)
8.5 Yields of British and French securities, 1770–1820

depicted in figure 8.6. Taxes, as in the British case, were a relatively constant but lower share of output, as seen in figure 8.7.

The first French interest rate in figure 8.5 is the monthly yield on the stock of the Compagnie des Indes, the French East India Company. The series begins in 1770 when the Crown took over the Compagnie des Indes and converted its stock into 5 percent consols. After soaring to well above 10 percent in the wake of the monarchy's partial bankruptcy, the French yields

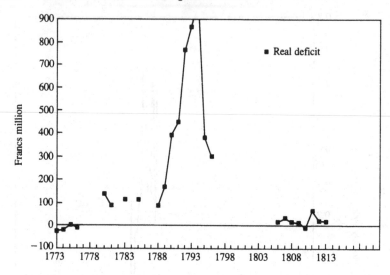

Sources: White (1989, 1990); Mollien (1945)
8.6   France, real deficit (surplus)

declined rapidly after a reorganization of the government's finances and fell to approximately 6 percent by 1776.

When the American War for Independence began there was considerable concern that support for the American revolutionaries would bring about a new financial collapse. Yields on the stock of the Compagnie des Indes increased, reaching as high as 8 percent in 1778. The financial markets' fears were calmed by Jacques Necker who was appointed finance minister in 1776. His reforms reaffirmed the Crown's commitment to fiscal prudence, enabling the state to finance the war almost entirely by borrowing with taxes held nearly constant. The estimated cost of the war from 1777 to 1782 has been calculated at 1,066 million livres and total borrowing at 997 million livres (Harris, 1967, p. 240–242). Direct taxes were increased late in the war, in 1782, by 27 million livres, most of which was a third *vingtième* of 21 million for the duration of the war plus three years. Complete budgets exist for only a few years. One extant budget for 1780 in table 8.1 shows total expenditures of 625 million livres, covered by revenues of 501 million and borrowing of 124 million.[6] Necker induced the public to lend to the state by reducing non-military expenditures and using the proceeds to cover the interest payments on the new debt. The minister's promise was that when the war ended and extraordinary military expenditures ceased the Crown would run a balanced budget, with the increased cost of servicing the war debt offset by reduced non-military expenditures. The financial

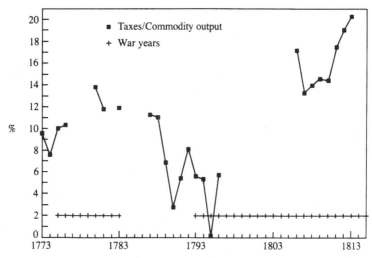

Sources: White (1989, 1990); Mollien (1945); O'Brien and Caglar (1978)
8.7 France, taxes as a percentage of commodity output

markets were convinced by this strategy, and after 1779 yields on government securities fell, leveling off at slightly above 6 percent for the *rentes
perpétuelles*.

The interest rate history of France thus parallels Britain's in figure 8.5. As
in the British case, a rise in the interest rate during the American War served
to reallocate scarce resources to the war effort. Likewise, after the war,
interest rates fell in the belief that the budget would soon be balanced.[7]
However, Necker was dismissed from office in 1781 and his successors did
not adhere to his financial strategy. They quietly restored many of the
budget cuts he had made and allowed other expenditures to rise. No new
taxes were imposed and the peacetime budget deficits were financed wholly
by borrowing. In 1785, the actual deficit was 125 million livres, covered
wholly by the issue of new debt. The projected budget for 1788 in table 8.1
shows total expected revenues of 472 million and expenditures of 565
million livres (of which 260 million were interest payments).[8] The minister
of finance planned to cover the deficit of 93 million by new borrowing.

The public in France only gradually became aware of the government's
deviation from its announced objective. In 1784 and 1785, the Crown had
explained its continued borrowing as the product of continued wartime
commitments and a need to convert short-term debt into long-term debt. In
1785, the government even attempted to set up a Sinking Fund to begin
retirement of the debt, although the funds committed to it were soon taken
back. Only in 1787 did the Parlement de Paris fully recognize that the

Table 8.1 *French budgets, 1774–1814*

	1774	1780	1781	1785	1788	5/1/1789–4/3/1790	1790	1791	1792
Total revenue	276.7	501.3	436.9		472.4	298.2	124.0	242.4	370.6
Direct taxes					153.0	136.6	38.7	151.7	
Indirect taxes					205.7	58.7	13.8	7.6	
Crown lands					50.3	49.6	17.9	19.4	
Foreign subsidies									
Other					63.4	53.3	53.6	63.7	
Total expenditure	258.5	625.0	526.6		565.2	500.2	487.9	772.1	1,362.9
Royal households					32.3	24.4	32.5	31.2	
Army/Navy/Colonies					150.7	165.0	166.7	205.4	
Interest payments					260.1	164.8	168.8	253.1	
Clergy								159.4	
Other					122.1	146.0	119.9	123.0	
Deficit	18.2	−123.7	−89.7	−124.7	−92.8	−202.0	−363.9	−529.7	−992.3
New borrowing	48.6	176.5	426.0	459.9	150.1	257.0	51.5	6.9	
Reimbursements	66.8	52.6	336.3	335.2	57.3	203.6	168.0	74.1	
Net borrowing	−18.2	123.7	89.7	124.7	92.8	53.4	−116.5	−67.2	
Money creation						190.0	424.1	609.8	998.2

Crown would not be able to balance its budget. The French monarchy was able to deceive the public because government finance was not open to parliamentary inspection as in Britain; there was no set of institutions in France to guarantee that the government would adhere to a time consistent policy. This was not the case in Britain (North and Weingast, 1989), where the parliament in Westminster voted on the budget, the Bank of England faithfully made daily redemption of its notes in specie and, as mentioned above, a Sinking Fund paid off the national debt. By contrast, the budget was not public in France, a project to set up a Sinking Fund had failed, and the Discount Bank had been forced to suspend more than once.

    This lack of institutional commitment in the absence of a good track record forced the French government to borrow at higher interest rates than the British could. The premium on French consols over British consols in figure 8.5 reflects the greater riskiness of French securities. The higher French rate may in part reflect a higher cost of capital, but this should not account for the whole difference.[9] There were large international capital flows between all countries in this period, and Dutch and Swiss investors placed several hundred million livres in French securities (Riley, 1973). Furthermore, there is considerable evidence that rates for private French borrowers were well below rates for the government. Although data on

1/1/1793–9/21/1793	Year II 9/22/1793–9/21/1794	9/22/1794–4/19/1795	10/27/1795–9/22/1796	9/1805–12/1806	1807	1808	1809	1810	1811	1812	1813
259.3	2,105.6	3,087.1	279.3	970.8	759.9	811.2	856.8	860.7	1056.3	1168.0	1263.8
			40.6	403.0	311.8	295.0	302.8	302.6	306.0	335.7	334.6
				195.9	219.7	206.6	284.6	294.9	401.0	436.0	472.8
			16.2	254.1	172.2	181.5	186.9	190.4	189.3	200.0	200.0
			122.4	43.7	34.2	36.1	30.0	30.0	112.3	30.0	48.0
			100.1	53.9	22.0	91.4	52.5	42.8	47.7	166.3	208.4
2,667.0	4,775.7	5,734.8	581.7	968.8	773.6	806.4	851.2	831.2	1103.4	1168.0	1263.8
				582.2	459.4	491.5	506.7	478.4	663.1	722.0	816.0
				128.1	103.8	104.7	108.0	109.7	148.0	148.0	129.5
−2,407.7	−2,670.1	−2,647.7	−302.4	−18.2	−33.9	−15.4	−14.6	9.3	−67.3	−20.2	−20.2
			13.5								
			13.5								
2,459.8	2,892.4	2,647.7	−288.9								

non-government interest rates is fragmentary, existing evidence suggests that in the last two decades before the Revolution private individuals could on average borrow at under 5 percent (Rosenthal, 1989).

The revolution: France's squandered reputation

The collapse of the French monarchy was initially accompanied by a loss of confidence in the nation's ability to meet its commitments, but the initial success of the Revolution convinced the public that a program of stabilization could work. Only by 1792 when war broke out again was it clear that it was unlikely that the government would be able to succeed. The civil and foreign wars in the next few years required vast resources. The tax base was substantially reduced and the government could have borrowed only at very high rates. The revolutionaries turned to confiscatory taxation, capital levies and the inflation tax to cover their expenditures. These methods of finance eventually proved to be self-defeating and destroyed initial good faith in the Revolution.

The Revolution began in 1787 when the Parlement de Paris and the government's own hastily organized Assembly of Notables refused to sanction new taxes or new loans. Although they were not given complete accounts of government finance, they seem to have correctly perceived that the Crown had almost exhausted its ability to borrow in the sense that a very large fraction of tax revenues was already pledged to pay the funded debt and that non-interest expenditures could not easily be reduced.

When a poor harvest in the summer of 1788 produced a drop in tax receipts, the minister of finance decreed a partial default on the debt. Unable to borrow any more from the market, the government covered its deficit by borrowing from the Discount Bank, while it waited for the Estates-General in the hope that it would raise taxes to solve the crisis. Continued dependence on this monopoly bank of issue forced it to suspend payment in September 1789 when a run began, turning its bank notes into fiat money.

In the year following the May 1, 1789 opening of the Estates-General, tax revenues declined to 298 million, as seen in table 8.1. The public refused to pay the traditional taxes, partly in the expectation that these would be abolished and partly because they were prompted by the Parlement and then the Estates-General-turned National Assembly to rebel against the Crown. Only 53 million livres of the deficit were covered by borrowing from the market. The remainder of the 202 million livres deficit was paid by money creation via the Discount Bank. Unwilling to raise taxes, the National Assembly chose to seize the lands of the Church and auction them off to cover the immediate deficit and repay the outstanding unfunded debt. To meet the state's urgent financial needs, the *assignats* were created. These notes were used by the state to pay its creditors, who could in turn employ them to buy the nationalized properties of the Church, the *biens nationaux*.

In 1790 the tax receipts were only 124 million livres while expenditures were 488 million. The *ancien régime's* indirect and direct taxes were abolished and replaced only with new taxes on income and property (Godechot, 1968, pp. 163–174; Marion, 1919, vol. 2, pp. 82–91). The deficit and the net reimbursements were covered by payment in *assignats*. While the immediate situation looked dismal, financial markets seem to have believed that the sale of *biens nationaux* could resolve the state's problems, and the interest rate in figure 8.5 fell back to pre-crisis levels in 1791, which were still well below the levels in 1770 after the partial default. This suggests that at most the public believed that the government might force them to accept slightly depreciated paper money in payment of interest for a brief period. Credibility was created by the more open budget process and more importantly by the sale of Church lands to retire the *assignats* that had been used to cover the deficit and pay off part of the national debt.

The outbreak of war in April 1792 and the vast increase in expenditures eliminated any chance of success for retiring the *assignats* by the sale of the *biens nationaux*. The markets lost confidence and the yields on government securities returned to 1789 levels until 1793 when the bourse was closed. The state's finances deteriorated rapidly and the growing deficit in figure 8.6 was covered entirely by the issue of *assignats*. During the revolutionary Terror, the government attempted to halt inflation with price controls and raise revenue by steeply progressive income taxes and forced loans. Although the price controls were briefly successful, these experiments failed and were abandoned after the overthrow of Robespierre in 1794. However, tax collections did not pick up and the government became wholly dependent on money creation to pay for its expenditures. Inflation began to rise very rapidly in early 1795, leading to a hyperinflation at the end of the year. In December the government abandoned the use of the *assignats* and imposed a forced loan to retire them from circulation. Still unable to secure anything but minimal tax collections, a new paper money, the *mandats*, was issued in 1796, generating a very short-lived inflation.

The government's fiscal state is captured in its budget for October 1795–September 1796 in table 8.1. Expenditures totalled 582 million livres. Valued in specie, payment of direct taxes raised 41 million, the forced loan 14 million, and income from state lands 16 million. The bulk of revenue was derived from two sources: taxes imposed on conquered territories of 105 million and money creation of 304 million livres.

Having exhausted its ability to use money creation, the Directory had to cut expenditures and raise taxes. In September 1797, the government wrote down the value of interest payments by two-thirds, reducing the *rentes perpétuelles* from 175 million to 58 million livres. This was further reduced by canceling the debts of émigrés and convicts, leaving annual payments at 40 million. The remaining *rentes viagères* required another 29 million in annual service. Adding the 6.1 million livres for the debts of annexed countries, the annual interest payments on the national debt stood at 75.3 million in 1799 – a drastic reduction from the 260 million of 1788. Nevertheless, the government did not make full payment in specie even on this reduced sum.

Unable to raise tax revenues which as seen in table 8.1 remained below the levels of the *ancien régime*, the government took new drastic measures. It delayed payment to government contractors, forcing them to queue for payment. In 1799, the Directory attempted a return to the economic policies of the Terror, including the imposition of a 100 million franc forced loan on the wealthy in July. The interest on the new consols, the *tiers consolidé* (Tiers) in figure 8.5 rose to 50 percent in this new crisis.

By 1799, revolutionary France had squandered its modest endowment of credibility, having failed to pursue any consistent policies. Its ability to finance the wars of the next decade and a half was in consequence sharply limited. Money finance and large-scale borrowing was ruled out by the loss

Table 8.2 *Revenue and expenditure, Great Britain, 1793–1816, million pounds*

	1793	1794	1795	1796	1797	1798	1799	1800	1801
I. Revenue									
(1) Net revenue	18.52	19.33	19.05	19.39	21.48	27.24	32.51	33.10	32.75
(2) Indirect taxes	13.57	14.20	14.79	14.53	16.22	18.58	21.37	20.00	23.39
(2a) Customs duties	3.65	4.35	3.42	3.65	3.94	4.74	7.06	6.78	8.78
(2b) Excise and stamp duties	10.01	9.85	11.37	10.88	12.28	13.84	14.31	13.22	14.61
(3) Direct taxes	2.95	3.03	2.95	3.02	3.36	4.59	8.12	9.60	10.44
(3a) Land and assessed taxes	2.95	3.03	2.95	3.02	3.36	4.59	6.45	5.09	4.64
(3b) Income and property taxes	0.00	0.00	0.00	0.00	0.00	0.00	1.67	4.51	5.80
(4) Other revenue (Post Office, Misc.)	2.00	2.10	1.32	1.84	1.90	4.06	3.02	3.51	2.95
II. Expenditure									
(5) Total net public expenditure	21.82	26.80	38.31	38.25	46.93	49.51	49.76	54.22	58.48
(6) Debt charges	9.15	9.80	10.47	11.60	13.59	16.20	17.09	17.20	19.05
(7) Civil government expenditure	2.34	2.07	2.25	2.52	3.91	4.60	4.79	5.31	5.85
(8) Military expenditure	10.33	14.93	25.59	24.13	29.43	28.71	27.88	31.71	33.58
(9) Deficit	−3.3	−7.47	−19.26	−18.86	−25.45	−22.27	−17.25	−21.12	−25.73
III. Composition of loans									
(10) Total loans	12.44	22.96	32.53	35.58	53.08	37.02	43.57	46.49	59.74
(11) Funded loans	3.92	12.91	18.79	28.58	42.84	22.77	16.35	20.50	36.15
(12) Unfunded loans	8.52	10.05	13.74	6.99	10.24	14.26	27.22	25.99	23.59
(13) Expenditure for loan reduction	8.76	15.91	12.73	14.28	24.64	14.74	29.38	25.52	32.73
(14) Net borrowing	3.68	7.05	19.80	21.30	28.44	22.28	14.19	20.97	27.01

Sources and Notes (by row):
(1)–(4) Gayer, Rostow and Schwartz (1953, Appendix IX, Table 223).
(5)–(8) Gayer, Rostow and Schwartz (1953, Table 226). Row (5) = (6) + (7) + (8). Debt charges are
interest on the public debt; civil government includes both civil government and civil list; military
expenditure is the sum of Army, Navy and Ordnance.

of reputation. Only taxation at home and abroad were available to the French.

British fiscal strategy, 1793–1815

The war against France was initially financed in the traditional eighteenth century manner; according to O'Brien (1967), 90 percent of wartime expenditures between 1793 and 1798 were covered by borrowing. The massive scale of expenditures led to a virtual doubling of the national debt by 1798. Table 8.2 shows the movements in expenditures and receipts for Great Britain from 1793 to 1816. The Napoleonic Wars required far greater expenditures and thus large deficits for a longer period of time than previous wars, as seen in table 8.2 and in figures 8.3 and 8.4. This increased pressure on government finance resulted in two new developments that

1802	1803	1804	1805	1806	1807	1808	1809	1810	1811	1812	1813	1814	1815	1816
35.17	37.81	45.07	50.13	54.93	58.74	51.31	62.72	68.39	66.55	66.09	72.57	73.75	78.45	65.51
26.40	30.39	34.43	37.40	39.19	39.74	40.64	40.59	43.72	42.18	40.48	42.67	44.85	44.24	40.50
7.73	8.19	9.47	10.15	10.81	10.55	10.28	11.90	12.42	10.94	11.58	11.87	12.61	11.95	10.08
18.67	22.20	24.96	27.25	28.38	29.19	30.36	28.69	31.30	31.24	28.90	30.80	32.24	32.29	30.42
8.65	6.18	9.71	10.85	12.55	17.19	19.02	20.85	21.23	20.60	20.57	22.18	22.56	24.12	19.15
5.32	5.80	6.02	6.26	6.39	7.03	7.62	8.44	7.74	7.39	7.50	7.91	8.04	9.50	7.35
3.33	0.38	3.69	4.59	6.16	10.16	11.40	12.41	13.49	13.21	13.07	14.27	14.52	14.62	11.80
3.47	3.85	3.94	4.93	6.27	5.38	5.51	5.10	7.35	7.64	9.11	11.84	10.61	14.43	10.23
48.46	47.24	57.36	67.38	66.63	66.89	71.11	74.53	78.21	82.29	91.67	106.15	107.37	99.52	64.81
19.63	19.92	19.84	21.49	22.41	23.02	22.34	23.39	23.68	23.86	25.58	26.43	29.11	31.39	32.19
6.26	5.67	7.74	8.82	6.08	6.85	6.66	6.93	8.97	6.81	8.47	9.19	9.19	14.72	6.90
22.57	21.65	29.78	37.07	38.14	37.02	42.11	44.21	45.56	51.62	57.62	70.53	69.07	53.41	25.72
−13.29	−9.43	−12.29	−17.25	−11.7	−8.15	−19.8	−11.81	−9.82	−15.74	−25.58	−33.58	−33.62	−21.07	0.7
42.50	30.86	32.86	53.01	51.01	49.98	59.34	58.73	59.32	64.97	80.70	105.30	88.89	95.49	55.84
26.05	11.95	14.15	25.34	20.11	15.52	14.22	22.64	21.60	23.75	34.92	51.14	36.62	50.66	9.25
16.45	18.91	18.71	27.67	30.90	34.45	45.11	36.09	37.72	41.22	45.78	54.16	52.27	44.83	46.59
28.32	22.43	19.13	35.23	39.61	39.43	48.98	47.12	50.31	49.27	56.25	67.93	56.42	73.99	57.54
14.18	8.43	13.73	17.78	11.40	10.55	10.36	11.61	9.01	15.70	24.45	37.37	32.47	21.50	−1.70

(10)–(14) Gayer, Rostow and Schwartz (1953, Table 229). Expenditure for loan reduction is also referred to as capital charge. Row (14) = (10) − (13).

deviated from the previous century's experience: the suspension of specie payments in 1797 and the introduction of an income tax in 1799.

Britain fought the wars of the eighteenth century on the gold standard, but the circumstances of the late 1790s forced a suspension of payments in February 1797. Pressure on the Bank of England's gold reserves began with a financial crisis at the outbreak of war in 1793. Faced with both an external drain, caused by capital flight and foreign remittances, and an internal drain, the Bank of England reduced its private loans; but this only exacerbated the internal drain. The crisis was finally alleviated by the government's issue of Exchequer bills to merchants in the City. Pressure on the Bank's reserves from external gold outflows continued so that by December 1795, the Bank reacted to its gold reserve ratio falling below 20 percent by discouraging accommodation of government securities. The government then turned to the money market (O'Brien, 1967, chapter 5). The sale of government securities, which otherwise would have been absorbed by the Bank, competed with private securities, forcing up interest rates to unprece-

Table 8.3 *The Bank of England's contribution to government finance, 1793–1815, million pounds*

	1793	1794	1795	1796	1797	1798	1799	1800	1801
(1) Bank of England notes	11.38	10.51	12.44	9.99	10.39	12.64	13.17	15.95	15.38
(2) Government securities held by the Bank	9.97	9.41	13.21	11.91	10.24	11.09	10.48	13.78	13.94
(3) Private securities held by the Bank	5.74	4.08	3.69	5.17	7.31	5.98	6.50	8.00	10.38
(4) Seigniorage	0.15	−0.59	0.47	−0.81	0.52	1.07	0.56	0.89	0.28
(5) Seigniorage as a percentage of the deficit	4.54	−7.89	2.44	−4.29	2.04	4.80	3.25	4.21	1.09
(6) Seigniorage as a percentage of total war revenue	1.9	−4.43	1.89	−2.28	1.56	4.15	1.59	2.35	0.72

Sources and Notes (by row):
(1) Mitchell and Deane (1962, p. 442) circulation.
(2) Mitchell and Deane (1962, p. 442) government securities.
(3) Mitchell and Deane (1962, p. 442) total securities − government securities.
(4) Gayer, Rostow, and Schwartz (1953, Appendix 3, Table 121 and Appendix 4, Table 138).

dented levels, as seen in figure 8.5. The 3 percent consol rate reached an eighteenth and nineteenth century peak of 6.3 percent in April 1797. Private borrowers then turned to the Bank, which responded by rationing credit in December 1795.[10] The credit stringency was in part alleviated, as it had been in 1793, by direct government lending to the City. According to O'Brien (1967), the response by the Bank to its dwindling gold reserves hindered the government's war finance. To prevent the perceived collapse of the Bank in the face of both a massive external drain and a run on the country banks, occasioned by fears of a French invasion, the government finally allowed it to suspend specie payments on February 26, 1797.

After the Bank suspended specie payments, the government was again able to sell much of its short-term debt to the Bank of England. Thus, until hostilities ceased, the share of unfunded loans in total loans increased dramatically from a low of 19 percent in 1797 to a peak of 76 percent in 1808 (see table 8.2).[11] The government's ability to float debt is also measured by the expansion in the Bank's holdings of public securities, seen in table 8.3. Accommodation of both government and private borrowing is generally viewed by historians – including Fetter (1965), Schumpeter (1938), Silbering (1923), and Viner (1937) – as the way in which the Bank contributed to war finance.

Both the Bank's note issue in figure 8.8 and the price level in figure 8.9

1802	1803	1804	1805	1806	1807	1808	1809	1810	1811	1812	1813	1814	1815
16.14	15.65	17.12	17.13	19.38	18.31	17.65	19.06	22.91	23.32	23.22	24.02	26.58	27.25
13.86	11.38	14.84	14.15	14.49	13.43	14.55	15.03	15.76	19.54	21.65	25.31	29.31	25.85
10.68	14.04	11.57	14.07	13.54	15.24	13.76	16.25	22.42	17.56	16.45	13.71	15.86	18.86
0.47	−0.12	0.52	−0.28	−0.05	−0.05	0.21	0.87	1.69	0.38	−0.05	0.35	1.30	0.00
3.54	−1.27	4.23	−1.62	−0.42	−0.61	1.06	7.37	17.20	2.41	−0.19	1.04	3.87	0.00
1.55	−0.42	1.28	−0.57	−0.11	−0.09	0.38	1.56	2.95	0.63	−0.07	0.45	1.45	0.00

(5) Row (4) divided by the deficit in row (9), table 8.1.
(6) Row (4) divided by column (13), table 4.12, O'Brien (1967).
  Total war revenue comprises total war loans (total taxes collected less the 1788–92 average) + total loans.

rose considerably during the period. Although there is considerable controversy as to whether the Bank caused the inflation by its note issue,[12] the unavailability of other than fragmentary data on London and country bank liabilities makes the case hard to test. Nevertheless, the fact that private borrowers could discount commercial and government paper freely at the 5 percent usury ceiling when the shadow nominal interest rate was surely higher, reflecting inflation rates up to 10 percent per annum, suggests that the indirect mechanism originally pointed out by Thornton (1802) was important.

While money creation by the Bank seems to have been responsible for inflation, and although real cash balances – the inflation tax base – maintained a rising trend in this period (see figure 8.10) in contrast to the French experience from 1794 to 1796 (White, 1990), it was not a principal pillar of war finance. One measure of the contribution of the Bank to war finance is seigniorage revenue (measured as the increase in bank notes divided by the average price level) expressed as a percentage either of the deficit or of war revenue. As seen in table 8.3, seigniorage was relatively unimportant in magnitude. However, these are downward biased measures of the contribution of inflationary finance because they omit the private banking system, whose liabilities, according to Presnell (1963) were at least as large as those of the Bank. Money creation did not make a large

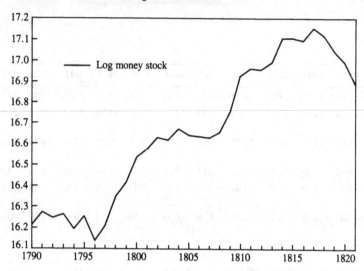

Source: Gayer, Rostow and Schwartz (1953)

8.8   Great Britain, log of the money stock

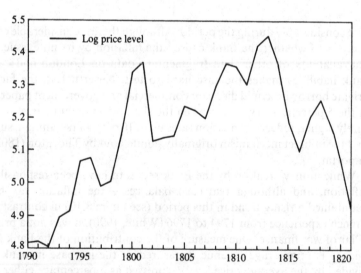

Source: as figure 8.8

8.9   Great Britain, log of the price level

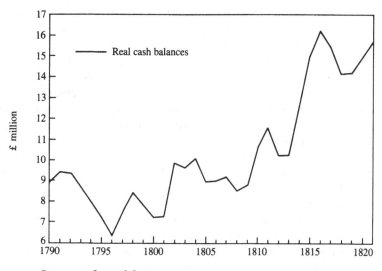

Source: as figure 8.8

8.10   Great Britain, real cash balances

contribution to war finance, but it did give the government critical flexibility in short-finance and debt management.

For this reason, the government viewed the Bank of England as an essential component of its war finance program. This can be seen in its opposition to a number of requests by the Bank (June 1797, October 1797, February 1803) to resume specie payments (O'Brien, 1967, chapter 5), its support of the Bank in the face of the withering criticism of the Bullion Report of 1810, its encouragement of the Bank to accommodate private demands for credit and its granting of *de facto* legal tender status to the Bank's notes in 1811 (Fetter, 1949).

Despite the government's opposition to resumption during wartime conditions, there also exists considerable evidence that the government wished to confirm its commitment to a return to the gold standard once hostilities ceased. The government's failure directly to confront the 1810 Bullion Report's criticism of the Bank for allowing the exchange rate to depreciate by over 10 percent (see Laidler, 1987) can be understood in this light. The government felt unable to argue that continued suspension was justified by wartime fiscal needs because it was concerned that this position would weaken both internal and external confidence in the paper pound. Instead, the government took the much misaligned positions of both disputing the facts of depreciation and presenting a list of non-monetary causes (O'Brien, 1967, chapter 6).

The second departure from the eighteenth century pattern of government finance was the institution of an income tax in 1799. Concern over the size of the national debt, the inability to raise further revenue from indirect taxes and the threat of defeat by the French revolutionaries were all arguments that Pitt used to overcome opposition to direct taxation by the propertied classes. The income and property taxes were immensely success- ful. In table 8.2, they rise from zero to approximately 20 percent of total tax revenue by the end of the war. Moreover, unlike the preceding wars, and especially the American war where net borrowing could rival and exceed tax revenues (see table 8.4), total taxes covered a far greater share of government expenditure than borrowing, which at its Napoleonic war peak covered approximately 30 percent. By contrast, in the same year that the British parliament levied an income tax, the French Directory attempted to impose a new forced loan. Property owners, large and small, had relatively little say in the government and remained outside the governing structure. They were not convinced that this was an appropriate means of raising funds, or that they would benefit. There was thus a high level of avoidance and the yield on the tax remained low.

The British experience during the Napoleonic wars suggests that the government followed policies consistent with the modern theory of tax smoothing. The theory of tax smoothing implies that an optimizing govern- ment will set tax rates over time so as to minimize deadweight losses (Barro, 1989). In a policy of tax smoothing, if future government expenditures are known with certainty, then the current tax rate will be set to reflect those expenditures and will remain constant over time. In an uncertain world, taxes will follow a martingale as the government attempts to forecast expenditures rationally and set the current tax rate consistent with its forecast of the future so that only unpredictable events will produce changing tax rates. Thus, in the event of a war of unprecedented severity and duration, such as the Napoleonic War, tax rates will increase signifi- cantly during the war to reflect the new, higher present value of government expenditures. However, the wartime rise in taxes will not fully match the rise in expenditures since they would be expected to decline after the war (Kochin, Benjamin and Meader, 1985).

The theory of tax smoothing implies that average tax rates should follow a martingale process. In table 8.5, we test for a martingale for Britain in 1700–1815, using two measures of the average tax rate: the ratio of tax revenue to commodity output and the ratio of tax revenue to national income. In both cases, the Dickey–Fuller test (see Nelson and Plosser, 1982) for the coefficient on the lagged average tax rate shows that the null hypothesis that the coefficient is equal to one cannot be rejected at the 1 percent level. This evidence supports the hypothesis that the British govern-

Table 8.4 Revenue and expenditure, Great Britain, 1776–85, million pounds

	1776	1777	1778	1779	1780	1781	1782	1783	1784	1785
I. Revenue										
(1) Net revenue	10.57	11.10	11.44	11.85	12.52	13.28	13.76	12.68	13.21	15.53
(2) Indirect taxes	8.06	7.66	7.72	8.14	8.85	9.13	9.32	8.43	9.17	10.68
(2a) Customs duties	2.68	2.41	2.35	2.52	2.77	3.02	2.90	2.95	3.03	4.54
(2b) Excise and stamp duties	5.38	5.25	5.37	5.62	6.08	6.11	6.42	5.48	6.14	6.14
(3) Direct taxes	2.04	2.45	2.64	2.58	2.65	2.77	2.86	2.76	2.66	2.97
(Land and assessed taxes)	1.87	2.30	2.50	2.45	2.52	2.63	2.72	2.59	2.46	2.67
(4) Other revenue (Post Office, misc.)	0.17	0.15	0.14	0.13	0.13	0.14	0.14	0.17	0.20	0.30
II. Expenditure										
(5) Total net public expenditure	14.04	15.26	17.94	19.71	22.60	25.81	29.23	23.51	24.24	25.83
(6) Debt charges	4.63	4.71	5.03	5.52	5.99	6.92	7.36	8.05	8.68	9.23
(7) Civil government expenditure	1.27	1.77	1.42	1.16	1.25	1.35	1.26	1.38	1.32	1.45
(8) Military expenditure	7.54	8.78	10.98	12.46	14.87	17.06	20.13	13.67	13.76	14.79
(9) Estimated deficit	−3.47	−4.16	−6.50	−7.86	−10.08	−12.53	−15.47	−10.83	−11.03	−10.30

Sources and Notes (by row):

(1)–(4) Mitchell and Deane (1962, p. 388).

(5)–(8) Mitchell and Deane (1962, pp. 390–391).

(9) = (5) − (1).

Table 8.5 *Tax smoothing in Great Britain, 1700–1815*
$T/Y = B_0 + B_1 * (T/Y)_{t-1} + e_t$

		Coefficients of independent variables				
variable	Period	B_0	B_1	$\bar{R}^2$	SEE	D–W
Taxes/	1715–1815	0.876	0.978	0.87	2.81	1.84
Commodity output		(0.918)	(25.94)[a]			
Taxes/	1700–1815	1.69	0.947	0.81	3.16	1.85
National income		(1.46)	(22.39)[a]			

$\Delta T/Y = B_0 + B_1 \Delta (T/Y)_{t-1} + e_t$

Taxes/	1715–1815	0.312	0.049	0.002	2.82	1.92
Commodity output		(1.09)	(0.47)			
Taxes/	1700–1815	0.29	0.017	−0.008	3.20	1.19
National income		(0.98)	(0.177)			

Notes:
t-values in parentheses.
[a] *t*-value not significantly different from 1 at the 5 percent level of significance.

ment was engaged in tax smoothing.[13] However, as the data on commodity output and national income are based on interpolations between benchmarks, these results should be regarded only as suggestive. Similar regressions were tried for France, using the ratio of tax revenues to commodity output for the period 1728–96. The results were comparable to those for Britain, however the even more fragmentary nature of the French data does not allow any but tentative conclusions to be drawn.

The ability to tax smooth is based on the government's credibility to ensure a flow of revenue after the war to service the debt. The British invested in credibility by their performance of debt service after the major wars. In addition, establishment of the Sinking Fund and its continued operation during the Napoleonic Wars strengthened this investment. This stands in striking contrast to the French monarchy which created a Sinking Fund in 1785 – attempting to enhance its reputation – only quickly to be forced to abandon it.

The British experience is also consistent with recent theoretical development on rules versus discretion (Bordo and Kydland, 1992). The experience of the suspension period can be viewed as being consistent with following a contingent gold standard rule. Under this rule, the government maintains the standard – keeps the price of its currency in terms of gold fixed – except in the event of a major war. In wartime, it may suspend specie payments and issue paper money to finance its expenditures, and it can sell debt issues in terms of the nominal value of its currency on the understanding that the debt will eventually be paid off in gold. The rule is contingent in the sense that the public understands that the suspension will last only for the duration of the wartime emergency plus some period of adjustment; it assumes that afterwards the government will follow the deflationary policies necessary to resume payments.

After hostilities ceased in 1815, several attempts were made to pick a date for resumption – 1816 and 1818 – but as each occasion approached, the Bank requested a postponement on the ground that the exchanges were unfavorable. Finally parliament agreed on July 2, 1819 (Peel's Act) on resumption in stages from February 1, 1820 to full redemption on demand on May 1, 1823 and it was agreed that the government would retire its outstanding securities held by the Bank and that the Bank would reduce its note issue to achieve the aim. Resumption was achieved on May 7, 1821. The tenor of the debate in parliament and the press, the lack of effective opposition to resumption, and the fact that resumption was achieved, despite the delays, before the final date suggests that observing the rule was paramount (Feaveryear, 1963, pp. 224–225; Fetter, 1965, pp. 73–76; Laidler, 1987).

The experience of the suspension may also be understood within the context of recent theories of optimal seigniorage and revenue smoothing. During the years of the paper pound, the government can be viewed as having two fiscal instruments: taxation and seigniorage (the inflation tax). According to the theory the government would at each moment of time set each tax rate so as to minimize the deadweight losses (excess burdens) of the instrument (Diamond and Mirlees, 1971). Over time an optimizing government would smooth revenue from both tax instruments and both instruments would evolve in a similar martingale pattern (Mankiw, 1987; Poterba and Rotemberg, 1990; Trehan and Walsh, 1990).

A simple test of the revenue smoothing hypothesis is to regress the rate of inflation on the average tax rate. If revenue smoothing occurs, a positive and significant coefficient is expected (Mankiw, 1987). We replicated Mankiw's regressions for the period 1797–1815, in both levels with a Cochrane–Orcutt adjustment for serial correlation, and first differences (see table 8.6). As can be observed, none of our results were consistent with the hypothesis – in every case the coefficient on the tax rate was of the wrong sign.[14] As Goff and Toma (1993) argue, seigniorage smoothing would not be expected to prevail under a specie standard where the inflation rate does not exhibit persistence.[15] Our results suggest that though specie payments were suspended the commitment to resume prevented the government from acting as it would under the pure fiat regime postulated by the theory. This

Table 8.6 *Revenue smoothing in Great Britain,*
1797–1815

Regression equations (*t*–values)

<hr>

(1) $\Delta \log P_t = -1.81 - 0.0008 \, (T/Y) + 0.001 \, (\text{time})$
　　　　$(-0.12) \, (1.27)$　　　　(0.14)
　　　　　$R^2 = 0.016 \; SEE = 0.119 \; D\text{–}W = 1.60 \; \rho = 0.33$

(2) $\Delta \log p_t = -7.77 - 0.007 \, (T/CO) + 0.004 \, (\text{time})$
　　　　$(-0.40) \, (-1.27)$　　　　(0.42)
　　　　　$R^2 = 0.004 \; SEE = 0.120 \; D\text{–}W = 1.56 \; \rho = 0.35$

(3) $\Delta^2 \log p_t = 0.007 - 0.01 \, \Delta \, (T/Y)$
　　　　$(0.207) \, (-1.87)$
　　　　　$R^2 = 0.121 \; SEE = 0.137 \; D\text{–}W = 1.77$

(4) $\Delta^2 \log p_t = 0.01 - 0.01 \, \Delta \, (T/CO)$
　　　　$(0.31) \, (-2.03)^*$
　　　　　$R^2 = 0.148 \; SEE = 0.135 \; D\text{–}W = 1.74$

<hr>

Notes:
(T/Y) represents tax revenues divided by national income.
(T/CO) represents tax revenues divided by commodity
output.
* signifies statistically significant at the 5 percent level.

suggests that though the British authorities may have used the inflation tax as a source of wartime finance, they did not follow an optimal policy of seigniorage smoothing.

The consulate and empire, 1799–1812

Although Great Britain, in spite of suspension, was able to finance a considerable portion of its war effort by borrowing, France relied almost entirely on taxation while it attempted to rebuild its reputation as a debtor. It had lost its credibility during the Revolution and was unable to follow a tax smoothing policy. Consequently, even at the height of the wars, the Empire covered most of its expenditures by taxation. Napoleon has traditionally been regarded by historians as a simple, obstinate hard-money man. In public, he adamantly professed to oppose any new borrowing. The collapse of the *ancien régime*'s finances from excessive borrowing and the Revolution's finances from excessive use of paper money may have irrationally colored his and his contemporaries' views of public finance. However, his pronouncements were necessary, to a certain degree, to restore confidence and many of his actions and statements should be judged in this light.

Napoleon's coup of November 1799 began sweeping changes in government finance that built on the tough measures taken by the Directory. The system of taxation was reorganized, new taxes were imposed, payment on the debt in specie was resumed and institutions – the Banque de France and a Sinking Fund – were established, which served as additional guarantees of the government's commitment to fiscal prudence. Nevertheless, even at its apogee, Napoleon's system of finance did not engender greater confidence, and it appears to have restrained any return to large-scale borrowing. The Imperial budget remained secretive and the public had no equivalent to the British parliament to monitor the Emperor's plans. In the absence of such an institution it was impossible for the government to make a completely convincing commitment to its announced fiscal program.

Immediately after his coup, Napoloen began to alter the tax system. The centralized agency for the collection of direct taxes established during the Revolution was abolished in the same month as the coup and replaced by separate offices in each *département* who reported to the minister. The practice of electing local tax officials was eliminated. The new government also returned to the *ancien régime*'s policy of requiring interest-bearing security deposits of its tax collectors. The monarchy's method of short-term borrowing was re-established with the tax collectors issuing *rescriptions* to make their monthly payments to the government in advance of the taxes they collected.[16] The bonds acted as a guarantee for the *rescriptions*, providing proper incentives for effective tax collection.

Although collection of direct taxes improved with these measures and a new *cadastre*, the government did not rely on direct taxes to cover its expenditures. Indirect taxes had been the largest component of royal revenues; in table 8.1, the budget for 1788 shows that they accounted for 43 percent of total revenue. These taxes were extremely unpopular, and under the Revolution, they had virtually disappeared by 1790. Only during the Empire were indirect taxes gradually reintroduced. The communes re-established the *octrois*; in 1802 the government demanded a portion of this revenue, which increased over time. New taxes, similar to those of the *ancien régime* were imposed on tobacco, alcohol, salt, and the prices of government monopolies, such as the post, were increased (Marion, 1925, vol. 4, pp. 297–304).

The result of this new policy regime was that France was taxed at a significantly higher level than before the Revolution. Even though the borders of France were expanded somewhat, this cannot fully account for the dramatic rise in tax revenue seen in table 8.1. French taxes as a percentage of commodity output in figure 8.6 were distinctly higher under the Empire, allowing the government to cover most of its expenditures without borrowing. The slow restoration of France's reputation began when the Consulate ordered the payment of *rentes* fully in specie in 1800, leading the yield on the *tiers consolidé* in figure 8.5 to drop below 10 percent for the first time.[17] To amortize the debt, the Consulate created a Sinking Fund in November 1799, which received the security bonds of the tax collectors. Half of these funds were then invested in the stock of the Banque de France, established in January 1800, and half placed on deposit. The Sinking Fund then used the dividends received from the bank plus revenue from the remaining *biens nationaux* slowly to retire the debt. In 1800 and 1801 alone it retired 3.6 million francs of 5 percent *rentes*. The general solvency of Napoleon's regime is reflected in the return, on March 28, 1803, to the bimetallic standard. The *franc germinal* was established, fixing the bimetallic ratio at 15.5:1. Throughout the Napoleonic wars the government adhered to this new standard.

The fiscal discipline of the Empire produced a continued decline in the yield of the *tiers*, which dropped below 7 percent during the middle years of the Empire. The growth of the public debt under the Empire was modest. On the eve of Napoleon's coup in November 1799, the *rentes perpétuelles* amounted to 46.3 million francs. When the Empire collapsed in April 1814, this had risen to only 63.3 million (Fachan, 1904; Vührer, 1886). Although Napoleon never had any major issue of new long-term debt, the Sinking Fund was authorized to issue bonds paying 6 or 7 percent. These bonds helped to consolidate some of the older debts and the small accumulating deficits, but they were not a major vehicle for war finance. Between 1806 and 1812, 224 million francs of these bonds were issued. Another source of borrowing was the Banque de France, established in 1800. In the first five years of operation, approximately one-third of the bank's discounts were advances to the government. This short-term borrowing was quite cheap, as the government could borrow from the bank at rates lower than the open market. Borrowing from the Banque de France was important for smoothing the flow of tax payments; but it was, in the overall picture of government finance, a relatively minor contribution to war finance. Even at the peak of 80 million francs in 1805, it was less than 10 percent of expenditures. This followed the pattern of British finance where the unfunded debt was bought by the Bank of England. The critical difference is that in Britain it was rolled over into long-term debt.[18]

While the Emperor's borrowing from the Banque was generally restrained, the government on one occasion did press the bank too far. By December 1805, the bank had made 97 million francs of discounts, 80 million of which were on obligations of the tax farmers (Courtois fils, 1881, pp. 116–117). The redemption in specie of this large increase in the Banque de France's notes from these loans led to a sudden drop in reserves and temporary and partial suspension of payments. This was also what happened in Britain and led to the suspension. But, unlike the British case, the government could not fully or permanently suspend payment, given its history, and the hope that the public would maintain its real balances. In the next few years, Imperial borrowing from the bank was more restrained. Only in 1811 did government borrowing from the bank begin rapidly to rise again.

France's borrowing during the wars from all sources was limited. Although the Empire may have been able to issue new *rentes*, the general opinion was that credibility was weak. This view was shared by ministers like Barbé-Marbois and diehard emigres like Ivernois.[19] Furthermore, it was feared that any large issue of debt would rapidly drive up yields. Mollien complained at times that even small sales of bonds of the Sinking Fund could not be carried out without quickly driving up the interest rate (Marion, 1925, vol. 4, pp. 347–351). Rightly or wrongly, the government interpreted these signs and popular opinion that the market would not be favorable to new large loans.

The fiscal discipline imposed on the Empire because of France's lack of credibility was, however, partially eased by taxation of its conquered territories and its allies. Before 1805, these revenues appear to have been relatively small. The largest subsidies were 4 million francs per month from Spain and 30 million per year from Italy. The transfers to France were thus limited and most of the taxation of conquered nations was to support French armies abroad. In 1805, Austria supplied 75 million and in 1809 164 million francs. Between 1806 and 1812, Prussia provided somewhere between 470 and 514 million francs. These enormous revenues meant that French armies abroad were not a drain on the French Treasury. While it may appear that France was able to pay for its wars cheaply by taxing the conquered countries, it should be noted that after 1814 France had to repay these countries with reparations. Although the reparations were not anticipated, *ex ante*, they were probably more expensive than a policy of raising all tax revenue in France or borrowing voluntarily from conquered nations.

French finances appeared victorious in early 1811. Britain was encumbered by a growing debt, the Bank of England's notes had depreciated, and the pound sterling stood at a substantial discount. France maintained the value of the franc, the Bank of France redeemed its notes at par, and the budget of the previous year was balanced. The *rentes* stood at above 80, implying a yield of just over 6 percent. What destroyed the Empire was the enormous expense and failure of the Russian campaign. There was a budget deficit of 46 million in 1811, and of 37.5 million in 1812. The *rentes* tumbled in 1813. The situation was sufficiently grave that the Empire attempted to cover the deficit with an old expedient – it offered the *biens communaux* for sale and imposed new taxes. The collapse of the Empire produced a huge deficit for 1814, leaving the restored monarchy with enormous arrears (Marion, 1925, vol. 4, pp. 372–380).

Napoleon's Hundred Days brought a crushing burden in the form of the

Treaty of November 20, 1815 – estimated at 1,290 million francs. The victorious allies imposed an indemnity of 700 million francs payable in five years, the cost of the army of occupation for five years, and reparations for individuals and towns that reached 320.8 million francs. Thus, in addition to ordinary expenditures, the French Treasury's budget for 1816 included 140 million francs for the indemnity and 130 million for maintaining foreign troops. To cover this, tax farmers' security bonds were increased, the *liste civile* was cut, salaries of employees were reduced, and a surcharge on direct taxes was levied.

The restored monarchy remained very weak and was rescued only by a series of new loans issued and managed by Hope and Baring in 1817. The end result was that the *rentes* which required annual payments of 63.3 million in 1814 now had an annual cost of 202.4 million francs in 1830. Ironically, these interest payments were not much different from the total cost of payments in the last years of the *ancien régime*.

Conclusion

While the Napoleonic wars after 1797 offered the curious spectacle of faithful Albion abandoning the gold standard and borrowing substantially while perfidious France maintained convertibility of the franc and borrowed very little, these war finance regimes were the consequence of each nation's credibility as a debtor. Given its long record of fiscal probity, coupled with its open budgetary process in parliament, Great Britain could continue to borrow a substantial fraction of its war expenditures at what were relatively low interest rates. British tax rates did not vary much over most of the eighteenth century as peacetime surpluses offset wartime deficits to pay off the accumulated war debts. Indeed, taxes would not have been greatly increased during the Napoleonic wars except that their duration imposed a debt burden much higher than the eighteenth century norm, requiring a rise in the tax rate to sustain the nation's credibility as a borrower. In addition, because of its longstanding record of maintaining specie convertibility, Britain had access to the inflation tax, although in practice it was not a major source of wartime finance.

France, on the other hand, had squandered her reputation in the last decade of the *ancien régime* and the Revolution. Her dependence on taxation did not reflect any superior fiscal virtues but rather the opposite. Borrowing would have been exceedingly costly and the public very skeptical of the Empire's fidelity. Moreover, the recent experience of *assignat* hyperinflation ruled out the inflation tax as a source of revenue. Inherited credibility resolves this paradoxical pairing of fiscal regimes.

Notes

For helpful comments and suggestions we thank Levis Kochin, Hugh Rockoff, Mark Rush, Forrest Capie, Stanley Engerman and Angela Redish. Howard Bodenhorn provided valuable research assistance.

1 See Barro (1987); Barro (1989).
2 See Kydland and Prescott (1977); Lucas and Stokey (1983).
3 These dates were chosen because the available French data begins in 1770.
4 For a similar pattern in earlier wars in the eighteenth century, see Barro (1987); Benjamin and Kochin (1984).
5 Barsky (1987) found that the inflation rate for Great Britain over the period 1729–1913 showed no evidence of persistence based on autocorrelations. Absence of inflation persistence also characterized the 1797–1815 period, as seen in n. 13 below. Such evidence is not consistent with an *ex post* Fisher effect (positive correlation between the nominal interest rate and inflation). For the period of the suspension, Black and Gilmore (1990) found that nominal interest rates only partially incorporated expectations of inflation and with a long distributed lag – evidence suggesting that nominal rate movements largely reflected movements in the real rate.
6 White (1989, p. 553).
7 Another factor that may have driven down French interest rates was a switch in Dutch investment from Great Britain to France during the Fourth Anglo–Dutch war. White (1989).
8 Braesch (1936, vol. 2, pp. 55–186).
9 A higher marginal productivity of capital is associated with a less developed economy. France has traditionally been regarded as lagging far behind Britain but more recent research by O'Brien and Caglar (1978) and others suggests that the differences were not great.
10 Williamson (1984) following Ashton (1959) provides evidence that government borrowing during the French war crowded out private investment. Heim and Mirowski (1987) dispute this conclusion. Evidence in favor of Williamson's position is presented by Black and Gilmore (1990). Also see Mokyr (1987) and Williamson (1990).
11 These figures do not account for the retirement of debt or conversions between funded and unfunded debt. Accounting for these factors, as O'Brien (1967, table 4) does, reduces the share of unfunded loans somewhat but does not change the pattern significantly.
12 Silberling (1923), Morgan (1939), and O'Grada (1989) argued that the Bank's note issue did not cause inflation based on evidence that price changes temporally preceded both note issue and the Bank's total advances. In agreement with this position, Gayer, Rostow and Schwartz (1953) view the Bank as passively accommodating private demands for credit. The counter view is taken by Viner (1937) and Schumpeter (1938). One difficulty with treating the fact that price changes preceded monetary changes as evidence for causality is that the bulk of the prices included in the indexes used in the tests were commodity prices whose

movements in an efficient market would predict future changes in monetary policy.

13 However, it should be recognized that the power of these tests is relatively weak. There is considerable controversy about their use (see McCallum, 1989). It has recently been suggested that these tests may sometimes pick up segmented trends in lieu of the unit roots (Rappoport and Reichlin, 1989).

14 We also ran the regression using the nominal interest rate as dependent variable as did Mankiw (1987). In every case the coefficient on the tax rate was insignificant and of the wrong sign.

15 Indeed the inflation rate over the period 1797–1815 does not display any evidence of persistence, as can be seen in the following autocorrelations:

Autocorrelations of inflation 1797–1815

Lags	Autocorrelations								
1–9	0.24	−0.54	−0.38	0.15	0.15	−0.16	0.02	0.15	−0.07
10–18	−0.25	0.04	0.35	0.13	−0.19	−0.17	−0.02	0.04	0.02

Notes:
Standard error of correlation = 0.23.
Q(18) = 16.4 is well below the critical value of 26.0 at the 10 percent level of significance.

Alternatively based on the insignificant coefficient of the following first order autoregression, the inflation rate in 1797–1815 did not follow the martingale postulated by the theory of seigniorage smoothing:

$$\log P_t = 0.003 + 0.209 \log P_{t-1} \quad R^2 = 0.037 \qquad D\text{–}W = 1.65$$
$$(t\text{-values}) \ (0.109) \ (0.804) \qquad\qquad SEE = 0.107$$

However, these results should be viewed as suggestive owing to the limited number of observations.

16 See Marion (1925, vol. 4, pp. 169–212) and Godechot (1968, pp. 643ff.).

17 The interest rate for France before the introduction of the *tiers consolidé* is the yield on the *inscriptions sur le grand livre de la dette publique*, which was a 5 percent perpetual.

18 Even the British rolled over their debt with varying degrees of difficulty, depending on the progress of the war. Two major conversions occurred during interludes of peace in 1803 and 1814.

19 Marion (1925, vol. 4, pp. 337–338).

References

Ancien Moniteur or *Moniteur Universal*, 1789–93. Paris.

Ashton, T.S., 1959. *Economic Fluctuations in England, 1700–1800*, Oxford: Clarendon Press.

Barro, Robert J., 1979. "On the determination of the public debt," *Journal of*

Political Economy, 87 (5) pt. 1 (October): 940–971.

1987. "Government spending, interest rates, prices and budget deficits in the United Kingdom," *Journal of Monetary Economics*, 20 (2) (September): 221–248.

1989. "The neoclassical approach to fiscal policy," in Robert J. Barro (ed.), *Modern Business Cycle Theory*, Cambridge, MA: Harvard University Press: 236–264.

Barsky, R.B., 1987. "The Fisher hypothesis and the forecastability and persistence of inflations," *Journal of Monetary Economics*, 19 (January): 3–24.

Benjamin, D.K. and L.A. Kochin, 1984. "War, prices and interest rates: a martial solution to Gibson's paradox," in M.D. Bordo and A.J. Schwartz (eds.), *A Perspective on the Classical Gold Standard: 1821–1931*, Chicago: University of Chicago Press: 587–612.

Black, R.A. and C.K. Gilmore, 1990. "Crowding out during Britain's industrial revolution," *Journal of Economic History*, 50(1) (March): 117–139.

Bordo, M.D. and F.E. Kydland, 1992. "The gold standard as a rule," Federal Reserve Bank of Cleveland, *Working Paper*, 9205 (March).

Braesch, Frederic, 1936. *Finances et monnaie revolutionaires*, vol. 2, Paris, La Maison du Livre Français: 55–186.

Brewer, John, 1989. *The Sinews of Power: War, Money and the English State, 1688–1783*, New York: A. Knopf.

Courtois, Alphonse C., 1877. *Tableaus des Cours des Principales Valeurs*, Paris, Librairie Guillaumin et Cie.

Courtois fils, Alphonse, 1881. *Histoire des Banques en France*, Paris: Librairie Guillaumin et Cie.

Diamond, P. and J. Mirlees, 1971. "Optimal taxation and public production," *American Economic Review*, 61: 261–278.

Dickson, P.G.M., 1967. *The Financial Revolution in England*, London: Macmillan.

Fachan, J.M., 1904. *Historique de la Rente Française*, Paris: Berger-Lavrault et Cie.

Feaveryear, A., 1963. *The Pound Sterling*, Oxford: Clarendon Press.

Fetter, F., 1949. "Legal tender during the English and Irish bank restriction," *Journal of Political Economy*, 63: 241–253.

1965. *Development of British Monetary Orthodoxy, 1797–1875*, Cambridge, MA: Harvard University Press.

Friedman, Milton, 1990. "Bimetallism revisited," *Journal of Economic Perspectives*, 4 (Fall): 85 104.

Gayer, A.D., W.W. Rostow and A.J. Schwartz, 1953. *The Growth and Fluctuation of the British Economy*, Oxford: Clarendon Press

Gazette de France, 1770–89. Paris.

Godechot, Jacques, 1968. *Les Institutions de la France sous la Révolution et l'Empire*, Paris: Presses Universitaires Françaises.

Goff, B.L. and M. Toma, 1993. "Optimal seigniorage, the Gold Standard and central bank financing," *Journal of Money, Credit and Banking*, 25 (February): 79–95.

Harris, Robert D., 1967. "French finances and the American war 1777–1783," *Journal of Modern History* (June): 233–258.

Heim, C.E. and P. Mirowski, 1987. "Interest rates and crowding-out during

Britain's industrial revolution," *Journal of Economic History*, 47 (1) (March): 117–139.

Kochin, L., D. Benjamin and M. Meader, 1985. "The observational equivalence of rational and irrational consumers if taxation is efficient," *Federal Reserve Bank of San Francisco*, West Coast Academic Conference.

Kydland, Finn. E. and Edward C. Prescott, 1977. "Rules rather than discretion: the inconsistency of optimal plans," *Journal of Political Economy*, 85: 473–491.

Labrousse, Ernest, 1970. *Histoire Economique et Social de la France, Vol II*, Paris: Presses Universitaires de France.

Laidler, D., 1987. "The bullionist controversy," in J. Eatwell, M. Milgate and P. Newman (eds.), *New Palgrave Dictionary of Economics*, London: Macmillan.

Lucas, Jr., Robert E. and Nancy L. Stokey, 1983. "Optimal fiscal and monetary policy in an economy without capital," *Journal of Monetary Economics*, 12: 55–93.

Mankiw, N.G., 1987. "The optimal collection of seigniorage – theory and evidence," *Journal of Monetary Economics*, 20 (2): 327–341.

Marion, Marcel, 1914–25. *Histoire Financière de la France depuis 1715*, vols. 1–4, New York: Burt Franklin.

Mathias, Peter and Patrick O'Brien, 1976. "Taxation in Britain and France 1715–1810. A comparison of the social and economic incidence of taxes collected for the central governments," *Journal of European Economic History*, 5: 601–650.

McCallum, Bennett, 1989. "On 'real' and 'sticky-price' theories of business cycles," *Journal of Money, Credit and Banking* (November): 397–411.

Mitchell, B.R. and P. Deane, 1962. *Abstract of British Historical Statistics*, Cambridge: Cambridge University Press.

Mokyr, J., 1987. "Has the industrial revolution been crowded out? Some reflections on Crafts and Williamson," *Explorations in Economic History*, 24 (3) (July): 293–319.

Mollien, François-Nicholas, 1945. *Mémoires d'un Ministre du Trésor Public*, vols. 1–4, Paris. Imprimerie de H. Fournier et Cie.

Morgan, E.V., 1939. "Some aspects of the bank restriction period," *Economic History* (February): 205–221.

Murphy, Antoin, 1986. *Richard Cauhillon: Entrepreneur and Economist*, Oxford: Oxford University Press.

Neal, Larry D., 1990a. *The Rise of Financial Capitalism: International Capital Markets in the Age of Reason*, Cambridge: Cambridge University Press.

1990b. "How the South Sea Bubble was blown up and burst: a new look at old data," in Eugene N. White, *Crashes and Panics: The Lessons of History*, Homewood: Dow Jones/Irwin.

Nelson, Charles R. and Charles I. Plosser, 1982. "Trends and random walks in macroeconomic time series: some evidence and implications," *Journal of Monetary Economics*, 14 (September): 135–162.

North, Douglass and Barry Weingast, 1989. "Constitutions and commitment: evolution of institutions governing public choice," *Journal of Economic History* (December): 803–832.

O'Brien, Patrick, 1967. "Government revenue 1793–1815: a study in fiscal and financial policy in the wars against France," unpublished D. Phil. thesis, Oxford University.

1988. "The political economy of British taxation, 1660–1815," *Economic History Review*, 2nd ser., 61(1): 1–32.

O'Brien, Patrick and Keyder Caglar, 1978. *Economic Growth in Britain and France 1780–1914*, London: George Allen & Unwin.

O'Grada, C., 1989. "The Irish paper pound of 1797–1820," University of Dublin (mimeo).

Poterba, J. and J. Rotemberg, 1990. "Inflation and taxation with optimizing government," *Journal of Money, Credit and Banking*, 22 (1) (February): 1–18.

Presnell, Leslie, 1963. *Country Banking in the Industrial Revolution*, Oxford: Clarendon Press.

Rappoport, P. and L. Reichlin, 1989. "Segmented trends and nonstationary time series," *Economic Journal*, 99 (Supplement): 168–177.

Report for the Select Committee on the High Price of Bullion [1810] (1978). New York: Arno Press.

Riley, James C., 1973. "Dutch investment in France, 1781–1787," *Journal of Economic History*, 33 (December): 733–757.

1986. *The Seven Years War and the Old Regime in France: The Economic and Financial Toll*, Princeton: Princeton University Press.

Rosenthal, Jean-Laurent, 1989. "Credit markets in Southeastern France, 1650–1788," UCLA, *Working Paper*, 589 (March).

Schumpeter, E., 1938. "English prices and public finance, 1660–1822," *Review of Economics and Statistics*, 20: 21–37.

Silberling, N., 1923. "British prices and business cycles," *Review of Economics and Statistics* (October): 223–261.

Thornton, Henry, 1802. *An Inquiry into the Nature and Effects of the Paper Credit of Great Britain*, London: Henry Thornton.

Trehan, B. and C. Walsh, 1990. "Seigniorage and tax smoothing in the United States: 1914–1986," *Journal of Monetary Economics*, 22 (1) (January): 97–112.

Viner, J., 1937 [1975]. Studies in the *Theory of International Trade*, Clifton, NJ: Augustus M. Kelley Publishers (reprint).

Vührer, Alphonse, 1866. *Histoire de la Dette Publique en France*, Paris: Berger–Levrau.

White, Eugene N., 1989. "Was there a solution to the Ancien Regime's financial dilemma?," *Journal of Economic History* (September): 545–568.

1990. "Deficits, inflation and the bankruptcy of the French revolution," (April). (mimeo).

Williamson, J., 1984. "Why was British growth so slow during the industrial revolution?," *Journal of Economic History*, 44 (3) (September): 687–712.

1990. "New views on the impact of the French wars on accumulation in Britain," Harvard Institute of Economic Research, *Discussion Paper*, 1480 (April).

9 Interpreting a change in monetary policy regimes: a reappraisal of the first Hungarian hyperinflation and stabilization, 1921–28

PIERRE L. SIKLOS

Introduction

Hungary's experience during the 1920s offers an interesting illustration of failed attempts at transforming the rules governing monetary policy. In other words, they represent examples of unsuccessful changes in monetary regimes. This chapter reconsiders the first Hungarian hyperinflation and stabilization in light of previously unused historical evidence, as well as econometric evidence based on a time-series analysis of the period 1921–28. Three potentially distinct monetary regimes are considered: the so-called Hegedüs reforms of 1921, which produced a temporary change in the prevailing monetary regime; the hyperinflation of 1921–24; and the post-hyperinflationary period of 1924–28. According to the rational expectations hypothesis a successful change in a monetary regime can be brought about only if the public has credibility in the policy makers' intentions. Otherwise, there is no reason for individuals to revise the future path of the variables of interest. Credibility is here defined as in Cukierman (1986, p. 6), as "the extent to which the public believes that a shift in policy has taken place when, indeed, such a shift has actually occurred."

Unfortunately, as Dornbusch (1988) has argued, economists have no adequate theory of credibility. Indeed, the literature contains a number of studies which have reinterpreted Sargent's view of history by calling attention to a variety of historical attempts to arrest inflation that failed, but which appeared credible by Sargent's standards (see Siklos, 1990a for a survey).[1]

It is for this reason that a mix of historical and statistical evidence is utilized in this chapter to gauge the significance of policy shifts during the period 1921–28. The present study argues that the 1921 reforms, previously largely ignored in the literature, produced a change in the monetary regime. By contrast, the post-1924 regime, previously assumed to be a distinct period (Sargent, 1986, chapter 4), turns out to be largely indistinguishable from the one which preceded it.

The present study is also of interest because the early 1980s has witnessed a resurgence in theoretical and empirical studies dealing with hyperinflation.[2] Interest in hyperinflationary episodes and their aftermath remains high, in part, due to the continued existence of persistently high rates of inflation in several countries around the world. Another important stimulus to research, as noted already, has been the impact of the so-called "rational expectations revolution." A re-examination of Hungary's first encounter with hyperinflation is undertaken with a view to reconsidering earlier studies (e.g., Sargent, 1986; Wicker, 1986), which suggested that the end of the first Hungarian hyperinflation was an illustration of a successful monetary regime transformation.

The belief that individuals form rational expectations about economic aggregates such as inflation requires that they evaluate a mathematical expectation of a variable conditional on some information set. Although the latter set probably consists of more information than is available to an econometrician,[3] it should at least include data on variables suggested by economic theory. Once such a view is accepted, policy implications are quite striking. For example, statistical causality[4] between money growth and inflation differs significantly as between hyperinflation and stabilizations.

During a hyperinflation, causality is predicted to run from inflation to money growth.[5] By contrast, the end of a hyperinflation is marked by a return to traditional modes of financing government spending (e.g., tax revenues and bond financing). In any event, the almost exclusive reliance on seigniorage to generate revenues is abandoned. Consequently, one would no longer expect past inflation to explain current money growth. Indeed, under a real bills interpretation of the link between money and price level movements, one would not expect causation to run in either direction following a return to price stability.[6]

A separate and somewhat contentious issue raised by Sargent's (1986, chapter 3) interpretation of the end of hyperinflations also involves assuming rationally-formed inflation expectations. A sudden and drastic return to price stability, and the apparent lack of associated transition costs,[7] is inconsistent with the Keynesian–neoclassical synthesis view of the tradeoff between inflation and output in which, at least in the short run, significantly higher unemployment, or lower output, would be expected. Sargent thus hypothesized that if expectations of inflation could be altered quickly, the termination of hyperinflation need not produce significant economic costs. Such a view presumes that the public is able to determine the credibility of government attempts at changing a policy regime. The conclusions of this chapter differ, therefore, from Sargent (1986, chapter 4), who assumed that the conditions required for credibility were fulfilled when price stability returned in 1924. The chapter's results also contradict Wicker (1986). He argued that the transition costs to price stability were significant in the Hungarian case. No such scenario is found based on the historical evidence, as well as the available econometric evidence.

The next section briefly outlines the state of Hungary's economy following the dismemberment of the Habsburg Empire. The following section reassesses the historical evidence related to two attempts to end hyperinflation in light of the issues surveyed above. The next section offers some econometric evidence while a final section concludes the study.

Hungary in the aftermath of the Habsburg Monarchy[8]

In this section I shall seek to outline broadly how sharp the economic dislocation may have been for Hungary following the dismemberment of the Austro–Hungarian monarchy.

Hungary entered the 1920s under the provisions of the Treaty of Versailles,[9] although the earlier Treaty of St. Germain (September 10, 1919) concluded with Germany was also to have some bearing on Hungary's future. Beyond forcing the Hungarian government to allocate funds in its budget for as yet unspecified reparations payments, and impose a lien on all Hungarian assets, thereby blocking the possibility of using them as collateral to secure external loans, the collapse of the monarchy led to other significant economic changes. The area of Hungary shrank to 28.6 percent of its former size (i.e., before 1914; see Pénzügyminisztérium Közlemény, vol. V, no. 1, 1929, p. 66, hereafter PK),[10] and the total population fell from 20.9 to 7.8 million between 1914 and 1921 (Berend and Ránki, 1979, p. 111, hereafter BR).

Since Hungary was essentially an agrarian nation (Siklos, 1991, chapter 3, and references therein) it is worth briefly considering the influence of the monarchy's dismemberment for the economy's primary sector. First, and despite an aborted attempt at land reform, the proportion of landed estates exceeding 1,000 cadastral yokes[11] remained approximately one-third of the total area. In general, the distribution of landed estate holdings remained unaffected (PK, p. 67). Similarly, the loss of livestock remained very much in line with population and territorial losses.[12]

However, only 15 percent of iron ore, and 11 percent of timber, remained in postwar Hungary (BR, 1979, p. 111). Virtually all copper, and other non-ferrous metals (e.g., bauxite), and salt deposits also disappeared with the shrinking of Hungary's borders (Macartney, 1965, p. 461). The ending of the customs union which existed under the previous monarchy meant that trading opportunities with the newly-formed countries bordering Hungary would become restricted. More important, perhaps, is the fact that the protective status of Hungary's agricultural sector under the monarchy vanished at one stroke (Eckstein, 1952).

As far as other sectors of the economy were concerned, gross coal output, an important commodity in Hungary's economy, was estimated at roughly two-thirds of the total for Greater Hungary,[13] thus raising its overall contribution to national output considerably. In the case of manufacturing output, 52.5 percent of it originated in Trianon Hungary in 1913 (PK, p. 70). Moreover, 80–90 percent of engineering and printing plants remained in Trianon Hungary (BR, 1979, p. 111). Hungary thus ended up with a disproportionate share of the industrial infrastructure and labor. Moreover, the hostility of its new neighbors,[14] combined with the unavailability of raw materials, and the imminent raising of tariff barriers, meant that there were virtually no external market outlets for Hungarian industrial output (Ferber, 1986). Finally, in the political arena, it would take several years before Hungarian politics, at least in diplomatic circles and to a lesser extent at the public level, managed to set aside Hungary's openly irredentist policy,[15] which doubtless contributed to its economic difficulties following the breakup of the monarchy.

The foregoing evidence must lead one to conjecture that Hungary began the decade of the 1920s, to use modern economic terminology, with natural levels of output or unemployment lower and higher, respectively, than they had been before the breakup of the monarchy. However, the economic literature on the first Hungarian hyperinflation (e.g., Sargent, 1986, chapter 4; Wicker, 1986) does not satisfactorily address the role of the transition to both a peacetime and a sovereign economy on the eve of its experience with hyperinflation.[16] Yet, such considerations are important if one is properly to assess the subsequent state of Hungary's economic development, as well as the prospects for stabilization.

Interpreting a change in policy regimes: the historical evidence

Introduction

Space limitations prevent a complete economic history of the 1922–28 period (see Lewis, 1970 for an international survey, and Hoensch, 1988 for a Hungarian history). I have therefore chosen to discuss three so-called policy regimes, namely the Hegedüs period of 1920–21, the hyperinflation of 1921–24, and the League of Nations (hereafter LON) stabilization plan of 1924, to illustrate the arguments of this study. While a policy regime, as defined in the Introduction, is viewed as being primarily monetary in nature it is, of course, difficult to divorce the fiscal and political elements from the purely monetary ones (see also Bordo and White, chapter 8 in this volume).

It is useful briefly to consider the events of 1920–21 by way of introduction. During 1920–21, irredentist forces dominated Hungarian politics. Individuals associated with this policy believed that a combination of military force and defiance toward the victorious nations in the war would lead to a reassessment of the terms of the Treaty of Trianon. Adding to these difficulties were the issues of prewar debt and note circulation. Although settlement of the debt question came only many years later[17] the immediate consequence of the dismemberment of the Empire was the presence of a large quantity of Austro–Hungarian bank notes in the newly-formed countries which desired to dump them into Austria or Hungary. A temporary solution consisted in the stamping of notes so that users could identify the country which purportedly undertook to accept the debt. Despite the fact that the Reparations Commission was responsible for overseeing these questions, the stamping policy was not introduced simultaneously in all countries (Boross, 1984, p. 195). Hungary's desire to regain lost territories through force,[18] combined with diplomatic obstinance, put immediate pressure on the Hungarian budget which led to the overissue of currency and thus contributed to the emergence of inflation.[19] The Hungarian government's political orientation meant the virtual abandonment of any policy aimed at reconstruction: it was clearly felt that territorial and reparations questions had to be dealt with first before other economic reforms could proceed (Péteri, 1985; Ferber, 1987).[20]

The Hegedüs plan

It was becoming increasingly clear to Bethlen, Hungary's ruler at the time (Macartney, 1961, chapter 4), that the Reparations Commission and the victorious powers would relax neither their intransigence with respect to Hungary's claim for the return of lost territory nor the financial obligations arising from the war. Yet it was also clear that France and Great Britain were competing to become the dominant powers influencing the future course of politics and economics in Central Europe (Kindleberger, 1984; Péteri, 1985b). Bethlen, one of the members of the Hungarian delegation to the Peace Conference in 1919, was also led to believe that the French would be sympathetic to a softening of the most onerous clauses of the Treaty, and wished to play a constructive part in the development of a newly independent Hungary (Déak, 1942, pp. 285–290, 330–338; Ránki, 1983, pp. 12–14). In the meantime, as Britain attempted to regain some measure of prominence in the area of international finance, contacts between the Hungarian banking establishment and the Bank of England were begun in order to assist Hungary's return to some semblance of economic and financial normality (Pogány, 1987/88).[21] As with the French, the object was to establish a sphere of influence over Central Europe.[22]

The Hungarian government consequently began to believe that a somewhat less adversarial stance toward the Reparations Commission might instead prove beneficial in the long run. However, the government did not intend to abandon its irredentist policy entirely; it would only tone it down, largely for the purposes of international consumption (Péteri, 1985b). An important step in this direction came with the appointment of the highly respected Roland Hegedüs as minister of finance in December 1920.[23] Hegedüs imposed two conditions for his appointment. First, that he be granted *de facto* dictatorial powers over the country's finances, in addition to unconditional government support for his proposed policies. Second, that he remain untouched by any future ministerial shuffles. Once these conditions were accepted, the Hegedüs plan called for radical reforms to put the government's budget into balance.[24] These may be summarized under three headings.

FULFILL ALL TREATY OBLIGATIONS

This was a complete reversal from the earlier policy of seeking modifications to Trianon. No doubt the Hungarian government realized that acceptance of the impending financial burden – the amount of reparations had yet to be fixed by the Commission[25] – would make reconstruction difficult, but Hegedüs was convinced that if his stabilization plan proved to be credible and sustainable[26] desperately needed foreign credits from the United States, Britain, and France, would follow and facilitate the transition to economic stability and thence growth. Indeed, this was the gamble Hegedüs proposed the Hungarian government accept to prevent financial collapse.

INTRODUCTION OF A COMPREHENSIVE SYSTEM OF TAXATION TO ENSURE THAT REVENUES EVENTUALLY MATCH EXPENDITURES

Taxes were to be imposed on bank deposits and foreign currencies held domestically. However, the novel feature of Hegedüs' plan was the way in which a tax on property and capital was to be administered. Property and capital holders could fulfill their tax liability based on the revenues generated by the property or, in lieu of such payments, the government would accept shares in capital or property. Hegedüs thus hoped not only to generate revenues from such an arrangement, but also to acquire collateral for the government which it could eventually use to finance some of the reconstruction costs. In developing such a policy, Hegedüs wished to tap the wealthiest segments of Hungarian society which, previously, had contributed a disproportionately small share to total tax revenues. His demand for unconditional government support was thus meant to deflect resistance from parliament, whose members were generally capital or property owners.

Hegedüs' economic thought was heavily influenced by that of the German economist Georg Knapp.[27] Knapp believed that the price level was determined independently of the quantity of money. Instead, "real" or institutional factors influenced price level changes.[28] Thus, Hegedüs attempted to formulate a monetary policy geared to ensuring that government debt would be backed not so much by generating anticipated future government budget surpluses,[29] at least initially, but by enabling the government to acquire some assets against which it could borrow, especially in international markets and, thereby, back future government spending.

THE CREATION OF A HUNGARIAN STATE NOTE INSTITUTE

This institution would issue currency but would not be independent of the government since effective control of monetary policy would remain in the hands of the minister of finance (and parliament). However, a legal ceiling of 22 billion crowns (hereafter K) was set on the note issue. The lack of independence of this quasi-central bank could be viewed as a flaw in the stabilization program but Hegedüs anticipated remaining in his post, at least until the country's fiscal and monetary policies were restored to some semblance of equilibrium, and he felt that he was the best bulwark against the possibility of currency overissue. Put differently, even a nominally independent central bank would not be immune from political pressures during these turbulent times. Hegedüs believed he had the moral authority and the reputation to prevent excessive monetary growth.

As Hegedüs' ministry lasted a short period of time (December 1920–August 1921), it is difficult to explore econometrically the results of the program except indirectly. Table 9.1 shows data for the exchange rate and wholesale prices measures in rates of change. The figures reveal a dramatic and persistent fall in inflation until July 1921 when it became clear that Hegedüs' resignation would be imminent. Meanwhile, the exchange rate showed signs of appreciating as Hegedüs had hoped in order to obtain foreign loans on more favorable terms.[30]

Hegedüs resigned (August 21, 1921) as much for domestic political reasons, that is, the unwillingness of parliament to back the taxation measures, as for external political reasons, principally the intransigence of the Reparations Commission,[31] and the refusal of the Little Entente to withdraw its lien on Hungarian assets. In sum, Hegedüs' gamble failed and, as a result, any determination on the part of domestic politicians to accept sharply higher taxes for its constituents to rescue the government from its perennial fiscal imbalance quickly dissipated.

While the Hegedüs period appears to be a minor one in terms of its duration it is nevertheless significant from the perspective of economists' views about what constitutes a regime change. After all, Hegedüs proposed

Table 9.1 *Inflation and exchange rates under Hegedüs,*
1921: MI–1921:M7, %

Year	Month	Inflation[a]	Exchange rate appreciation[b]
1921	Jan.	—	2.36
	Feb.	−4.45	12.67
	Mar.	−21.94	−44.09
	Apr.	−16.36	−18.48
	May	−6.90	−16.60
	Jun.	0.00	4.60
	Jul.	0.00	20.30

Notes:
[a] 100 log first difference in the wholesale price index on a
   month-to-month basis.
[b] 100 log first difference in the exchange rate on a month-
   to-month basis. A positive number indicates a
   depreciation while a negative number means appreciation
   of the K relative to the Swiss franc.
− not available.
Source: Appendix.

a dramatic departure from the past, and one which would appear to have
been credible since the minister was careful to craft a plan based on
resources available to Hungary at the time. Moreover, in the area of
taxation, Hegedüs' plan would be similar to the plan later imposed on
Hungary by the LON in 1924. Viewed from a modern perspective, therefore, the Hegedüs reforms seemed to have all of the ingredients necessary
for credibility. The difficulty was that the plan relied on a set of domestic
and foreign political expectations that did not materialize.

The hyperinflation of 1921–24 and the stabilization plan of 1924

The emerging world-wide postwar economic slump implied greater urgency
than before regarding the reconstruction of Europe. As a consequence,
Hungary was admitted into the LON in September 1922 and it immediately
requested financial assistance. By July of the following year, all the powers
agreed to lift Treaty charges on Hungarian assets, thereby freeing them for
use as collateral for an external loan. Experts from the LON were brought
in, as elsewhere in Central and Eastern Europe (e.g., Austria), to restore

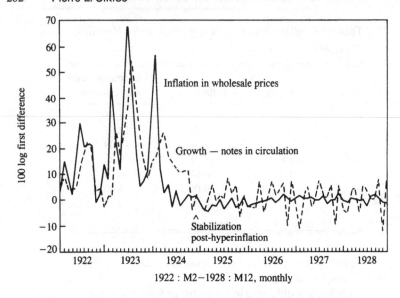

9.1   Inflation and money growth, 1922:M1–1928:M12

financial order and set the framework for a reconstruction loan. The basic plan for stabilization consisted of the following three parts:

1   the creation of an independent central bank which would henceforth largely be forbidden to discount government debt;
2   the introduction of a comprehensive system of taxation and customs tariffs; and
3   a requirement that the government balance the budget by June 1926.

Figures 9.1 and 9.2 plot the development of some financial variables in Hungary before and after the hyperinflation ended. During the hyperinflation (February 1922–June 1924), inflation in wholesale prices averaged 19.34 percent, while average money growth was 16.29 percent, both values computed on a monthly basis.[32] Following July 1924, when the reforms which were to lead to price stability took effect,[33] there is a noticeable drop in both inflation and money growth. However, since some but not all of the necessary policies were in place a few months prior to July 1924, the sharp reductions in both series can be traced to earlier in 1924.[34] A similar story emerges from figure 9.2 which plots real balances, that is, the purchasing power of the note circulation. There is a steady drop in the series until the middle of 1923 and, after a temporary recovery,[35] real balances begin consistently to rise only around the time of the stabilization.

From all appearances, the stabilization appeared successful. However, appearances can be deceptive. Figure 9.2, for example, reveals that even by

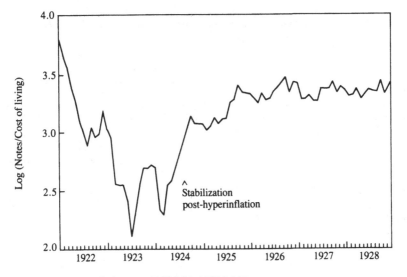

9.2   Real balances, 1922:M1–1928:M12

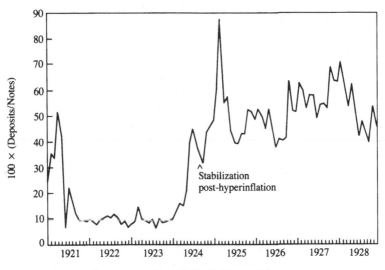

9.3   Deposit to note ratio, 1921:M1–1928:M12

the end of 1928 real balance holdings were consistently below levels reached in early 1922 when inflation in the cost of living index averaged 19.48 percent on a monthly basis (February–April 1922; 9.43 percent in the wholesale price index for the same period). Figure 9.3, which plots the deposit–note ratio, which provides an indication of the extent of reinterme-

Table 9.2 *Hungarian government: revenues, expenditures, deficits, 1924/ 25–1931/32, annual, million pengő*

Year	Revenues[a]	Expenditures	Extraordinary balance[c] Budget[b]	Ordinary	All
1924/25	1143.1	1179.4	0.0	−36.3	36.3
1925/26	1228.1	1145.0	110.8	83.1	27.7
1926/27	1380.3	1250.0	135.0	130.3	−4.7
1927/28	1435.0	1354.3	190.0	80.7	−109.3
1928/29	1478.7	1472.8	164.2	5.6	−158.6
1929/30	1461.5	1478.2	48.5	−16.7	−65.2
1930/31	1397.3	1628.0	33.9	−230.7	−264.6
1931/32	1206.8	1387.6	7.1	−180.8	−187.9

Notes:
[a] Includes revenues and expenditures from State enterprises. The budget year is from July to June of the following year.
[b] Extraordinary expenditures by the Hungarian government and State enterprises, ostensibly for investment in infrastructure.
[c] Revenues less expenditures.
Source: Magyar Nemzeti Bank (National Bank of Hungary), economic research and statistics department materials in the Hungarian National Archives.

diation following the hyperinflation, reveals that levels in this series were not much different following stabilization than during Hegedüs' brief reign in 1921.[36] There are also additional reasons to doubt the credibility of the stabilization. First, the nominal yield on the LON loans averaged approximately 8⅓ percent per annum. This implies an *ex post* real interest rate of between 8.18 percent and 8.56 percent, depending whether a cost of living or a wholesale price index, respectively, is used.[37] Given that Hungarian economic growth averaged around 1.4 percent (see below) it is clear that a balanced budget could not be sustained in the long run.[38]

Second, the LON requirement that the Hungarian government balance its budget almost immediately (18 months after the end of hyperinflation) was draconian even by modern standards since it was to be accomplished during a period when both reconstruction and reparations costs would represent a significant drain on the government's budget. In fact, as table 9.2 shows, deficits were not eliminated at all but generally rose over time, at least until 1931–32. Previous authors (e.g. Sargent, 1986, chapter 3; Wicker, 1986) who assumed that the stabilization was credible formed their views on the basis of planned budgets, which were scrutinized by the LON, and

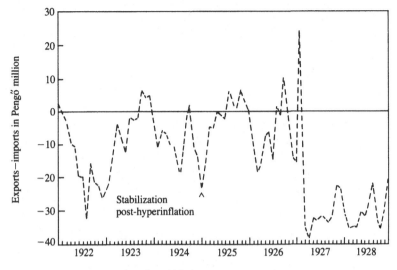

9.4   Balance of trade, 1922–28

not actual budget figures which included increasingly large amounts voted by the Hungarian parliament but excluded from official budget estimates.[39] Third, the stabilization plan did nothing to correct the severe disadvantage faced by Hungary imposed by the high tariff barriers and other trading restrictions emanating from still hostile neighbors. Hungary's balance of trade, as shown in figure 9.4, thus showed no sign of improving. Indeed, foreign exchange losses averaged 3.46 percent of net national product between 1924 and 1929, a not inconsequential amount. Finally, while Britain's return to the gold standard, in April 1925, resulted in a severe deflation in the United Kingdom. Hungary experienced the opposite problem as inflation in the cost of living index during the period 1925: M5–1928: M12 was 33⅓ percent higher than during the initial months following the end of hyperinflation (1924: M7–1925: M4).[40] The reasons were, in large part, the high tariffs imposed on imports which rose throughout the period in question, as well as domestic shortages in most commodities caused by the attempt to divert as much production as possible towards exports. Moreover, even if the central bank was independent of the Hungarian government, it became entirely dependent on UK monetary policy as the stabilization plan effectively called for such a policy (see, *inter alia*, Mitzakis, 1925).

Given historically higher relative Hungarian prices, a legacy of the customs union with Austria, trade balance difficulties further hampered economic recovery. Thus, as shown in figure 9.4, Hungary's trade balance

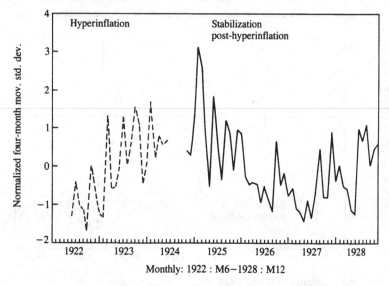

9.5   Moving standard deviation of inflation

had worsened considerably by the second half of 1926. Finally, in 1924 and 1925, reparations represented 14.3 percent and 11.7 percent, respectively, of exports (Eckstein, 1952) and, consequently, meant a further drain on foreign exchange.

I have also computed a monthly proxy for income velocity based on output data for lignite, a key indicator of aggregate Hungarian economic activity and notes in circulation as a proxy for the money stock (see Figure B1 in Appendix B, not reproduced in this volume). Since velocity is considered a proxy for expected inflation, it can also serve as an additional indicator of the public's confidence in the stabilization program. Average velocity levels rose sharply during the hyperinflation, as one would expect, and dropped with the ending of high inflation. Yet, average velocity levels were not significantly lower during, say, 1922 than during the entire stabilization period considered (1925: M1–1928: M12). Such an outcome may be construed as an indication of higher expected inflation.

Alternatively, even if expectations of inflation fell somewhat from hyper-inflationary levels, at least in the short run, as the government was forbidden to issue currency to underwrite a deficit,[41] uncertainty about the future course of inflation could not have fallen concomitantly, given the circumstances surrounding the ending of hyperinflation discussed above. In this regard, figure 9.5 plots the four-month moving standard deviation of inflation separately for the hyperinflation and post-hyperinflation samples.

This kind of statistic is often used as a proxy for inflation uncertainty.[42] The plot is on a normalized scale so that the results for the two different samples may be compared. Not surprisingly, inflation uncertainty rose during the course of the hyperinflation but, on average, does not show signs of being significantly lower in the stabilization phase considered.

The existence of high inflation uncertainty, combined with the lack of credibility in the long-run viability of the stabilization plan, casts doubts on Wicker's study of the post-Habsburg hyperinflation, which purported to show significant transition costs in the return of price stability (Wicker, 1986), and in which it was presumed that a regime transformation took place. The significant transition costs found by Wicker may, if present at all, equally well be explained by the influence of inflation uncertainty on the inflation–unemployment or output tradeoff relationship in a manner reminiscent of Friedman's (1977) hypothesis.[43] However, the apparent rise in unemployment rates following the return to price stability detected by Wicker loses significance if one fails to account for possible changes in the natural rate of unemployment or output. As noted, these aggregates were in all likelihood significantly different after 1921 than they had been previously, thereby raising for the Hungarian case the same point introduced by Garber (1982) for the German hyperinflation and, more recently, by Siklos (1989) for the Hungarian hyperinflation after the Second World War. That is, simply comparing unemployment rates before and after hyperinflation takes place without due consideration to possible changes in the natural rate of unemployment will bias the interpretation of the consequences of ending a hyperinflation toward the conclusion that transition costs were indeed significant when, in fact, they were not.[44]

In any event, there are still other reasons to question the transition costs hypothesis as it applies to post-Habsburg Hungary. Table 9.3 shows annual data for industrial production from 1924 to 1931. Following stabilization, and until the great depression, output grew on average 8.4 percent. By contrast, as shown in table 9.4, long-term growth rates in national income and *per capita* income measures averaged around 0.69 percent–1.49 percent per annum which cannot be considered deficient relative to European experience.[45] Hence, much like the 1980s, the late 1920s in Hungary and elsewhere were characterized by relatively high unemployment rates and significant economic growth.[46]

Because annual data may mask some interesting variations in month-to-month figures, figure 9.6 plots inflation in the cost of living index on the vertical axis and the unemployment rate on the horizontal axis for the hyperinflation (1922: M1–1924: M6) and post-hyperinflation (1924: M7–1928: M12) samples, respectively.[47] Combinations of the two series are indicated by the + symbol and some are dated to facilitate tracing their

Table 9.3 *Industrial output in Hungary, 1924–31*

Year	Index (1913 = 100)
1924	88.1
1925	100.0
1926	113.0
1927	121.3
1928	130.0
1929	132.4
1930	121.4
1931	102.2

Source: Eckstein (1952, table 25, p. 141).

Table 9.4 *Comparative economic growth data, average annual, %*

Period	National income		*Per capita* income	
	Hungary	Europe	Hungary	Europe
1913/29	1.49	0.95	0.83	0.42
1929/38	1.42	2.61	0.69	1.81
1913/38	1.46	1.55	0.78	0.92

Source: Eckstein (1952).

development over time. No clear pattern emerges in either sample[48] nor can one conclude that unemployment was persistently higher following the return to price stability since, except initially, unemployment rates fell consistently, approximately six months after the period of high inflation ended.

Thus, while there is no doubt that the LON loan permitted the return to lower inflation, there are considerable doubts about whether the regime in place after June 1924 was fundamentally different from the one which preceded it. As Eckstein (1952, p. 126) remarks, in discussing the LON's role in Hungary's financial affairs:

Practically no attention was paid to the question of overall economic viability, as affected by the balance of trade, the country's competitive position in its export

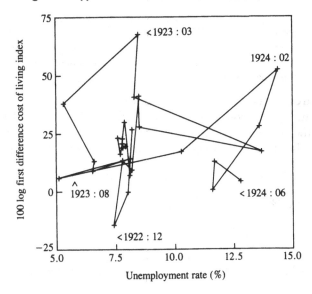

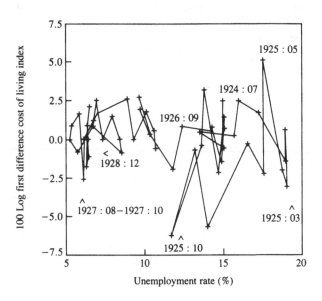

9.6   Inflation and unemployment rates
(a) Hyperinflationary period, 1922:M2–1924:M6
(b) Stabilization period, 1924:M7–1928:M12

markets, levels of agricultural and industrial productivity, and relative stage in economic development. In a word, there was no attempt to define Hungary's basic economic problems and draw up a comprehensive economic program. The fallacy and weakness of the narrow financial approach was clearly demonstrated when the collapse of reconstruction came in 1931.

The final element in the list of events which cast doubts on the existence of a regime transformation in 1924 is the resignation of Finance minister Kállay at the time the stabilization plan was introduced. Statistical evidence about whether regime changes can be detected during the period under study is presented below.

Econometric evidence

Introduction and some preliminary test results

In what follows, I shall concentrate on the question whether the sharp reduction in inflation in 1924, in particular, constitutes a regime change in a statistical sense.

The evidence presented below, in common with much econometric evidence, can be sensitive to the choice of models, how these are estimated, the selection of variables to include, their lag length, and so on. Although there are a number of tests available which can improve our understanding of economic relationships there is, nevertheless, disagreement about the econometric methodology best suited to discovering the underlying truth about economic relationships. A large number of tests were consequently applied to time series either individually, in reduced-form models with other available variables, or in what are called vector autoregressive models (hereafter VAR), which is a type of simultaneous equations technique popular and useful in estimating interrelated or jointly-determined series. Since there exists a large literature on the various tests to be performed, the discussion about these will be necessarily brief. Readers are asked to consult the references, although these are not meant by any means to be exhaustive or complete. Finally, as the econometric methodology and the number of tests applied create a large volume of output only a selection of the results is presented. Many others are relegated to Appendix B.

One set of tests was conducted to determine whether there are any unit roots in the data. Since economic theories are concerned with cyclical variation in economic variables, that is, with time series which are stationary,[49] considerable importance is attached to the question of how best to extract that particular portion of a time series. Based on received evidence, which is not altogether uncontroversial,[50] many economists believe that aggregate time series tend to behave like a random walk, possibly with a drift, which is to say that the level of a series contains a unit root, labelled I(1) series, and perhaps a changing mean.[51] Available evidence (Evans, 1978; Siklos, 1990b) also suggests that in the case of two other hyperinflations this century, namely the German and second Hungarian (1945–46) hyperinflations, money and price log-level data, in particular, contain two unit roots, and are thus labelled I(2) series. By contrast, data from a more stable period (e.g., a stabilization period) appear generally to contain only one unit root.[52]

Tests applied to several time series available for this study confirm the foregoing dichotomy in unit root behavior for many time series, such as notes in circulation and prices, both in log levels. However, for several other series, most notably the (log) exchange rate, the unemployment rate, and (log) real balances, only one unit root was found in both the hyperinflation and stabilization samples. Moreover, even in the case of the notes and prices series one cannot entirely reject the null hypothesis of two unit roots when the two supposedly different policy regime periods are combined. In addition, the last result is robust to subsample selection, as confirmed by tests of coefficient stability. To avoid possibly biasing the results the appropriate time series for the hyperinflation sample were treated as stationary in second log differences, whereas data from the stabilization period were considered stationary in first log differences.

A second round of preliminary tests consisted in performing bivariate causality tests.[53] As noted in the Introduction to this chapter, causal relationships between money and prices would be expected to differ between hyperinflation and stabilization phases. Test results suggest that one cannot entirely dismiss the possibility that, for example, causation runs from prices to notes during *both* policy regimes under study.[54] Put differently, the evidence of a regime shift in the notes–prices nexus is not overwhelming. Also, causality tests between the exchange rate and notes and prices, or causation between prices and output or unemployment rates, appear largely unaffected by the breakdown of the data set into hyperinflation and post-hyperinflation periods.[55]

The data

Monthly observations on a wide range of series for the period 1922: M1–1928: M12 were utilized. Some data are available from 1919: M7. Cagan (1956, table 1) dates the beginning of the hyperinflation at 1923: M3, and its termination at 1924: M2. It could be argued, apart from the fact that Cagan's definition is a rather arbitrary one, that Hungary faced conditions leading to hyperinflation immediately following the war. Moreover, while March 1923 is indeed the first month the inflation rate exceeded 50 percent on a monthly basis some of the intervening months until February 1924 experienced inflation rates considerably less than 50 percent. Finally, dating the beginning of hyperinflation from January 1922 increases the sample size by 14 observations. It is clear that the econometric estimates will be enhanced by the additional degrees of freedom.

As far as dating the end of the hyperinflation, suffice it to note that the evidence below was unaffected by the addition of the observations from March to June 1924, inclusive. In any event, as discussed, the June 1924 date appears to be preferred on historical grounds.[56]

The Hegedüs era

Unfortunately, there are too few observations to perform comprehensive statistical tests of the Hegedüs period. Nevertheless, Granger-type causality tests conducted for the sample 1921: M2–1921: M8 reveal that there is no causality from either money growth to inflation or vice versa, which is consistent with a regime in which resort to seigniorage is abandoned.[57] Nevertheless, one may understandably feel uncomfortable with a sample of only seven observations[58] although this bit of evidence is instructive, especially in light of the text's discussion, and the fact that significantly different results are obtained for the hyperinflation sample.

Cointegration tests

An alternative to testing whether pairs of series are causally related to each other is to examine whether one series acts as an attractor to another series. Thus, for example, if we expect notes and prices to be highly correlated with each other during a hyperinflation, because everyone understands that the government finances its deficit almost exclusively through the note issue, it is also possible that these same series display a common trend. Similarly, once a credible regime change takes place and terminates hyperinflation, one would predict that notes reflect the effects of remonetization while prices would no longer be governed by the need to debase the currency. Hence, the common trend previously in existence may disappear.

Suppose the model being considered is a version of the quantity theory $(MV = Py)$ written in regression form as

$$P(t) = bM(t) + e(t). \tag{9.1}$$

All the variables have been defined (in the Appendix) and are in the logarithm of the levels. If real income (y) effects are negligible (9.1) implies that (the log of) velocity is stationary. Moreover, if the linear combination $e(t) = P(t) - bM(t)$ is also stationary, P and M are cointegrated, that is, the two series are said to possess a common trend (Engle and Granger, 1987).

Table 9.5 *Cointegration tests*

Model	Hyperinflation (*H*)			Stabilization (*S*)		
	$r=0$ 17.84*		$r=1$ 6.48	$r=0$ 19.27*		$r=1$ 4.15
$N=f(P)$		$r=0/r=1$ 11.36*			$r=0/r=1$ 15.12*	

Notes:
All series in the *H* sample are in first log differences while for the *S* sample the data are in log levels. The values given in table 9.5 represent the likelihood ratio statistics for cointegration. See also Johansen and Juselius (1989). *r* represents the number of cointegrating vectors.
* signifies that the null hypothesis that there are, at most, *r* cointegrating vectors is rejected at the 5% level of significance.
The test $r=0/r=1$ is for the null hypothesis that $r=1$ *conditional* on $r=0$.

To conserve space, two cointegration tests are presented for model (1) only and are given in table 9.5. A unique cointegrating relationship between N(notes in circulation) and P(price level) is found in both samples, which is contrary to what one would expect if the samples were indeed distinct. The results suggest, therefore, that even if some remonetization took place after June 1924 it did not overcome an underlying equilibrium relationship of the type embodied in (9.1).[59] Combined with the earlier causality test results there appears to be a strong statistical basis for questioning the existence of a regime change in 1924.

Model estimation results

We consider in this section the short-run relationship between series of interest modeled by the vector autoregressive approach. As there exists a large theoretical and empirical literature which uses this technique, only a brief sketch of the VAR approach is given.

The essence of the VAR technique is to treat each endogenous variable as a function of its own past as well as the past of other endogenous variables in a system of equations. Such a framework essentially views the problem of the evaluation of policies as one which assumes that some economic variables are interdependent.[60] Estimating such a system can be carried out by ordinary least squares but, as the coefficient estimates are difficult to interpret, it is more common to examine, among other statistics, variance decompositions (VD). These show the percentage of forecast error variance attributable to specific shocks or innovations in the system of equations. Innovations represent that part of the variation in an endogenous variable which is not explained by any of the right-hand-side variables in an equation of the system (i.e., the error term). Forecast errors for a variable at a particular time horizon will be due to errors in forecasting that series, as well as to errors in forecasting the other variables in the system.[61]

Unfortunately, unless the error terms across equations of the system are uncorrelated, interpretation of such VD is rendered difficult since the errors have a common component which cannot easily be identified. Consequently, the usual practice is, first, to order the equations based on *a priori* economic theory, or on the degree to which the innovations appear to be correlated.[62] Changing the order of the equations can, of course, influence the results so the ordering of equations imposes restrictions on a model. Further difficulties arise because, among other issues which cannot be addressed here, the series may be cointegrated.

In the results reported below, two models were considered. Both can be written as follows:

$$By(t) - Cx(t) = e(t), \tag{9.2}$$

where y represents a vector of endogenous variables, x is a vector of exogenous variables, and e represents the error term. Two versions of equation (9.2) are considered as shown below in vector notation:

Model 1: $y = [WPI, N]'$
                  $x = [BOT, FNEWS]'$

Model 2: $y = [ycyc, WPT]'$ or $[U, WPI]'$
                  $x = [BOT]'$.

The series WPI, N were defined in Appendix B. BOT represents the balance of trade (i.e., exports less imports), included to proxy aggregated supply shocks, and FNEWS is an impulse dummy variable,[63] which captures the possibility that fiscal news may also have an independent influence on the money–prices relationship.[64] The events considered to have a potential effect on money and prices were as follows: the admission of Hungary into the LON (1922: M8), the lifting of Treaty charges on Hungarian assets (1923: M7), the resignation of Finance minster Kállay on the eve of the LON stabilization plan's implementation (1924: M2), Britain's return to the gold standard (1925: M5), the withdrawal of the LON from Hungary (1926: M6), and the introduction of the pengő currency to replace the K (1927: M1).

In the second model, U represents the unemployment rate while $ycyc$ represents a proxy for cyclical output (see Appendix B(a) for a discussion of the derivation of this series). The purpose of this model is to examine the evolution of the inflation–unemployment, or cyclical output, relationship. All the series were estimated for the entire available sample as well as the hyperinflation and post-hyperinflation samples, separately, when sufficient data allowed estimation. For the complete sample, as well as the post-hyperinflation period, the series were measured in first log differences, except for FNEWS. For the hyperinflation samples, the data are in second log differences, again except for FNEWS.[65]

The results of interest are plotted in figures 9.7 and 9.8, and are derived from Models 1 and 2, respectively, in which the endogenous variables also enter in the order listed above.[66] Figure 9.7 shows the response of prices to innovations in N, and vice versa, conditional on the vector x in Model 1, for a 12-month horizon. Overall, there seems to be little influence from N to WPI (see figure 9.7(b)), in either the stabilization or hyperinflation samples, since the responses vary between 2 and 4 percent, after two months, and remain stable at the same level thereafter. In other words, notes are a poor forecaster of prices. When the response of N to innovations in WPI are considered (figure 9.7(a)), however, the VDs reveal for all samples that the Hungarian government appears to have responded to inflationary shocks in the issue of N. Thus, after four months, innovations in WPI produce a large response (between 60 and 70 percent) in the note issue for the 1922–28 sample. Note also the larger response of notes to inflation shocks during the hyperinflation sample relative to the post-hyperinflation sample (45 percent during hyperinflation compared with 15 percent in the post-hyperinflation sample, after four months). This result simply reflects the comparatively greater sensitivity of the note issue to inflation during the hyperinflation phase, as one would expect. In summary, it appears that the monetary authorities injected notes based on past prices rather than on an expectation of future prices. Therefore, a model in which prices are used to forecast money growth would have done reasonably well for the entire data set (i.e., 1922–28).

A similar conclusion is drawn from an examination of figures 9.8(a) and (b) which reveals that a considerable amount of persistence exists in both the U and $ycyc$ series, since well over 80 percent of their variance over a 12-month horizon is due to innovations in the same two series.[67] Again, however, there does not appear to be a large difference in the responses of U or $ycyc$ to own past shocks as between the hyperinflation and post-hyperinflation samples. If the regime change was not credible, and output costs from the end of hyperinflation were insignificant following the end of the hyperinflation as argued in this chapter, then one would expect the responses of U and $ycyc$ to be largely autonomous of WPI, especially if a kind of natural rate-hypothesis view of output or unemployment is

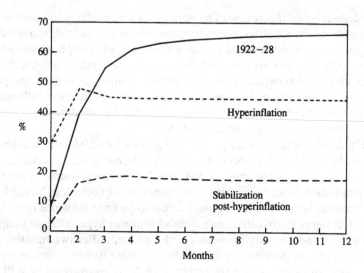

(a) Response of notes to innovations in WPI

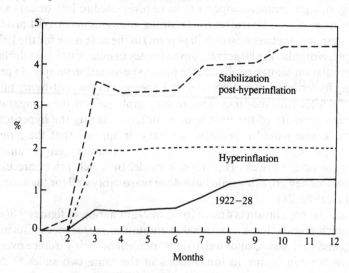

(b) Response of WPI to innovations in notes

9.7   Variance decomposition: prices and notes

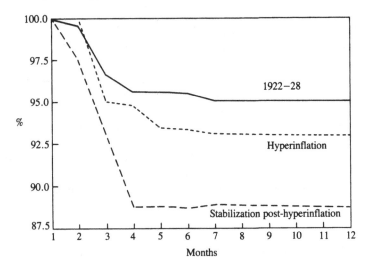

(a) Response of *U* to innovations in *U*

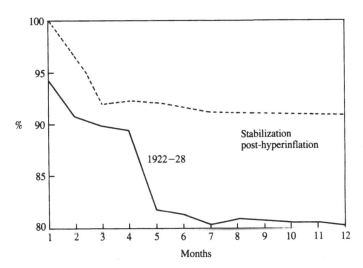

(b) Response of *ycyc* to innovations in *ycyc*

9.8   Variance decompositions: *U* or *ycyc* and WPI

assumed to operate throughout the period in question. Since innovations in WPI explain less than 5 percent of the variance in U (less than 10 percent of the variance in $ycyc$, plots not shown) the results are broadly consistent with the arguments in this chapter. In any event, there again appears to be less evidence to distinguish the hyperinflation and post-hyperinflation samples than previous studies referred to would have led us to believe.[68]

Conclusions

This chapter had two objectives. First, to set the record straight about the economic consequences for Hungary from the breakup of the Austro–Hungarian monarchy. Hungary experienced a deep structural change in its economy which thereafter affected both the costs and the political motivations of successive Hungarian governments. Second, to argue, on both historical and econometric grounds, that the advent of the LON-sponsored economic reforms were not credible and did not produce a significant regime change in the modern-day economic sense of the word. Thus, while inflation was sharply reduced, other indicators point to the failure of the LON policies to correct the economic problems which led Hungary to resort to hyperinflation. Hungary was therefore doomed eventually to repeat the experiment, as it did following the Second World War, and to impoverish its economy and citizens, as it also did during the 1930s, in order to escape very high inflation (see Siklos, 1991). All that the LON reforms accomplished was an externally-financed reduction in inflation. It is, however, difficult to draw definitive conclusions regarding the long-run effects of the period under study because of the emergence of the great depression only five years after the so-called stabilization. Nevertheless, it is not unreasonable to conclude, as did the Hungarian Institute for Economic Research (MGKI, 1943), that the stabilization of 1924 was illusory ("A Stabilizàció Illuziója").[69]

There are also some lessons for modern economies currently experiencing high inflation and a high external debt load (see also Webb, 1988). Policies implemented externally, which focus on the narrow objectives of the budget and the exchange rate, without regard to the structural state of the domestic economy, or knowledge of the necessary ingredients to sustain long-term economic growth, not to mention the imposition of historically high *ex post* real interest rates, are doomed to failure. It must, therefore, be concluded that one should either be somewhat less sanguine than Sargent (1986) about the simplicity with which the ending of a hyperinflation can be deemed successful, or be rather careful in formulating a "credible" set of policies. In the latter case, the lessons of Sargent's analysis remain valid.

Appendix: data description and sources

Notes to the data: Series label, definition, explanation and sources

N: notes in circulation
In K/10. To obtain a consistent series all values were converted into P (12,500K = 1P). Figures are in thousands.
Sources: League of Nations (1926); Young (1925); Mitzakis (1925); *Magyar Statisztikai Szemle* [*Hungarian Statistical Review*]; Boross (1984).

M1: notes and deposits
In thousand P; see notes on series **N**.

ER: exchange rate
K per 100 Swiss francs, as quoted on the Zurich exchange. After 1926, P per 100 Swiss francs. There were no quotes in 1926. Estimates were generated from quotes of the paper crown (K) relative to the gold crown.
Sources: Magyar Statisztikai Évkönyv [*Hungarian Statistical Yearbook*]; Young (1925); Mitzakis (1925).

WPI: wholesale price index
Basis 1913 = 1. Average prices prevailing in the following industries: food, mining, leather, paper products, and miscellaneous related industries. See also notes to **COLI** series below for an explanation of how the data for 1927–28 were adjusted. After December 1926 a comparable index based on New York gold prices is available. To convert these values to the 1913 base year index I used the nearest values for the wholesale price index base year 1913, corresponding to the WPI in terms of gold prices which prevailed during the 1924–26 period. Thus, for example, in November 1926, the WPI in terms of gold prices stood at 1.27 corresponding to a WPI (1913 = 1) of 18319. Accordingly, the WPI (1913 = 1) for January 1927 was assumed to be 18319 since it stood at 1.27 in terms of gold prices. Where missing values existed, linear interpolation was used. There is some confusion about the base of the index since the pattern of prices for 1922 (1914 = 1) in Mitzakis (1925) is virtually identical to the one based on 1913 prices and used by some authors. The relevant issues of Pester Lloyd were unavailable to me but I believe that the data are 1913 = 1. The date in Boross (1984) is also apparently 1913 = 1 but the price index values are considerably higher than the data reported in Mitzakis (1925). There is, unfortunately, too little information in Boross to resolve the question one way or another.
Sources: Magyar Statisztikai Szemle; Mitzakis (1925); Boross (1984). The data for 1922–23 (January–November) are from the Pester Lloyd index of retail prices for 60 commodities.

COLI: cost of living index
Cost of Living Index 1913 = 1, including rent. For data in 1927–28, see notes to **WPI**

series. Other missing data were 1925 January–February, 1922 January–June, 1922 August, and 1922 October–November. For missing data from 1922 the series entitled "Price Index for food for a family of four based on 82800 calories" was used as a proxy. For missing data in 1925, Budapest quotes for the US dollar exchange rate with the gold K were used.

Sources: Mitzakis (1925); *Magyar Statisztikai Szemle*; *Economic Bulletin of the Central Corporation of Banking Companies.*

URATE: unemployment rate
Unemployed in the Social Democratic Union as a percentage of union membership. Data for 1925 January–December 1928 were estimated by assuming that the total membership was equal to the average number of unemployed divided by the average unemployment rate for the period 1922 December, 1923 March–May, and 1923 July–1924 December. Membership data were only available for these periods.

Sources: See notes to UN series, and Wicker (1986).

ADV: advances to the Treasury
In million K.

Sources: Young (1925), Mitzakis (1925).

BOT: balance of trade
Exports less imports; converted into million P at par. For the gold K = 20.26 US cents; for the P = 17.49 US cents. Both are New York quotes.

Sources: League of Nations (1926), Magyar Gazdaságkutató Intézet [Hungarian Institute of Economic Research] *Helyzetjelentései* [*Situation Reports*]; Young (1925).

X: exports
See notes to **BOT** series.

IM: imports
See notes to **BOT** series.

UN: unemployment
Number of unemployed in the Social Democratic Union.

Sources: Annuaire Statistique Hongrois [*Hungarian Statistical Annual*]; *Economic Bulletin of the Central Corporation of Banking Companies.*

LIGNOUT: output of lignite
Forms the basis of the estimates of ycyc or cyclical output of the Hungarian economy. Production of Lignite in thousand metric tons.

Source: the *Economist, Monthly Supplement,* various issues, 1923–29.

UKWPI: wholesale price index in the United Kingdom
The *Economist*'s index of wholesale prices (1901–1905 = 2200) for cereals, meats,

and other foods, textiles, minerals, and miscellaneous products (rubber, timber, oils, etc.).
Source: the *Economist*, various issues, 1923–29.

UKURATE: unemployment rate in the United Kingdom
Unemployment rate among insured working persons in Great Britain and Northern Ireland. Data for 1926: M5–1927: M1 inclusive exclude coal miners during a strike when the government declared these workers uninsured.
Souce: the *Economist*, various issues, 1923–29.

Notes

I am grateful to the Social Sciences and Humanities Research Council of Canada, and to the Hungarian Academy of Sciences, for initial funding for this project. Subsequent research was carried out while I was on leave during 1988–89, in Oxford at St. Antony's College and the Institute of Economics and Statistics, and at the University of California, San Diego. Financial support from Wilfrid Laurier University, which enabled me to visit the collections of the Hoover Library at Stanford during the summer of 1989 and from the International Economic History Association, which permitted me to travel to the Tenth Conference in Leuven, Belgium, is gratefully acknowledged. A diskette containing the data used in this chapter is available on request while a data appendix, together with another appendix with detailed econometric results not given in the chapter, appear in the Wilfrid Laurier University *Working Paper* series. K. Ferber, of the Budapest School of Economics, made available valuable information pertaining to the historical circumstances facing Hungary during the 1920s, as well as a number of archival and statistical documents. Comments on a previous draft by Michael Bordo, Richard Burdekin, Forrest Capie, Anna Schwartz, and Elmus Wicker are greatly appreciated.

1 Advocates of Sargent's views point out that only in the episodes he considered has a statistical break been found either in the money–price correlations or in causality test results. Dornbusch and Fischer (1986), however, counter that credibility in the historical episodes considered by Sargent was accomplished by high interest rates and a suitably picked exchange rate.

2 In a recent survey, Siklos (1990a) lists no fewer than 65 books, articles, and chapters published since 1980 dealing with hyperinflations. However, the list is, by no means, exhaustive.

3 An argument of this kind is used in Lucas (1980) in testing what he considers to be the fundamental propositions of the quantity theory of money.

4 Causality is used here in the Granger–Sims sense of the term. See Granger and Newbold (1986, chapter 8).

5 This occurs when current money growth is set on the basis of expected inflation or the current prevailing rate of inflation. For an analysis of the implications of

imposing such conditions on the behavior of the monetary authorities, see Christiano (1987).

6 A real bills theory of money, rejuvenated by Sargent and Wallace (1982), predicts that money–price correlations depend on how the government finances anticipated deficits. If seigniorage (i.e., base money) is the vehicle, money–price correlations will be high. Otherwise, the same two aggregates need not be correlated at all. Whether such a theory is a more general one than the quantity theoretic view of money–price correlations is one that has sparked considerable debate.

7 These are the unemployment and output losses of an abrupt return to price stability.

8 In what follows, I shall ignore the period of the so-called "Red Terror" during which a Bolshevik revolution, led by Béla Kun, briefly ran the country and was later overturned. Also, Hungary after the First World War will be referred to as Trianon Hungary while pre-1914 Hungary will be called Greater Hungary (see also n. 9 below).

9 Known also, in Hungary, as the Treaty of Trianon. Signed June 4, 1920 and ratified by the Hungarian Parliament November 13, 1920. See *Survey of International Affairs* (hereafter *SIA*) (1928, Supplement, p. 150).

10 That is, from an area of 325,411 square km to 93,010 square km. 330,000 Hungarians also returned to Hungary from areas subsequently under foreign rule. This imposed an additional burden for the State since many of these individuals had helped Hungary's balance of payments through remittances. Finally, immigration, long a safety valve of sorts, was severely hampered by restrictions imposed by the United States. See Macartney (1965, p. 463; 1961, chapter 4).

11 A cadastral is equivalent to approximately 1.42 acres.

12 Horned cattle, horses, pigs, and sheep, being the vital constituents of livestock; Trianon Hungary values as a proportion of those for Greater Hungary were, respectively, 29.4 percent, 38.1 percent, 43.8 percent, and 28.1 percent. The comparisons are based on 1911 figures. Additional losses occurred because of the First World War, but these do not appear to have been very large (PK, p. 69). The above figures also do not reflect the fact that Hungary was defaulting on her reparations obligations in 1921–22 regarding the delivery of cattle (*SIA*, p. 151).

13 Figures are for 1913, and are slightly lower in 1921 (around 60 percent of Greater Hungary output) mainly because of the impact of the Red Terror.

14 Principally the so-called "Little Entente" nations of Czechoslovakia, Yugoslavia, and Romania.

15 This policy consisted in advocating the return of territories lost as a result of Trianon.

16 A recent exception is Franco (1990) which I found after writing this chapter. Wicker (1986) addresses in some detail the structural changes explaining unemployment, with special emphasis on the post-hyperinflation phase of Hungarian economic history during the 1920s. It is argued below, however, that he drew the wrong conclusions about the Hungarian experience relative to Sargent's thesis about ending hyperinflations.

17 The issue appears to have been settled only by 1928. See the *Economist* (1928). For more extensive discussions of the controversies surrounding the apportionment of the prewar debt as between Hungary and Austria, see Boross (1984); Mitzakis (1925); Pasvolsky (1928); Pogány (1987/88).

18 Such as the taking of Sopron, a town currently on Hungary's western frontier with Austria.

19 In an inconsequential attempt to control inflation early in the aftermath of the Red Terror (1920) the then minister of finance, Korányi, introduced a policy of withholding a fraction (50 percent) of the notes to be stamped as a "forced" loan of sorts to aid in temporarily financing government expenditures. Interestingly, a similar policy was to be implemented 25 years later during Hungary's second experience with hyperinflation. See Siklos (1990b).

20 Monetary arrangements following the breakup of the monarchy led to the creation of the Hungarian State Note Institute, a pseudo-central bank with no autonomy from the government (see p. 280 below). See Ferber (1987); Pogány (1987/88); Boross (1984); Mitzakis (1925).

21 Advice and, later, administrative involvement through the LON Reconstruction plan were, eventually, to be the means by which Britain would be involved in Hungary's financial affairs.

22 See Sayers (1976, chapter 6). Apparently, the Governor of the Bank was personally interested in fostering international banking relations. Again, see Sayers (1976, p. 122).

23 Hegedüs had a distinguished career both as an academic, a member of the Hungarian parliament, and as a Bank Director.

24 More details can be found in Mitzakis (1925, pp. 151–163).

25 The size and burden of German reparations was, however, known and, presumably, could serve as a guide.

26 Although these terms have, strictly speaking, a particular modern meaning, as defined in the Introduction to this chapter, Hegedüs clearly felt that the plan had to be believed by the public and, perhaps more importantly, by foreign governments and financial markets, in order to succeed.

27 Boross (1984, p. 189) claims that Hungarian views of theories of inflation followed the "traditional quantity theory," by which I take her to mean that monetary changes (eventually) lead to price changes in the same proportions. This is the position taken by North American economists such as, most notably, Milton Friedman (see Friedman, 1989). Knapp's views (1924), by contrast, appear to be closer to the version of the real bills doctrine espoused by Sargent and Wallace (1982) in which, essentially, money derives its value from how well it is "backed" by the earning power of the government.

28 Knapp was primarily interested in what explains the existence of money. See Schefold (1987); Bonar (1922); Sanger (1906), for reviews of Knapp's rather difficult *State Theory of Money* (1924). See also Frankel (1977), who also examines Knapp's views and contrasts them with the ideas of the German economist Simmel. I am grateful to David Laidler for the reference.

29 Hegedüs' plan called for a modest budget deficit until 1923 because of planned investment expenditures in infrastructure.

30 Money growth also slowed considerably, since it averaged 1.42 percent per month from January 1921 to July 1921. Previously (August 1919 to December 1920), money growth had averaged 4.63 percent per month.

31 Although no amount for reparations had been set, the Commission protested to the Hungarian government because its budget made no provision for such expenditures. This accentuated the irritation and frustration of Hungarian government officials.

32 These calculations are based on 100 times the first log difference in the wholesale price index (WPI) which somewhat understates rates based on proportional changes.

33 The LON loan to Hungary was also made available that month.

34 For example, the independent central bank, the National Bank of Hungary, was created in April. See also the discussion in the text below.

35 The brief rebound may be attributed to the lifting of the lien on Hungarian assets by July 1923.

36 The average for this ratio is 50.97 percent (1924: M7–1928: M12) while the same ratio stood at 51.87 percent in April 1921. Interest on deposits was arbitrarily fixed. Since the real return on these deposits was higher following the end of hyperinflation, one would have anticipated a much stronger recovery in the deposit – note ratio in the absence of other mitigating factors such as credibility in the stabilization program.

37 Also, the debt burden on a *per capita* basis was substantially higher than elsewhere in Eastern Europe. The term structure of the debt burden changed dramatically from being largely long-term during the late 1920s to essentially short-term in the early 1930s. See Spigler (1986) and Nötel (1986). Total debt outstanding averaged 4.3 billion pengő – the new currency introduced in 1927 to replace the K – during the period 1924–30 (MGKI, 1943), of which 42 percent was short-term debt. Total debt represented around 86.1 percent of average national income for the years 1924/25–1929/30. See MGKI (1947). Moreover, the cost of servicing the debt remained fairly stable at, on average, 150 percent of total exports until 1927/28. These data are based on National Bank of Hungary materials in the Hungarian National Archives.

38 This is the so-called unpleasant monetarist arithmetic of Sargent and Wallace (Sargent 1986, chapter 5). Suppose a government's budget constraint can be written

$$D_t + \rho B_t = (\Pi + g)M_t + gB_t,$$

where D is the deficit net of interest payments, B is the stock of public debt, ρ is the real interest rate, π is inflation, and g is output growth. If $\rho > g$, so that real interest costs are greater than the economy's ability to finance them, it can be shown that M would grow in an explosive fashion since deficits cannot be indefinitely financed via bonds.

39 The data in table 9.2 cannot be explained by the approaching great depression since government spending did not respond automatically to rising unemployment or other social problems. Apparently, the practice of extraordinary

budgets, that is expenditures arising from off-budget items in modern parlance, was not solely a Hungarian practice. Franco (1990, p. 181) argues that the Polish government used the same device following their own post-First World War experience with high inflation.

40 Wholesale prices, however, were deflating at a rate of 0.61 percent until April 1925, but the rate of deflation fell sharply to a rate of 0.14 percent thereafter. It is not unusual for currencies to be overvalued following the end of a hyperinflation (Bernholz, Gartner, and Heri, 1985). For Hungary this was to prove disastrous (Péteri, 1985a).

41 The public was aware of the existence of extraordinary budgets, although only official estimates were published.

42 See also Friedman and Schwartz (1982). Whether the moving standard deviation proxy is a good one is debatable. Engle (1982), for one, suggests that it is not. I have derived the so-called ARCH (Autoregressive Conditional Heteroskedasticity) residuals, by using a model of inflation as a function of money growth, and these confirm the inference based on figure 9.5. Indeed, the ARCH residuals are statistically insignificant for the hyperinflation sample but are statistically significant at the 5 percent level for the post-hyperinflation sample.

43 In his Nobel Lecture, Friedman (1977) proposed that inflation and output were negatively correlated instead of the positive correlation which stems from the expectations – augmented Phillips Curve relation. Friedman explains these results as originating from the fact that inflation uncertainty, proxied by the variability of inflation, reduces the efficiency of an economic system which, in turn, produces more unemployment and less output relative to an economy experiencing low inflation volatility.

44 In the German case the natural rate of unemployment was influenced by the ending of subsidies to the capital goods-producing sector. In the Hungarian hyperinflation of 1945–46 it was the dismantling of postwar reconstruction projects at roughly the same time as the stabilization reforms were introduced which, in all likelihood, raised the natural rate of unemployment.

45 The agricultural sector was, however, hit hard by a combination of poor weather, relatively high Hungarian prices, and high tariffs, as neighboring countries began to practice "beggar thy neighbor" policies. Economic growth was widely distributed across the industrial sector. Based on data in Fellner (1930), output growth in 11 of 18 industries sampled averaged over 10 percent in the period 1926–28.

46 Hungarian and UK unemployment rates are roughly comparable over the period studied despite widely divergent inflation rates. (See Figure B2, Appendix B.)

47 A difficulty in interpreting the end of this episode of hyperinflation is that the great depression of 1929–33 makes it unclear what the long-term effects of the loan and reparations arrangements would have been on the Hungarian economy. The great depression clearly resulted in credits to Hungary drying up but it is equally clear that loan and reparations costs together represented a burden which, historically, the Hungarian economy was not in a financial position to

tolerate for long. Time and time again, throughout the 1930s, Hungary asked the LON to extend further credits, and to reduce the interest rate on outstanding loans, generally with little success. It is also evident from a reading of Hungarian journals and the press at the time that Hungarian officials in the Finance Ministry, the National Bank of Hungary, as well as academic economists, did not feel that the stabilization plan was formulated on a sound economic basis. See Péteri (1985b); Ferber (1986).

48 A simple regression of unemployment as a function of inflation yields the following results: $u = 8.47\ (0.71) + 0.02p(0.03)$, $R^2 = 0.01$, 1922: M2–1924: M6; $u = 11.33(0.6) - 0.24p(0.3)$, $R^2 = 0.01$, 1924: M7–1928: M12. Standard errors are in parenthesis, R^2 is the coefficient of multiple determination, u is the unemployment rate, and p is inflation in the cost of living index. None of the coefficients are statistically significant at the 10 percent level.

49 A stationary series is essentially one with a constant mean and variance.

50 Appendix B provides some references.

51 The choice of models with which to extract the cyclical portion of a series is between a random walk, so that stationary series are expressed in differences of the levels, or one which follows a deterministic trend.

52 There is a large relevant literature. For a recent survey, see Diebold and Nerlove (1990).

53 See Granger and Newbold (1986, pp. 259–262) for a description. Essentially, the information set available is assumed to consist of the series $X1(t)$ and $X2(t)$ for which we have current and past observations alone. If $X1(t)$ causes $X2(t)$ it is because, roughly speaking, past values of $X1(t)$ jointly explain (in a statistical sense) $X2(t)$ but lagged values of $X2(t)$ do not explain $X1(t)$. An F-test is used to determine the direction of causality.

54 This is the causality test result predicted in a hyperinflationary environment.

55 All the causality tests were carried out by assuming the series should be modelled in their stationary form through differencing. Christiano and Ljunqvist (1988) have suggested that differencing can introduce spuriousness in causality tests. This does not appear to be true for the present data set since the tests were also conducted in first differences (H sample) and log levels (S sample) and the conclusions reached above generally hold.

56 Another reason to prefer the June 1924 date arises because the LON's loan almost fell through when the US opted out of loan guarantees at the last minute. The "loan crisis" was resolved when Britain agreed to back a large fraction of the debt. See, for example, Nötel (1986).

57 The computed F-statistics were, with degrees of freedom in parenthesis, $F(1,3) = 1.09$ for the test whether money growth causes inflation, and $F(1,3) = 0.90$ for inflation causing money growth. The significance levels are, respectively, 0.37 and 0.41.

58 Sargent and Wallace (1982, p. 419) in one case tested for causality with only two degrees of freedom remaining.

59 Those familiar with tests for cointegration will note that the test differs from the one popularized by Engle and Granger (1987). The test statistics given in table 9.5 are based on Johansen's test (E-G) for cointegration. Space limitations

prevent a fuller description except to note that the *E-G* test rejects the null of no cointegration less often than one would expect. However, application of the *E-G* test to the present data set did not affect the conclusions insofar as the test is consistent with the absence of a regime change. Readers are asked to consult the references provided in the notes to table 9.5. One word of caution is in order here. Johansen's test is designed for I(1) series and not the I(2) series which apply in the *H* sample. Nevertheless, the conclusions are unaffected when the *E-G* test is applied to the *H* data. The implied stationarity of velocity would also be inconsistent with the hypothesis of explosive inflationary expectations (Flood and Garber, 1980, 1983). Hoffman and Rasche (1991) have recently found that variables forming the usual money demand function are cointegrated even during the highly volatile period of the Great Depression in the United States. It would seem that one may perhaps not learn very much from tests of cointegration of the type conducted above. Note, however, that in the present study one is testing whether a postulated change in a monetary regime took place, which suggests that different cointegrating relationships would take place over the samples considered. By contrast, Hoffman and Rasche analyze a *single*, albeit turbulent, monetary regime.

60 There may also be exogenous or predetermined variables in the system.

61 Granger causality inferences may also be derived from VDs.

62 VDs are based on the moving-average representation of the system of equations.

63 Takes the value of 1 in the month of a particular event, and −1 the following month. Thus, it is assumed that fiscal news influences the endogenous variables only temporarily.

64 Webb (1986), and Siklos (1991), have also argued that fiscal news may be an important variable in understanding the progress and end of hyperinflations.

65 If the series are not cointegrated, as is the case for these models (results not shown), no error correction term is necessary.

66 Changing the order of the endogenous variable does, of course, influence the VD results quantitatively but the main qualitative conclusion, namely that a regime change is comparatively difficult to detect, is unchanged. Results using all the possible permutations in the vector **y** are available on request.

67 There were too few observations to estimate a VAR using *ycyc* for the hyperinflation sample.

68 Also, Chow tests do not reveal any coefficient instability when the VARs are estimated for the entire available sample.

69 Dornbusch (1990) is, therefore, correct in pointing out that stabilization of prices is insufficient to guarantee long-term economic growth, but he is incorrect in arguing that, insofar as the Hungarian case is concerned, the European experience stands in contrast to the modern South American one.

References

Berend, I.T. and Gy. Ránki, 1979. *Underdevelopment and Economic Growth: Studies in Hungarian Social and Economic History*, Budapest: Akadémiai Kiadó.

1984. *Economic Development in East-Central Europe in the XIXth and XXth Century*, New York: Columbia University Press.

Bernholz, P., M. Gartner and E. Heri, 1985. "Historical experiences with flexible exchange rates: a simulation of common qualitative characteristics," *Journal of International Economics*, 19: 21–45.

Bonar, J. 1922. "Review of the *State Theory of Money*," *Economic Journal* (March): 39–47.

Bordo, M.D. and E.N. White, "British and French finance during the Napoleonic Wars" NBER working paper no. 3517 (November 1990).

Boross, E.A., 1984. "The role of the state issuing bank in the course of inflation in Hungary between 1918 and 1924," in G. Feldman (ed.), *The Experience of Inflation: International and Comparative Studies*, Berlin: De Gruyter: 188–227.

Cagan, P., 1956. "The monetary dynamic of hyperinflation," in M. Friedman (ed.), *Studies in the Quantity Theory of Money*, Chicago: University of Chicago Press: 25–117.

Christiano, L.J., 1987. "Cagan's model of hyperinflation under rational expectations," *International Economic Review*, 28 (February): 33–49.

Cukierman, A., 1986. "Central bank behavior and credibility: some recent theoretical developments," Federal Reserve Bank of St. Louis, *Review*, 68 (May): 5–17.

Déak, F., 1942. *Hungary at the Peace Conference: The Diplomatic History of the Treaty of Trianon*, New York: Columbia University Press.

Diebold, F.X. and M. Nerlove, 1990. "Unit roots in economic time series: a selective survey," in T.B. Formby and G.F. Rhodes (eds.), *Advances in Econometrics: Co-Integration, Spurious Regressions and Unit Roots*, Greenwich, CT: JAI Press.

Dornbusch, R., 1988. "Notes on credibility and stabilization," *NBER Working Paper*, 2790 (December).

1990. "From stabilization to growth", *NBER Working Paper*, 3302 (March).

Dornbusch, R. and S. Fischer, 1986. "Stopping hyperinflations past and present," *Weltwirtschaftliches Archiv*, 122 (1): 1–47.

Eckstein, A., 1952. *The Economic Development of Hungary, 1920–1950: A Study in the Growth of an Economically Underdeveloped Area*, Ph.D dissertation, University of California, Berkeley.

Engle, R.F., 1982. "Autoregressive conditional heteroskedasticity with estimates of the United Kingdom inflation," *Econometrica*, 50 (July): 987–1007.

Engle, R.F. and C.W.J. Granger, 1987. "Co-integration and error correction: representation, estimation and testing," *Econometrica*, 55 (March): 251–276.

Evans, P. 1978. "Time series and structural analysis of the German hyperinflation," *International Economic Review*, 19 (February): 195–209.

Fellner, Fr., 1930. "Csonka Magyarország Nemzeti Jövedelme" [Dismembered Hungary's National Income], Budapest: Magyar Tudományos Akademia.

Ferber, K., 1986. "A controversy on the indebtedness of Hungary at the end of the 1920s," *Acta Historia*, 32 (1–2): 113–125.

1987. "Lépéshatrányban. A Magyar Kormány Kölcsönszerzési Kisérlete 1930–31-ben" [A Step Behind. The Attempt of the Hungarian Government at Gaining a Loan in 1930–31], *Történelmi Szemle*, 30(2): 137–54.

Flood, R.P. and P.M. Garber, 1980. "An economic theory of monetary reform," *Journal of Political Economy*, 88 (February): 24–58.

1983. "Process consistency and monetary reform," *Journal of Monetary Economics*, 12: 279–295.

Franco, G.B.H., 1990. "Fiscal reforms and stabilizations: four hyperinflation cases examined," *Economic Journal*, 100 (March): 176–187.

Frankel, Sir Herbert, 1977. *Money: Two Philosophies, the Conflict of Trust and Authority*, Oxford: Basil Blackwell.

Friedman, M., 1977. "Inflation and unemployment: Nobel Lecture," *Journal of Political Economy*, 85 (June): 451–472.

1989. "Quantity theory of money," in J. Eatwell, M. Milgate and P. Newman (eds.), *Money: The New Palgrave*, New York: Norton: 1–40.

Friedman, M. and A. Schwartz, 1982. *Monetary Trends in the United States and the United Kingdom*, Chicago: University of Chicago Press for the NBER.

Garber, P.M., 1982. "Transition from inflation to price stability," in K. Brunner and A.H. Meltzer (eds.), *Carnegie-Rochester Conference Series on Public Policy*, 16, Amsterdam: North-Holland: 11–42.

Granger, C.W.J. and P. Newbold, 1986. *Forecasting Economic Time Series*, 2nd edn., New York: Academic Press.

Hoensch, J.K., 1988. *A History of Modern Hungary 1867–1986*, London: Longman.

Hoffman, D. and R.H. Rasche, 1991. "The demand for money in the U.S. during the great depression: estimates and comparisons with the post war experiences," unpublished ms.

Johansen, S. and K. Juselius, 1990. "Maximum likelihood estimation inference on cointegration – with applications to the demand for money," *Oxford Bulletin of Economics and Statistics*, 52(2): 169–207.

Kindleberger, C.P., 1984. *A Financial History of Western Europe*, London: George Allen & Unwin.

Knapp, Georg Friedrich, 1924. *State Theory of Money*, London: Macmillan.

League of Nations, 1926. *The Financial Reconstruction of Hungary, General Survey and Principal Documents*, Geneva: League of Nations.

Lewis, W.A., 1970. *Economic Survey 1919–1939*, London: George Allen & Unwin.

Lucas, R.E., Jr., 1980. "Two illustrations of the quantity theory," *American Economic Review*, 70 (December): 1005–1014.

Macartney, C.A., 1961. *October Fifteenth: A History of Modern Hungary*, 2nd edn., Edinburgh: Edinburgh University Press.

1965. *Hungary and Her Successors*, London: Oxford University Press.

MGKI, Magyar Gazdaságkutató Intézet, 1943. "Az Elsó Világ Haború Gazdasági Kóvetkezményei" [The Economic Consequences of the First World War], Budapest.

1947. *Magyar Nemzeti Jövedelme* [The National Income of Hungary], 31 (March), Budapest.

Mitzakis, M., 1925. *Le Relèvement Financier de la Hongrie et la Société des Nations* [The Financial Restoration of Hungary and the League of Nations], Paris: Presses Universitaires de France.

Nelson, C.R. and C.I. Plosser, "Trends and random walks in macroeconomic time series: some evidence and implications," *Journal of Monetary Economics*, 14 (September): 135–162.

Nötel, R., 1986. "International credit and finance," in M. Kaser and E. Radice (eds.), *Economic History of Eastern Europe*, vol. II, Oxford: Clarendon Press: 170–295.

Nurkse, R., 1947. *International Currency Experience: Lessons of the Inter-War Period*, Geneva: League of Nations, 1944; reprinted by United Nations.

Pasvolsky, L., 1928. *Economic Nationalism of the Danubian States*, New York: Macmillan.

Péteri, Gy., 1985a. "Nemzetközi Likviditás és Nemzetgazdasági Szempont a Magyar Monétáris Politikában 1924–1931 között" [International Liquidity and Economic Points of View about Hungarian Monetary Policy 1924–1931], *Történelmi Szemle*: 1203–1211.

1985b, "Montagu Norman és a Magyar szanallási mü." Az 1924- ós Magyar Pénzügyi Stabilizációrol" [Montagu Norman and the Reconstruction Plan. On the 1924 Hungarian Financial Stabilization], *Századok*, 1: 121–151.

Pogány, A., 1987/88. "Két Szempont a Magyarországi Infláció Vizsgálatához (1914–1924)" [Examining the Hungarian Inflation from Two Points of View], *Történelmi Szemle*, 2: 1204–1215.

Ránki, Gy., 1983. *Economy and Foreign Policy: The Struggle of the Great Powers for Hegemony in the Danube Valley 1919–1939*, New York: Columbia University Press.

Sanger, C.P., 1906. "Review of the *State Theory of Money*," *Economic Journal* (June): 266–267.

Sargent, T.J., 1986. *Rational Expectations and Inflation*, New York: Harper & Row.

Sargent, T.J. and N. Wallace, 1982. "The real bills doctrine versus the quantity theory: a reconsideration," *Journal of Political Economy*, 90 (December): 1212–1236.

Sayer, R.S., 1976. *The Bank of England 1891–1944*, Cambridge: Cambridge University Press.

Schefold, B., 1987. "Knapp, Georg Friedrich," in J. Eatwell, M. Milgate and P. Newman (eds.), *The New Palgrave: A Dictionary of Economics*, London: Macmillan.

Siklos, P.L., 1989. "The end of the Hungarian hyperinflation of 1945–1946," *Journal of Money, Credit and Banking*, 21 (May): 135–147.

1990a. "Hyperinflations: their origins, development, and termination," *Journal of Economic Surveys*, 4: 225–248.

1990b. "The link between money and prices under different monetary regimes: the case of postwar Hungary," *Explorations in Economic History*, 27: 468–482.

1991. *War Finance, Hyperinflation and Stabilization in Hungary, 1938–1948*, London: Macmillan, New York: St. Martin's Press.

Spigler, I., 1986. "Public Finance," in M. Kaser and E. Radice (eds.), *Economic History of Eastern Europe*, vol. II, Oxford: Clarendon Press: 117–169.

Vágo, J., 1925. "Le Chômage en Hongrie" [Unemployment in Hungary], *International Labour Review*, 12 (September): 370–389.

Webb, S.B., 1986. "Fiscal news and inflationary expectations in Germany after World War I," *Journal of Economic History*, 46: 769–794.

1988. "Latin American debt today and German reparations after World War I," *Weltwirtschaftliches Archiv*, 124 (4): 745–774.

Wicker, E., 1986. "Terminating hyperinflation in the dismembered Habsburg Monarchy," *American Economic Review*, 76 (June): 350–364.

Young, J.P., 1925. *European Currency and Finance*, vol. I, Serial 9, Commission of Gold and Silver Enquiry: United States Senate, Washington DC: Government Printing Office: 232–327.

10 Halting inflation in Italy and France after the Second World War

ALESSANDRA CASELLA AND
BARRY EICHENGREEN

Introduction

In the aftermath of the Second World War, Italy and France like the other European belligerents experienced persistent, rapid, disruptive inflations. Within four years of the armistice, however, both countries had succeeded in bringing the era of postwar inflation to a close. This chapter is an attempt to understand what made their stabilizations possible.

Doing so is no easy task. There is an abundance of potential explanations for the two stabilizations: fiscal correction (tax increases and expenditure reductions), monetary restriction (reserve requirements and credit controls), changes in domestic politics (the exclusion of the Communists from postwar governments), and foreign aid (notably the Marshall Plan).

The challenge is not to formulate hypotheses, but to reject them. This is analogous to the problem faced by players of the board game "Clue," whose object is to determine who committed the murder in which room using what weapon. Players roll dice and draw cards to eliminate suspects until only one person, room, and weapon remain.

In this chapter we utilize international comparisons in place of dice and cards. Comparisons discipline the argument. Although many of the explanatory factors we consider appeared simultaneously in Italy and France, the two countries stabilized at very different times (Italy in the summer of 1947, France at the end of 1948). Given the difference in timing, either events that occurred simultaneously in the two countries cannot account for both stabilizations, or else other critically important differences across countries determined the lag with which those events brought inflation to a halt.

For example, it is argued that the Italian stabilization was caused by a provision affecting banks' reserve requirements enacted in October 1947 which restricted bank advances to business. However, a similar provision adopted simultaneously in France did not affect inflation there. This implies either that changes in reserve requirements were not central to the stabilization, or that certain subtle differences in the Italian and French banking reforms provide the key to understanding the different national experience. (We suggest below that, while the change in reserve requirements in Italy was more stringent than its French analog, in both countries changes in reserve requirements played at best a subsidiary role in stabilization.) Similarly, it is argued that the exclusion of the Communists from the Italian government in 1947 moderated inflationary expectations by promising to usher in a new era of fiscal discipline. But the Communists were excluded from the French government at the same time, and inflation there continued for another 18 months. Another popular argument in the Italian literature is that George Marshall's Harvard speech in June 1947 helped to halt the inflation by signalling that foreign finance would be made available in quantities sufficient to eliminate Italy's trade and budget deficits. Yet the same speech promised Marshall Plan aid for France but had no noticeable impact on French inflation, which continued for another 18 months.

To understand the nature and timing of the two stabilizations, it is first necessary to understand the inflations. We characterize inflation in both countries as symptomatic of a distributional conflict. In the aftermath of the Second World War, distributional disputes remained unresolved. The notional demands of government, households and firms summed to more than 100 percent of national income. Inflation, fueled by central and commercial bank credit, reconciled these incompatible claims. As in the model of Alesina and Drazen (1991), so long as distributional interests, uncertain about the patience of their adversaries, delayed offering concessions in the hope that others would give in first, inflation persisted. Eventually, the least patient groups offered concessions sufficient to bring the inflation to a halt.

This framework points to the Marshall Plan as a key element in the Italian and French stabilizations and to differences in political complexion and in national investment strategies as the explanation for differences in the timing of the stabilizations. The Marshall Plan increased the size of the pie to be shared out among distributional factions, reducing the sacrifices required to eliminate excess demand. By reducing the benefits of delay relative to the costs, it increased the likelihood of early stabilization.

In Italy, stabilization followed the announcement of the Marshall Plan almost immediately. In France, on the contrary, the conflict between interest groups was not speedily resolved. We discuss three possible explanations for the delay. First, politics may have been more polarized in France than in Italy, so that a larger penalty would be suffered by the group that offered concessions. Second, even though the Left ultimately lost in both countries it was stronger in France than in Italy and was therefore willing and able to keep fighting longer. Finally, French governments were pursuing an ambitious program of investment motivated by international ambitions and perceived threats to domestic security. Since all social groups were committed to the program, the entire reduction in excess demand had to come from the share of national income that remained after the portion devoted to investment was removed. In terms of immediate consumption shares, therefore, the sacrifices required to bring the inflation to a halt were larger in France than in Italy, and each distributional interest in France had a greater incentive to hold out. Hence stabilization took longer to complete.

Shifting the focus from proximate determinants of the two stabilizations, such as changes in fiscal policies and commercial bank reserve requirements, to their underlying determinants, namely distributional conflicts and the international initiative that promoted their resolution, is not to deny a role for those proximate factors. Government budget deficits and commercial bank liquidity creation provided the immediate impetus for inflation in both Italy and France. Our argument is simply that budget deficits and high levels of liquidity creation were themselves symptoms of underlying distributional conflicts, and they were successfully removed only when the Marshall Plan intervened to encourage an early distributional settlement. Inflation and stabilization in Italy and France, in other words, cannot be adequately understood purely in terms of these proximate determinants.

The chapter proceeds as follows. In the next section we sketch the development of inflation in the two countries. We then analyze evidence relevant to the competing explanations for the stabilizations: the monetary hypothesis, the fiscal hypothesis, the change in government, and the Marshall Plan. Having reviewed the standard arguments, we then discuss the inflations as a reflection of distributional conflicts and present our interpretation of the timing of the two stabilizations. A final section draws some conclusions.

The historical background

Both Italy and France endured significant economic hardship in the aftermath of the Second World War. At the end of 1945, agricultural production in both countries had fallen to little more than 50 percent of prewar levels; industrial production was similarly impaired in Italy and declined to no more than 70–75 percent of its 1938 level in France. Despite extensive destruction of capital equipment, the subsequent recovery was rapid: by 1946, GDP in real terms was above 80 percent of the prewar level in both countries (see table 10.1).

In both France and Italy, inflation proceeded rapidly through the

Table 10.1 *National income in constant 1938 prices, 1938 and 1945–50*

Year	Italy (billions lire)	% 1938	France (billions francs)	% 1938
1938	165	100	380	100
1945	91	55	207	55
1946	133	81	315	83
1947	149	90	341	90
1948	157	95	366	96
1949	164	99	414	109
1950	175	106	445[a]	117

Note:
[a] Taken from Maddison (1982, p. 174).
Sources: Italy: Ercolani (1969, p. 422); France: INSEE (1966, p. 556), except as otherwise noted.

beginning of 1947 (see figure 10.1). Italian prices had declined in the months immediately following the armistice, but a change had taken place in the spring of 1946 as inconclusive debates over policy had led to worsening expectations. In the 12 months between May 1946 and May 1947, wholesale prices rose by 105 percent, and the free exchange rate rose by 250 percent.

A break in the pattern occurred at the beginning of the summer, coincident with the formation of the fourth de Gasperi government, the first postwar coalition to exclude the Communists, and with Marshall's Harvard speech committing the United States to a program of financial support for European reconstruction. Italy's free exchange rate strengthened substantially in June and appreciated steadily over the summer. Prices continued to rise but at a decelerating rate, while the gap between black market and legal prices narrowed. Imports of goods free of administrative controls (so-called "franco-valuta" imports), typically a vehicle for repatriating capital, increased substantially over the summer, reaching for the entire year a volume five times larger than in 1946. In October, new commercial bank reserve requirements were put in place, and prices began to fall. The quarterly rate of wholesale price inflation swung from 16 percent in 1947:2 to − 11 percent in 1947:3. At the beginning of 1948, prices stabilized, aside from a readjustment in the summer of 1948 when the subsidy on wheat was abolished. Overall, Italian wholesale prices rose by 3 percent in 1948, and declined slightly but continuously until June 1950.[1]

In France, prices rose by 80 percent over the year ending in December 1946. The interim Blum government of late 1946 and the Ramadier

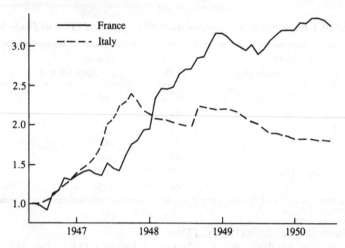

10.1   Monthly wholesale price index, May 1946–June 1950
Sources: Italy: Bolletino Mensile di Statistica, various issues; France:
INSEE (1966, p. 376).

government that succeeded it in January 1947 attempted to impose a price
freeze. A New Year's Day decree cut all retail prices by 5 percent. A second decree mandated another 5 percent cut in retail prices, effective from March 1.
Citizens' committees were formed to verify that the requisite reductions had
taken place. Model shops were established to sell goods at official prices and
make it easier for the public to identify cheating by retailers. This so-called
"Blum Experiment" achieved a temporary pause in inflation: retail prices in
Paris fell by 2 percent between January and April 1947.

Shortages were quick to develop, however, encouraging transactions at
black-market prices. The attempt to halt inflation by decree collapsed in the
spring. Inflation accelerated from May through the end of 1947, with retail
prices in Paris rising by 50 percent and prices in other urban areas rising
even faster.

In the first half of 1948 the French government imposed a capital levy and
impounded all 5,000-franc bank notes, producing a temporary cash surplus
for the Treasury and reducing aggregate demand. Retail prices in Paris rose
by less than 1 percent between January and July 1948. But in the second half
of the year the budgetary problem reappeared, and inflation accelerated
again. By December 1948 retail prices in Paris were up by 26 percent over
July.

At this point the French stabilization finally took hold. With the help of a
good harvest in the summer of 1948, wholesale prices stabilized, rising by

Table 10.2 *Bank credit to business in Italy, January–October 1947*

Period	Increase in deposits (%)	Increase in advances (%)	Advances/deposits end of period (%)	New advances/ new deposits (%)
Jan.–Mar. 1947	11.8	18.8	63.6	94.8
Apr.–Jun. 1947	11.9	24.1	70.6	129.1
Jul.–Sep. 1947	8.3	14.7	74.7	124.9
Oct.–Dec. 1947	7.2	2.3	71.3	24.0

Source: Bank of Italy (1948, p. 160).

only 1.4 percent between the ends of 1948 and 1949. In 1950 wholesale prices increased by less than 2 percent over the first half of the year.

The monetary hypothesis

A first possible explanation for the two stabilizations is monetary correction. According to this view, excessive money and credit creation by the consolidated banking system fueled inflation in both countries. Central banks provided money finance not just for the government budget deficit but to businesses requiring credit for reconstruction. Commercial banks, unrestrained by reserve requirements, lent freely to the private sector. Restraint by the central bank plus the imposition of reserve requirements on the commercial banks were necessary and sufficient, according to this argument, to bring the inflation to a halt. This is the leading explanation for the Italian stabilization, and we analyze it in considerable detail.[2]

The new reserve requirements, designed by Luigi Einaudi, the Minister of the Budget, required banks to hold government bonds or blocked accounts at the Bank of Italy equal to as much as 15 percent of existing deposits and 40 percent of additional deposits.[3] Simultaneously with the enactment of these restrictions at the beginning of October 1947, the Bank of Italy's discount rate was raised from 4 to 5.5 percent. As mentioned above, the aggregate wholesale price index began to decline in October 1947, in perfect synchronization with the credit measure.[4] The credit institutions had been expanding advances to the private sector at a rapid rate. In the second and third quarters of 1947, credit extended had exceeded deposits collected by over 25 percent (table 10.2). In the last quarter of 1947, advances continued to rise but at a much lower rate. By the end of December, banks were holding excess reserves of 44 billion (or 4.5 percent of deposits). In 1948, the growth rate of private credit remained low during the first half of the year but increased subsequently as economic activity recovered. Hence the argument that the imposition of the reserve requirements should be credited with the stabilization.

A difficulty with this argument is that the new regulations had been anticipated for months. In January, Einaudi, then Governor of the Central Bank, had written to the credit institutions urging them to limit the expansion of their advances to the private sector. The following month he had minuted the Treasury minister on the same topic, proposing the imposition of new reserve requirements. Both letters were examined in the *Annual Report* of the Bank of Italy, published at the end of March. By then, the reform of reserve requirements was already the subject of public debate: for example, Libero Lenti had discussed it in *Corriere della Sera* at the end of February.[5] In April, the specific form of the provision was exposed to the government. In mid-June, speaking before the Assemblea Costituente, Einaudi had once more analyzed the need to control bank credit and described his proposal. Finally, the new regulations were approved and discussed with the banks in August, more than 30 days before their application, and detailed in the major newspapers (see, for example, Einaudi's articles in *Corriere della Sera* on August 31 and September 7). In Einaudi's words: "It is obvious that the restriction has neither been unexpected, nor sudden, nor draconian: it has been slow, foretold and discussed at great length." Hence it is difficult to see the reserve requirements as an abrupt change in regime that would have caused a break in price level trends at the moment of their imposition.[6]

The bank regulations had three purposes. First, they were intended to reduce the quantity of money. Second, they aimed at providing automatic financing to the Treasury through the banks' subscription of bonds. Finally, they were designed to break the vicious circle linking speculation against the currency to credit and inflation.

As shown in table 10.3, the new regulations failed in their first goal. Although the rate of growth of deposits declined in 1947:4 (from 8 to 7 percent for all deposits, and from 7 to 4 percent for business deposits), this decrease was offset by a rise in the rate of growth of central bank credit. Currency circulation increased by 15.6 percent between June and September but by 18 percent from September to December. Circulation grew because of a seasonal effect but also because of the support the government granted to the industries hurt by the credit measure itself, support that the central bank financed. Firms found it hard to cope with credit stringency. As nominal interest rates rose in the last quarter of 1947, the real interest rate on bank credit jumped from something on the order of -90 percent to as much as $+50$ percent on an annual basis.[7] The government felt compelled to intervene in support of the mechanical and shipbuilding industries, among other sectors. In the financial year 1947–48, the increase in the

Table 10.3 *Italian money supply, June 1946–December 1948, billion lire*

Period	Notes[a]	Business deposits[b]	Money supply	Change in money supply (%)
Jun. 1946	394.7	229.8	624.5	
Dec. 1946	505.0	369.0	874.0	40.0
Jun. 1947	577.6	455.0	1,032.6	18.1
Dec. 1947	788.1	503.5	1,291.6	25.1
Jun. 1948	816.0	628.0	1,444.0	11.8
Dec. 1948	963.0	740.0	1,703.0	17.4

Notes:
[a] Notes exclude Treasury currency (which accounted for 1–1.5 percent of notes in circulation) and circular checks. Circular checks accounted for 13–14 percent of notes in circulation over the entire period.
[b] Business deposits ("conti di corrispondenza coi clienti") are used as proxy for checking deposits.
Source: Bank of Italy (1949).

endowment of the Istituto per la Ricostruzione Industriale (IRI) and direct subsidies to industries amounted to 71.5 billion lire, up from 9 billion lire in 1938–39 (both in constant 1947 prices).[8] In the last three months of 1947 the Bank of Italy's credit to the government was 10 percent higher in constant prices than in the previous 15 months.[9] In effect, the reserve requirements diverted loans to business from the commercial banks to the central bank (which extended loans to enterprises via the public sector), without much net effect on overall rates of growth of money and credit. The rate of monetary growth slowed between the years ending September 1947 and September 1948, but only slightly.

In achieving their second objective, increasing commercial bank financing of the public deficit, the reserve requirements were more successful. Credit to the government rose from 10.5 percent of total private bank credit between July 1946 and September 1947 to 29.3 percent in the following 15 months. (Correspondingly, the banks financed 12.3 percent of the deficit in the first period and 20.4 percent in the second.)[10] But since nominal bond yields did not fall after the stabilization, it is not clear that bond subscriptions by banks effectively reduced the debt burden of the Treasury.

The effect of the credit measure on prices is more difficult to assess. The standard story is that firms, anticipating further price increases, had been postponing sales and accumulating inventories, which served only to

Table 10.4 *Change in
inventories in Italy, 1945–49,
billion lire, 1938 prices*

Year	
1945 ·	− 3.2
1946	2.3
1947	8.6
1948	− 0.7
1949	1.3

Source: Ercolani (1969, p. 441).

restrict supply and fuel additional inflation. They financed their current labor costs and possibly capital flight through bank advances. When credit was tightened, producers and retailers were forced to sell goods from their inventories to collect revenues sufficient to cover their costs. Prices declined dramatically as a result.

Inventory data appear in table 10.4. Although these estimates are not particularly precise, they point strongly to the accumulation of inventories in 1947, in conjunction with the large amounts of credit extended by banks to firms, supporting the interpretation summarized above. The decline in stocks accompanying the stabilization is far from dramatic, but annual data may conceal more dramatic changes over shorter periods.

Ultimately, these data merely establish the existence of a correlation between inflation and inventory behavior. Additional evidence is required to evaluate the direction of causation. Disaggregated price indices are a possible source of useful information.[11] These show that the largest declines in prices were those for food, even though 1947 was a very poor harvest year. In contrast, prices of manufactures, which should most dramatically reflect the effects of inventory liquidation, declined less than the aggregate index. The price decline seems to have been negatively correlated with the labor content of the good: whereas the price of swine fell by 41 percent, for example, the price of pork fell by 19 percent; similarly, the price of the iron industry's goods fell by 6 percent, while the price of mechanical products actually rose.[12]

It is thus difficult to sustain the hypothesis that price declines were caused by firms in distress suddenly unable to borrow. In fact, the industry hurt most seriously by the credit crunch and the increase in wages, and which had ultimately to be rescued by the government, was the mechanical industry, whose output prices increased steadily. It is probable, however, that firms and stores did liquidate their inventories, and that they did so because of a combination of tighter credit and expectations of declining prices. How much the change in expectations owed to the credit restriction and how much to other developments remains an open question.

Another reason to question the role of the credit measure in halting the Italian inflation is that credit controls and reserve requirements were imposed almost simultaneously in France, without a concomitant effect on inflation.[13] In January 1947 French banks were instructed by the National Credit Council (NCC) to refuse credits that might have been used to finance commodity hoarding.[14] The banks were required to provide extensive documentation of all requests for advances of 2 million francs or more and to obtain approval from the Bank of France for advances of more than 30 million francs.[15] Two months later reserve requirements were imposed on all commercial banks. The Banking Control Commission required all commercial banks to maintain liquid assets equal to at least 60 percent of their demand deposits. In October the banks were instructed by the NCC to cut down or cancel existing credits to customers not engaged in the production of goods.

The reason for the ineffectiveness of this first round of French credit controls and reserve requirements is not difficult to ascertain. The 60 percent reserve requirement defined liquid assets to include not just cash and Treasury securities but commercial bills as well.[16] Moreover, commercial bills were exempted from NCC and Bank of France oversight on the grounds that self-liquidating credits provided in connection with normal business transactions were not inflationary. With advances controlled but discounts of commercial bills unrestricted, firms shifted toward the use of the latter.[17]

A second set of credit controls was imposed in September 1948 in response to resurgent inflation. The timing makes it tempting to credit them with having halted the inflation at the end of that same year. These controls required banks to hold Treasury paper equal to at least 95 percent of that in their possession on September 30, 1948, and to invest 20 percent of new deposits in government securities. Commercial bills were made subject to the same oversight as other loans. Commercial banks were forced to justify to the central bank individual discounts that exceeded 5 million francs. Strict limits were placed on the amount of central bank credit commercial banks could obtain.[18] For the first time commercial bills were no longer perfectly liquid in the sense that they could be rediscounted at the Bank of France upon demand.

Importantly, however, exemptions from rediscount ceilings were extended to commercial bills arising out of transactions associated with agricultural production, with exports and with the provision of working

Table 10.5 *Sources of increase in money supply in France, 1947–49, billion francs*

Source	1947	1948	1949
Gold	− 30	—	—
Foreign exchange	—	—	49
Postal deposits with Treasury	23	58	44
Domestic credit, Bank of France	34	27	41
and commercial banks combined	287	484	460
(to government)	(143)	(104)	(111)
(to business)	(182)	(380)	(349)
Total	322	507	544

Source: Kriz (1951, p. 90).

capital to industry for re-equipment. Of the 147 million francs of credit provided to business by the Bank of France in 1949, 105 billion francs were rediscounts not subject to ceiling.[19]

Table 10.5 shows the rate of increase of the money supply in France and its proximate determinants. Monetary growth accelerated sharply in 1948 and failed to slow in 1949. Since reserve flows were small in both years, domestic credit creation was far and away the most important source of monetary growth.

Table 10.6 shows the composition of the increase in domestic credit. Again, there is little sign in the French data of change between 1948 and 1949. Loans, advances and discounts for business accounted for 79 percent of the increase in domestic credit in 1948, 76 percent in 1949. The commercial banks supplied 69 percent of the credit provided by the consolidated banking system in 1948, 52 percent in 1949. Direct advances by the Bank of France to the government declined abruptly in 1948, but rediscounts for commercial banks rose dramatically in 1948 and again in 1949, reflecting the exemption from credit ceilings of commercial bills generated in connection with re-equipment. Thus, insofar as Bank of France policy was less inflationary in 1948–49 than in 1947, this reflected a decline in the provision of direct advances to the Treasury. And since the government budget remained deep in deficit, the decline in direct advances reflected the Treasury's greater ability to place bonds with the public (as shown in Table 10.7, p. 326). This surely was a consequence of the stabilization rather than an independent cause.

That the share of domestic credit provided by the commercial banks fell in 1949 suggests that the September 1948 commercial bank reserve requirements may have had some small effect. However, the ratio of new commer-

Table 10.6 *Composition of increase in bank credit in France, 1947–49, billion francs*

Source	1947	1948	1949
Credit to government	143	104	111
By Bank of France	199	39	76
Direct advances	116	43	5
Other	83	−4	71
By commercial banks (Treasury bill holdings)	−56	65	35
Credit to business	182	380	349
By Bank of France	34	113	147
Rediscounts	34	107	131
Open market purchases and advances	0	6	16
By commercial banks	148	267	202
Commercial bill discounts	119	228	179
Loans and advances	29	39	23

Source: Kriz (1951, p. 94).

cial bank loans to new commercial bank deposits showed no tendency to decline between 1948 and 1949: it in fact rose from 0.93 to 1.32.[20] It is thus hard to attach much importance to reserve requirements as a restraint on the lending activities of French commercial banks.

In summary, there is little evidence of a significant monetary correction in either Italy or France around the time of stabilization. Credit controls may have had a larger impact on the ratio of new commercial bank credit to new deposits in Italy, but due to the response of the central bank and public enterprise, that impact was in any case insufficient to slow the rate of monetary growth.

The fiscal hypothesis

Although stabilization took place without a concomitant contraction in money supplies, it still may have reflected anticipated future changes in rates of money growth. This points to a change in the budgetary situation as a plausible explanation for stabilization. Even if current monetization was still large, a decrease in the accumulation of debt could signal a future decline in the rate of growth of money supply and, through the power of expectations, lead to immediate price stability.

In both Italy and France, postwar budget deficits were large. In the prevailing climate of political uncertainty, it was not clear whether taxes could be raised sufficiently to service existing debt, much less to pay the interest on new loans. As inflation accelerated, tax receipts lagged and budget deficits widened, requiring additional monetization. Only if legislators marshaled the resolve needed to raise taxes and reduce public spending would it be possible to bring this vicious spiral to a halt.[21]

In Italy, the public displayed a surprising willingness to subscribe government bonds at low interest rates immediately after the war. The first loan launched in the summer of 1945 took the form of a five-year bond at a 5 percent interest rate (the so-called Soleri loan, after the name of the Treasury minister). It was well received, and the government succeeded in financing its deficit of the first postwar financial year without resorting to credit from the central bank. While advances from the Bank of Italy became necessary in following years, nominal interest rates did not rise significantly despite the acceleration of inflation: the average government bond yield was 5.4 percent in 1946 and 6.2 percent in 1947.[22] This reflected not just the strong influence of the government on the credit institutions (partly through the direct control to which the largest banks were subject) and the lack of alternative assets, but also public confidence. Commenting on the favorable outcome of the Reconstruction Loan issued in the winter of 1946–47 (a 30-year bond yielding 5 percent), Einaudi wrote that its success should be attributed "not to predictable economic reasons, but to the patriotism of the lenders."[23]

The government's inability to face fundamental political choices gradually undermined public enthusiasm for bond issues. Contradictory measures fueled inflation. Two examples are the administration of wheat prices and the debate over monetary reform and the capital levy.

Until the summer of 1948, the price of wheat in Italy was controlled. The government collected the crop from farmers at a fixed price and sold it to mills at an artificially low price. Farmers naturally shifted into the production of other crops whose prices were free. In May 1946 the government therefore decided to increase the price it paid for wheat by 300 percent, restoring its real value to 1938 levels, but without raising the price it received from the mills. The banks that financed government wheat purchases rediscounted the bills issued in conjunction with this operation at the Bank of Italy. As a result, public wheat purchases were financed entirely by monetary expansion. The association of government policy and inflation was strengthened.

The possibility of a monetary reform, involving the substitution of a new currency and a tax on liquid wealth, had been debated since the German raid on the Bank of Italy and the feared theft of the plates with which the Italian currency was printed. With the end of the war the problem became less urgent, but arguments for substituting a new currency for the existing one were used to support the case for a capital levy (a special one-time tax on monetary assets). The Left favored reform and the capital levy while the Center-Right opposed them. Conflicting announcements followed on one another's heels: in January 1946 the issue of a new currency was officially postponed *sine die* by the Treasury minister, but the following April it was announced that enough new notes had been printed to make the conversion possible and that it was likely to take place soon. In June it was reported that the newly printed notes had to be destroyed because they had been produced illegally. In September 1946 the debate was reopened. Only in February 1947 was currency reform definitely rejected. The effect of the debate on the public's willingness to hold financial assets, and therefore on the velocity of money and inflation, was dramatic.[24] Risk-averse investors attempted to minimize their holdings of currency and other finance assets, and velocity rose. The capital levy that was supposed to accompany the currency change was approved in March 1947, but its revenue covered less than 4 percent of government spending for the fiscal year 1947–48.[25]

France, too, experienced a sequence of budgetary crises between the armistice and early 1949. Typically, the finance minister demanded some combination of tax increases and expenditure reductions, which was blocked by the Assembly. The government fell, to be replaced by another of slightly different political complexion, and the process was repeated. The most serious crisis occurred in the first half of 1947. After an extended deadlock, in July the Assembly agreed to a package of expenditure reductions and tax increases. But increased wage demands by public sector employees quickly upset the budgetary equilibrium. As soon as this became apparent, the public allowed maturing Treasury bills to run off, forcing the government to solicit credit from the Bank of France. The ceiling on advances from the Bank of France to the state was doubled, creating fears of renewed inflation.

In October 1947, the Ramadier government again attempted to reduce public spending and to increase revenues by reorganizing the tax system. Employment in the Veterans' Ministry and the military courts was cut.[26] But internal disorder, in part reflecting demands for higher wages, forced Ramadier to call up an additional 80,000 men into the armed forces. To forestall a threatened strike by government employees, public sector pay and benefits were increased by 100 billion francs. The budget deficit for 1947 was nearly 300 billion francs, more than 80 percent of 1946 levels. The crisis showed no sign of passing; the Schuman cabinet that took office in November 1947 was greeted by another wave of strikes and sabotage, which it met by increasing all wages by 25 percent in January 1948.

In the first half of 1948, Finance minister René Meyer imposed an

Table 10.7 *Budget deficits, 1945–49*

Italy, billion lire

	1945–46	1946–47	1947–48	1948–49	1949–50
Budget deficit	458	564	897	547	332
% of national income[a]	34	18	14	7	4

France, billion francs

	1945	1946	1947	1948	1949
Budget deficit	308	353	292	570	611
% of national income	40	17	8	9	8

Note:

[a] The deficit–income ratio for Italy is calculated with respect to the income of the calendar year in which the corresponding financial year began.

Sources: Italy: Ercolani (1969, pp. 433, 423, 425); ISTAT (1957), p. 251); France: INSEE (1958, pp. 224, 228); INSEE (1966, p. 556).

exceptional capital levy, which raised 150 billion francs.[27] To punish speculators and black marketeers, all 5,000-franc notes (300 billion francs' worth) were recalled. Some subsidies for nationalized industries were eliminated, and civil servants were laid off. The government received additional funds as Marshall Plan aid finally came on stream. Together these revenues were sufficient to balance the budget for the first half of 1948.[28]

Unfortunately, the budget deficit re-emerged thereafter. The capital levy and the recall of large-denomination banknotes were one-time expedients. Wages were still rising and public enterprises were running large and growing deficits. The budget deficit for the calendar year 1948 came to nearly 600 billion francs.

Tables 10.7 and 10.8 confirm that the fiscal situation in both countries remained in disarray. Table 10.7 shows the budget deficit, as a share of national income, and its financing. Table 10.8 shows debt–income ratios. The Italian budget deficit as a share of GDP declined between the years ending June 1947 and June 1948, from 18 to 14 percent. The decline was due to an increase in revenues, as income tax collection was reorganized; without substantial changes in tax rates, income tax revenues more than

Table 10.8 *Public debt at the end of the financial year*
Italy, 1946–47—1949–50, billion lire

Debt	1946–47	1947–48	1948–49	1949–50
Domestic debt				
Long-term	488.7	479.3	453.6	648.5
Short-term	278.9	482.6	743.7	719.2
Other	188.0	295.0	479.0	628.3
Total	955.6	1257.0	1676.3	1996.0
(% of national income)[a]	(29.8)	(20.0)	(22.5)	(25.3)
Debt to the Bank of Italy[b]	365.9	473.4	470.5	561.6

France, 1945–48, billion francs

Debt	1945	1946	1947	1948
Domestic debt				
Long-term	600.5	641.7	638.9	754.5
Short-term	746.0	754.2	724.5	951.6
Other	475.8	578.1	754.2	744.6
Total	1822.3	1974.0	2117.6	2450.7
(% of national income)	(235)	(96.7)	(58.8)	(41.4)
Advances from the Bank of France	− 14	73	115	43[c]

Notes:
[a] The debt–income ratio for Italy is calculated with respect to the income of the calendar year in which the corresponding financial year began.
[b] Changes in the official accounts with the Bank of Italy were only one of the possible sources of advances to the Treasury.
[c] Taken from Kriz (1951, p. 94).
Sources: Italy: ISTAT (1949–50, p. 432); Ercolani, (1969, p. 423); France: INSEE (1958, pp. 93, 224, 228); INSEE (1966, pp. 376, 556), except as otherwise noted.

doubled.[29] The French deficit as a share of NNP rose between 1947 and 1948 and was concentrated in the second half of the year. This hardly seems like the type of development that would lead to stabilization. As in Italy, there was a decline in the deficit as a share of GDP in 1949.

Debt–income ratios show a more pronounced decline in each country in the year of stabilization. While this could have led to a positive revision of expectations, it may also have reflected the impact of inflation on the stock of debt and the increased difficulty encountered by the two governments in raising funds on financial markets. In the case of Italy, the decline is due entirely to the reduction in the stock of long-term debt. (Short-term debt rose by almost 70 percent.) In the absence of a corresponding decrease in the deficit figures, the numbers show increased reliance on monetization.

In conclusion, there is only very weak evidence of fiscal correction in either country prior to or coincident with stabilization.

Changes in government composition

If inflation came to a halt, this must have been due to a change in expectations about future monetary and fiscal management rather than concurrent changes. In this section and the next, we analyze the two events most likely to have altered expectations in a favorable way.

Though the Italian price level started falling only in October 1947, coincident with the imposition of reserve requirements, the free exchange rate had already begun to strengthen the previous June, wholesale food prices had stabilized, and the change in the aggregate price level had slowed to the point where it was rising less quickly than the quantity of money. These events followed on the heels of dramatic political changes. Specifically, exclusion of the Communists from the government is said to have enhanced public confidence in the ability of officials to implement anti-inflationary policies.

Previous Italian governments had featured protracted disputes over economic policy between the Center-Right and the Left. Treasury ministers had been Liberals or Christian Democrats who favored fiscal discipline and the abolition of subsidies and price controls. In contrast, finance ministers, overseeing taxation and social spending, had been Communists who possessed very different views of the responsibilities and priorities of the state. In February 1947, the two ministries had been merged as the Ministry of the Budget, under the Christian Democrat Corbino, who still lacked the power required to impose restrictive economic measures. The outlook changed in May 1947 when the Communists were expelled from the government. The new Minister of the Budget and Vice Premier was Luigi Einaudi, whose commitment to economic orthodoxy and fiscal rectitude was beyond reproach. The formation of a government whose conservative budget minister was also Vice Premier may have sent an important signal: Italy was prepared to move to a free market system without the hesitation of previous years. The political basis of the new coalition was the middle class, the principal source of private savings. Anti-inflationary policies would have to be implemented to guarantee its support.[30]

This argument has two limitations. First, the change in Italian government composition in 1947 did not reflect a shift in the underlying balance of political power. There was no decline in support for the Communist Party. Its support had risen steadily in the wake of the 1946 election, in which the party had received 19 percent of the vote (compared with 35 percent for the Christian Democrats and 21 percent for the Socialists). In January 1947, the Socialist party split into two factions, rendering the Communists the second largest party in the country and the leading representative of the Left. In April 1947, immediately preceding their expulsion from the government, the Communists won important victories in local elections in Sicily.

It was not clear therefore why the new Center-Right government, comprised of parties that had previously garnered insufficient support to govern alone, could govern now. Since the Communists continued to control the trade unions, they could continue to press for improved living standards for the working class and foment public unrest. According to many commentators this was de Gasperi's fear: that strikes and disorder provoked by a Communist party freed from government responsibilities could lead to the political defeat of the Christian Democrats.[31] The moment was especially delicate because general elections were scheduled to take place in October 1947. (Ultimately, the elections were postponed to April 1948.) Following the credit measure of October 1947, strikes and terrorism did take place, with massive demonstrations in Milan and Rome and bombings and assaults on political headquarters and newspapers. By the end of November, however, when the occupation of the Prefettura (the seat of the central government's representative) in Milan failed to yield concessions from the government, the authorities regained control. It was, as many called it, the "farewell to the revolution." The general strike called for December 10 failed; Repubblicani and members of the Center-Left joined the government, and social peace followed. The last US troops, who had remained in the country a few extra days, finally departed. All through the time of unrest, prices continued their decline.

The second limitation of the argument is that the Communists were expelled from the government simultaneously in France, but the change had no impact on inflation. Like their Italian counterparts, the French Communists had done well in the 1946 elections; with 185 seats, they were the single largest party in the Assembly.[32] The Socialists, occupying the pivotal position between Left and Right, initially chose to form a Center-Left coalition with the Communists and Radicals. The occasion for the change was not any decline in Communist support or influence but rather a bitter dispute over wage policy, brought to a head in April 1947 by a strike in the Renault works. The Communist ministers objected to the government's attempt to stabilize wages and opposed it when a vote of confidence was called. Ramadier immediately replaced them with Socialists and members of the clerical party, the Mouvement Républicain Populaire.

The question, as in Italy, is why the new coalition was able to govern in the absence of an obvious decline in support for the Communist opposition. The Communists were as capable of pressing for increased wages when in opposition as when in office; if anything, it was now easier to coordinate the Party's actions with those of the Communist trade unions. Strike activity intensified rather than diminishing after May 1947;[33] it began to decline only after October 1948, more than a year after the Communists had been expelled from the government. That October saw a great strike wave led by the miners and with the participation of railwaymen, dockers, seamen, and steelworkers. Strikes were organized primarily by the Confédération Générale du Travail (CGT) although the non-Communist unions did not disassociate themselves from them. Police and troops occupied the mines in order to keep them operating, and strikers responded with sabotage. The Queuille government that had taken office the previous month refused to give in, and eventually the strikers began to drift back to work. The Queuille government strengthened its grip over French politics, retaining office for nearly 13 months, the longest of any cabinet in the period.[34] The Communists lost ground in the March 1949 cantonal elections.

Clearly, something other than declining support for the Communists contributed to the permanent change in government complexion in France and Italy in the spring of 1947. That something else was the Marshall Plan.

The Marshall Plan

It is impossible to understand political events in either France or Italy without reference to the Marshall Plan. The Americans made exclusion of the Communists from Western European governments a precondition for Marshall Plan aid. While this was publicly admitted by Marshall only in March 1948 (during a speech at the University of California at Berkeley), the implicit link between American aid and local politics was previously understood. On May 7, 1947 the US Ambassador to Italy, James Dunn, had written Marshall to suggest that US aid "should perhaps be based upon the quid pro quo of necessary changes in political orientation and policy." Only the previous day de Gasperi had told the Ambassador that it was "not wise to form a government without the Communists." Marshall's response indicated an awareness that US aid could buttress a non-Communist government.[35] Rumors of US pressure were widespread. As the *Economist* wrote, "It is universally believed in Italy . . . that American support encouraged the Prime Minister, and that further American economic aid was made conditional upon the construction of a 'purged' Cabinet." The

Table 10.9 *ERP funds from April 1948–March 1952, and 1948 GDP,
million dollars*

Country	Amount	GDP 1948	% GDP 1948
Italy	1,466.8	12,980.4	11.3
France	2,444.8	22,230	11.0

Sources: Italy: CIR (1952, p. 100); Ercolani (1969, p. 422); France: INSEE (1966, p. 528).

Communists may have left the French government for independent reasons, namely the dispute over wage policy, but it is likely that their exclusion from all subsequent governments was not independent of US influence.

Was the Marshall Plan responsible for bringing the two inflations to a halt? Even though shipments of goods started only in April 1948, announcement of the plan the preceding June came at the same time as the break in inflationary expectations in Italy. Although it was not guaranteed in June 1947 that the US Congress would approve the plan, there is little evidence of uncertainty in the Italian newspapers or in Einaudi's description of the program before the Assemblea Costituente on June 18. The anticipated amounts were large: Einaudi mentioned a total transfer to Italy of between $2 billion and $3 billion, equivalent to 20–25 percent of Italian GNP. (Ultimately, the total transfer to Italy amounted to $1.5 billion.)

Table 10.9 shows total Marshall Plan funds disbursed to Italy and France, in absolute amount and as a percentage of the two countries' GDP in 1948.

Could the announcement of the Marshall Plan have brought about stabilization in Italy? One problem with this argument is that American aid to Europe had been generous since the end of the war. From 1945 to the end of 1947, Italy and France had received grants and loans roughly equivalent to the amounts that came later under the European Recovery Program (ERP). But US aid had tailed off in 1947. Moreover, the Marshall Plan was a systematic program scheduled to last several years. It could therefore contribute not only to the two countries' immediate needs but also to their requirements for long-term growth. It minimized uncertainty over future aid and freed European governments from the need to bargain constantly for new sources of assistance.

Marshall Plan funds might be expected to have relieved inflationary pressure through three channels. First, foreign grants could have narrowed the government budget deficit, allowing the authorities to reduce their dependence on advances from the central bank. Second, they could have relaxed the external constraint, eliminating incipient excess demand for imported wage and capital goods that otherwise would have forced a further devaluation of the lira and the franc and, by raising import prices, have fueled domestic inflation. Third, Marshall Plan aid could have eliminated the gap between domestic investment and domestic savings.[36]

ERP aid took the form of grants of goods and services, conditional on the presentation of programs and budgets by the countries involved. Recipient governments then sold the imported goods to domestic business in exchange for domestic currency. The revenues so generated ("counterpart funds") had to correspond to the going US price for the goods transferred and were kept in special accounts. Their utilization was to be agreed upon by the United States and the local government.[37]

Marshall Plan funds covered a large share of government budget deficits in France and Italy. Table 10.10 shows that foreign funds (principally Marshall Plan aid) financed almost a quarter of the French budget deficit in 1948 and nearly half in 1949. In Italy, where the funds were utilized with a lag, they played a negligible role in financing the deficit for the 1948/49 financial year, but they financed almost a quarter of the deficit of the following 12 months. In the first years of the program the volume of funds approved, which was much larger than the volume effectively utilized, is a better gauge of the impact of the Plan on expectations: in Italy funds approved for the period from April 1948 to June 1949 were equivalent to 70 percent of the deficit for the financial year 1948/49, and those approved for the following 12 months financed more than three-quarters of the corresponding deficit.

ERP funds played an even more important role in financing current account deficits. Marshall Plan aid in relation to the components of the French and Italian balances of payments is shown in Table 10.11. The franc zone's 1948 current account deficit was $1.74 billion. American aid was $0.75 billion, leaving just under $1 billion to be financed by reserve losses and capital inflows. In 1949 the French current account deficit fell to $0.7 billion, and Marshall Plan aid financed it fully. In Italy, the current account deficit was $0.24 billion in 1948, and $0.2 billion in 1949. In both years aid received was approximately 30 percent larger than the deficit, leading to current account surpluses.

Table 10.11 makes clear that the main difference in the external positions of the two countries lay in the trade balance. In 1948, for example, the French trade deficit was four to five times as large as the Italian, even though French GNP was only twice Italian GNP. Clearly, domestic absorption behaved quite differently in the two countries. Since only part of

Table 10.10 *Italy and France, ERP funds and government deficits, million dollars*

Italy

Period	Assigned ERP funds	Utilized ERP funds	Government deficit[a]
Apr. 1948–Jun. 1948	159.0		
Jul. 1948–Jun. 1949	510.0	23.9	951.3
Jul. 1949–Jun. 1950	402.8	131.7	553.3
Jul. 1950–Jun. 1951	236.0	255.4	918.4

France

Period	Assigned ERP funds	Utilized ERP funds	Government deficit
1948[b]	951.0	456.0	2,142
1949	746.4	840.5	1,751
1950	436.1	508.2	1,629
1951	267.5	244.0	1,440

Notes:
[a] The Italian government deficit is translated into dollars using the exchange rate officially used in the calculation of the counterpart funds.
[b] Calendar years.
Sources: Italy: CIR (1962, p. 100); ISTAT (1949–50, p. 431); Ercolani (1969, p. 433); France: ERP data from Quarterly Reports of the Economic Cooperation Administration (various issues); deficit data from INSEE (1966, p. 228).

the discrepancy can be imputed to the government accounts, the behavior of private saving and investment was crucial.

The question of how ERP funds affected the French savings–investment balance directs attention to the Monnet Plan. The Monnet Plan guided the French reconstruction effort from the beginning of 1947. Highest priority was attached to reconstruction and modernization of the country's capital stock. Initially the plan was intended to speed the reconstruction and modernization of six key industries: coal, electric power, steel, cement, agricultural machinery, and transport. It was expanded subsequently to include a variety of other sectors.[38]

Table 10.12 shows that finance for the Monnet Plan was provided initially by government borrowing and bank credit. The contribution of bank credit declined sharply in 1948. In part, the capacity of French industry to finance investment out of retained earnings increased in 1948

Table 10.11 *Balance of payments on current account, 1947–50, million dollars*

Italy

Item	1947	1948	1949	1950
Commodity imports	1,326.9	1,388.0	1,420.6	1,358.4
Commodity exports	665.6	1,067.6	1,114.4	1,200.7
Balance	− 661.3	− 320.4	− 306.2	− 157.7
Services	− 77.7	83.7	111.8	110.4
Current account excluding aid	− 739.0	− 236.7	− 194.4	− 47.3
Government aid[a]	254.2	312.4	306.4	238.8
Current account	− 484.8	76	112	191.5

Franc zone

Item	1947	1948	1949	1950
Commodity imports	2,491.7	2,510.3	2,034.7	1,958.2
Commodity exports	1,040.0	1,081.9	1,567.1	1,879.9
Balance	− 1,451.7	− 1,428.4	− 467.6	− 78.3
Services	− 224.0	− 309.2	− 239.0	− 161.7
Current account excluding aid	− 1,675.7	− 1,737.6	− 706.6	− 230.0
American aid	0	754.0	855.4	508.7
Current account	− 1,675.7	− 983.6	148.8	278.7

Note:
[a] Government aid corresponds to amounts actually received during the year.
Sources: Italy: CIR (1952, p. 94); France: INSEE (1966, p. 366).

and again in 1949. But the single biggest difference between the three successive years lies in Marshall Plan funds. By 1949 they accounted for nearly half of Monnet Plan spending.

In Italy, on the other hand, no long-term national investment program was formulated until the creation in 1950 of the "Cassa del Mezzogiorno," the government agency supervising and coordinating investment plans in the South. The lack of a comprehensive public program and the timidity of private investment were considered the main obstacles to development by Marshall Plan administrators.[39] Especially during the first two years of the

Table 10.12 *Sources of finance of the Monnet Plan, 1947–49, billion francs*

Source	1947	1948	1949
Tax revenues and domestic government borrowing	8	84	119
ECA counterpart funds	—	104	225
Self-financing	30	80	104
Capital issues	34	27	41
Bank credit	88	33	45
Total	138	328	534

Source: Kriz (1951, p. 102).

Marshall Plan, Italian economic policy was explicitly directed at rebuilding foreign reserves, which had been severely depleted in 1947. This involved a conscious effort to curb aggregate demand and increase private savings. The policy was controversial since, in the short term at least, it gave priority to financial stability over growth. Nonetheless, the Italian authorities persisted in their program, as reflected in the narrowing trade deficit.[40]

Thus, by 1949 the Marshall Plan fully financed the current account deficit in France and Italy and substantially reduced both countries' budget deficits. It is tempting to conclude that the announcement of the Marshall Plan, in June 1947, was the central event that reversed inflationary expectations in Italy and led to price stability. But why then did the same announcement not trigger stabilization in France? Why were the two stabilizations separated by 18 months?

Delay in stabilization as a distributional war of attrition

The Marshall Plan reduced the need for fiscal retrenchment, but did not eliminate it. For price stability to be sustained, the public had to be convinced that the government had adopted a policy of fiscal discipline leading to persistent declines in future money growth rates. Fiscal discipline was painful: the two countries were rebuilding their economies after the destruction wrought by the war while simultaneously striving to provide acceptable standards of living to the population. The pressure of demand clashed with a tight supply constraint, and incompatible claims could be reconciled only by fiscal deficits, monetization, and price increases. Stabilization required that some of these claims be abandoned.

It is natural to think of the inflationary process as reflecting a distributional struggle between political factions enjoying roughly equal popular support and locked in uncompromising positions. In both Italy and France the principal rivals in the distributional conflict were recipients of labor income on the one hand and recipients of profits, interest, and rents on the other. Strikes for higher wages and lobbying for retail price controls and cheap public services (public transport, for example) were labor's way of fighting for a larger distributional share. Producers, to protect their share, attempted to pass along higher wages in the form of higher prices. Insofar as they failed, profits were squeezed, and firms demanded subsidies and cheap credit from the government. The budget moved into deficit due to higher public sector pay, cheap provision of public services and subsidies to enterprise, combined with the resistance of different groups to higher taxes. The deficit was financed by central bank credit, and inflation was the result. This is an obvious interpretation of the repeated fiscal crises in France. Equally, it explains the most important episodes of accelerating inflation in Italy, as when for example the government increased the price paid to wheat farmers but, when that increase could not be carried forward to the consumers, financed it with credit from the Bank of Italy.

As these examples make clear, fiscal imbalance and inflation represented an unsatisfactory solution to the conflict. They inflicted costs on the economy. Nevertheless, stabilization was delayed until one side – in both countries the Left – agreed to shoulder the burden of deflation.

If we accept this interpretation, we are left with three questions. First, could the delay in stabilization be the result of rational choice by political actors? Second, what role was played by the Marshall Plan? Finally, how can we explain the difference in the timing of stabilization in Italy and France?

An answer to the first question is provided by Alesina and Drazen (1991), who model the delay in stabilization as the outcome of a war of attrition between rational players. The idea is as follows. Suppose that the burden of stabilization, in the form of policies reducing some group's distributional share, is unevenly distributed. The group conceding first incurs the larger share of the costs. If rival factions differ in their ability to shoulder the costs of inflation yet are uncertain about the cost-bearing capacity of the others, each will refuse to concede, hoping to outlast the others. Over time, the costs of inflation rise and with them the perceived probability that the other factions are in fact more patient. Ultimately, the distributional interest least able to bear the costs concedes, and stabilization occurs. Delay is rational: even if inflation is finally halted through the adoption of policies identical to those deemed unacceptable initially, different groups still have an incentive to hold out as long as the costs of stabilization are borne unevenly and there is uncertainty about the staying power of their rivals. Until the moment

Table 10.13 *Unemployment rate,ᵃ 1946–50*

Year	Italy	France
1946	n.a.	0.6
1947	8.5	0.5
1948	9.4	0.9
1949	8.7	1.2
1950	8.4	1.2

Notes:
[a] The unemployment rate is calculated as the
ratio of unemployed to total labor force. For
Italy, the labor force was obtained by
multiplying the participation rate in 1951,
the only year when the number is available,
by the population.
n.a. not available.
Sources: Italy: International Labor Office
(1949–50, p. 85), ISTAT (1951, p. 23, 1952, p.
29); France: Carré *et al.* (1975, p. 58); INSEE
(1966, p. 117). When missing, the data were
interpolated linearly.

they concede, the probability that others will concede first and bear the
costs of stabilization is sufficient to justify the ongoing loss from inflation.

In both countries, stabilization was associated with a consolidation of
power in the hands of the Center-Right, and it was the Left at bore the costs.
In Italy, stabilization coincided with the change in government in June 1947
and was confirmed by the outcome of the general elections in April 1948.
The Christian Democrats received 48.5 percent of the vote (versus 35.2
percent in the 1946 elections), while the share of the Communists and
Socialists together fell from 39.7 percent to 31 percent. In France, the end of
social conflict in 1949 is clearly captured by the decline in the number of
working days lost in labor disputes, which fell from 13 million in 1948 to 7
million in 1949.[41]

The unequal distribution of stabilization costs should be reflected in
income shares. These are difficult to construct and evaluate because of data
problems and concurrent changes in the structure of the economy. Tables
10.13 and 10.14 report estimates of unemployment rates and industrial
salaries for France and Italy. In France, real wages fell continuously from
1946 to 1950. Unemployment was low but rising. There can be little doubt
that the decline in labor disputes signaled the acceptance by labor of a

Table 10.14 *Real industrial salary index,*[a]
1950 = 100, 1946–50

Year	Italy	France
1946	48.8	109.8
1947	74.8	100.4
1948	94.8	97.1
1949	99.2	96.7
1950	100	100

Note:
[a] For Italy, the industrial salary index is
deflated by the private consumption
deflator. For France, it is deflated by the
retail price index.
Sources: Italy: Ercolani (1969), pp. 425,
455); France: INSEE (1966, pp. 428, 328).

smaller distributional share. In Italy, real wages rose, albeit at a declining
rate, over the entire period. The large increase in 1947 reflects the backward
indexation of nominal wages, coupled with the decline in prices during the
final quarter of the year. Although wages continued to rise in the following
years, Italian unemployment also rose from 1947 to 1948. This was a
dramatic development, given that unemployment was already high and was
generally regarded as the major threat to social peace. Overall, then, the
Italian evidence on distribution is more ambiguous than the French.
Nonetheless, the Italian literature is unanimous in describing a shift towards cautious, conservative policies, and the loss of political influence of
the Left is clearly reflected in the election results.[42]

The coincidence of the Italian stabilization with the announcement of the
Marshall Plan complements the rest of the story. The Marshall Plan was
not sufficient to eliminate the budget deficit, but it increased the size of the
distributional "pie" to be shared out among rival factions, reducing the
magnitude of the sacrifices required to eliminate aggregate excess demand
and bring the inflation to a halt. By lowering the costs of conceding relative
to the benefits, the Marshall Plan increased the likelihood of early
stabilization.

There is no doubt that expectations of substantial American aid contributed to the Italian Communists' peaceful exit from the government. When
de Gasperi met the Communist leader Togliatti to explain and justify the
change in government, he is reported to have said: "You have to under-

stand . . . it is a matter of bread."[43] On June 7, 1947 the Communist newspaper *L'Unità* appeared with the headline "Italy Needs the Solid Help of the Generous American Nation."

Announcement of the Marshall Plan was not sufficient to end the distributional conflict in France. Since the funds granted to the two countries were comparable, relative to income, the difference must lie in factors that made the costs of conceding and agreeing to shoulder a disproportionate share of the stabilization higher in France than in Italy. There exist three possible explanations for the contrast.

First, in France stabilization may have entailed a more asymmetric division of costs. With more at stake, the different groups would have been willing to hold out longer. This hypothesis can be tested with evidence on the shift in distributional shares following stabilization. In both countries, the Left ultimately conceded; if the cost of doing so was higher in France than in Italy, the income share of labor should have declined more dramatically in France. As mentioned above, this implication is difficult to verify. Tables 10.13 and 10.14 support it, but more data are required before a firm conclusion can be drawn.

A second possible explanation is that the Left was stronger in France than in Italy. Even though it still turned out to be the weaker faction, so long as there remained uncertainty over the staying power of the Right, postponing stabilization would have been rational. The stronger the Left, the greater the perceived likelihood that it would ultimately outlast the Right, and the longer the delay it would have been willing to tolerate. The French Left commanded a larger share of the vote than the Italian, and its influence on labor was not weakened by a high unemployment rate. On the other hand, the absence of wage indexation in France made inflation more costly for wage earners. Overall, the evidence on this hypothesis, while suggestive, is not definitive.

Finally, stabilization may have been delayed longer in France than in Italy because its absolute cost was higher. There may have been a larger disparity between desired income shares and feasible income shares or, equivalently, between notional demand and supply.

Unlike Italy, France was committed to an ambitious program of domestic investment, and all reductions in desired income required to achieve *ex ante* balance between demand and supply had to be taken from consumption. Insofar as social groups were fighting over immediate consumption shares, since neither group was willing to imperil the investment program, the distributional stakes would have been higher in France than in Italy. Table 10.15 shows gross investment net of inventories as a percent of GDP in the two countries. In Italy the investment share remained below prewar levels. Indeed it fell in the years following the stabilization, suggest-

Table 10.15 *Gross investment net of inventories as share of GDP^a, 1938 and 1945–50*

Year	Italy	France
1938	16	13.4
1945	6.1	n.a.
1946	12.1	15.3
1947	14.2	17.1
1948	14.2	20.2
1949	13.1	18.8
1950	12.9	n.a.

Notes:
[a] The investment share is calculated at current prices.
n.a. not available
Sources: Italy: ISTAT (1957, p. 265); Ercolani (1969, p. 422); France: Carré *et al.* (1975, p. 106).

ing that part of the decline in expenditure required for stabilization took the form of a decline in investment. In France, in contrast, the investment share was above prewar levels and rose strongly from 1946 through 1948.

The French investment program has been identified previously as playing a major role in the inflation. As Rosa described the French dilemma,

There was not enough capacity available, even with the foreign assistance provided ... to reconstruct and to raise living standards at the same time. Hesitating to accept this inevitability, the French permitted continued increase in their money supply – new money purchased the materials and labor needed for reconstruction and to a considerable extent new money met production costs in undamaged sectors of the economy as well ... That is, instead of rationing their limited resources through direct controls, or of rationing in effect through heavy taxation which would divert purchasing power directly into payment for reconstruction, the French chose to do their rationing by means of rising prices.[44]

The different behavior of investment in the two countries reflected different international aspirations and threats. The Monnet Plan stemmed from the French desire "to reconstruct and modernize French heavy industry in order to increase its strength relative to that of Germany."[45] Heavy investment was required to insure that French exports would displace the products of German heavy industry at home and on international markets. The sectors favored by the Monnet Plan, notably coal, steel, and transport, were those viewed as critical for France's national security and international political aspirations.

American influence reinforced France's commitment to the investment program. The US State Department made clear that America opposed amputation of the Ruhr and Rhine and told Charles de Gaulle that "the best guarantee of French security lay in devoting all of France's energies to the reconstruction of the French economy."[46]

In Italy, on the other hand, political and economic realities rendered international ambitions out of the question. Successive Italian governments' first and only economic goal was to promote internal reconstruction. Living standards were too low to support an aggressive investment policy without creating financial instability. Policy makers believed that long-term development would result from monetary discipline and investor confidence, and that immediate growth should be sacrificed for the sake of monetary stability. Unlike in France, in Italy investment did not absorb a high and rising share of national income, and its share could be compressed to moderate the sacrifices required of other claimants.

Conclusion

Inflation in Italy and France after the Second World War must be understood, we have argued in this chapter, as the outcome of a distributional conflict. The Marshall Plan, while not sufficient to eliminate the imbalance between desired and feasible distributional shares, reduced the magnitude of the concessions required of domestic interest groups to bring inflation to a halt. It thereby increased the likelihood of an early stabilization, and indeed triggered it in Italy.

The transition to price stability occurred later in France because the conflict was more intense. This may have been reflected a stronger and more aggressive Left or higher distributional stakes. The last possibility arises from France's ambitious program of investment in heavy industry, which set aside a larger share of domestic income for uses that would translate into increased production and higher living standards only with a lag.

To some, our analysis would appear to have more in common with the historical literature in which inflation is viewed as a political phenomenon than with the literature in economics in which it is viewed as the outcome of economic processes. Our central message is that there is no incompatibility between the two views.[47]

Notes

Earlier versions of this chapter were presented to the International Economic History Association Conference in Leuven, Belgium, and to seminars at the

University of California at Berkeley. Along with seminar participants and the editors of this volume, we thank Allan Drazen for helpful comments.

1 Inflation accelerated in the second half of 1950, reflecting the rise in world commodity prices consequent on the Korean crisis.

2 Authors subscribing to this view include Baffi (1967); Castellino (1964); Foà (1949); Hildebrandt (1965); Hirschman (1948); Lenti (1966); and Lutz and Lutz (1950).

3 The ratio of reserves to deposits was not to exceed 25 percent overall.

4 While the primary objective of the regulation was to control the "multiplicative" role of the banks, at the same time the new reserve requirements were designed to avoid too severe a contraction of credit. Consulted at the end of August, the banks had agreed that the provision could be fulfilled with the funds currently at their disposal. Aggregating over all banks, it required them to immobilize Lit 112.2 billion. Free reserves at the end of September amounted to Lit 115.4 billion. Bank of Italy (1948, p. 160).

5 *Corriere della Sera* (February 27, 1947).

6 Einaudi, speech to the Assemblea Costituente (October 4, 1947) in Atti Parlamentari (1947, p. 861). The coincidence of timing is also noted skeptically by Dornbusch and Fischer (1986).

7 Nominal interest rates rose slightly between September and December 1947, falling thereafter to their previous levels. The yield on short-term Treasury bonds was 7 percent in August, 8 percent in October, and 6 percent in January 1948 (Bank of Italy, 1948, p. 275).

8 Bank of Italy (1948, pp. 126, 127), adjusted to constant prices.

9 Disregarding the expense for the wheat subsidy (Lutz and Lutz, 1950, p. 6).

10 Baffi (1967, pp. 948–949).

11 ISTAT (1946, 1947, 1948).

12 See Bank of Italy (1949).

13 Our analysis of credit controls in France draws primarily on Hirschman and Rosa (1949) and Kriz (1951).

14 The Bank of France and the four leading banks had been nationalized by legislation passed in December 1945. The National Credit Council (NCC), dominated by the Bank of France but including also representatives of the big banks, of government, of business, and of consumer groups, was created to coordinate the lending policies of the banks with the monetary policies of the government.

15 Supporting data had to include information on the financial situation of the applicant for credit and an explanation of why the borrower could not obtain the necessary funds by liquidating surplus assets or by discounting commercial bills.

16 Only long-term loans, non-marketable securities, overdrafts and certain advances did not qualify. See Kriz (1951, p. 87).

17 The ratio of commercial bills to all bank loans increased from 45 percent at the end of 1945 to 60 percent at the end of 1948. Hirschman and Rosa (1949, p. 350).

18 Rediscount ceilings had already been applied to the smaller banks. The legislation of September 1948 made them universal.

19 Kriz (1951, p. 96).
20 Ratios are constructed from tables in Kriz (1951).
21 An influential statement of this theory of hyperinflation, as applied to post First World War experience, is Sargent (1986).
22 Bank of Italy (1948, p. 275).
23 *Corriere della Sera* (January 19, 1947). In the same article, Einaudi also mentioned priests' sermons, during Sunday Masses, urging subscription of the loan.
24 The Reconstruction Loan issued in November 1946 was exempt from the still-to-be decided wealth tax.
25 ISTAT (1949–50, p. 425).
26 Snider (1948, p. 323).
27 Lubell (1955, p. 49); Pickles (1953, p. 87).
28 Lubell (1955, p. 49).
29 ISTAT (1949–50, p. 430).
30 For overviews of the political developments of the period in Italy, see Gambino (1975) and Grindrod (1955).
31 See Montanelli and Cervi (1985).
32 In addition, the Socialists had 104 seats, the moderate Mouvement Républicain Populaire 164 seats, the Radicals 43, and the conservative parties a total of 119. See Pickles (1953, p. 71).
33 Pickles (1953, pp. 80–85) provides an account of strike activity and labor negotiations. She concludes on p. 80, "wage negotiations and price increases followed each other with monotonous regularity, at intervals of only a few months."
34 See Jeanneney (1956, chapter 2).
35 United States Department of State (1948, pp. 890–916); the *Economist* (June 7, 1947, p. 881).
36 The effects of a transfer in the presence of gaps between government revenues and spending, between domestic savings and investment, and between imports and exports are analyzed in Bacha (1989).
37 For a detailed description of the program, see Eichengreen and Uzan (1992).
38 Two accounts of the Monnet Plan are Uri (1950) and Lynch (1984).
39 Economic Cooperation Administration (1949, p. 35).
40 For a critical view of the Italian use of Marshall Plan funds, see De Cecco (1968).
41 International Labor Office (1949–50). No equivalent numbers are available for Italy.
42 Scholars all seem to agree on this point, independent of their political persuasion. See for example, Baffi (1967) and De Cecco (1968).
43 Montanelli and Cervi (1985, p. 150).
44 Rosa (1949, pp. 154–170). See also Lynch (1984, pp. 240–241) for a similar statement of this view.
45 Lynch (1984, p. 229).
46 Lynch (1984, p. 229).
47 An influential statement of the historian's view is Maier (1976), while the consensus view among economists is well stated by Sargent (1987). Another

author who takes an eclectic view consonant with our own – and who like us stresses a foreign loan, although to a very different end – is Siklos (chapter 9 in this volume).

References

Alesina, Alberto and Allan Drazen, 1991. "Why are stabilizations delayed?," *American Economic Review*, 81: 1170–1188.

Atti Parlamentari, 1947. *Assemblea Costituente, Assemblea Plenaria, Discussioni*, Rome.

Bacha, Edmar, 1989. "A three-gap model of foreign transfers and the GDP growth rate in developing countries," *Journal of Development Economics*, 32: 279–296.

Baffi, Paolo, 1967. "L'evoluzione monetaria in Italia dall'economia di guerra alla convertibilità (1935–58)," *Letture di politica monetaria e finanziaria*, Tomo 3, Milan: Giuffré.

Bank of Italy, various years. *Annual Report*, Rome: Bank of Italy.

Carré, J.-J., P. Dubois and E. Malinvaud, 1975. *French Economic Growth*, Stanford: Stanford University Press.

Castellino, Onorato, 1964. *Gli intermediari finanziari e la politica della moneta e del credito*, Tourin: Giappichelli.

De Cecco, Marcello, 1968. "Sulla politica di stabilizzazione del 1947," in *Saggi di politica monetaria*, Milan: Giuffré.

Dornbusch, R. and S. Fischer, 1986. "Stopping hyperinflations past and present," *Weltwirtschaftliches Archiv*, 122: 1–47.

Economic Cooperation Administration, 1949. *Italy Country Study*, Washington, DC: US Department of State.

Eichengreen, B. and M. Uzan, 1992. "The Marshall Plan: economic effects and implications for Eastern Europe and the former USSR," *Economic Policy*, 14: 117–176.

Ercolani, Paolo, 1969. "Documentazione statistica di base," in G. Fuà (ed.), *Lo sviluppo economico in Italia*, vol. III, Milan: Franco Angeli.

Foà, Bruno, 1949. *Monetary Reconstruction in Italy*, New York: King's Crown Press.

Gambino, Antonio, 1975. *Storia del dopoguerra dalla liberazione al potere DC*, Rome: Laterza.

Gavanier, M., 1953. "Le revenue national de la France: production et disponibilités nationales en 1938 et de 1946 a 1949," *Statistique et études financiers*, supplement finances françaises, no. 20.

Grindrod, Muriel, 1955. *The Rebuilding of Italy*, London: Royal Institute of International Affairs.

Hildebrandt, George, 1965. *Growth and Structure in the Economy of Modern Italy*, Cambridge, MA: Harvard University Press.

Hirschman, Albert O., 1948. "Inflation and deflation in Italy," *American Economic Review*, 38: 598–606.

Hirschman, Albert O. and Robert V. Rosa, 1949. "Postwar credit controls in France," *Federal Reserve Bulletin*, 35: 348–360.

INSEE, 1966, *Annuaire statistique de la France: Résumé rétrospectif*, Paris: INSEE.

International Labor Office, 1949–50. *Yearbook of Labor Statistics*, Geneva: ILO.

ISTAT, 1946, 1947, 1948, 1951, 1952. *Bolletino Mensile di Statistica*, various issues, Rome: Poligrafico dello stato.

　1949–50. *Annuario statistico italiano*, serie V, vol. II, Rome: Poligrafico dello stato.

　1957. "Indagine statistica sullo sviluppo del reddito nazionale dell'Italia dal 1861 al 1956," *Annali di statistica*, serie VII, vol. IX, Rome: Poligrafico dello stato.

Jeanneney, Jean-Marcel, 1956. *Forces et faiblesses de l'économie française 1945–56*, Paris: Armand Colin.

Kriz, M.A., 1951. "Credit controls in France," *American Economic Review*, 41: 85–106.

Lenti, Libero, 1966. *Inventorio dell'economia italiana*, Milan: Garzanti.

Lubell, Harold, 1955. "The role of investment in two French inflations," *Oxford Economic Papers*, 7–8: 47–56.

Lutz, Friedrich and Vera Lutz, 1950. "Monetary and Exchange Policy in Italy," *Princeton Studies in International Finance*, 1, Princeton: Princeton University Press.

Lynch, Frances M.B., 1984. "Resolving the paradox of the Monnet Plan: national and international planning in French reconstruction," *Economic History Review*, 37: 229–243.

Maddison, Angus, 1982. *Phases of Capitalist Development*, New York: Oxford University Press.

Maier, Charles, 1976. *Recasting Bourgeois Europe*, Princeton: Princeton University Press.

Montanelli, Indro and Mario Cervi, 1985. *L'Italia della repubblica*, Milan: Rizzoli.

Pickles, Dorothy, 1953. *French Politics: The First Years of the Fourth Republic*, Oxford: Oxford University Press.

Rosa, Robert V., 1949. "The problem of French recovery," *Economic Journal*, 59: 154–170.

Sargent, Thomas, 1982. "The end of four big inflations," in R. Hall (ed.), *Inflation*, Chicago: University of Chicago Press: 41–98.

Snider, Delbert A., 1948. "French monetary and fiscal policies since the liberation," *American Economic Review*, 38: 307–327.

United States Department of State, 1948. *Foreign Relations of the United States, 1947*, Washington, DC: Government Printing Office.

Uri, Pierre, 1950. "France: reconstruction and development," in Howard Ellis (ed.), *The Economics of Freedom*, New York: Harper.

11 The rise and fall of credit controls: the case of Sweden, 1939–89

LARS JONUNG

Introduction

Why do economic policies change? Why do policy makers replace one policy regime with another? An answer to this question is provided here by using Swedish central bank policy over the past 50 years as a case study.[1] Swedish authorities moved in the 1940s and 1950s from a traditional monetary policy based on open market operations, discount changes and unregulated international flows of money and capital to a policy based on foreign exchange and capital controls, central allocation of credit flows of all financial institutions and regulation of interest rates. Then in the 1980s these controls were gradually dismantled and Sweden returned to a monetary policy regime similar in several ways to that which had prevailed before the outbreak of the Second World War.

In short, Swedish monetary policy from 1939 to 1989 can be summarized as a process of financial regulation which prevented financial markets from functioning "freely," replacing them with centrally-given orders, followed eventually by a process of financial deregulation re-establishing previously fossilized markets or establishing markets for new financial instruments; hence the title for this chapter: the rise and fall of credit controls. This change in policy regime encompasses not only the choice of monetary instruments in a narrow sense, it involves two different sets of rules of behavior for all decision making units in the Swedish economy: the central bank (the Riksbank), the government, the commercial banks, and other financial institutions, as well as private firms and households.

This chapter examines first the transition from a monetary regime based on market incentives to a monetary regime based on bureaucratic controls, and then back again to a regime based on market incentives.[2] The chapter is organized in the following way. First, the characteristics of the two monetary regimes are briefly presented. Then, the rise of credit controls is discussed. Next, the demise of these controls in the 1980s is considered. A broad approach to the framing of monetary policy is adopted and the actions of the central bank are discussed from a wider political and ideological perspective than is commonly the case. The movement towards regulation is given more attention than the process of deregulation; since the deregulation is so close in time, it is difficult to give a balanced account of its causes.

Market versus non-market oriented monetary regimes

The major difference between the two types of monetary regimes considered here is the choice of system of coordination adopted; one is based on market oriented techniques of monetary control, the other on non-market oriented instruments. The first regime, that is the regime in existence prior to 1939 and in the late 1980s, is market oriented, being based on the existence of efficiently functioning financial markets where prices (that is, interest rates) and quantities (that is, credit and capital flows) are allowed to move more or less "freely" with no attempt by the monetary authorities to prevent the workings of these markets. Instead, the Riksbank relies on such markets to carry out its policy. It thus has an interest in the maintenance of well-functioning financial markets. Here, monetary policy works more or less anonymously through price signals, basically through open market operations. This is an equilibrium regime in the sense that financial markets are allowed to clear. There is no need for the central bank to meet regularly and directly with representatives from various financial intermediaries to convey its intentions; they are communicated through the market. Such a monetary system is open towards the rest of the world. Exchange controls or capital controls are not required to isolate the domestic financial markets. In short, this type of regime is associated with the traditional institutional framework for the conduct of monetary policy. Many would associate it with the liberal economic order.

The second and alternative type of monetary regime, roughly prevailing from the outbreak of the Second World War until the mid-1980s in Sweden, was based on a non market approach. The major prerequisite for this regime was the existence of exchange and capital controls that isolated Sweden from the outside world financially, allowing the monetary authorities to establish a structure of interest rates and a distribution of credit according to political preferences, not according to market outcomes. (These controls were gradually modified but remained in force for capital transactions until 1989.) The financing of the public sector and the housing sector was subsidized at below market rates. New instruments were introduced to accomplish this aim such as liquidity ratios, lending ceilings and controls on the emission of new bonds. Interest rates were set by administrative decisions. The financial system, in particular the commercial banking system, was closely monitored by the Riksbank. Few financial innovations were forthcoming during the credit control regime of the 1950s, 1960s, and 1970s compared to the deregulation of the 1980s.

As a consequence of this choice of non-market coordination, the Riksbank met regularly with representatives from various financial institutions to convey its opinions as they no longer could be communicated through markets: "open mouth operations" replaced open market operations. "Voluntary" agreements between the Riksbank and financial institutions were a common element of this policy. Basically, this was a disequilibrium system where financial markets were prevented from functioning "freely," characterized by queues of borrowers in both the short and the long end of the market. In this regime the actions of the authorities were framed in terms of credit aggregates while the rate of interest was kept at a "low" and "stable" level. The policy of the Riksbank was aimed not only at stabilizing the business cycle, but allocative and distributional goals were also fostered by the central bank. The Riksbank behaved as a price controller; a regulatory agency in charge of a program of controls of interest rates and domestic and foreign flows of credit and capital.[3]

To sum up, the main difference between the two types of monetary regimes considered here is that in the first type, the credit control regime, the Riksbank used direct monetary controls, primarily quantity restrictions, commonly applied on a selective basis, while in the second type, it used indirect procedures of monetary control relying on price incentives. This is a major distinction between a non-market oriented and a market oriented policy regime.

The two policy regimes, the traditional one and the credit control regime, have fundamentally different implications for the degree of independence of the central bank. In the first type of "liberal" regime, the central bank can be assigned the traditional task of maintaining a fixed exchange rate and/or a stable price level and remain relatively independent from the government. Such a market-determined allocation of credit and interest rates was not accepted by the Swedish authorities during most of the post-Second World War period. Instead, monetary policy became an integral part of overall allocative and distributional policies. As a consequence, the Riksbank was forced into a subservient role, being administratively responsible for the financing of the building sector as set out in various policy documents (see below). As a consequence of the financial deregulation of the 1980s, a new interest in establishing a more independent Riksbank developed. Steps were also taken in the late 1980s to reduce political pressure on the Riksbank.

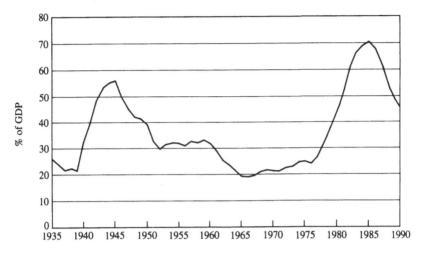

11.1   Swedish government debt as ratio of GDP, 1935–90, %

The rise of credit controls

The behavior of the Riksbank

Prior to the Second World War the Riksbank followed a traditional type of monetary policy. Even during the depression of the 1930s, the Swedish financial system remained fairly unregulated compared to the American system. The outbreak of war marked the end of that regime. Exchange and capital controls were introduced in 1940, effectively isolating the Swedish money and capital markets from outside influence. These exchange controls were initially regarded as emergency measures but they remained in force, although modified, until 1989.

During the Second World War, Swedish government debt increased rapidly (see figure 11.1). Commercial banks became major purchasers of bonds during these years. This is seen from figure 11.2 which displays the ratio of bonds to deposits of the commercial banking system from 1930 to 1990. During the war, the Riksbank stabilized the rate of interest at a low level (figure 11.3).

Immediately after the war, commercial banks made large sales of bonds in order to increase their lending to other sectors, in particular to industry. As the Riksbank aimed at maintaining a "low" and stable discount rate of around 2.5 percent and a long-term bond rate of 3 percent, the Bank was forced to make large purchases of bonds. It also started to exert moral pressure on commercial banks and other institutions holding bonds in

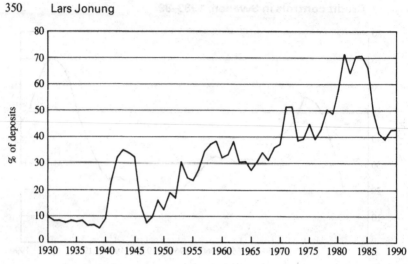

11.2   Ratio of bonds to deposits of commercial banks, 1930–90,%

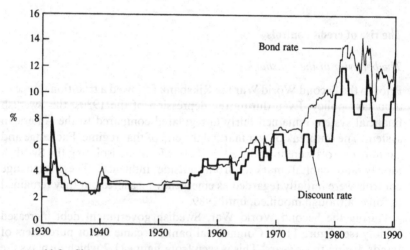

11.3   Short- and long-term interest rates, 1930–90,%

order to keep interest rates unchanged. The governor of Riksbank, Ivar Rooth, objected to this policy, viewing it as ultimately inflationary. He tried in vain to convince the majority of the Board of the Bank to allow an increase in the rate of interest. Eventually, he chose to resign in 1948 in protest, a unique step in the history of the Riksbank.

It turned out to be increasingly difficult for the Riksbank to maintain low interest rates using traditional monetary instruments. Eventually, the Bank made an internal investigation searching for methods of controlling interest rates. The outcome was a report recommending a series of measures inspired by the system of price controls of goods and services applied during the Second World War. The Bank turned to parliament and asked for new legislation in this spirit. Consequently, parliament in the fall of 1951 passed a stand-by law introducing new instruments encompassing direct controls of lending and deposit rates. Using this stand-by law as bargaining pressure, the Riksbank reached a "voluntary" agreement with the commercial banks in the early months of 1952. According to this agreement the Riksbank determined both deposit and lending rates. The commercial banks agreed to maintain the liquidity ratios recommended by the Riksbank. These ratios constituted a method for allocating funds to the government and the building sector as government and housing bonds were included together with cash items in the "liquid" assets that formed the numerator of the liquid asset ratio. The volume of commercial bank deposits represented the denominator of this ratio. At the same time, the system of credit controls was extended to the bond market through the control by the Riksbank of new issues of bonds. The timing, size, and interest rates of every new bond issue had to be approved by the Bank.

This control system contributed to the establishment of monthly meetings between the Riksbank and the commercial banks held from the early 1950s onwards. These meetings represented a way for the Riksbank to inform and sometimes to order commercial banks what to do. At the beginning of every meeting, the asset and liability side of the commercial banking system was reported and commented on as part of the regular business. The governor of the Riksbank was known personally to criticize commercial bank managers that did not fulfil the intentions of the Bank.[4]

In two periods, 1955–57 and 1970–71, the Riksbank introduced ceilings on commercial bank lending to sectors that were not regarded as "priority" sectors, that is to all sectors except the public and the housing sector. Other quantitative controls were used from time to time.

At the end of the 1950s, the national pension fund (the AP fund) was established after a heated political debate. The AP fund rapidly became the major purchaser of bonds. Its monopoly position is displayed in figure 11.4. The fund could purchase only bond issues that the Riksbank had permitted through the issue control. The Bank thus controlled the rate of interest as well as the volume of bonds issued. The AP fund had to follow tight rules concerning the composition of its bond portfolio. Basically, priority was given to the housing sector, the government sector, and the export industry. Now, the Swedish capital market virtually ceased to exist. There was no

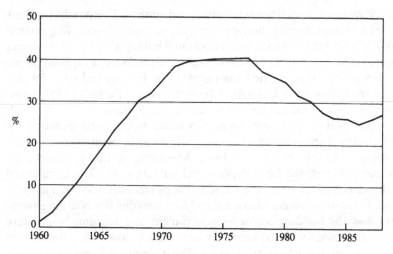

11.4   The national pension fund's (AP) share of total outstanding
bonds, 1960–88,%

active "thick" secondary bond market, rather, it became a political market
where the volume, the distribution, and the price of long-term capital was
determined according to political preferences.

The effect on the balance sheet of the consolidated commercial banking
sector of the Riksbank's actions in the 1950s, 1960s, and 1970s is summarized in figure 11.2, displaying the ratio of bond holdings to deposits of
commercial banks, which roughly corresponds to the aggregate liquidity
ratio of the commercial banking system. The fall in the ratio in the second
half of the 1940s was arrested after the introduction of the liquidity ratios in
the early 1950s. Gradually, the ratio increased in the 1950s reaching a level
of around 30 percent in 1960. The establishment of the AP fund reduced the
pressure on the commercial banking system to purchase bonds. However,
as a consequence of the rapid and huge increase in government debt
following the energy price increase in 1973–74 (OPEC I), the Riksbank
gradually raised the ratio, reaching around 50 percent by 1980. This
marked the peak of the credit control regime.

To sum up, in the 1950s an encompassing system of domestic credit
controls was introduced, protected and supported by the exchange controls
put into effect in the beginning of the Second World War. This system
allowed the Riksbank to control the flow of long-term as well as short-term
credit to every major sector in the Swedish economy and gave it the power
to determine, within broad margins, the rates of interest offered by all
financial intermediaries. This system of command and control replaced the

earlier system of market allocation. There were basically no functioning secondary markets for financial assets in Sweden with the sole exception of government-issued lottery bonds which were in high demand because of the prevailing tax laws.

All commentators on Swedish monetary policy in the 1950s through the 1970s argue that the credit market was strictly regulated and that interest rates were kept below market rates. However, there are no answers to the question of how far the regulated interest rates were from market equilibrating rates. Ideally, we would like to have an empirical measure of the degree of credit rationing prevailing but no such single aggregate measure is available. The extent of disequilibrium varied over time. It is commonly asserted that in periods of expansionary policies the system was closer to an equilibrium situation than during periods of contractionary monetary policy, when the selective controls were usually tightened. Besides, it is difficult to find a representative international interest rate to use as a benchmark, as most European countries relied on domestic credit controls and exchange and capital controls in this period as well.

The causes of the rise of credit controls

Several forces contributed to the rise of credit controls. They can be traced to the monetary program of 1944 that was inspired by the experience of the 1930s and the Second World War, the shifting balance of power in the market for political ideas, prevailing views on the aims and means of fiscal and monetary policy, pressure from vested interests, and demonstration effects from abroad. As these developments interacted, it is difficult to rank them according to a precise degree of influence.

THE MONETARY PROGRAM OF 1944

In 1943 the Board of the Riksbank appointed a committee of five influential members to prepare a report concerning the aims and means of monetary policy after the end of the war. The proposals of the committee formed the basis of a program accepted by parliament in 1944. Parliament basically accepted David Davidson's monetary norm, which stated that nominal income should be stabilized and that the price level should move in inverse proportion to the growth of real income. Most importantly, the policy of stabilizing interest rates, set forth during the war, was to be continued. The bond rate should not be allowed to increase, and instead other measures, not specified, should be used. Reductions of the rate were to be accepted in times of depression in order to fight unemployment.

The monetary program exerted an important influence on the conduct of Swedish central bank policy in the following decades. It codified a policy of low and stable interest rates and eventually forced the Riksbank to introduce non-market oriented techniques of monetary control as it could not raise its discount rate and thus other interest rates to an equilibrating level.

THE EXPERIENCE OF THE SECOND WORLD WAR

The experience of the Second World War exerted a profound influence on postwar economic policies in Sweden. The outbreak of war in 1939 came as no surprise, rather it was expected. The authorities acted quickly. Most importantly, a system of exchange and capital controls was instituted in 1940, a system that remained in effect until 1989. The Swedish economy became the subject of far-reaching controls of wages, prices and rents. As a result of the war, the country became isolated internationally which facilitated the system of rationing and controls. Business, labor, and government cooperated closely in the framing of economic policies. A considerable number of regulatory or semi-regulatory agencies were founded during the war and some of them survived the outbreak of peace. Actually the war effort contributed to a permanent rise in the size of the public sector.

The regulatory system established during the war was commonly regarded as successful. It was viewed as proof that economic planning and far-reaching government intervention in the market economy could work in Sweden, suggesting that this could also be the case under peacetime conditions. It increased public belief in regulations and disbelief in markets, which facilitated the establishment of credit controls.

THE LEGITIMACY OF GOVERNMENT INTERVENTION AND ECONOMIC PLANNING

Government actions like economic policies have to be acceptable and regarded as legitimate by the public in order for them to work. The fact that Sweden was able to stay out of the war as a neutral country while the rest of Europe was devastated lent legitimacy to government actions, *per se*. This legitimacy carried also over to domestic affairs, contributing to greater acceptance of government intervention in the economy after the war.[5]

The *Zeitgeist* was positive towards far-reaching government intervention in fields previously left to private initiative. One such field was the economy. Leading economists within Sweden were pro-planners in a broad sense like Gunnar Myrdal and Ingvar Svennilson. Myrdal (1951), for example, was of the opinion that economic planning was inevitably bound to increase in the future.

POLITICAL FORCES: THE DOMINANCE OF THE SOCIAL DEMOCRATIC PARTY

The Social Democratic Party came into power in the election of 1932. It

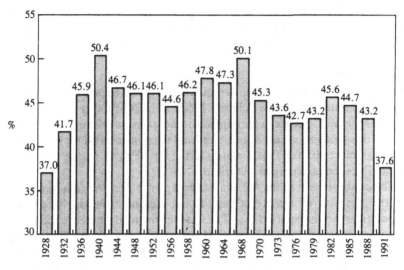

11.5   Vote share of the Social Democratic Party, 1928–91,%

launched a "crisis" program in 1933 based on expansionary fiscal policy which was commonly regarded as bringing Sweden out of the depression. The party remained in power during the rest of the 1930s. In the election of 1940 it received a majority of its own (figure 11.5 shows the vote share of the Social Democratic party from 1928 to 1991). The Social Democrats laid the foundation in the 1930s for their unique dominance of Swedish politics in the post-Second World War period. During the war all parties, with the exception of the Communist party, were represented in the government. Shortly after the end of the war, the Social Democrats formed a new government by themselves, with a pronounced ideological profile. A new party program had been written in 1944 which asked for extended government intervention and government planning. The financial sector was one area where socialization and government controls were asked for and Gunnar Myrdal, as a member of the government, emerged at this time as a leading proponent for government controls.

Throughout the post-Second World War period socialization and economic planning has been high on the agenda of the Social Democratic Party. At every party congress in the past 50 years proposals for socialization of the banking system have been raised. The leadership of the party has turned down these requests, sometimes promising government investigations or more government controls of the financial sector as a substitute for outright socialization. This political milieu, dominated by a strong socialist party, facilitated the introduction and administration of credit controls. The financial sector was apt to enter "voluntary agreements" and abide by them, knowing that there was a strong political sentiment against private ownership of financial institutions.

THE EFFECT OF THE AP FUND
The political dominance of the Social Democrats was cemented for many years by the introduction in the early 1960s of the AP fund, a pension fund set up as the consequence of the supplementary pension reform of 1959. The idea of this fund met strong opposition from the non-socialist parties, but in a special referendum in 1958 the proposal of the AP fund, supported by the Social Democrats, emerged victorious.

The establishment of the AP fund made it possible for the government to control the flow of long-term capital and eliminate the rise of private alternatives for financial savings. The fund represented a massive socialization of savings in Sweden. Through the establishment of the AP fund, the consolidated public sector acted as a net lender; in this position, the government could more easily control credit and capital markets compared to the case of being a net borrower, as revealed by the events of the 1970s.

THE DOMINANCE OF KEYNESIANISM AND THE LOW INTEREST RATE DOCTRINE
Keynesian theories formed the intellectual basis of much of the Social Democrats' economic policies. Keynesian economic thinking made a rapid and lasting impact on Swedish economic policies. One reason was the affinity between the Keynesian message of that period and the political outlook of the Social Democrats, another reason was the affinity between Keynesianism and the views of the Stockholm School as they emerged in the 1930s. Both groups were favorably inclined towards government intervention in a market economy which was regarded as unstable, prone to display large cyclical swings, if left by itself. Swedish economists who held leading positions at the universities, as advisers and as politicians in the 1940s, 1950s, and 1960s were as a rule members of the Stockholm School. Several of them went into political service as Social Democrats like Gunnar Myrdal, Karin Kock and Alf Johansson. Some of their students who made political careers were pro-planners.

The Keynesianism of that day strongly recommended government intervention to stabilize the economy as well as to foster economic growth, primarily by enhancing investment. Fiscal policy was regarded as superior to monetary policies. Direct controls and regulations were accepted as part of this outlook. One aspect of the new approach was the stress on planning. A national medium-term budget was set up at the end of the 1940s and medium-term plans have been published regularly since then. The role of

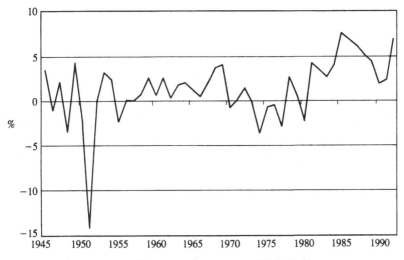

11.6 *Ex post* real long-term interest rate, 1945–91,%

monetary policy in this framework was to guarantee the financing of the plans. Much of the Swedish economic policy in the 1940s, 1950s, and 1960s was geared towards maintaining a high level of investment. A number of new instruments were introduced for this purpose.

Belief in the beneficial effects of low interest rates characterized economic thinking. Several arguments were presented in support of low interest rates: a rise in rates would have adverse effects on the distribution of income by raising rents and might reduce the volume of investment. The low interest rate doctrine was a major driving force behind the selective controls, when aimed primarily at keeping the rate below the equilibrium rate. During several years between 1950 and 1980 *ex post* real rates were negative (figure 11.6), suggesting that the credit control regime transferred wealth from saving units to investors. (The *ex post* real rate is calculated as the nominal rate minus the rate of inflation taking no account of tax effects. If these were included, the *ex post* rate would be negative for almost the entire post-Second World War period for private individuals.)

THE ROLE OF THE HOUSING POLICY AND THE "MILLION PROGRAM"
The housing sector became the prime example of a centrally-planned sector after the Second World War. Here the Social Democrats made a large political commitment. The aim was to eliminate the housing shortage that had developed during the Second World War by new construction while maintaining low rents. Political bodies decided on the volume of new housing units to be built and its composition.

11.7   Housing construction: number of completed dwellings, 1940–90

In the mid-1960s the government launched the "million-program," aimed at building 100,000 new housing units per year for 10 years. The program was given much political weight and was regarded as successful by the Social Democrats. The million program is displayed in figure 11.7. The Riksbank became directly involved in the housing policy as it was given responsibility for the financing of the housing program at interest rates that were regarded as "low." As the financing of new construction was cost-based, any increase in interest rates would spill over in higher rents. The Riksbank did not decide the annual amount of new constructions, however, as the planning process involved the Board of Housing, the Ministry of Finance, and other groups.

THE ROLE OF ORGANIZED INTEREST GROUPS
The influence of vested interests on the framing of economic policies has been stressed by Mancur Olson (1982, 1989). Lobbyists and pressure groups are given an important role alongside ideas and ideologies in Sweden, and as the credit control regime developed, a number of interest groups reaped benefits from it. One influential group was the "housing industrial complex," consisting of cooperative non-profit construction firms with close political ties to the Social Democrats and the union movement (the LO), in particular the construction union, as well as the Tenants' National Association. This group, which also encompassed the private construction industry, actively lobbied for support for the housing sector in terms of low interest rates and other forms of subsidies.

Another influential group was the farming community. Traditionally the farming interest in parliament has advocated low interest rates.[6] The Farmers' Party formed a coalition with the Social Democrats during the period 1951–57, and in this position exerted pressure for low rates. For example, when the governor of the Riksbank, who was a Social Democrat, asked at a board meeting of the Bank in July 1957 for a rise in the discount rate, the representative of the farmers' party was the only one to propose lowering it.

The business sector, in particular the dominating large export industries, were also in favor of low rates. Export companies were given priority after the government and housing sector in the queue for new bond issues. Big business was thus no major opponent of the credit controls.

Traditionally, those who save form a pressure group that asks for "high" rates of interest; they could counteract the pressure groups that ask for "low" rates. However, in Sweden, a society permeated by organized interests, savers were not organized in any pressure groups protecting their interests. The main reason was that the savings activity had been socialized by the introduction of the AP fund. The public reacted by exit, not voice, that is, private savings out of private disposable income fell secularly in Sweden after 1960, reaching a level below zero at the end of the 1980s. The life insurance companies, which represented the savers indirectly and could be viewed as the only pro-saving interest group, were critical of the controls, but could not prevent their introduction.

INTERNATIONAL DEMONSTRATION EFFECT

Sweden was influenced by the conduct of economic policies in other countries as well as by prevailing political and economic ideas. Low interest rates were a goal in countries like the United Kingdom and the United States. Many other countries maintained exchange controls and experimented with selective controls as well. Norway and Finland carried out monetary policies similar to Sweden's. Keynesian policies were dominant in the industrialized world, and Sweden was no exception to the international pattern. The growth performance of the Swedish economy also appeared impressive in an international context. Inflation was not a major problem and the "Swedish model," as it developed in the 1950s and 1960s, appeared highly successful, which lent legitimacy to the policy of credit controls.

CENTRAL BANK CONTACTS

The Swedish Riksbank was influenced by its international contacts through BIS, IMF, and OECD. The governor of the Riksbank met monthly in Basle with other governors of central banks to discuss policy matters. Starting in the mid-1950s, Swedish economic policies, including monetary policies, were monitored regularly by the IMF. The Swedish authorities also had regular contact with the OECD. These contacts apparently did not have a major impact on the framing of the Riksbank's policy.

To sum up, a number of factors, reflecting political and economic ideas as well as vested interests, contributed to the rise of the regime of credit controls. There was some opposition to the regime stemming from commercial bankers such as the Wallenbergs and from academic economists, in particular from Erik Dahmén and Erik Lundberg, who also served as advisers to commercial banks. The liberal and conservative parties were also critical of the system of selective controls, but they remained out of power until 1976.

The Riksbank, formally the bank of parliament, was commonly regarded as subservient towards the government in this period, but it attempted in its non-official contacts to maintain independence and counter the pressure from outside. One prominent public case was the "coup" of July 1957 when the board of the Riksbank raised the discount rate without asking for a prior approval from the government. The government, in particular the Finance minister, reacted strongly and forced the chairman of the board to resign, replacing him with a former Finance minister. Following this event the Riksbank made no major public attempt to defend its position relative to the Ministry of Finance. On the other hand, the Bank had demonstrated a certain independence.

The demise of credit controls

The behavior of the Riksbank

The oil price increases of the 1970s (OPEC I and OPEC II) marked a new era for Swedish economic policy. As a response to these events Swedish exports declined rapidly, economic growth slowed, and the Swedish budget deficit increased dramatically. Stabilization policies, strongly inspired by the prevailing Keynesian doctrine, aimed at maintaining full employment through a high level of aggregate domestic demand, counteracting the reduction in exports. Fiscal policy was highly expansionary.

Government debt as a ratio of GDP rose from 20 percent in the mid-1970s to a peak above 60 percent 10 years later (see figure 11.1, which reveals that the post-OPEC debt ratio for Sweden was higher than after the Second World War). The new and major goal of monetary policy was now to finance the twin deficits: the budget deficit and the balance of payments deficit. To this end the Riksbank first extended the system of credit controls, most prominently by raising the required liquidity ratios in several steps

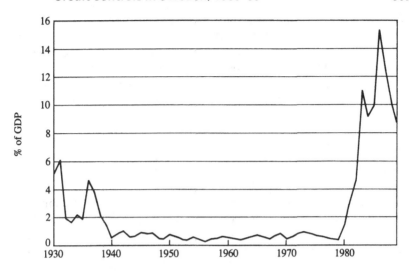

11.8   Stock market turnover as a ratio of GDP, 1930–89,%

towards their maximum limit of 50 percent. It also introduced new controls
to regulate the activities of the finance houses. These institutions had
merged as a way of evading the controls that covered the commercial banks;
however, this process was arrested after a while and replaced by financial
deregulation which started around 1983. A number of selective credit
controls were abolished in the 1980s: the liquidity ratios in 1983, regulations
of the lending rates and lending ceilings of commercial banks in 1985, and
finally the exchange controls in 1989.

New financial techniques and instruments emerged as part of the deregulation. Something of a financial revolution occurred in Sweden in the 1980s
when financial markets woke up from the freeze of the credit control
regime.[7] The stock market displayed an impressive growth in the 1980s
after being dormant since the start of the Second World War (figure 11.8).

The policy of the Riksbank eventually focused solely on stabilizing the
exchange rate of the Swedish currency to a basket of currencies, ignoring
attempts of regulating the flow of capital domestically. This priority of the
Riksbank emerged after four devaluations of the krona in 1977–82; in order
to defend the exchange rate, the "low" interest rate policy had to be
abolished and replaced by a market oriented interest rate policy. The
Riksbank held the Swedish level of nominal rates above the international
level for substantial periods in order to induce an inflow of capital to
finance the balance of payments deficit.

The institutional setup was completely transformed during the deregulation. The Riksbank worked actively in establishing financial markets, new financial instruments, and techniques. This was a period of transition from one regime to another, which required new behavior. A whole new class of financial analysts and traders arose, creating political tension; the monthly meetings between the Riksbank and the commercial banks lost their importance as the Riksbank carried out its policy through the financial markets.

The causes of deregulation

By 1989 practically all selective controls had been eliminated. The Riksbank had by then the first priority to defend the exchange rate, using as its main instrument open market operations, that is changes in the short-term interest rate. What are the factors behind this rapid deregulatory process – that took less than a decade? A mixture of negative shocks to the Swedish economy, new ideas and new priorities all contributed to the new order.

The system of credit controls was based on financial isolation of Sweden from the rest of the world. The purpose of the exchange controls was to maintain this isolation so that the Riksbank could determine domestic interest rates and the domestic allocation of capital. Current account transactions were not hindered by the exchange controls but all capital transactions were the subject of close supervision. The rapid rise in the budget deficit and in the current account deficit in the 1970s and 1980s undermined Sweden's financial isolation.

THE BUDGET DEFICIT

The huge rise in the size of the government deficit starting in the mid-1970s is probably the major factor behind the deregulation (figures 11.1 and 11.9); the authorities had to develop new ways of finding buyers of government debt. The ability of the organized credit market to finance the rising government debt was limited. They thus gradually started to issue new instruments such as Treasury bills and bonds with interest rates attractive enough to find buyers among firms and private individuals outside the regulated sectors. As these instruments became popular, second-hand markets started to develop, eventually allowing the Riksbank to carry out open market operations.

The Riksbank aimed initially at keeping the "organized" financial sector regulated, even extending some regulations. However, this policy was eventually reversed and the whole financial sector became the subject of deregulation since it turned out to be difficult to isolate the old regulated segments from the newly emerging unregulated ones.

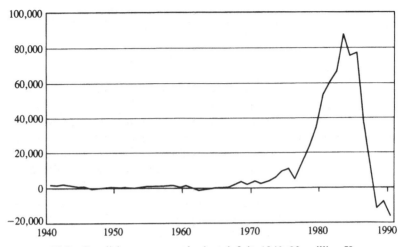

11.9   Swedish government budget deficit, 1940–90, million Kronor

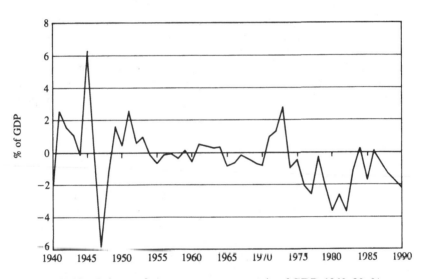

11.10   Balance of current account as a ratio of GDP, 1940–90, %

THE BALANCE OF PAYMENTS DEFICIT

Major and persistent deficits were registered in the Swedish balance of
payments after OPEC I (figure 11.10). The deficits forced Sweden to borrow
from abroad. Both the private sector and the public sector acted as
borrowers. Because of this, the efficacy of the exchange controls was

reduced. The foreign borrowing was a break with the past, as Sweden had not been active as a borrower after the Second World War.

EVASION (INTERMEDIATION OUTSIDE THE "ORGANIZED" FINANCIAL SECTOR)

A major reason behind the deregulation was the growth of the "grey market," that is the credit market outside the regulated market. As time went by, a number of techniques were devised to evade or reduce the effects of the selective controls. Basically, lenders and borrowers met outside commercial banks, or as a result of commercial bank intermediation. Commonly commercial banks could benefit from this by supplying bank guarantees as collateral behind loans.[8]

This process was a threat to the power of the Riksbank as well. It ran the risk of having a smaller base from which to operate. According to some observers, commercial banks tended to turn into safety vaults for government bonds, with liquidity ratios close to 50 percent (figure 11.2), while commercial bank functions proper were taken over by new financial institutions like the finance houses. These expanded rapidly in the 1970s and 1980s prior to the deregulation. After the deregulation their growth was arrested, and they are now in a process of decline. The regulatory system was thus gradually being undermined by evasion, but this was a long-run process that by itself would hardly have created the rapid deregulation. The authorities made several attempts to reduce the size of the grey markets.

INSTITUTIONAL CHANGES

The breakdown of the Bretton Woods system of fixed exchange rates increased demand for financial sophistication among Swedish companies to deal with increased uncertainty on markets for foreign exchange. Finance departments were created that grew rapidly in size. Volvo, ASEA and other large non-financial firms performed many financial services that were close to commercial bank activities.

The size of the financial market expanded and the number of financial intermediaries grew rapidly in the 1980s. This trend towards more agents and more sophistication within the financial sector made it increasingly difficult to carry out monetary policy based on credit controls and close supervision of every financial unit. Instead it became more attractive for the Riksbank to move to a market oriented regime.

IDEOLOGY AND POLITICAL BELIEFS

The deregulatory process was not initiated by a change in the views of the ruling Social Democratic Party. Deregulation was not on the agenda of the party congresses in the 1980s, nor was it expressed as a popular demand on the grass roots' level. Rather, new requests for socialization were made, although less frequently than in the 1970s. Most likely, if there had been a vote among "hard-core" Social Democrats (the "fundamentalists") concerning deregulation, in particular the abolition of the exchange controls, the "nos" would have dominated. Deregulation was asked for by the liberal and conservative opposition, but not made a major political issue.

The fact that the Social Democrats lost the elections in 1976 and 1979 and faced great difficulties in retaining their earlier powerful position, induced some rethinking. The Finance Minister in 1982–90, Kjell-Olof Feldt, was a leading proponent of a more market oriented approach, including the movement towards financial deregulation. Actually, the deregulation movement was initiated by the Ministry of Finance and the Riksbank; practically all of the deregulatory measures were decided with no or only minor political debate. They gave the impression of being "technical" adjustments rather than viewed as fundamental changes in the policy regime.[9]

THE GENERATION EFFECT

A new generation of decision makers came into political power in the 1980s with no memories of the 1930s and the Second World War. This generation gradually came to control the Ministry of Finance and the Riksbank, replacing the old guard that had based their careers on introducing and/or administrating the controls. This new group had no vested interest in the existing system and was probably more open to changing it. The Finance minister and the governor of the Riksbank also sought advice from a new generation of economists that was more market oriented than their predecessors. It is, of course, difficult to assess the possible impact of this "generation effect." Such an effect is stressed by Hirschman (1985), however. He envisages a private–public cycle oscillating between collectivism and individualism, where disappointment with the present system is a driving force for change in preferences. These changes take place when one generation of decision makers is replaced by another.

In the 1980s the collectivism that characterized Swedish society, epitomized in the Swedish model, was gradually put in question and replaced by a growing acceptance of individualism and requests for greater freedom from government intervention. This shift in the intellectual balance of power contributed to the acceptance of deregulation and greater private freedom in financial affairs.

THE DECLINE OF KEYNESIANISM AND THE RISE OF NEW ECONOMIC IDEAS

The credit control regime was consistent with Keynesianism as it developed in Sweden after the Second World War. However, gradually in the 1980s this view was undermined, most prominently when the policy of fiscal expansion in the mid-1970s turned out to give rise to an unexpectedly bad results in the form of a rising budget deficit, growing current account deficits, large foreign borrowing, slow growth, mounting inflationary pressure, and eventually four devaluations between 1977–82 to restore international competitiveness. The demise of Keynesianism did not mark the rise of any other school like monetarism. Rather it was replaced by an eclectic approach influenced by the international trend towards stabilization policies based on market oriented philosophies like monetarism and rational expectations. Furthermore, ideas stemming from the public choice school also contributed to a skeptical attitude towards interventionism.[10]

The new generation of economists that reached positions as professors, advisers, and consultants in the 1980s held a much more positive view towards markets than the older generation. Even some of the professed Keynesian and pro-interventionist professors of the older generations made the transition to a more critical attitude towards government intervention.

VESTED INTERESTS

The system of credit controls was supported by the housing–industrial complex. However, a change in the housing subsidies in the mid-1970s reduced this sector's dependence on changes in interest rates. Furthermore, as a consequence of the "million program" and the economic problems emerging following OPEC I and II, demand for new housing fell sharply by the mid-1970s (see figure 11.7). The housing–construction lobby was thus not as interested or as powerful as earlier in promoting its case by asking for controls on interest rates.

Gradually, the deregulation found support among a new breed of financial analysts and economic journalists that received employment due to the rapidly expanding financial sector. This group was active in pushing for deregulation. As the Swedish public has been accustomed to the new situation: adopting new financial techniques and new instruments, investing abroad by buying foreign stocks and real estate, it has become increasingly difficult politically to return to the old regime. The AP fund has lost relative importance and the public has shown great interest in private insurance. Deregulation has received support from a broad segment of Swedish society. As the process continues, this support will form a pressure group for maintaining the new order.

Perhaps the strongest opposition towards deregulation has stemmed from the labor union movement, the powerful LO. Its leader has publicly criticized the employers in the financial sector and pushed for taxation of financial services. LO has been highly critical of the abolition of the exchange controls as these controls contributed to the power of the unions by giving them the possibility of influencing the investment activities of domestic firms. When the controls are gone, the unions and the firms face a different incentive structure. If the unions push for high wages, firms may simply emigrate – a step made easier with no exchange controls – making the unions less powerful than before, and fundamentally changing the rules of the game as once set out in the "Swedish model." It is consistent with this line of argument that economists at LO have strongly opposed various proposals to make the Riksbank more independent from the parliament than before. They fear that such a Riksbank would carry out a tighter monetary policy than it would if it remained under closer political control. Such a tight policy would create higher unemployment, and thus reduce the power of the union movement.

DEMONSTRATION EFFECT FROM ABROAD

The international trend towards deregulation has influenced thinking and policies within Sweden. There has been a fear that Sweden would be left behind in this process of competitive deregulation, in particular as the growth performance of Sweden lagged behind the rest of the OECD in the 1980s. Furthermore, European integration put pressure on the Swedish authorities to revise methods of monetary control. The international pattern thus lent legitimacy to Swedish deregulation.

CENTRAL BANK COOPERATION

The Riksbank and the Ministry of Finance have been influenced towards accepting deregulation through their contacts with various international organizations such as BIS, IMF, and OECD. It has been increasingly difficult to defend the Swedish exchange controls as long as the rest of the world is deregulating and Swedish financial institutions have been allowed to set up operations abroad.

The governor of the Riksbank in a newspaper article in 1986 summarized his views of the causes of the deregulation. In short, in his opinion the deregulation was due to a combination of exogenous events and evasion that made the old system of controls unsustainable:

it is neither noble thoughts nor economic models that have induced the Riksbank to deregulate but a reality that has made the old instruments of credit controls more and more useless. In the old days, when the liquidity in the economy was low and the commercial banks were the dominant financial intermediary various forms of regulations were effective to restrict the supply of credit. When the budget deficit increased rapidly and liquidity was flowing – later supported by the expansion in profits due to the devaluations of 1981 and 1982 – the regulations became more and more inefficient. In 1982, when the whole set of instruments of controls was in force, the Riksbank was roughly controlling a shadow of the real world.

The strategy of economic policies changed in many OECD countries in the 1980s. A case study of eleven countries, including Sweden (see OECD, 1988), concluded that "sustainability" was an important concept when explaining the reason for policy changes. The old system of controls was not sustainable in Sweden. It broke down primarily as a consequence of the expansion of the public deficit. The process was then facilitated by changes in economic and political ideas, these changes interacting with actual economic events. Furthermore, the financial crisis that occurred in Sweden in the early 1990s took place several years after the deregulation, although the deregulation was one important cause. Due to this time lag, the deregulation was not called into question. When it occurred, it was regarded as successful.

Conclusion

The design of the monetary regime is not framed in a political and ideological vacuum. Instead it is influenced by a number of developments. This chapter stresses primarily the following set of factors as accounting for the rise and fall of the regime of credit controls in Sweden during the period 1939–89: major exogenous macroeconomic disturbances, prevailing economic ideas, and dominating political ideologies. The monetary isolation caused by the Second World War and the wartime exchange controls, the monetary policies during the war, the acceptance of the doctrine of low rates of interest, the rise of Keynesianism and the political power of the Social Democrats all contributed to the rise of selective monetary controls. Likewise the oil price rises of the 1970s, the ensuing application of expansionary fiscal policies (inspired by Keynesianism) causing a sharp rise in the budget deficit and in the balance of payments deficit, and a rapid growth of evasion undermined the credit control system and paved the way for a new monetary regime based on deregulation.[11]

Basically, the life-cycle of credit controls has been described here. This description also suggests that the present monetary regime, based on a market oriented approach, may change again in the future. This will occur if and when the present regime is regarded as unsustainable. A combination of negative disturbances, changing political priorities and new interpretations of the historical record can initiate a movement towards reregulation in the future. The history of the Riksbank, the world's oldest central bank, thus provides several examples of processes leading to changes in a prevailing monetary regime.

Notes

This chapter is part of a study in preparation of Swedish monetary policy from 1945 to 1990 carried out under the auspices of the Riksbank. The views are those of the author and should not be interpreted as reflecting those of the Riksbank.

I owe a great debt to Per Frennberg. He has skillfully drawn all the illustrations and given me valuable comments on earlier drafts. Krister Andersson, Michael D. Bordo, Forrest Capie, Lars Hörngren, Carl-Göran Lemne and Anthony Santomero have given me valuable comments on earlier drafts.

1 These questions are answered in a recent OECD publication (see OECD, 1988). This report deals with the economic policy changes in a number of OECD countries in the 1980s. In this chapter the record of one country, that is Sweden, covering 50 years is considered.

2 Here the Lucasian distinction between policy regimes appears to be highly appropriate.

3 The similarities between the behavior of the Riksbank as a price controller and "standard" Swedish price control practices are striking. See Jonung (1990).

4 Notes from these meetings for the period 1956–73 have recently been made available. They are currently being analyzed in a study of Swedish monetary policy.

5 This argument is stressed by Mancur Olson (1982) who suggests that it is easier for countries that lost wars than countries that won wars to deregulate their economies.

6 This theme runs through the history of the Riksbank, where the farm members of parliament have always been prone to ask for low interest rates.

7 For an account of the emergence of new financial instruments and of the institutional details of the deregulatory process, see Jonung (1986) and Englund (1990). The instruments and targets of the Riksbank after the deregulation are described by two "insiders" in Hörngren and Westman-Mårtensson (1991).

8 Evasion and financial disintegration as a driving force behind financial innovations and deregulation is considered, for example, by Artus and de Boissieu (1988) and Kane (1981).

9 This interpretation is supported by a comparison of the treatment of monetary policy issues in *Tiden*, the ideological journal of the Social Democratic Party, in the 1940s and in the 1980s. In the second half of the 1940s, several articles, written by leading party members, asked for controls and economic planning. In the 1980s, hardly any articles of this kind appeared, indicating an absence of an ideological interest in monetary controls and/or acceptance of the newly emerging order.

10 The gradual demise of Keynesianism and the rise of new economic ideas in Sweden is strikingly illustrated by the annual reports of the SNS group of economists. In the 1970s this group was strongly Keynesian. It changed gradually in the early 1980s, emphasizing monetary norms, greater independence for the Riksbank, and less government intervention.

11 The account also illustrates the interpretations of Hirschman (1985) and Olson

(1982). They have presented different views on why economic policies are changed. Hirschman argues that there is a cycle of private and public involvement; disappointment and frustration concerning private behavior lead to public involvement, which in their turn lead to frustration concerning public policies which cause the return of private concerns. This explanation is consistent with the Swedish pattern of financial regulation followed by financial deregulation. Hirschman looks primarily at the sentiments of the voters – the public; much of the conduct of monetary policy has been carried out by non-elected public servants, however, Olson argues that vested interests are important in the framing of economic policies. His views are helpful in explaining the introduction and the long life of the selective controls. The demise of the controls is directly related to the exogenous events that forced the authorities to rethink their policies. Vested interests were too weak in preventing the revision of monetary policy caused by these events.

References

Artus, P. and C. de Boissieu, 1988. "The process of financial innovation: causes, forms, and consequences," chapter 5 in Arnold Heetje (ed.), *Innovation, Technology, and Finance*, Oxford: Basil Blackwell.

Englund, P., 1990. "Financial deregulation in Sweden," *European Economic Review*, 34 (May): 385–393.

Hirschman, A., 1985. *Shifting Involvements*, Oxford: Basil Blackwell.

Hörngren, L. and A Westman-Mårtensson, 1991. "Swedish monetary policy: institutions, targets, and instruments," *arbetsrapport*, no. 2, (May), Stockholm, Sveriges Riksbank.

Jonung L., 1986. "Financial deregulation in Sweden," *Skandinaviska Enskilda Banken Quarterly Review*, 15 (4): 109–119.

  1990. *The Political Economy of Price Controls. The Swedish Experience 1970–1987*, Aldershot: Avebury.

Kane, E., 1981. "Accelerating inflation, technological innovation and the decreasing effectiveness of banking regulation," *Journal of Finance*, 36 (2): 355–367.

Myrdal, G., 1951. "Utvecklingen mot planekonomi," [The trend towards the planned economy], *Tiden*, 43.

OECD, 1988. *Why Economic Policies Change Course*, Paris: OECD.

Olson, M., 1982. *The Rise and Decline of Nations*, New Haven: Yale University Press.

  1989. "How ideas affect societies: Is Britain the wave of the future?," in *Ideas, Interest and Consequences*, *IEA Readings*, 30, London: Institute of Economic Affairs.

Part IV

Perspectives on monetary regimes

12 An assessment of monetary regimes

ANNA J. SCHWARTZ

Introduction

Is there a common denominator for the varied monetary regimes that the chapters in this volume deal with? More than a dozen countries figure in the papers, most of them during periods when their monetary regimes were commodity-based, some of them (England, France, 1789–1821; the United States 1862–78; Hungary, 1921–28; Italy, France, 1945–49) at other periods when they either suspended or were seeking to re-establish commodity standards, and finally one country (Sweden, 1939–89) whose monetary regime is tracked over 50 years under fixed and floating exchange rates.

The common denominator that I propose is the degree of success each regime experienced in maintaining actual and expected price stability. This is not necessarily the perspective of the authors of the chapters. In commenting on their contributions, I note their focus before assessing the price performance of the monetary regimes they deal with. The section headings I use are my own.

Commodity money standards in transition

Gallarotti and Redish in chapters 2 and 3 provide complementary descriptions of the forces that accounted for the switch to gold in the second half of the nineteenth century.

For Redish, a fall in the price of gold had created by 1860 a *de facto* gold standard in the bimetallic monetary regimes of Belgium, Switzerland, and France. While *de facto* monometallism had occurred in the past and had occasioned changes in the mint ratio, this time no change in the mint ratio was made. Instead these countries and Italy introduced a token silver coinage to provide small-denomination currency, and the Latin Monetary Union, which they organized in 1865, agreed on a uniform token silver circulation. Although the price of gold rose thereafter, the partner countries decided not to return to a *de facto* silver standard, taking actions to prevent silver from driving gold out of circulation: each of them freely minted only gold but gave the existing silver 5-franc coins unlimited legal tender. In 1878, they suspended the coinage of the silver 5-franc coin.

Gallarotti covers a broader range of countries than the Latin American Union that switched to gold during the 1870s, and does not refer to the *de facto* gold standard there as of 1860, although he says the "environment" for a switch was ripe after 1850. Presumably, the environment includes the change in the relative prices of gold and silver. What Gallarotti discusses are the structural and proximate forces that led to the switch. He identifies as structural forces, ideological attraction to gold and aversion to silver, industrialization, and economic development, as well as shifts in political power from agriculture to industry, from exporters and debtors to importers and creditors. The proximate forces in the late 1860s were a rise in world silver and decline in world gold production, the decline in India's silver imports, and a fear of soft money. Germany's adoption of gold in 1871 determined a similar preference by its trading partners in the Scandinavian Monetary Union and in Holland, just as the decision by France to adopt a gold standard determined the preferences of its Latin Monetary Union trading partners.

Redish does not refer to the price stability implications of the international gold standard that emerged; Gallarotti does. He interprets the late nineteenth century switch from silver to gold as a choice of stable money, and contrasts it with the support of soft money by the welfare state in the twentieth century. For this reason he believes there would be strong political resistance to a shift from today's inflationary fiat money regimes.

On the counterfactual question of what price behavior would have been, had the demand for silver been sustained and had the bimetallic standard remained the concerted choice of the countries that shifted to gold in the 1870s, Gallarotti is skeptical of Friedman's argument that greater price stability might have prevailed than the international gold standard provided during the deflationary years before 1897. Gallarotti is even more dismissive of such an outcome had the United States unilaterally returned to a bimetallic standard in the mid-1870s, in line with Friedman's analysis, and had it thereby influenced the rest of the world to follow suit. Readers must weigh for themselves these contrary judgments.

Gallarotti describes the shift from a silver- to a gold-based monetary system as a monetary regime transformation, although the rule governing monetary authorities or their reaction function, I believe, is invariant to the commodity that serves as the standard. Calomiris in chapter 4, however, definitely deals with a monetary regime change in discussing the US resumption of the gold standard in 1879 after seventeen years of a fiat money system.

Calomiris focuses on the effects of anticipations of possible regime switches in determining prices and nominal interest rates, not only during the greenback suspension of convertibility but also during the silver agitation of the 1890s. His main point is that expected deflation during the greenback episode in anticipation of resumption and expected inflation during the silver episode in anticipation of the collapse of the gold standard were unrelated to current changes in monetary aggregates or exchange rates. Nominal interest rates underestimated *ex ante* real rates in the first, and overestimated real rates during the second episode. By using financial returns data, however, Calomiris distinguishes between periods of expected and unexpected price change to correct the misleading assumption of covariance stationarity for money and price processes during the nineteenth century.

For the greenback episode, Calomiris stresses fiscal policy news about the probability and timing of resumption as an important determinant of innovations in the exchange rate and price level. For him the supply of greenbacks was irrelevant to exchange rate and price movements, except through an effect on expectations of resumption.

For the silver episode, Calomiris challenges the view that the short-run fiscal deficits of the 1890s and potential growth of the silver currency supply posed a threat to the long-run maintenance of the gold standard. Instead, he finds that the main threat to the gold standard in the 1890s was an expectation of the Treasury's suspension of convertibility. The decline in gold tax payments and increase in silver tax payments measured the threat in mid-1893 and late 1895 through mid-1896. Had the suspension occurred, it would have resulted in a fall in the dollar exchange rate to only a small discount – as judged by the small interest rate differential between London and New York.

Calomiris' emphasis on expectations in influencing exchange rate and price movements is entirely acceptable, but I reject his emphasis on news. If expectations in both episodes were unrelated to current changes in monetary aggregates or exchange rates, how can news be important? The public clearly was sensitive to the possibility of a change in regime suggested by current data. News may influence, say, daily movements in a variable, but it does not explain longer-run movements. The only way exchange rates moved during the greenback period was as expectations affected the demand for and supply of foreign exchange, by producing greater or lesser willingness on the part of foreigners to hold assets whose value was fixed in terms of greenbacks, or on the part of US residents to hold assets fixed in terms of foreign currencies.

Successful and unsuccessful adherence to the gold standard

Of the three country gold standard studies, the one by Martín-Aceña in chapter 5 devoted to Spain is a report on its switch from a bimetallic standard to a brief period of gold convertibility that it abandoned in 1883, when the Bank of Spain's gold reserve was sharply reduced from its peak in 1881. Paradoxically, Spain continued to maintain legal reserve requirements against note issues, in fact increasing the requirements in 1891, 1898, and 1902. The Bank of Spain's gold reserves rose with few setbacks from 1883 to 1914, the total exceeding requirements and suggesting that convertibility was feasible at least from 1890 on, if not earlier.

The question that Martín-Aceña raises, but does not answer, is why Spain failed to resume. The chief loss that failure imposed on the economy was the cessation of foreign investment after 1883. Successful resumption at the parity prevailing before 1883 in 1885 would have required a price fall of 8 percent, and in the early 1890s a price fall of 15 percent, according to Martín-Aceña's estimates. Apparently Spain was unwilling to pay the price of deflation in order to resume.

Spain could still have adopted the gold standard after 1900. Yet it did not do so, although its liquidity ratio compared favorably with that of the new gold standard adherents of that period and its margin of reserves was large enough so that any temporary balance of payments deficit would not have been daunting.

Martín-Aceña mentions that imports of both repatriated and foreign capital are recorded after 1900, but he does not link the failure to resume to this development. If the advantage of the gold standard to an underdeveloped economy was that it attracted capital from abroad for industrialization, then it would seem that Spain's conservative financial policies, although it did not bind itself to the formal discipline of the gold standard, nevertheless earned it that advantage.

Because Spain left the gold standard, Martín-Aceña argues that the capital imports it was denied during the last two decades of the nineteenth century reduced its rate of growth relative to that of other European countries. The growth rate of its GNP and industrial production decelerated not only from 1883 to 1900 but also from 1900 to 1914. Only the growth of exports accelerated after 1900. He supports the argument by estimating the ratio of the external flow of real resources (the current account deficit) to national income in the pre-suspension period, in 1890, 1900, and 1913, as 3.2, 1.1, 1.9, and 2.4 percent, respectively. Foregone inflows of resources could have been on the order of 1–2 percent of GNP between 1883 and 1900, slightly less thereafter. Hence Martín-Aceña concludes that the failure to resume was a serious error of the authorities that contributed to Spanish economic backwardness.

My reaction to the chapter is that Spain does not fit any model of the gold standard. Spanish experience flouts the view that countries prefer fixed exchange rates because they bind monetary authorities to a rule. Spain observed a rule, in the sense that it limited the deviation of its price level from world prices, although it abandoned fixed peseta exchange rates for floating rates. Moreover, Spanish experience does not conform to the view that countries regard floating exchange rates as temporary arrangements in response to a shock, although it might have been misguided in its prolonged attachment to floating rates. Another model of the gold standard stresses that the access to international capital markets that it provided was an incentive for countries to adopt it, but Spain is not an example.

The chapters by Dick and Floyd (chapter 6) on Canadian and by Pope (chapter 7) on Australian experience take a tack that is quite different from the chapter on Spain. The main concern of each of the former chapters is how to model balance of payments adjustment under the pre-First World War gold standard. For Dick and Floyd the issue in interpreting Canadian experience is the contrast between the price-specie-flow and the portfolio balance approach to balance of payments adjustment. In the Australian case Pope discriminates between the price-specie-flow and the monetary approach to the balance of payments.

The monetary approach may be regarded as a special case of the portfolio balance approach. Asset holdings in the former are classified as money and non-money assets. In the portfolio balance approach, there are three assets: money, dometic assets, and foreign assets. If domestic and foreign assets are perfect substitutes, the model becomes the monetary approach, with interest parity prevailing, given an appropriate risk premium. In the portfolio balance approach, domestic and foreign assets are not perfect substitutes, and each asset demand depends on the rate of return from each asset, the domestic interest rate, and the foreign interest rate. Operations on different assets are expected to have different effects on macroeconomic variables, because they imply different changes in asset composition.

Based on their econometric results, Dick and Floyd conclude that the Canadian balance of payments adjustment is better explained by the portfolio balance model, which develops the implications of international capital mobility, than by the price-specie-flow approach. Interest rates are the result of portfolio choices. Long-term capital inflows in Canada responded to domestic investment opportunities. By raising the Canadian price level relative to foreign price levels, capital inflows induced portfolio changes, which led to foreign reserve inflows that brought the supply of and demand for money into equality. The endogenous money supply adjusted through the balance of payments without affecting the balance of trade. The monetary authorities could not control the domestic money stock; they could determine only the allocation of the monetary base between domestic credit and foreign assets. Dick and Floyd are sympathetic to the McCloskey–Zecher (1976) emphasis on integrated commodity markets in explaining balance of payments adjustment, but they prefer emphasis on capital mobility as the essence of the monetary nature of that adjustment.

Pope concludes on the basis of his econometric tests that the price-specie-flow mechanism is not an adequate description of Australia's gold movements, trade, and capital flows. Gold exports from Australia mirrored production rather than trade deficits. Capital flows are not well explained by intercountry interest rate differentials. The only satisfactory explanation, Pope finds, is that "the world money stock was redistributed through capital movements in a way that *tended* to equilibrate" different countries' demands for and supplies of money with their currencies fixed in relation to one another through gold. Because capital flows directly offset autonomous changes in exports, imports, and net property transfers, maintenance of the gold standard was easier and more automatic than it would otherwise have been.

In my judgment, the analysis of balance of payments adjustment should not be treated in the manner of these chapters as a contrast between the price-specie-flow approach and the monetary or portfolio balance approach to the balance of payments. I believe that changes in commodity prices, changes in spending, changes in interest rates, and changes in capital flows are all involved in the adjustment process. In some episodes, one set of changes may be more important than another, but that does not rule out a role for other changes.

With respect to price performance in the two gold standard regimes, the chapters emphasize that Canada and Australia were small countries that could not influence the world price level. What did vary for each country was the price level of domestic non-traded goods relative to prices of non-traded goods in the rest of the world. Traded goods' prices in each country were determined by world traded goods prices.

Wartime upheaval and postwar stabilization

It is hard to find links between the four chapters in this section covering 200 years and dealing with disparate issues. Each chapter occupies a different time frame and centers on different historical concerns.

The question Bordo and White in chapter 8 pose concerning the Napoleonic Wars is why Britain, which abandoned gold in 1797 and did not resume until 1821, was able to borrow a substantial fraction of its war expenditures at relatively low interest rates, whereas France, which maintained convertibility of the franc from 1805 on, had to rely on taxes to finance its war expenditures.

Their answer is that the British government had credibility as a borrower because of its long record of fiscal probity, while France was not a credible borrower, having squandered her reputation for creditworthiness in the last decade of the *ancien régime* and during the Revolution.

The notion of juxtaposing the experience of the two belligerents is certainly attractive, and one must admire the authors' initiative in assembling the extant statistical record, however incomplete, of fiscal and monetary actions in the two countries. On the theory that a government will increase tax rates during a war that will not fully match its forecast of future expenditures since a decline in postwar expenditures would be expected, they test for tax smoothing in the two countries. The result is inconclusive, although they regard the results for Britain as supportive of the hypothesis that Britain invested in credibility by establishing a Sinking Fund for debt service. On the theory that a government would smooth revenue from both legislated taxes and the unlegislated inflation tax, they also test for revenue smoothing by Britain. They find no evidence for that hypothesis. Despite these innovative efforts to interpret historical experience in the light of present-day theoretical approaches, I must note my reservations about the thesis the chapter offers.

For two reasons I wonder if the difference in reputation between Britain and France is the full explanation of the difference in the historical record of the two countries. The first reason is the following point. France's egregious fiscal and monetary transgressions dated from the 1789 revolution. By 1796 both large budget deficits and excessive money creation had ceased. When Napoleon seized power in 1799, he adopted policies of fiscal and monetary prudence. Bordo and White explain Britain's move to inconvertibility of the pound that lasted for 24 years as consistent with the public's belief that a commitment to the gold standard was contingent on the absence of war. If this explains Britain's continued esteem despite its abandonment of the standard, why should there not have been a corresponding public belief that a commitment to balanced budgets and non-inflationary money growth in France was contingent on the absence of revolution? In that event, France should not have had a tarnished reputation any more than Britain had.

The second reason for wondering if the different experience of the two countries is attributable wholly to reputation is that Britain was a far more potent economic power than France during the war. It had begun to industrialize in the 1780s, and France was at least 50 years behind Britain when it started in the 1830s. The two countries were certainly not equal in industrial strength, even if the recent research to which Bordo and White refer suggests that there was less difference between them than has traditionally been the view. Relative to France, Britain was capital-rich, France, capital-poor. It seems dubious to me that the difference in reputation between the two countries fully explains the higher interest rate at which France borrowed up to 1820. The authors refer to large international capital flows in this period, implying that the flows should have equalized rates of return. That is not, however, the case. The United States imported capital in the last decades of the century that yielded higher returns to lenders than they could earn domestically. The reference to "several hundred million livres in French securities" that Dutch and Swiss investors placed, moreover, weakens the argument that France had to resort to taxation because it couldn't find lenders. The evidence to which Bordo and White refer of lower interest rates for private than government French borrowers concerns the *ancien régime*, not the Napoleonic period. They should have presented evidence that Napoloen would have preferred to borrow but found no willing lenders. If Napoleon was a stickler for convertibility of the franc, could he not also have been a stickler for limited borrowing?

Siklos in chapter 9 examines the first Hungarian hyperinflation (1922: M2–1924: M6) and the subsequent stabilization (1924: M7–1928: M12) to determine whether the reduction in inflation constituted a regime change. His verdict is negative, based on both statistical and econometric evidence.

The statistical evidence includes the following items: although real balances began to rise with stabilization, even by the end of 1928, they had not reached the levels of early 1922, when cost of living was rising 19 percent on a monthly average. The deposit–note ratio by 1928 was also slightly lower than in 1921 during the pre-hyperinflation period. With an *ex post* real interest rate of about 8 percent during the stabilization period, compared to a 1.4 percent rate of Hungarian economic growth, the sustainability of the regime was doubtful. The condition of the budget led to the same conclusion. The League of Nations imposed a requirement of budget balance by June 1926, yet reconstruction and reparations costs drained the budget, so that deficits were rising until 1931. Official budget estimates, moreover, excluded extraordinary expenses. In addition, Hungary's balance of trade worsened; it lost foreign exchange from 1924 to 1929, in part because of the payment of reparations. Finally, inflation rose after the initial year of stabilization, and neither velocity nor inflation uncertainty was significantly lower in 1925–28 than in 1922.

The econometric tests, including a search for unit roots in the data; causality tests between money and prices, between exchange rates and notes and prices, or between prices and output or unemployment rates; cointegration tests between money and prices; and a vector autoregression, all raised questions on the validity of the distinction between the pre- and post-June 1924 periods.

Siklos concludes that no regime change occurred when hyperinflation ended, contrary to Sargent's view that a cold-turkey return to price stability alters price expectations of inflation quickly because the public regards the change in policy regime as credible. He accepts neither Sargent's view that the change in Hungary was associated with no transition costs of higher unemployment and lower output, nor Wicker's contrary view that the transition costs of higher unemployment and lower output were significant. Siklos finds unemployment and output behavior essentially similar over the whole period from 1921 to 1928. Credibility on his evidence requires more than emphasis on the budget and exchange rate. It also entails emphasis on the ingredients to sustain long-term economic growth. The chapter seems to me to support Siklos' findings.

There is a contrast between the analysis of the first Hungarian hyperinflation and its aftermath and the analysis of the experience of Italy and France after the Second World War. For Casella and Eichengreen in chapter 10 neither a monetary nor a fiscal correction can explain stabilization in Italy and France. For Siklos, had stabilization actually been achieved in Hungary, it would have been by these traditional factors.

Casella and Eichengreen argue that concurrent changes in monetary and fiscal management and the permanent change in government complexion in France and Italy in 1947, with the ouster of the Communists, cannot explain a change in expectations that led to stabilization. The critical link in their view was the announcement of Marshall Plan aid, even though shipment of goods only started in 1948. Marshall Plan funds covered a large share of government budget deficits, and also helped finance current account deficits. Yet stabilization in France occurred 18 months later than in Italy. The question is why.

The answer that Casella and Eichengreen offer is that a distributional struggle between recipients of labor income on the one hand and recipients of profits, interest, and rents on the other explains the difference in the timing of the outcome in the two countries. Stabilization was delayed until one side yielded. Delay increased inflation and made stabilization more costly, but the group that could hold out longer came off best since the costs were unevenly distributed.

The Marshall Plan improved supply and reduced the cost in reduction of aggregate demand that stabilization required. In Italy the Marshall Plan generated a quick and not so painful end to inflation without opposition of the Left. In France, determination to launch a major investment plan created additional pressure on demand that raised the cost of ending inflation, even with Marshall Plan aid. The cost of surrendering was too high for the Left, given the effects of investment demand on consumption, so 18 months passed before the resolution in the form of stabilization came.

To verify their analysis, Casella and Eichengreen suggest, first, that the income share of labor should have declined more dramatically in France than in Italy, but lack confirming data; second, that the Left was stronger in France and so could hold out longer, but again find the evidence inconclusive; third, that the struggle over consumption shares was more intense in France because gross investment, in current prices, was higher there relative to the prewar level than in Italy.

I find some inconsistencies in the analysis, especially with respect to the timing relations Casella and Eichengreen discuss. They dismiss the effect of the introduction of reserve requirements on commercial banks in Italy that coincided with stabilization on the ground that the new regulations had been anticipated for months. Yet the announcement of the Marshall Plan in June 1947, although anticipated for months and in advance of actual goods' shipments in April 1948, is taken to account for stabilization in Italy almost immediately after the announcement.

All the data the authors have assembled, admittedly far from ideal, bear a heavy burden of interpretation to sustain their view that monetary and fiscal corrections cannot explain the end of inflation in the two countries and that investment played a measurably greater role in France than in Italy to account for the delay in the French stabilization. I also wonder whether Casella and Eichengreen regard the model as applicable to other end-of-inflation episodes and, if so, which ones.

Jonung in chapter 11 gives a detailed account of the monetary regime that operated in Sweden prior to 1939 and reappeared in the late 1980s, and another that prevailed from the outbreak of the Second World War.

The first of the two regimes is a traditional market oriented one, in which monetary authorities do not interfere with the movement of market-determined interest rates and with the allocation of credit in financial markets. The central bank conveys its intentions through its open market operations. Traditionally, its main responsibility was maintaining a fixed exchange rate, and it was relatively independent of the government. A reversion to this model, in a managed floating exchange rate world, is now in process as financial deregulation proceeds.

The second type of regime is a non-market oriented one, in which monetary authorities allocate credit according to political preferences. Subsidies are extended to the public, housing, and export sectors at the expense of other sectors, with the help of commercial bank liquidity ratios, lending ceilings, and controls on bond issues. Interest rates are subject to administrative controls. Commercial banks are closely supervised and financial innovations hindered as threats to administrative control. In such a system, as Jonung notes, the central bank communicates with financial institutions through "'open mouth' operations."

Jonung gives an exhaustive discussion of the political, intellectual, and institutional forces that contributed, first, to the rise of credit controls and then to their dismantling. He notes the link between the spread of domestic credit controls and exchange controls that were put into effect at the start of the Second World War, and the link between deregulation in the 1980s and the difficulty of defending exchange controls, which were abolished in 1989. Yet Jonung does not isolate, as I would, the influence of exchange controls as a fundamental factor in promoting domestic credit controls or the freeing of exchange rates as essential to the breakdown of credit controls. The chapter as a whole is straightforward and informative about two monetary regime transformations in Sweden.

Concluding observations

The variety of monetary regimes in this volume affords the reader insights into different historical circumstances, different institutional settings, and different constraints on the individuals who played a role in the countries concerned. Given these external conditions, every monetary regime is associated with price behavior that results from actions of authorities, financial intermediaries, and the public.

Most of the examples of price behavior in this volume deal with inflation and its aftermath. Some authors have interpreted experience in light of models they regard as illuminating the past; others have not imposed conceptual structures on the material. In both cases, readers should profit from an introduction to wide-ranging views of a distinguished group of economists.

References

McCloskey, Donald N. and J. Richard Zecher, 1976. "How the gold standard worked, 1880–1913," in J.A. Frenkel and H.G. Johnson (eds.), *The Monetary Approach to the Balance of Payments*, London: George Allen & Unwin: 357–385.

Index